SF in Dimension:
A Book of Explorations

SF IN DIMENSION

A BOOK OF EXPLORATIONS

Revised and Enlarged Second Edition

by Alexei and Cory Panshin

Advent:Publishers, Inc.

Chicago: 1980

Acknowledgments

"The Magic of Their Singing," copyright © 1970 by Ultimate Publishing Co. Inc.

"The Elizabethan Theatre in 1590," copyright © 1969 by Mercury Press, Inc.

"The Short History of Science Fiction," copyright © 1971 by Ultimate Publishing Co. Inc.

"Searching for the Heartland," copyright © 1972 by Mercury Press, Inc.

"The World Beyond the Hill," copyright © 1972 by Thomas D. and Alice S. Clareson.

"Fragmentation," copyright © 1973 by Mercury Press, Inc.

"Science Fiction: New Trends and Old," copyright © 1974 by Reginald Bretnor.

"The Special Nature of Fantasy," copyright © 1974 by The Fantasy Association.

"Reflections and Commentaries," copyright © 1974 by Mercury Press, Inc.

"Reading Heinlein Subjectively," copyright © 1974 by Richard E. Geis.

"Time Enough for Love," copyright © 1976 by Alexei and Cory Panshin.

" 'Found in Space' by R. Monroe Weems," copyright © 1974 by Ultimate Publishing Co. Inc.

"Retrospection," copyright © 1974 by Mercury Press, Inc.

"The Unicorn and the Mirror," copyright © 1975 by Mercury Press, Inc.

"Farewell to Yesterday's Tomorrow," copyright © 1974 by UPD Publishing Corporation.

"Intuition and Mystery," copyright © 1976 by Mercury Press, Inc.

"The End of the Ghetto?" copyright © 1977 by Avenue Victor Hugo Publishers.

"The Past and the Future of SF," copyright © 1978 by Mercury Press, Inc.

"Dealing with Higher Realities," copyright © 1979 by Mercury Press, Inc.

This book is for
JAMES BLISH
who opened the door.

CONTENTS

"We are at our human finest, dancing with our minds, when there are more choices than two. Sometimes there are ten, even twenty different ways to go, all but one bound to be wrong, and the richness of selection in such situations can lift us onto totally new ground. This process is called exploration and is based on human fallibility. If we had only a single center in our brains, capable of responding only when a correct decision was to be made, instead of the jumble of different, credulous, easily conned clusters of neurones that provide for being flung off into blind alleys, up trees, down dead ends, out into blue sky, along wrong turnings, around bends, we could only stay the way we are today, stuck fast."

—*Lewis Thomas*

"The fact of thinking in terms of stories does not isolate human beings as something separate from the starfish and the sea anemone, the coconut palms and the primroses. Rather, if the world be connected, if I am at all fundamentally right in what I am saying, then thinking in terms of stories *must be shared by all mind or minds, whether ours or those of redwood forests and sea anemones.*"

—*Gregory Bateson*

PREFACE: SF IN DIMENSION

SF in Dimension presents the evolution of a new paradigm of SF that is different from the traditional construction of science fiction as fiction about science. In this book there are twenty-two essays on the past, present and future of SF. They were first published in a wide variety of places over a period of eleven years, from 1969 to 1980. The order in which they are presented here is roughly but not strictly the order in which we wrote them. Three essays—"Fiction and Human Development," "A New Worldview," and "The Death of Science Fiction"—were written especially for this book.

We were married and first began working together in 1969. In the spring of that year, Alexei had won the SFWA Nebula Award for his first novel, *Rite of Passage*. Also that spring, he wrote *Masque World*, the third of his novels celebrating the adventures of Anthony Villiers and Torve the Trog, all three written in the space of a year and a half on the festive energy of the time, the same energy that would manifest itself later that summer at the Woodstock Festival.

What a great rollercoaster ride the Sixties were! What a series of running battles! America was divided against itself—North against South, white against black, dove against hawk, rock against folk, cop against hippie, straight against stoned, child against parent.

Science fiction was divided, too. The radical party, the New Wave, flatly rejected what it took to be the wornout materials, crude writing and obsolete story structures of traditional pulp-born American science fiction. Their opponents, the Old Wave, raised the banner of John W. Campbell and furiously defended the values of the Golden Age of *Astounding* and *Unknown*.

To us there seemed to be a certain measure of right in the arguments of both sides, but neither side seemed worth joining. As we perceived it, neither side was addressing itself to the real underlying problem of which the outward quarrel was only a symptom.

This was only two years before the death of Campbell—"John W. God" to his detractors (and in a sense to his partisans as well). Campbell was still editing *Astounding* (renamed *Analog*) as he had since 1937. His burly presence still dominated the genre. But the signs of the time were as clear to us as they were to any New Waver: science fiction in the Campbellian sense had run its course. It was out of touch with present reality.

Long ago, in a visionary moment, Campbell had had a glimpse of the nature and purpose of science fiction. But the SF that most closely fit this vision was the science fiction of *Astounding* in 1941, and not the stories of the present moment. As editor of *Astounding* and *Analog*, he had led and directed the progress of science fiction for thirty years and more, but now his attitudes and theories had become constricting to creativity, an impediment to further progress.

And just how was it that John Campbell saw things? On at least one occasion late in his life he explicitly expressed his sense of science fiction's true majesty and power.

Campbell was sitting in a circle of SF writers who were going on at length, speculating as to the relative place and merit of science fiction within English letters. Campbell—the Grand Sachem and Great Father Bear of Modern Science Fiction—terminated the discussion by embracing the question and hugging it to death.

He spread his arms wide:

> "This is science fiction," he said, from open-armed fingertip to fingertip. "It takes in all of time, from before the universe was born, through the formation of suns and planets, on through their destruction and forward to the heat death of the universe. And after." His hands came together so that his index fingers delimitated a very tiny measure of space. "This is English Literature, the most microscopic fraction of the whole."

Harry Harrison, who tells this story, says that Campbell's listeners took him as being humorous, as being deliberately outrageous. But our sense of Campbell is that he was doing no more than speaking the truth as he saw it. He was saying that which he had believed and lived by every day of his editorial career.

Campbell's vision was broad enough to stimulate and encompass SF for a generation. The great limitation of his view was that it was strictly an engineering-and-physics interpretation of the universe, founded in the science and the values of 1930. There were vast areas of human thought and expression which Campbellian valuation held of very small account—of which English Literature was only one example. There were persons and facts and even science that Campbell's modern science fiction excluded from its view.

The literature that Campbell's guardianship of science fiction produced was strong where it was strong—primarily in imaginative intellection. Otherwise it was severely limited. It was often narrow, crude and juvenile. Beyond any denying, its chief appeal was to an audience of technocrats and teenagers, persons who were lacking in mature sensibility.

The alternative to Campbell's science fiction that was offered by the New Wave may be taken as literature's revenge on Campbell for his pride and his philistinism. Everything Campbell believed in, the New Wave rejected. In the typical New Wave story, the universe collapsed forever yesterday. In place of physical science and galactic adventure, the New Wave substituted literary experimentation based on the fifty-year-old models of Alfred Jarry, James Joyce, and John Dos Passos.

The contention of the New Wave was that long ago—sometime between the great master H. G. Wells and the unspeakable magazine publisher Hugo Gernsback—science fiction had gone astray. SF was to be saved from the likes of Gernsback and Campbell by traveling back in time to a point before science fiction became pulpish and dumb and starting over, as though the way backward were the way forward.

The New Wave was highly effective as criticism. As a demonstration of rebellion it shattered the hypnotic spell of Campbell.

It made it possible to entertain the thought of non-Campbellian or post-Campbellian SF.

But the New Wave was not post-Campbellian. Absurdism, surrealism and naturalism, however well they might serve to show up Campbell's weaknesses and limitations, in themselves offered no positive alternative to Campbell.

Indeed, to a real degree they were a philosophical step backward. Campbell was born and raised in a time when Jarry, Joyce and Dos Passos and the attitudes they represented were current. The universe offered to Campbell was one of futility, purposelessness and cosmic alienation. That was the universe of H. G. Wells. During the Thirties, in his story-writing career as Don A. Stuart, author of "Twilight" and "Forgetfulness," and in his series of articles in *Astounding* on the planets of the solar system, Campbell had painfully worked out the basis of an alternative—modern science fiction.

Campbellian science fiction might have distinct limitations, but it was a step forward. The artistic cynicism and stylistic doodah of the New Wave could never be sufficient cause to reject all that science fiction had been and done under Hugo Gernsback and John W. Campbell. That was the period in which British and European writers had all but completely turned away from SF, finding the empty and purposeless universe that Campbell had embraced and triumphed over too overwhelming and unbearable to face. When they did come back to SF, it had been within Campbell's terms. It is no accident at all that British writers of the Forties and Fifties, like Arthur C. Clarke and Eric Frank Russell, wrote Campbellian science fiction.

American pulp science fiction was an honorable, meaningful and ofttimes brilliant phase in the development of SF. It was a past that SF should not lightly toss away—and certainly not for mere experimental technique, technique that was no longer even current in the literature from which it was adopted.

Be reminded that the year was 1969—the first year of Richard Nixon's presidency, the last year of the Sixties. Nixon perceived himself as having been elected to bring a divided country together again—and had set out to do it by suppressing dissent and separating out rotten apples. The battles were ending. The atmosphere was darkening. Altamont, Kent State and Watergate were in the air.

What we had always loved best in Campbellian science fiction was the way in which it built on itself, criticized itself and extended itself in a constant game of can-you-top-this? It was that same quality that we had loved the Sixties for. But now it all seemed to be ending, both in science fiction and in the culture at large. The energy was being turned off.

To us, the problem of the time seemed to be how to keep and value all the best of what modern science fiction had been while pressing on beyond Campbell. In a time like this, with creative energy failing, whose lead should we follow? What path should we take?

The Old Wave? The attitudes and facts of the Old Wave were out of touch with present reality.

The New Wave? Even less in touch with present knowledge and lacking in comprehensive vision besides.

What kind of science fiction could it be possible to write without reference to contemporary thought, without universal vision, and without creative energy? It was not only Watergate that could be sensed waiting ahead in the Seventies—it was novels like Barry Malzberg's *Beyond Apollo* and Robert Silverberg's *Dying Inside*. We didn't want to write work like that.

There is an SF story that we read in more than one form and under more than one title when we were young. In this story, a character is shown a fork in time. Two futures are outlined for her, both with a certain allure, neither one ultimately satisfying. Rather than accepting either given choice, the character strikes out into the unknown. And somehow, through a radical random action, a third alternative comes into being.

Our own alternative to the New Wave and the Old was to cease writing science fiction stories, to step back a distance, sit down and begin a complete and fundamental examination of every aspect of science fiction. We wanted to look into crucial questions—the origins of science fiction, the relationship between cultural energy and SF, the multiple meaning of science fiction, and the relevance of SF to the present and to the future. This book of critical and theoretical essays is the result.

We set out at the beginning to doubt all and to believe all—to doubt as acutely as the New Wave, and to believe as encompassingly as the Old Wave. It is to this end that these essays are both visionary and highly specific.

The models for our criticism have been those earlier SF writers who have struggled with the problems of the genre, those pioneer writer-critics who have attempted to explain to themselves, and to all of us, where science fiction came from, what it is for, and how it might be made better. Our SF criticism is founded upon the book reviews of Damon Knight and James Blish, the historical investigations of L. Sprague de Camp and Sam Moskowitz, the plainspoken writing advice of de Camp, and the psycho-literary speculation of Knight and Cyril Kornbluth.

The most visible characteristic of this school is its practicality and specificity. It has been written for evident reasons and whenever possible for paying markets. These essays are in that tradition. They are book reviews, essays on the climate of the time, historical investigations, and psychological speculation written to suit the needs of a a wide variety of magazines and books.

Here you will find essays of three general sorts. There are reviews of sixty books—novels by established writers, first novels, anthologies, history, criticism, bibliography and memoirs. There are essays on the nature of science fiction. And there are three reconsiderations of the early stories of Robert Heinlein, the pre-eminent writer of Campbellian science fiction.

In a real sense, this book is a workshop of new ideas. It is no accident that one of these essays will refer to books or ideas considered in another, or that the same ground may be covered once, twice and again from different angles, as in the case of Heinlein. With no sense at all of apology, we would be the first to say that this book is full of errors in fact, mistakes in judgment, reconsiderations and amendments, and claim it as a virtue. What is important here is the whole.

SF in Dimension is the record of a process. Our aim has been to pose every fundamental question concerning science fiction that we could think of, to turn away from nothing. We wanted to discern the actual nature of science fiction, separate from what Campbell or anyone else might think or say about it. Like John W. Campbell before us, we aimed to stand on the shoulders of our predecessors and peer more deeply into the mystery than they. This is the central purpose that binds the essays in this book together and makes it a whole despite its variety of approaches to its subject and its sometime apparent self-contradiction.

One other thing that this book is is a reflection of the Seventies. Underneath their superficial appearance of decadence and triviality, the Seventies were a decade of private experiment and openness to change. Instead of battles and confrontation, no one paid attention to anyone else. The result is that 1980 is very different from 1969.

The attitudes of the onetime counterculture of the Sixties have become naturalized, absorbed into the culture as a whole. Rock music and marijuana, blue jeans and ecology are everyone's property now. Ideas that John W. Campbell would have found very strange and unsettling have been adopted from the past and from other cultures. Most important, the central science of this new day is no longer John Campbell's physics, but a strange new biology that must be called the science of life. It may be seen in signing gorillas, two-brain psychology, genetic experimentation and the increasing validation of the priorities of ecology.

Our image of the universe is no longer the same. In the new climate of the Eighties, science fiction in the old-fashioned mechanistic Campbellian sense is clearly no longer relevant, no longer viable. It is not the leading edge of SF. As for the New Wave, it made its protest felt, and then with the passing of the Sixties, dried up and blew away.

Through the Seventies, the outlines of a new successor form of SF have slowly been taking shape. It is our hope that the cumulative effect of these essays will be to make that new shape manifest. In the final essay, "The Death of Science Fiction," the threads that weave through this book are brought together explicitly in a piece that is simultaneously a review of current books, a commentary on Robert Heinlein and a portrait of the new SF.

For us, these essays have been a bridge from the past to the future. We hope they may serve the same purpose for others.

We have included a short bibliography at the end of *SF in Dimension*. Some of the books listed have had a direct influence on these essays. Others, encountered along the way, have served to confirm certain ideas and approaches we have taken and are included to indicate the framework of current thought to which our book is related. Readers who find these essays serving to open new lines of thought and possibility may wish to pursue them further through these books.

Alexei and Cory Panshin
Elephant, Pennsylvania
February 1980

Part I: The Nature of SF

1/ THE MAGIC OF THEIR SINGING

[*Fantastic*, June 1970]

During the past few years there has been a noisy fight in science fiction between drumbeaters for a supposed "New Wave" and the guardians of all that science fiction is supposed to have been since 1926. The writers of science fiction have been muttering amongst themselves and snarling from the sidelines, but they haven't, for the most part, declared themselves for one party or the other. The actual battlers have been editors and fans, people as central to the creation of science fiction as Judith Merril and John Jeremy Pierce.

It's a murky quarrel. It seems that both sides have chosen up on the emotional strength of one label or the other, and then found that no one else in their camp agrees on right and proper definitions. Both the New Wavers and the Old have laid claim to the same writers. Roger Zelazny has been split like a wishbone.

Insofar as there is emotional agreement within factions, a biased outsider might say that the New Wave seems to be in favor of literary experimentation, non-linearity and a remergence with the so-called "literary mainstream." And the Old Wave flag-wavers endorse the good-story-well-told, healthy social values, and fiction about science.

Neither package seems entirely worth having. Is science fiction indeed fiction about science, as the assumption has been since Hugo Gernsback founded *Amazing Stories*? It is my feeling that it is not. It is no more reasonable to expect sf to be about science than to expect all historical novels to restrict themselves to military history or the state of the marketplace. On the other hand, is science fiction actually inferior to the mainstream? In recent times, the apparent movement has been by a "mainstream" of frustrated social literature that is moving toward science fiction and fantasy. The experiments of Barth, Barthelme, Burroughs, Coover, Vonnegut and Nabokov may indicate a direction.

The New Wave-Old Wave argument, as its partisans have put their cases, has been an empty one, but the edginess and bad temper of the writers have been real. These are uncertain and often frightening times in science fiction. Things are unclear. Things are changing. What the shape of science fiction will be in five years, no one would be confident to say. But some of the idols of Golden Age science fiction have turned to writing popular science or other forms of fiction, and some have stopped writing altogether in the face of pressure. And among younger writers there seems to be a sense of a new universe to be opened, though none of them have yet proved their belief with books.

Joanna Russ has characterized science fiction as the Elizabethan theatre after Marlowe, but before Shakespeare. I want to believe it. I can see the empty Elizabethan theatre waiting to be filled with giant magics—and see science fiction as an unknown universe impossible to fill. But Russ's nominations for the part of Marlowe are Asimov and Heinlein and I don't think they qualify. They seem more akin to the morality dramatists who came twenty years before Shakespeare. In the place of Thomas Kyd, who was the first versifier, the last of the moralists and the first of the tragedians, we might name Zelazny or Delany. But science fiction has still to produce its Marlowe, let alone a Shakespeare.

Still, the potential of a real rift appears between technicians content to write formula moralities and melodramas all in the same limp gray prose, and experimenters curious to know the true range of science fiction. The rift is more potential than actual because the experimenters have yet to fully justify themselves. Roger Zelazny and Samuel R. Delany have superseded their predecessors but not surpassed them.

If this were Afterward, and all the possible changes of science fiction had been rung, this column would be more organized than I actually expect it is going to be from one issue to the next.* Since I think that we actually stand well before science fiction's hour, this column will be a random collection of suggestions, arguments, opinions and dreams. If the New Wave and Old are drum-beaters and flag-wavers, I invite you to see me as the fellow with the piccolo playing "Over the Hills and Far Away."

I have been reading science fiction for twenty years, writing it for ten, and criticizing it for six. My opinions on the subject have been changing all the while, and you can assume that they will continue to change, possibly from one column to the next. What I say is by way of suggestion. It isn't authoritative, objective or final. Treat it accordingly—pick through what I say and accept what you can.

Science fiction has been a literary genre since the founding of *Amazing* in 1926. It has been a naive, insular, uncertain and impolite literature. That's from our side, the inside. The outside world has looked on us with righteous contumely.

Sf has been innocent of ordinary literary standards. Since 1950, when the editors H.L. Gold in *Galaxy* and Boucher and McComas in *Fantasy and Science Fiction* began setting new standards for the field, science fiction has at least been literate. But even today most science fiction continues to be written in a dull utilitarian prose that remains much the same not only from story to story, but even from author to author. Prose that sings or cuts is rare. Variations in prose can distinguish characters, set a tone, produce a range of effect and stimulate a drowsy reader. But most science fiction, among all the musical effects of prose, has been aware only of pace—drone notes set to the beat of a drum.

Sf has primarily been published in pulp magazines and, more recently, in paperback books, and been shaped by their requirements. Among these is that the drum should beat very fast. Melodrama. Action.

Most science fiction has been short until recent times. Even novels

---

* This essay was the first in a series that appeared in *Fantastic* between June 1970 and July 1973, under the title *SF in Dimension*. The earliest of these were signed by Alexei Panshin alone.

have been, most usually, no longer than 60,000 words—which is short. This would seem unnecessarily limiting for a fiction about the unfamiliar.

Science fiction is associated in the popular mind with horror movies and with comic strips and with the worst excesses of scientism. Who among us could say that this is unjustified?

And even after forty years, there still is no generally accepted definition of the field.

Except . . .

Even under deserved criticism and contempt, science fiction has not withered. It has continued to expand its subject, its techniques, and its ideas of its limits. Other popular magazine fiction has almost completely disappeared. But in 1968, science fiction magazines supported by readers—not advertisers, as is the usual case—published three hundred original stories. I think the science fiction short story is an irrelevance that deserves to disappear, but it is a fifteen-year-old fact that science fiction is the present home of the American short story. And *Amazing* is not only still being published after more than forty years, it is the most vigorous present science fiction magazine, literarily if not economically.

But not only has science fiction proved durable beyond all reasonable expectation, its audience is unusual. Until recently, that audience has been intense but limited in size.

However, at any one time, this limited audience supports amateur magazines by the hundreds, and has done so for forty years. With only a few recent exceptions—college club magazines and the like—these journals have been published without sponsorship, endorsement or subsidy. This is a common fact to us within the sf world, but from the outside it is unique and remarkable.

And every year—again without sponsorship, endorsement or subsidy—science fiction supports conventions by the dozen. In the past few years, the number and size of these conventions has leaped. The first World Science Fiction Convention that I attended was the Seventeenth, in Detroit in 1959. The attendance was 371 people. This year there will be any number of regional conventions with that kind of attendance, and the attendance at the Twenty-Seventh World

Science Fiction Convention in St. Louis last September [1969] was over 1600 people.* And all on the basis of voluntary association.

Is it fiction about science that has brought this many people together this strongly? Or is there another more important element that binds them?

Until recently, to be published as science fiction meant that a book had an assured limited sale to the traditional narrow but loyal science fiction audience. I used to think it was the general audience that was missing the point, that it was fear and ignorance that kept them from science fiction.

There may have been some truth in this. Science fiction, well ahead of its time and all that, may only at last have been caught up to by laggard minds. On the other hand, it seems a more likely possibility that what has kept a larger audience away has been the imperfections of science fiction: the melodrama, the crudeness and the insistence upon featuring science to the exclusion of other aspects of life. Whatever the element that has bound the science fiction audience so tightly, is it so foreign to all other readers that the appeals of science fiction must inevitably pass them by? Or is it science fiction that has failed to explore its own possibilities?

There is no question that working in a pulp literature with pulp standards and pulp economics has inhibited science fiction writers from exploring the range of the field. Write a novel longer than 60,000 words? Nonsense—there is no market for such a book. Write a story about daily life in a strange society? The readers would never hold still for it. Write a legitimate tragedy? How? About what? You must be kidding. How?

But now a larger audience has shown an interest. Risk-taking books like *Stranger in a Strange Land* and *Dune* have been published as science fiction, but been seized upon by a new, large, educated, hip young audience. Are these pure accidents? I don't think so. It certainly isn't predictions about science that have caught these people. It must be some other rarer magic. But the intensity of this new appeal has been as great as it has always been within our limited

* The attendance at the Thirty-Second World Science Fiction Convention, held in Washington, D.C. in September 1974, was 4000 people.

audience. And the magic—is it our own secret heart's delight? Is it an accident that Paul Williams of *Crawdaddy* should hand John Lennon *The Three Stigmata of Palmer Eldritch* to read? Is it an accident that the *Whole Earth Catalog*, whose stated purpose begins, "We *are* as gods and might as well get good at it," and which lists appropriate tools, should list *Dune*? Is it an accident that much rock music should be about science fiction and that rock musicians should read science fiction?

What magic touched the people who saw *2001*?

What would science fiction be like if it regularly and surely engaged this audience, instead of occasionally and erratically?

This is hypothetical, because if someone actually knew the answer he would be writing fiction like nothing any of us has seen before and enchanting us all, science fiction's old audience and its new one. It is this vision of possibility that frightens some writers out of the field altogether and sets others to writing strange experiments.

At the same time, the spectre of respectability and academic acceptance is haunting sf writers with requests for library donations of manuscripts and old laundry lists. It may mean only that the hunt for material to analyze has become insanely intense, but the degree of interest is enough to make some typing fingers shaky. The Modern Language Association has begun to publish its own science fiction fanzine, *Extrapolation*. It has held general meetings on science fiction. One of the sessions at its just past winter meetings was devoted to John Brunner's *Stand on Zanzibar*. A Science Fiction Research Association is now being formed. And science fiction writers like Joanna Russ, William Tenn and Jack Williamson teach college courses in science fiction.

It can be frightening. Especially if the safe common sort of science fiction is all you know. Especially if you haven't a clue to an alternative. There are people who would like to see the colleges and the new people go away. Strange to say of science fiction writers, but there is fear of the unknown.

What is science fiction?

In his contribution to the Advent symposium, *The Science Fiction*

Novel, Robert Heinlein divided fiction into "the possible" and "the impossible" — Realism and Fantasy. He divided these categories again into past, present and future scene, and found most science fiction under the heading, "Realistic Future-Scene Fiction." And Heinlein in his discussion hinged his "realism" on science. This is the standard ideal of science fiction set by Hugo Gernsback—but it has never strictly been followed.

Science fiction cannot depend for its legitimacy on science. No matter how accurate a story may seem to be, or may prove to be, if it doesn't involve or move readers, it will surely die. And science alone is insufficient to explain a good story.

Cleve Cartmill's story "Deadline," which predicted the atomic bomb in 1944 and brought the FBI out to investigate him and *Astounding*, is not much better than a curiosity today. On the other hand, Alan Nourse's story "Brightside Crossing," set on a Mercury we now know to be impossible, still has the power to move.

In fact, if science fiction did derive its legitimacy from science, last year's science fiction would be thrown out on the same rubbish heap as last year's scientific textbooks. Science is a constant corrective procedure. Science fiction based on present science has to be insufficient. Science fiction based on hypothetical science has to be ingenious nonsense.

Science fiction has never done better than pretend to be about science—often to its great cost. L. Sprague de Camp wrote in his *Science-Fiction Handbook*, "The science-fiction magazines persist in publishing stories of strange worlds, the future, marvelous journeys, and utopias with little or no science — no pseudo-science even." Not quite true. Pseudo-science is science fiction's greatest crudity. Gernsback's rules said that science fiction ought to be about science, and the practical result was pseudo-science. De Camp himself was purist enough to try to follow Gernsback. He wouldn't write about faster-than-light travel, for instance, because he didn't believe it was possible. And eventually de Camp gave up writing science fiction for historical novels, where the facts stand still.

The quarrel about the relation of science and science fiction is as new as Larry Niven and R.A. Lafferty, and as old as Verne and

Wells. Verne said of Wells:

> It occurs to me that his stories do not repose on a very scientific
> basis. No, there is no rapport between his work and mine. I make
> use of physics. He invents. I go to the moon in a cannon-ball dis-
> charged from a cannon. Here, there is no invention, He goes to
> Mars in an air-ship, which he constructs of a metal which does away
> with the law of gravitation. *Ça, c'est tres joli*, but show me this
> metal. Let him produce it.

But science and the times have abandoned Verne, while Wells, who
was never "right," continues to be relevant. Science fiction does not
depend on accuracy, which is impossible, but on inner consistency.
The subject of science fiction is not the world as it will be, but the
limitless world of the imagination.

Science fiction, as a few have always insisted, is fantasy. What we
are used to thinking of as fantasy is a conscious re-creation of myths
and symbols that are no longer believed, but merely expected to
entertain. The world of fantasy is Earth. The spirit is medieval—
historical and nostalgic. Familiarity is half the appeal.

But this is not the only possible fantasy. Fantasy can be disciplined and creative and relevant. It has been crowded out of the
last empty spaces on Earth only to find an empty and inexhaustible
universe. All time. All space. And that is the world of "science
fiction."

For forty years, we have been gingerly feeling our way out into
this vast emptiness, first exploring our backyard and our neighborhood, and tied to the "realistic" world all the while by the safety line
of "science."

Now is the time to cut the line. To sing. To dance. To shout up
the dawn. To hurl rainbows. To discover marvels and populate the
darkness. And perhaps find ourselves.

2/ THE ELIZABETHAN THEATRE IN 1590

[*Fantasy and Science Fiction*, November 1969]

It may just be the current general unrest misleading us—as we have been misled before—but these feel like transitional times in science fiction. No one—writer, reader, fan, editor or critic—yet knows with any certainty what is happening, or what science fiction will look like five years from now, but the feeling persists that these are times of change.

There have been portents:

Until recently, to be presented as science fiction meant small risk of failure and an absolute limitation on success. We have spent forty years as a self-sufficient, self-supported and generally ignored magazine literature. Our proudest boast has been that we have survived when other magazine literatures have died. We have been poor, proud and honest in the years of wandering in the wilderness, and our chief audience has been engineers and bright fifteen-year-olds. Throughout our long ordeal we have been sustained by faith that we were destined for better things—Serious Attention, even Popularity.

And now . . . Two science fiction novels, *Stranger in a Strange Land* and *Dune*, have been vogue items, even though packaged and presented as science fiction. This year's Hugo ballot offers a choice in Drama among *2001*, *Charly*, *Rosemary's Baby*, *Yellow Submarine* and *The Prisoner*, a list of productions that can more than stand comparison with Hollywood's standard. Science fiction is a direct influence on the new rock music. Titles like "2000 Light Years from Home," "Interstellar Overdrive," "Progress Suite" and "Who Are the Brain Police?" are not uncommon. Universities have been vying for the papers of science fiction writers—*living* writers, *beginning* writers—and one loser in this competition even intends to publish a Union List of everyone else's holdings. Sf conventions, once a meeting ground for friends, are becoming congregations of four times as many strangers. And the report is that during the storm the other night on the Capitoline Hill, Lucius Tigelinus saw the statue of Hugo Gernsback bathed in a ring of fire.

What it all means is unclear—and we have been fooled before. Now? Why now? What now?

Is the coziness gone? Is it possible to be both Popular and Virtuous? Is popularity worth having? Is it too late to ask the outside world to just forget the whole thing?

Two disturbing points do present themselves. One is that the portents are coming at a time when the magazines, which have been the mainstays of science fiction for forty years, seem to be in difficulty. And another is that by any serious standard science fiction has yet to produce more than a handful of titles that someone other than an engineer or a fifteen-year-old can read without apology.

In the last several years, we've come to the conclusion that science fiction does not have to be a juvenile literature. That—set the pea patch of technology to one side—science fiction is an undiscovered universe. And we think this is the secret belief of many in the younger generation of science fiction writers. Joanna Russ, speaking to the Eastern Science Fiction Association in January, said, in effect, that science fiction is the Elizabethan theatre in 1590—waiting . . . We have every reason to think she was perfectly serious.

Our basic premise as critics is that it *is* 1590, and to judge books accordingly. In that light, the five books on hand for review are interesting examples of the curious, uncertain and half-formed state of the field of science fiction.

The Andromeda Strain by Michael Crichton is science fiction and a Book-of-the-Month Club selection. It has been favorably reviewed by *Life*, *Look* and the *New York Times*, and it has sold to the movies for an impressive sum. It is also cheap, sensationalistic, hastily-written trash—ultimately no more important to science fiction than *Seven Days in May*, ultimately no more important than *Seven Days in May*, period. The most interesting thing about the book is that although it has not been marketed as a science fiction novel, it has been reviewed as one. But it is no credit to the field.

In *The Andromeda Strain* we are menaced—or, rather, since this is a report on a past crisis, we *were* menaced—by a plague brought to Earth by a "Scoop satellite." The satellite was sent up for that very purpose by our own Chemical and Biological Warfare people, but has been broken into with pliers and chisel by an Arizona country doctor.

The story is either a plausible thriller—that is, you believe in the plague and in the efforts of the scientific and medical team to cope with it—or it is nothing. Crichton bolsters his story with easy expertise and massive documentation, but the story never hangs together. The main reason is that Crichton invents his story as he goes along and is satisfied to put down the first thing that comes to mind—and one lie contradicts the next.

Thus you have a bacteriologist who has won the Nobel Prize for work done in his spare time from his real career as a law student—Crichton consistently oversells—but who must be reminded that he has a vein in his wrist.

Thus you have a surgeon who has been placed on the project team by the Department of Defense and the AEC over the objections of our bacteriologist leader. But some year or more later the surgeon has yet to even familiarize himself with the basic purpose of the project. We are told that his reason for being present is that he is single, and thus more likely to make a "correct decision" involving "thermo-nuclear or chem-biol destruction of enemy targets," the "Index of Effectiveness" of single males in such matters being .824, compared to .343 among married males (*sic*, God help us).

Thus you have an Army van with a rotating antenna on top tacking back and forth across the Mojave Desert taking triangulations every twenty miles on a grounded satellite—the landing site of which has already been predicted with an error of a few hundred yards. Two such vans, we are told, would be suspicious.

Thus you have a portentous scientific report on the probability of contact between man and other life forms, with all figures to four places and a list of possibilities adding to unity. But which ignores the possibility of encountering a life form more advanced than our own—the "7+" level of data handling, if you please. Or the possibility of encountering a life form radically different from our own. Or the possibility of encountering no life at all.

Crichton's documentation is fake. His expertise is fake. And even his basic problem turns out to be a fraud—after a few days, the plague ups and goes away.

In a way, it may be the very implausibility of *The Andromeda Strain* beneath its officious and authoritative surface that is the basis of its success. People like to be scared, but they don't like to be *really* scared. An *Andromeda Strain* done with true care and attention might be too scary for real enjoyment. We had a book like that earlier this year in Thomas M. Disch's *Camp Concentration*. The problem posed was so hairy and so final as to scare even the author into bringing the Marines onstage at the last moment to save the day. Far more people are likely to read *The Andromeda Strain* than will ever read *Camp Concentration* precisely because it is less real. Its implausibilities are a constant reminder that it need not be taken seriously. It should make a perfectly terrible movie.

Arthur C. Clarke's *The Lion of Comarre and Against the Fall of Night* and Fritz Leiber's *A Specter Is Haunting Texas* are both leftovers from science fiction's juvenile days, though Clarke's stories were written in the Forties and Leiber's novel was first published in *Galaxy* last year.

Against the Fall of Night was Clarke's first novel. It jumps a billion years into Earth's future to the sand-encircled city of Diaspar. Its appeals are emotional—the thirst for knowledge at all costs, the nostalgia of time (" 'Ah, here's Bensor with the latest ten million years of history.' "), and the wonder of strange isolated places. At the same time, the story is curiously unemotional. Clarke's characters, truth to tell, are no better developed than Crichton's. The zombies of *2001* are rather more the rule than the exception in Clarke's fiction. More important, in this case, is that the story is largely undeveloped—too much is asserted, too little is examined. It is a good juvenile novel with faults serious enough that Clarke rewrote it completely as *The City and the Stars* eight years after its initial publication.

"The Lion of Comarre" is padding, a thin novelet from a 1949 issue of *Thrilling Wonder*, previously unreprinted, and included here to add sixty pages to a short book. Its appeals are much the same as *Against the Fall of Night,* and its twelve hundred years in the future don't look, taste or smell very different from the billion years of Diaspar.

Curiously, too, the narration of both stories has one foot stuck in 1945. The stories are dated by an uncritical scientism—again not much different from Crichton and his "Indexes of Effectiveness," though infinitely more honest—by tin cans, by vacuum tubes, and by haste and shortcuts. It would be interesting to see if a modern sense of wonder story could be written that would not date as easily as these.

A Specter Is Haunting Texas resembles Fritz Leiber's very first science fiction novel—*Gather, Darkness!*, serialized in 1943—in being an intermittently satirical melodrama about revolution. The target of both satire and revolution in *Gather, Darkness!* was organized religion. The target in *A Specter Is Haunting Texas* is Texas—which is to say the American impulse toward gigantism.

The Specter is Christopher Crockett La Cruz, an 8'6" (or 8'8", depending on which page of the book you choose to take for authority) ninety-seven pound Shakespearean actor co-opted into a Mexican revolution against the hormone-enlarged rulers of a post-World War III Greater Texas. The differences that twenty-five years have made are that the satire in *Specter*—while it lasts—is painted in broader strokes than the satire in *Gather, Darkness!* and that the revolution in the newer book is a temporary failure rather than a success. Otherwise, the books are much of a piece.

At its best, *Specter* is not particularly original. It covers ground covered better in the Fifties by H. Beam Piper and John J. McGuire in *A Planet for Texans* and by Richard Wilson in *The Girls from Planet 5*. Its greatest strength, in fact, is in conceits and occasional lines. And two-thirds of the way through it falls apart, its satire forgotten in favor of the melodramatic requirement of movement at any cost.

Specter is not the first science fiction book crippled by melodrama. Melodrama is a legacy of science fiction's forty years in the pulp wilderness. Melodrama has been the main vehicle of science fiction expression, first by requirement, latterly by habit, with only occasional exceptions such as the work of Pangborn or Clarke. Ultimately, however, melodrama will blur and distort where necessary for the sake of color, movement and superficial excitements, and this makes it an uncertain medium for any work that would make fine distinctions. Robert Heinlein's *Beyond This Horizon* is a good example of a serious and superior book twisted out of shape by the 1942 assumption that novels need melodramatic conflict. *Beyond This Horizon* would be a finer book without its melodramatic revolution, and *A Specter Is Haunting Texas*, like *Gather, Darkness!* before it, is, without the same claims to stature, similarly spoiled.

Donald A. Wollheim and Terry Carr's anthology *World's Best Science Fiction: 1969*, is not a book we would recommend to the uncommitted. It is more a genuine reflection of the state of health of the science fiction short story than a failure on the part of the editors that this is a large trivial book. Almost any collection of last year's sf short stories would inevitably be more of the same, and would probably be less literate and varied.

This year's *World's Best* is a collection of retreads like H.H. Hollis's version of John Collier, Colin Kapp's version of Poul Anderson's "The Sky People," and Fred Saberhagen's version of Orpheus and Eurydice—which alters the original legend in one significant regard: Saberhagen's Ordell chooses to join his Eury in death, while Orpheus retired to Thrace after his loss and consoled himself with the company of boys. *World's Best Science Fiction: 1969* further contains short fragments like Fritz Leiber's "The Square Root of Brain" and

Kurt Vonnegut's "Welcome to the Monkey House," and long fragments like Brian Aldiss's "Total Environment" and Samuel R. Delany's "Time Considered as a Helix of Semi-Precious Stones." But most of all, this anthology contains story after story about comic, threatening, or comic/threatening machines, like Sheckley's, like Silverberg's, like Knight's, like von Wald's, like Van Scyoc's, like Saberhagen's, like Lafferty's.

The science fiction magazines are few in number, low-paying and conservatively edited. This means that the few good short sf stories written are published in *Playboy*—like "Welcome to the Monkey House," and Damon Knight's "Masks," probably the best-realized sf short of the year—or turn up in original anthologies like Poul Anderson's "Kyrie," Brian Aldiss's "The Worm That Flies," and Terry Carr's own "The Dance of the Changer and the Three," all three of which come from a single anthology, Joseph Elder's *The Farthest Reaches*, and which have to be the rest of what passes for cream in this *World's Best*.

The trouble ultimately lies not in the magazines—which are no more to blame than this annual anthology, which has consistently been the best of its kind. The trouble is that the science fiction short story is the limited corner of an extremely large field. It is an almost inherently trivial form used for forty years for the illustration of moralities, for the drawing of fine scientific distinctions, and for the building of psionic sandcastles. There simply seems to be no room left for much beyond restatement or the trivial refinement of the already trivial. There may be a truism here—that science fiction to be good needs careful, extensive and intensive development.

In any case, it is a fact that much of the short science fiction that does seem worthy—like several recent prize winners—has proved to be part of a series or an integral piece of a longer work.

The Left Hand of Darkness by Ursula K. Le Guin is a long, serious and overwhelmingly detailed book. It comes with the cachet of the Ace Science Fiction Special line—a monthly series which has shown what an intelligent editor, in this case, Terry Carr, can do with a limited budget and a good eye. The large number of original first novels in the series is no accident. Le Guin's novel is not her first, but her previous adult novels have all been garden variety Ace books. *The Left Hand of Darkness* is well above the average in literacy, invention and ambition in this our year of 1590, but ultimately as a story it is a flat failure.*

The story, carried by illustrative folk tales, by the narration of a native he/she and by the musings of a lone Earth envoy, relates the opening of the closed, isolated and divided planet of Winter to the worlds of the human Ekumen. Le Guin's interest is in her world of Winter and its hermaphroditic humans, and she gives us detail after detail about them. Her story, however, is a public story, her characters are consistently held at arm's length, and her action is summarized rather than shown. Nonetheless, to the end of the story and past it into an appendix, we are still being given statistics, facts and anecdotes, as though this were a color travelogue and our only interest in raw information. Even her hermaphrodites, seen only in public function, eventually seem purely male, partly because she chooses always to call them "he." What we have at last is not so much a novel as the theory for one, but with all the vital arguments yet to be made. There is hope in a book like this—its intent is far from juvenile and that is an absolute necessity if we are ever to have a truly first-rate science fiction—but it is only the faintest taste of what science fiction might be.

Pray—all of us trying to write science fiction need your prayers—but don't hold your breath.

---

* In fairness to this widely-admired novel, we should point out that it won both the Hugo and Nebula awards, and deserved to win.

3/ THE SHORT HISTORY OF SCIENCE FICTION

[*Fantastic*, April 1971]

On October 25, 1963, Hugo Gernsback gave an address before the M.I.T. Science Fiction Society. He said:

> What I detest is the parading of pure fantasy stories as science fiction and their sale as such to gullible readers. I consider this an out-and-out fraud. It was particularly humiliating to me when I read the 1962 volume of the *Hugo Winners*, which the publisher, on the cover, lightheartedly labeled "*Nine prize-winning science fiction stories.*" Well, in my book it should have read "Eight fantasy tales, plus one science fiction story."

Hugo Gernsback invented the term "science fiction." The Hugo Awards, presented annually at the World Science Fiction Convention, were named for him. And yet he disowned eight of the first nine winners of the short fiction Hugo Award. The stories were "The Darfsteller" by Walter M. Miller, Jr.; "Allamagoosa" by Eric Frank Russell; "Exploration Team" by Murray Leinster; "The Star" by Arthur C. Clarke; "Or All the Seas with Oysters" by Avram Davidson; "The Big Front Yard" by Clifford D. Simak; "The Hell-Bound Train" by Robert Bloch; "Flowers for Algernon" by Daniel Keyes; and "The Longest Voyage" by Poul Anderson.

What a puzzle: Which of the stories was legitimate? Was it one of the five stories from *Astounding*, the technical man's science fiction magazine? Was it "Exploration Team" by Murray Leinster, whose story from the 1919 *Argosy*, "The Runaway Skyscraper," was re-

printed in the third issue of *Amazing* and who wrote again for Gernsback's last science fiction magazine, *Science Fiction +*, in the Fifties?
Was it "The Star" by Arthur C. Clarke, whom Gernsback in this same
speech calls "the most outstanding true science fiction personality"?
Was it "The Longest Voyage" by Poul Anderson, whose story was
scored for its astronomy in a letter to *Astounding* by Hal Clement
and in a reply by Anderson himself, two moves in what authors of
this bent are pleased to call The Game?

Our best guess is Daniel Keyes' "Flowers for Algernon" from *Fantasy and Science Fiction*. That's just our best guess. But whichever
story it was, remember, the other eight, whichever they were, were
not science fiction.

By 1963, Gernsback had had a good look at the transformation of
the genre. He didn't like it. He called it "decadence." Like Sturgeon, who has said that ninety per cent of science fiction is crud,
Gernsback said that ninety per cent of science fiction was fantasy
and unacceptable. The question is whether the ten per cents of Sturgeon and Gernsback would be the same.

The Science Fiction Writers of America—Gernsback's heirs—have
put together an anthology of vintage short science fiction, stories
that might have been Nebula winners had the Nebula Awards existed
before 1965. The book is called *The Science Fiction Hall of Fame,
Vol. I*, edited by Robert Silverberg, and its contents are a fair history
of science fiction. These are the writers and stories that we in the
science fiction world have respected. If any stories belong in Sturgeon's ten per cent, it is these. But how many of these stories would
Hugo Gernsback have acknowledged as *really* science fiction?

Here is Gernsback in 1963:

> When, in April 1926, I launched the first issue of *Amazing Sto-
> ries*, I called it "The Magazine of Scientifiction." Not a very elegant
> term, I admit, but I had the fixed idea, even in those early days of
> science fiction, that *Amazing Stories* henceforth was to be known
> as a scientific fiction monthly, to distinguish it from any other type
> of literature.
>
> Not content with that slogan, after a good deal of thought I
> added a second, more explanatory one: "Extravagant Fiction Today
> —Cold Fact Tomorrow."

I carried both of these slogans on the editorial page between 1926 and 1929, as long as I published *Amazing Stories*.

Later, for Vol. I, No. 1, of *Science Wonder Stories* in June, 1929, I wrote another descriptive slogan: "Prophetic Fiction is the Mother of Scientific Fact." I think this still means what it says. Science fiction—under *any* term or name—must, in my opinion, deal first and foremost in futures.

It must, in story form, forecast *the wonders of man's progress to come*. That means distant exploits and exploration of space and time.

[But not two of these three stories: "The Star," "Exploration Team," and "The Longest Voyage." Or perhaps not any of them.]

Contrary to the opinions of many latter-day, so-called science fiction authors, the genre of Jules Verne and H.G. Wells has now been prostituted to such an extent that it often is quite impossible to find any reference to science in what is popularly called science fiction today.

The classic science fiction of Jules Verne and H.G. Wells, with little exception, was serious and, yes, instructive and educational. *It was not primarily intended to entertain or to amuse*. These stories carried a message, and that is the great difference between technological science fiction and fantasy tales. I repeat: either you have *science* fiction, with the emphasis on *science*, or you have fantasy. You cannot have both—the two genres bear no relation to each other.

Of the stories in *The Science Fiction Hall of Fame*, Gernsback published only one, the earliest, Stanley G. Weinbaum's 1934 story, "A Martian Odyssey." Would that qualify as *science* fiction, with the emphasis on *science*, or is it fantasy? According to Gernsback, you cannot have both.

For comparison, here is a genuine Gernsbackian scientifiction story for you: "Sam Jones, Radio Tube Bootlegger," by Volney G. Mathison. Gernsback blurbed it this way:

A story of the bad old days when there were sharp practices in radio—and how some of the practitioners came to grief in carrying out their designs on the unwary public. If it is not true, it is well enough invented to convey a moral to radio-set owners in their purchasing of supplies.

Whatever this story may be, it is something other than Zelazny's "A Rose for Ecclesiastes," or Leiber's "Coming Attraction," or Matheson's "Born of Man and Woman," or even Weinbaum's "A Martian Odyssey."

If Gernsback is right—and we have to assume that he is, since he wrote the definitions—when did false science fiction start being passed off for the real thing? Why did it happen?

Gernsback founded *Amazing Stories* in April 1926 with the same clear vision of science fiction that he continued to hold in 1963. From the first issue, he sounded the same themes—science fiction was prophetic, educational and clean:

> A scientifiction story should be seventy-five per cent literature interwoven with twenty-five per cent science.

And:

> Science Fiction . . . is a tremendous new force in America. They are the stories that are discussed by inventors, by scientists, and in the classroom. Teachers insist that pupils read them, because they widen the young man's horizon, as nothing else can. Wise parents, too, let their children read this type of story, because they know that it keeps them abreast of the times, educates them and supplants the vicious and debasing sex story.

And Gernsback knew how to honor his own ideas. In one of his magazines, he held a "What Science Fiction Means to Me" letter contest. Second Honorable Mention went to Edward E. Smith, Ph.D.: "To the scientists no class of fiction has a lure even approaching that of carefully considered and well written science fiction." First Honorable Mention, Jack Williamson: "A new era dawns . . . Science will answer the call, with a thousand new inventions—inspired by science fiction."

First Prize in this contest went to B.S. Moore, unlike Smith and Williamson not a science fiction writer himself. Moore wrote:

> A few months ago I could not understand the fourth-dimension, that is, as the scientific world regards it. Today I do understand it, as it is understood in theory, of course, and I owe it to science fiction. True, the majority of writers are practically individual in their theories, but by weighing these and comparing them one can eventually reach the general explanation.

Gernsback wanted to call his magazine *Scientifiction*. He settled on *Amazing* when "after mature thought, the publishers [i.e., Gernsback] decided that the name which is now used was after all the best one to influence the masses, because anything that smacks of science seems to be too 'deep' for the average type of reader."

Gernsback had been publishing science fiction since 1908 in his various magazines, particularly in *Radio News* (which printed "Sam Jones, Radio Tube Bootlegger") and *Science and Invention*. *Science and Invention* was a magazine rather like *Popular Mechanics*, but livelier and more interesting. Along with more conventional material, *Science and Invention* printed prophetic articles and their fictional equivalent. Gernsback had a taste for dramatized prophecy. He wanted fiction in *Amazing* about the unknown that respected the known.

What did he publish? He published stories by Edgar Allan Poe —"the father of 'scientifiction'." He published Jules Verne: "He predicted the present day submarine almost down to the last bolt!" He published H.G. Wells.

Gernsback published stories by himself, establishing a tradition that has been respected by science fiction magazine editors ever since. His stories were the short stories "The Magnetic Storm," "The Electric Duel" and "The Killing Flash," and the novels *Ralph 124C 41+* and *Baron Munchausen's Scientific Adventures*, this last narrated by one "I. M. Alier."

He published reprints from the Munsey adventure magazines by writers like Murray Leinster. He published reprints from *Science and Invention*, and some reprints of reprints.

Eventually, Gernsback published new writers, most frequently David Keller, Harl Vincent, S.P. Meek, Ed Earl Repp, A. Hyatt Verrill, and Stanton A. Coblentz—names now nearly forgotten. These stories that Gernsback published, both the new and the reprints, were in the main about inventions to come.

The most famous new story that Gernsback published in *Amazing* —by a writer who is *not* forgotten—was Edward E. Smith's *The Skylark of Space*, a story of the first trip to the stars. Gernsback described it thus: "Plots, counterplots, hair-raising and hair-breadth escapes, mixed with love, adventure and good science seem to fairly tumble all over the pages." And: "By the time you finish reading the final instalment of *The Skylark of Space*, we are certain that you will agree with us that it is one of the most outstanding scientifiction stories of the decade."

With this as background, we may ask again: Where did Gernsback's dream of prophetic and educational fiction go wrong? When did science fiction get turned into unacceptable fantasy?

From April 1926 until Gernsback lost ownership of *Amazing* in 1929, he published every bit of scientifiction in existence. He had no competition. He set the rules. He made the definition and then illustrated it with stories to his own liking. He said what science fiction was, and he showed what it was. But then from June 1929 through December, there were three science fiction magazines.

There was *Amazing*, at first nominally edited by Arthur T. Lynch, and after November edited by T. O'Conor Sloane, who had been editor-in-fact for Gernsback. *Amazing* did its best to continue Gernsback's successful policies. They published stories by Jules Verne, David Keller, Harl Vincent, S.P. Meek, Bob Olsen, Stanton Coblentz, and Clare Winger Harris.

Gernsback started two new magazines, *Science Wonder Stories* and *Air Wonder Stories*. The slogan of *Air Wonder* was: "The Future of Aviation Springs from the Imagination" and the stories were to be "SOLELY flying stories of the future, strictly along scientific-mechanical-technical lines, full of adventure, exploration and achievement." *Air Wonder* quickly failed, and in 1930 Gernsback's two magazines were combined into one: *Wonder Stories*. In his new magazines, Gernsback published H.G. Wells, David Keller, S.P. Meek, Stanton Coblentz, Ed Earl Repp, A. Hyatt Verrill, and Clare Winger Harris.

Still, at that moment in 1929, there was the possibility of science fiction that did not fit Gernsback's definition. There were two editorial judgments at work instead of one.

T. O'Conor Sloane was born in 1851. When he became editor of *Amazing*, he was nearly eighty. He wore a long white beard, and he continued to edit *Amazing* until 1938.

Sloane was a man of the Age of Invention, like Gernsback.

Sloane's son had married the daughter of Thomas Edison. Sloane might be presumed to have shared Gernsback's tastes and beliefs.

But, as is well known, Sloane did not believe in the possibility of space travel. He was not a True Believer. Nonetheless, he did publish stories about space travel, stories that he could only think were fantasy. In 1930, Sloane published the first six stories of John W. Campbell, including the novel *The Black Star Passes*. He published *The Universe Wreckers* by Edmond Hamilton. And he published Edward E. Smith's second novel, *Skylark Three*.

Were these stories *really* science fiction, or fantasy masquerading as science fiction like all those Hugo prize-winners that Gernsback spoke so harshly of in 1963? Sloane couldn't know. He himself couldn't tell the difference. If he wanted to know, the only person he might have asked was Gernsback, the keeper of the keys to the true kingdom of science fiction, and we don't believe that he did.

Then, in January 1930, another competitor appeared, *Astounding Stories of Super-Science*, edited by Harry Bates. *Amazing* and *Science Wonder Stories* were the brethren of popular science magazines. They aspired to good paper, when it could be afforded. And they were always of a respectable so-called "bedsheet" size—eight and a half inches by eleven, or eleven and a half. On the other hand, *Astounding* was the offspring of a line of adventure fiction magazines. It was printed on cheap paper, and it was published in the less reputable "pulp" size—seven inches by ten. It looked racier and less educational, and it was.

Harry Bates had distinctly different ideas than Gernsback:

> *Amazing Stories*! Once I had bought a copy. What awful stuff, I'd found it! Cluttered with trivia! Packed with puerilities. Written by unimaginables!

Bates says:

> I had thought up about a dozen possible names. Of them all, the one I liked best was *Tomorrow*, but I didn't even show this one to Clayton, because it was too mild and indefinite and sort of high-brow. My second preference was *Science Fiction*, which was generic and like the other had dignity, but I killed this one with arguments that as a phrase hardly anyone had ever seen or heard it (*Amazing*

preferring the horrible "scientifiction") and that as a name it would promise only mild and orthodox stories concerned with *today's* science. . . . It was my third preference which I advocated: *Astounding*. As a name it lacked dignity, but no matter: it was gutsy and would compel attention, and it generally resembled *Amazing* and could be counted on to attract the eye of that magazine's readers while pleasantly promising others that the stories would stun them. It was a little better than *Fantastic* and much better than *Astonishing* and *Future* and the remaining ones on my list. I think I remember Clayton's trying it aloud, tasting it. I am not sure that the rest of the name was decided that morning, but I can tell you the reasons for our choice. "Of Science Fiction" would in time have become redundant. "Of Super-Science" was perfect. The word Science was in it, also that great promiser of extras: Super. As a phrase, the flavor was a trifle vulgar, but the meaning was right on the beam. Super-Science means *above* and *more than* science. The science fiction of the early writers was indeed above and more than science.

(To state it bluntly, the science fiction of the early writers had little relation to the science of the scientists. However, it had as much relation as it has had since, in the main. The extrapolations of most science fiction writers rocket starward from pads much too narrow and rickety. If the writers were solidly grounded in the sciences, *and* if they were aware of the intermeshings of the sciences, *and* if each one had a stiff conscience, there'd be very little science fiction written. . . . The naked fact is, almost all of what is called science fiction is fantasy and nothing else but. This has increasingly come to be recognized, but when I began privately saying so, near the beginning, I would get arguments. Do you aging buffs really think there is more science in science fiction nowadays? Do you really think the stories are less impossible? Of course they are better written, many of them, and more thought-provoking, some of them —but science? Hurrah for our honest old *Super*-Science!)

Bates further says:

Some of you clamored for occasional stories of the kind appearing in *Amazing*, but we knew that large numbers of the other readers would have been repelled by them. You still say that certain of *Amazing*'s stories were classics? Okay, I take your word for it . . . I'll tell you a secret. Eventually I tried to get a couple of hybrids combining the most conspicuous qualities of *Astounding* and *Amazing*, but I failed. It seemed we could not make them mix . . .

So that was two votes out of three against Gernsback. One editor,

T. O'Conor Sloane, didn't know for certain *what* science fiction was. The other, Harry Bates, knew it was fantasy.

By 1936, *Astounding*—under the editorship of F. Orlin Tremaine —was the only monthly sf magazine. *Amazing* was bi-monthly. And in that year, Gernsback sold a faltering and bi-monthly *Wonder Stories* to Standard Magazines, a pulp chain. In short, Gernsback's science fiction lasted as a working ideal for exactly as long as there was no alternative to it. When there was an alternative, Gernsback failed.

Recall Gernsback's words. Science fiction

> ... was serious and, yes, instructive and educational. *It was not primarily intended to entertain or to amuse.* These stories carried a message, and that is the great difference between technological science fiction and fantasy tales. I repeat: Either you have *science* fiction, with the emphasis on *science*, or you have fantasy. You cannot have both—the two genres bear no relation to each other.

The "real" science fiction of the Twenties, when Gernsback was running the show, was prophetic fiction about inventions, stories like Gernsback's own *Ralph 124C 41+*. Gernsback's science fiction was written by David Keller, Bob Olsen, Clare Winger Harris and Ed Earl Repp.

The false science fiction of the Thirties, when Gernsback had lost control, was primarily intended to entertain and amuse. It was published in *Astounding* and it was written by Edward E. Smith, John Campbell, Murray Leinster and Jack Williamson. It was exuberant fantasies of super-science. It was, as well, the more tightly-conceived fantasies of metaphorical science that Campbell had begun to write under the name Don A. Stuart and would encourage when he became editor of *Astounding*. It was these sorts of stories that Gernsback considered fantasy when they won the Hugo Award.

In the June 15, 1970 issue of *Library Journal*, a basic science fiction bibliography was published under the imprimatur of the Science Fiction Writers of America. This bibliography was compiled by Alexei Panshin from lists by himself, James Blish, L. Sprague de Camp, Damon Knight, Andre Norton, Joanna Russ, Robert Silverberg and Jack Williamson. It can stand as an indication of the science fiction valued by the practitioners of science fiction.

In this bibliography, sixty-two novels were listed that first saw publication since Gernsback founded *Amazing Stories* in 1926. Thirty-two of these were published in part or in whole in one or another of the sf magazines. None of these was published by Hugo Gernsback.

The earliest novel, Jack Williamson's *The Legion of Space*, was serialized in *Astounding* in 1934. The earliest nine—all of those titles published before 1948—appeared in either *Astounding* or *Unknown*. They were *Sinister Barrier* by Eric Frank Russell; *Lest Darkness Fall* by L. Sprague de Camp; *Gray Lensman* by Edward E. Smith; *The Incomplete Enchanter* by Fletcher Pratt and L. Sprague de Camp; *Slan* by A. E. van Vogt; *Beyond This Horizon* by Robert Heinlein; *Conjure Wife* by Fritz Leiber; and *The World of Null-A* by van Vogt. How many of these classics would Gernsback allow to be science fiction, and how many would he have considered fantasy?

The history of science fiction is very short. Generously, one might say that it lasted from April 1926 to December 1929. The Era of Gernsback.

But it is as fair to say that science fiction as Gernsback defined it never existed, that it was a dream of Gernsback's that was never realized. Gernsback wanted something narrower than he was forced to publish. If science fiction turned into unacceptable fantasy before his eyes, it was Gernsback who started the change.

Gernsback called his magazine *Amazing* instead of *Scientifiction*—and that was a fatal compromise. In his *Science Wonder* letter contest on "What Science Fiction Means to Me," his chosen winners honored fantasy as much as the spirit of prediction. Gernsback not only published the fantastic space opera *The Skylark of Space*, he praised it highly. He published Edmond Hamilton's novelet "The Comet Doom," indistinguishable from the fiction Hamilton was writing for the out-and-out fantasy magazine *Weird Tales*. He published Edgar Rice Burroughs' *The Master Mind of Mars* and described it as "entirely new, packed chockful of adventure and excellent science." (Gernsback's personal copy of the *Amazing Stories Annual* in which the story appeared was bound in his private collection together with his company's publication, *The Secrets of Your Hands, or Palmistry Explained*.) He published the space opera of Stanley Weinbaum.

And, in his last science fiction magazine, *Science Fiction +*, published for seven issues in 1953, Gernsback printed two stories by Harry Bates. Yes, Harry Bates.

Either Gernsback himself could not always tell the difference between science fiction and fantasy, or else he printed stories he could only think were fantasy and compromised with the truth when he said how much he liked their science, or else he had a unique notion of science. Perhaps the kindest thing to be said is that *Science Wonder Stories*—the home of "science fiction"—was as limited in conception as *Air Wonder Stories* and was as impossible to sustain.

Gernsback won only a single battle. His idea of what the field should be in practice was repudiated. However, his name for the genre was adopted. By 1932, *Amazing* was calling itself "The Magazine of Science Fiction" instead of "The Magazine of Scientifiction." By 1938, *Astounding Stories* had become *Astounding Science-Fiction*.

The name survived, we suggest, because it was concise, comparatively unrestricting, and respectable in sound. If you didn't look too closely, it fit the field. And it sounded pretty good. But the respectability it gave was always spurious and usually transparent, and depended on things like taking credit for predicting the atom bomb.

Today, the genre no longer needs false respectability. The books and stories in the SFWA bibliography and in the *Science Fiction Hall of Fame* volume are sufficient grounds for self-respect. Science and prophecy have nothing to do with it. Our self-respect is based on the fact that the genre is an art form, a valuable and sophisticated way of talking about ourselves and our feelings and perceptions. As much as has been accomplished in sf, the best is yet to be done.

Even a cursory glance shows that the term "science fiction" no longer can pretend to fit the actualities of the genre. Gernsback was right in 1963. We do misuse his name. We are fantasy-writing frauds. We should acknowledge the fact.

As Sam Moskowitz has said: "The real 'Father of Science Fiction' is Hugo Gernsback and no one can take the title away from him."

Science fiction was Hugo Gernsback's dream. We should bury it decently with him.

4/ SEARCHING FOR THE HEARTLAND

[*Fantasy and Science Fiction*, March 1972]

There is a question that used to be raised, long, long ago when science fiction was a thoroughly dubious enterprise, that doesn't get asked much anymore, and ought to be: what is science fiction good for? What goes on in science fiction that makes it worth reading?

This is not a question for readers. That they read science fiction at all—at least for a time—is sufficient justification. They read sf because they do find something in it. The question is for writers, editors, and critics, those people whose business it is to make science fiction and to make science fiction better. If we have any interest in keeping the readers we attract for longer than the traditional three years or five, if we have any interest in attracting more readers, if we have any interest in what we are doing beyond the mere dumb fact of doing it, this is a question that we need to know the answer to.

Hugo Gernsback answered the question back when the world was new. He said that sf was instructive and educational. That wasn't a true answer. That was a political answer. And Gernsback lost his audience to editors whose instincts were sounder. Twenty years later, John Campbell answered the question again. He said that sf was predictive. Again an untrue political answer. Campbell didn't insist on his answer as strongly as Gernsback, but he too lost his audience.

Since sf has gained legitimacy, the question of its value has been allowed to be tucked away, but it still deserves to be answered. It is the very lack of an answer that is the cause of some of our most whirling confusions and desperate battles.

Here's a whirling confusion for you: A year ago, Harry Harrison, a former Vice President of the Science Fiction Writers of America, declared that he was withdrawing all his books and stories from contention for the SFWA Nebula Awards as a protest against all the good stories that had lost and the bad stories that had won. As evidence for this critical judgment, he pointed to the fact that none of the short fiction winners had ever been selected by him for the annual best of the year volume that he and Brian Aldiss edit.

Here's a more humble confusion for you. In last November's issue of *Galaxy*, Algis Budrys publicly resigned as house book reviewer. There were, he said, admirable stories and popular stories. He knew an admirable story when he saw one, though he didn't always enjoy it very much. As for what was enjoyable and popular—well, Budrys had lost his innocent eye and couldn't entirely tell anymore what was likeable, and when he could identify something that was enjoyable, the remnants of his innocence tripped his tongue and prevented him from being able to say what it was. So he was quitting.

These are considerable problems that Harrison and Budrys raise. And in both cases, they reduce to the confession that a writer-editor and a writer-critic don't know why people do read science fiction. Both are sure of intellectual excellences, but emotional excellences —the heart of any art—leave them baffled. Harrison doesn't seem to know they exist and Budrys can't locate them.

The five anthologies on hand for review may give us some clues. Each is ordered around a premise. Premises are a way that an editor who doesn't know why people read sf can give readers a formal excuse for the existence of his book. In each case, the premise is written large on the book jacket:

The Hugo Winners, Vol. II is FOURTEEN PRIZE-WINNING SCIENCE FICTION STORIES.

Orbit 9 is An Anthology of Brand-New SF Stories.

Best SF: 1970 is The Best SF stories of the year from the best SF magazines in the world.

SF: Author's Choice 3 is THIRTEEN SF GREATS PRESENT THEIR FAVORITE STORIES.

Other Worlds, Other Gods is ADVENTURES IN RELIGIOUS SCIENCE FICTION.

Let us take a look at the actualities that lie behind these slogans and see what they can tell us about the true-blue heart of sf.

The key, if there is a key here, is in *The Hugo Winners*. The editor, Isaac Asimov, had his stories pre-selected for him with the guarantee that people had found them extraordinarily enjoyable, an advantage unshared by the editors of the other four anthologies, who had to take their chances. The result provides an effective commentary on both Harrison and Budrys. These stories have not been Harrison's choices any more than the Nebula Award stories have been. And though Budrys seems to believe that stories are either admirable or popular, these stories largely manage to be both—which is what we should want for science fiction. Awards may be given for external reasons or for bad reasons, and some stories may appeal at one moment and in retrospect seem less worthy, but overall this is an excellent collection, easily the most readable of the five we are considering. If any stories can give us clues to the reasons that people read science fiction, these should.

There are five obvious constancies in *The Hugo Winners*. The first is that the stories are recent, dating from 1962 through 1969. The second is that the stories are long. Only three, all by Harlan Ellison, are less than twenty pages in length. The seven longest range from fifty pages for "Nightwings" by Robert Silverberg to ninety pages for "The Dragon Masters" by Jack Vance. The third is that the stories are all well-removed from the familiar present, being set on other planets, or on parallel worlds, or on a sharply discontinuous future Earth. The fourth is that these strange worlds are developed in some detail, most particularly in the longer stories. And the fifth is that the stories are positive. With the exception of the Ellison stories, which are still positive enough to scream about the failings of the world ("The Beast That Had No Mouth, But Had to Scream 'Repent, Harlequin!' at the Heart of the World"), these stories show men responding well to crisis, human culture evolving, or men becoming something a little nearer the gods.

This last point clearly sets these science fiction stories apart from so-called mainstream fiction. Mimetic fiction, confined to our society and our time, shows men crushed by crisis, human culture as static, and men as all too definitely something less than the gods. And mimetic fiction is a negative drag of a literature. Sf allows the possibility of stepping outside the limitations of the present moment and considering alternatives.

The other constancies of this anthology reinforce this point. It is the removal from the present that allows alternatives to be presented. It is the development in detail that shows alternatives to be meaningful. Length in itself is not an absolute virtue, but it is length that allows the detailed presentation and development of alternatives. It is no accident that a series of short stories should have won the short fiction Hugo Award in 1962, or that when there has been but one short fiction award presented, it should go to longer stories like Poul Anderson's "No Truce with Kings" and Gordon Dickson's "Soldier, Ask Not" rather than to shorter stories. And finally, while the recent origin of these stories is of no particular importance, being built into the premise of the anthology—that is, that these are the most recent winners of this particular award—the fact that stories like these should be rewarded again and again over a period of years is important. These are the stories that people come to science fiction to find.

If there is any hope for us in our present moment of societal agony, it must be in the possibility of new alternatives. Science fiction, in its freedom from the limits of this moment, can offer its freedom to readers as a promise of the possibility of new alternatives, and this is sf's great virtue.

If this is what we can learn from *The Hugo Winners*, our other anthologies, particularly *Orbit 9*, *Best SF: 1970*, and *SF: Author's Choice 3*, offer the other face of the same lesson: that is, sf which rejects its freedom to be positive is as big a bummer as mimetic fiction. If *The Hugo Winners* is any guide, the stories in these anthologies will win no awards and may well give readers won to science fiction good reason to go away again. Most of these stories are almost perverse in their courting of unnecessary limitation. These stories are no worse technically than those in *The Hugo Winners*. They simply offer the reader no reward but technique, just like mimetic fiction.

Start with length. Again, length in itself is no virtue. But of fifty-four stories in these four anthologies, only four are longer than twenty-five pages. No room for development of new alternatives —if new alternatives were present. In *Orbit 9*, *Best SF: 1970* and *SF: Author's Choice 3*, they mostly aren't.

In Damon Knight's *Orbit 9* and in Harry Harrison and Brian Aldiss's *Best SF: 1970*, this may be laid on the doorstep of that particularly desperate failure of understanding, the New Wave. These two claustrophobic collections are the children and step-children of the New Wave.

Along about the middle Sixties, it was noticed by some writers and editors of science fiction that many of the devices of sf were tired and clichéd to the point of non-usability. Check back—there was a dreadfully thin period in sf at the end of the Fifties and into the early Sixties when writers were doing little more than ringing endless tiresome changes on the materials of the Forties. However, the answer that was found was not to invent new devices, but to chuck out of science fiction everything that makes it science fictional. The result was the New Wave. The result was these two anthologies.

The stories in these two books are not removed from the present. With all time and all space as possibilities, they choose to huddle. The settings are close-range tomorrows that differ from now only by the addition of a single whimper-making innovation. Or familiar todays that do the same. Or, even worse, surrealistic todays in which the universe makes less sense than it does for us, and the alternatives are even more limited than those we ordinarily know.

Almost inevitably, both collections are sinkholes of negation. There are a few exceptions in the twenty-eight stories in these two books. In *Best SF: 1970*, there is " 'Franz Kafka' by Jorge Luis Borges" by Alvin Greenberg, about a set of mysterious symbols invading our world to some unknown purpose, which ends: "I would imagine that the cake is still fresh. It is decorated with a unique set of symbols, which, like the cake, are sweet and edible. It is not my birthday either, but what danger could there be in a little taste?" In some hands and in some magazines, that could be taken as a negative ending. In these hands and in the context of *New American Review*, the original place of publication of this story, it must be taken as suggesting renewal. And in *Orbit 9*, there is R.A. Lafferty's "When All the Lands Pour Out Again." Lafferty is a man from whom the New Wave should have taken direction. He is prodigiously inventive of new devices, and though his story is not far removed, it offers the promise of all the new alternatives anyone could hope for.

There is one difference between these two anthologies. *Orbit 9* is the more depressing.

Harrison's *SF: Author's Choice 3* is neither as claustrophobic nor as negative, but it is no more recommendable. This third time around, the list of authors is getting thin. It's now down to David I. Masson, Piers Anthony, Langdon Jones and Barry Malzberg. And the authors seem to have been restricted to stories not previously reprinted, which makes the contents even thinner.

The main fault of the anthology is that it seems to have got caught in the mid-Sixties pinch. All of the stories date from 1964 or later. The Old Wave stories like Piers Anthony's "Phog" and Larry Niven's "Bordered in Black" use tired old devices. And the New Wave stories, like Brian Aldiss's "Sober Noises of Morning in a Marginal Land," aim for significance while disdaining all but the inescapable minimum of sf apparatus, and founder in vagueness. There are no exciting new alternatives here, no prizewinners actual or potential, and nothing to hold a hungry reader.

Other Worlds, Other Gods, edited by Mayo Mohs, is something different and something better than these last three anthologies. Half of its stories are from earlier periods than any in the other four books. There is more removal in these stories than in the Knight or two Harrison anthologies. Even the title seems to promise new alternatives of a sort that science fiction is well able to deliver.

If there is a fault in this anthology, it is that the premise is very narrowly construed. The editor, raised a Roman Catholic and presently the editor of *Time*'s Religion department, has restricted his selections to variations on Christianity. Two of the stories concern challenges to Catholicism in the contact of alien races. Four stories, two of them by Anthony Boucher, are about saints and saviors, all couched in Christian terms. And all the other stories are literalized Christian blasphemies. Perhaps the worst of these are "Evensong" by Lester del Rey and "Shall the Dust Praise Thee?" by Damon Knight, both reprinted from Harlan Ellison's anthology *Dangerous Visions*. Perhaps the best is Arthur C. Clarke's "The Nine Billion Names of God," a Christian horror story, but something quite different in Buddhist terms. It might have been more interesting if it had been written from a Buddhist point of view.

This is a more-than-adequate anthology. It suffers to some extent by the fact that very similar alternatives are set cheek-by-jowl. Perhaps some more enterprising editor will try another anthology of religious science fiction and present a wider range of material.

If all the stories in these five anthologies say anything to us, it is this: To write science fiction, a writer must necessarily be visionary enough to look for new alternatives and be brave enough to write them in discouraging times. If he is unwilling or unable, he wastes the medium and he surely has nothing to offer the readers who have discarded mimetic fiction for its emptiness.

5/ THE WORLD BEYOND THE HILL

[*Extrapolation*, May 1972]

Every story teller has the choice of setting his stories—his commentaries on the universe—in one or the other of two realms of the imagination. One is a world in which the facts of direct perception dominate. This world is the mimetic image of the common everyday places his listeners all know—the Cave, or the City, or the Global Village. The other is a world beyond fact where speculative fantasy runs free—the World Beyond the Hill.

At first glance, this may not seem like much of a choice, even though our own experience may be made both of what direct perception can explain and of what it cannot. We live in an age that respects fact, and in our time most literature has attempted to mirror our common world.

However, historically, this has not been the case at all. Village fiction has been domestic farce, crude humor, bloody anecdote, and simple adventure. It has been Aristophanes' *The Clouds*, with Socrates suspended in a basket, and *The Merry Wives of Windsor*, with Falstaff stuffed in a laundry hamper. It has been New Comedy, *The Satyricon*, "The Miller's Tale" and Robin Hood. It has been distinctly the smaller and lesser part of Western literature.

On the other hand, the fruit of the unhistorical, ungeographical World Beyond the Hill has been *The Odyssey*, *The Oresteia*, *Beowulf*, *Tristan*, *Parzival*, *The Divine Comedy*, *Morte D'Arthur*, *Gargantua and Pantagruel*, *The Faerie Queene*, *Doctor Faustus*, *King Lear*, *The*

Tempest, and *Paradise Lost*. The World Beyond the Hill has been
the heartland of our literature. It has owned all our best and most
meaningful stories. Until the past two centuries, it has been the
comedians and light entertainers who have told stories of the factual.
The serious have spun dreams.

This is no accident. The reason was stated by Aristotle in *The
Poetics*, commenting on tragedies like *The Oresteia*, which he called
poetry:

> It is not the function of the poet to relate what has happened,
> but what may happen,—what is possible according to the law of
> probability or necessity. The poet and the historian differ not by
> writing in verse or in prose. The work of Herodotus might be put
> into verse, and it would still be a species of history, with metre no
> less than without it. The true difference is that one relates what has
> happened, the other what may happen. Poetry, therefore, is a more
> philosophical and a higher thing than history: for poetry tends to
> express the universal, history the particular.

Until 1700, literature was more interested in expressing universal
cases than in reporting the particularities, fleeting and ephemeral,
of any single time and place. Indeed, the possibility of historically-
bound mimetic fiction would no more have occurred to most writers
than it did to Aristotle. Even the lightest stories of love and separation were automatically set in the World Beyond the Hill. The
audience for fiction was the superior literate few. To them, what
was local and common was irrelevant and uninteresting. And they
were enough of a kind that they felt no need to discover the facts
about themselves. Holding a simple mirror to perception was not
the purpose of literature.

After 1700, however, serious literature migrated from one fictional
realm to the other, from the World Beyond the Hill into the tight
confines of the Village. The reasons were three.

First, the rediscovery of our history and the exploration of the
world left no room for the imagination in those vast blank areas of
time and space that had previously been its playing fields. The World
Beyond the Hill must have psychological distance in order to exist.
Nothing ruins a story of universals more than particular criticism:

> Sheakspear, in a play, brought in a number of men saying they had suffered Shipwrack in Bohemia, wher ther is no sea near by some 100 miles.

Through the Middle Ages, the chief setting of removed literature was time—the a-historical past. The geography of *The Odyssey* and *The Oresteia* was only a stone's throw from the front doors of their audience. The same is true of medieval epic and romance. It may well have added to the power of Greek tragedy and *Tristan* and *Parzival* that they were displaced only a sufficient time to allow miracles, but that the giant heroic men they spoke of walked in familiar lands. It raised the slim possibility that what had happened once might happen again.

The Renaissance, however, in unearthing Classical literature, made for itself the beginnings of a new and more particular history that, as it became more detailed during the next two centuries, left less and less room for the marvelous. As the history of England was pieced together, it finally became necessary for the poets to admit that they had told several lies about King Arthur.

The World Beyond the Hill then seated itself in *terra incognita*, the remoter corners of the Earth, opened to literature by the voyages of discovery of the fifteenth and sixteenth centuries. Out there might be found Atlantis, El Dorado, or Lilliput. But, as the planet is finite, by the eighteenth century the voyages of exploration had replaced the universals of the imagination with the particulars of Africa, Asia and the Americas. The names of the magical mythical lands of Brazil, California and Terra Australis had, so to speak, been appropriated for new suburban developments by shrewd real estate agents. This planet, once the potential home of all the infinite possibilities the mind can conceive, stood revealed in its limitation. Once again, the World Beyond the Hill had to admit that it did not exist as it had said it did.

There was no longer houseroom in history and geography for the unfactual. It could not be taken seriously by men who knew nothing but history and geography. Eviction was the first reason for the replacement of the World Beyond the Hill by the Village.

The second reason was the rise of the middle class, practical men by the myriad, and the general spread of literacy throughout the population. The audience for fiction suddenly became far broader and more diverse than it had ever been before. This new audience— numerically, economically and politically dominant—was interested in learning what might be made of the broad, malleable, Modern world of fact they found themselves inhabiting. Even more, this audience had an insatiable interest in hearing about itself, in all its particular variation.

And third, at the same time that Captain Cook was mapping the Pacific and the middle class was staring at itself in its new mirror to its own great delight, literature realized for the first time the fictional potentials of the particular. The result was the rise of the mimetic novel, a new form discovering new possibility.

Village fiction now claimed title to the whole of the Earth. If you looked at things its way—and it forced you to as surely as lines of perspective force an angle of view in a painting—it promised that there was no place in this world that it could not touch and nothing it couldn't explain. It was a jealous landlord and it wanted its due.

Don Quixote (1605, 1615) was the first brilliant and devastating statement of this perception. The story is a commentary on the knightly romances like *Tristan* and *Parzival* that had summarized the ideals of Europe for four hundred years. It forces us to look at them from a Village point of view. Don Quixote is a citizen of the Village (like us all, the story would like us to believe and admit), who mistakenly places his faith in the objective reality of the World Beyond the Hill. He believes himself to be one with Tristan and Parzival, and time and time again he is ruthlessly undone by fact. The story says that if we share his delusion and try to live as he tries to live, we will be undone as well. In an acknowledgment of the World Beyond the Hill in an era (Shakespeare's) when it was still necessary to acknowledge the power of the World Beyond the Hill, Don Quixote is ultimately ennobled by his idealism, but still, in the very nicest of ways, Cervantes has handed mythic literature its eviction notice. The giants of this world have been forever put out of business by mad old men and windmills. They can leave now.

Robinson Crusoe (1719) is less nice about the same message. In this earliest of mimetic novels, a bourgeois invades the world of the non-factual—a remote island beyond the reach of maps, which in former times might have been the home of a Prospero—and hammers it into shape. The story says that given a shipwreck full of the necessary particulars, *that* is what practical men can do to the World Beyond the Hill any place they happen across it. They can set it to rights. They can make a bit of England of it.

By the end of Robinson Crusoe's century, the World Beyond the Hill was in a state of crisis. From its former flourishing, dominant state, it was now reduced to four slender forms. There were literary fairy tales from the court of Louis XIV. Some of these yet survive. "Beauty and the Beast" and "Cinderella," originally written for the entertainment of adults, still are read to children. There were Utopias, like Louis Sebastien Mercier's *Memoirs of the Year Two Thousand Five Hundred*, none of which are still read—which appears to be the universal fate of Utopias when their particular time of origin and pertinence is past. There were Gothic horror stories like *The Castle of Otranto* and *The Monk*, which clung to a precarious existence in the shadows of the past in a manner equivalent to the geographical compromise with the map of Europe that allowed Graustark its existence a hundred years later. Of such Gothics, only these two novels are even dimly-remembered curiosities. And finally, there were marvelous voyages, hundreds of them, only two of which still have any currency: *Gulliver's Travels* and that invader of the imaginary, *Robinson Crusoe*. They survive, not so much by their appeal to children, as by their continuing presence in children's libraries.

This is work of a minor order. It cannot compare to *King Lear* or to *Paradise Lost*. It is a clear decline from the seventeenth century.

The reason is the limitations in realms of existence for the World Beyond the Hill. They were few and narrow by 1800. There were the far corners of the Earth. Even into the twentieth century, innermost Africa and lost Tibet supported the stories of H. Rider Haggard, Edgar Rice Burroughs, and Talbot Mundy. But if the World Beyond the Hill had attempted to survive only here, it would at last have found itself huddling in the Himalayas, hoping to be overlooked, as it does in James Hilton's *Lost Horizon* (1933). In this final statement of the relationship between the Village and the World Beyond the Hill on this Earth, when the immortals of the fabulous land of Shangri-La are exposed at last to the light of the mimetic world, they must wither and die of old age, dissolving "like all too lovely things, at the first touch of reality."

There was even less room in the dimension of time by 1800. All the way back to the creation of the world, only those unimportant moments were available when no one had been watching and noting down particularities. For example—as in one of the forgotten Gothics of the eighteenth century, Clara Reeve's *The Old English Baron*—within a cupboard back in the fifteenth century, for exactly as long as no one looks within.

The alternatives to this Earth were just as limited. Heaven and Hell were possibilities, as in *The Divine Comedy* and *Paradise Lost*. But the range of stories allowed by these settings is small. More important, except for believers, stories of Heaven and Hell can only be entertainments. They cannot engage, as they could do in their own proper time.

The same is true of the setting of fairy tales and children's fantasies. We can call it by the common name of Never-Never Land. It is the place where William Morris set his re-creative medieval romances like *The Wood Beyond the World* (1894) and Lord Dunsany his *The King of Elfland's Daughter* (1924). It is a place quite firmly *of* Earth, but it is no place *on* Earth. Not with our histories and geographies sitting open on our laps. It is another remnant realm, the last memory of all the unhistorical, ungeographical places that formerly existed. It is invisible; it is underfoot or underground; it is the path you don't take; it is the space over your left shoulder; it is at the end of the rainbow. Never-Never Land is a limited, tightly-bound place that continues to exist by compromise, like those last floating islands that are forever dodging the mapmakers. It is a small place and it cannot grow larger. All its marvels are familiar, therefore limited in their meaning and power.

This was the state of the World Beyond the Hill at the end of the eighteenth century. A fading, failing world. In order to survive, and to regain the power it had formerly had, removed fiction had to find realms over which the Village had no sway and phenomena that rationalistic theories could not explain: new metaphors to compel the attention, understanding and assent of men.

Since 1800, speculative fantasy has been incubating new arguments. It has never been completely lost. There have always been some readers in every age with a hunger for the marvelous, and there have always been some writers to keep the old traditions alive. But while it has been busy, it has had to take its audience where it could find it. At its rare best, sf has been a minor tradition in major letters. At worst, it has taken refuge where it could, as children's literature or as crude popular entertainment.

For two hundred and fifty years, then, mimetic fiction has held stage center. It has had every opportunity to display itself, to present its case, to force its perspective. The result has been overconcentration, even an overdose of the particular. And now the day of the secular novel as the exclusive vehicle of serious fictional consideration of the universe is over. It has reached its natural limits while the World Beyond the Hill has been in exile. We have explored the Earth and turned it into a single Global Village. Asia, Africa, Australia, the Americas and Antarctica share the same telephone exchange, and any person in the world is at the other end of a direct dial phone call. In the process, we have discovered that not all problems worth acknowledging have social causes, and that not all social problems are amenable to present solution, as were the beliefs of the mimetic novel, the beliefs of the Modern world that began in 1700. We have not yet assimilated the fact, but this is the Modern world no longer. We are Post-Modern, and the limitations of the mimetic are now as apparent as the limitations of the removed in 1800.

Our main vehicle of serious literature today is still the Modern man's mimetic novel. Its history is glory piled on glory: Henry Fielding, Jane Austen, Dickens, Dostoevsky, and Tolstoy, and, in our century, the master accumulators of the particular, Joyce and Proust. But after them, there have been no new glories.

The mimetic novel has reached a dead end. Its claims have been shown to be as partial and subject to question as the claims of *Tristan* and *Parzival*. A look at any issue of the *New York Times Book*

Review in these days of the Global Village will show that the best understanding of the contemporary world by the secular novel is an impassioned bleat of bafflement. Something is definitely happening, but the mimetic novel doesn't know what it is.

The "mainstream" novel is a congeries of endless repetition of what has already been seen and said, ever-increasing miniaturization, autobiography disguised as fiction, "masterpieces" that are dead and forgotten in five years or one, catatonia, and black comedy that is as much the mirror of stasis as it is attempted exception. Its audience is deserting it because the mimetic novel can offer nothing sustaining. Far from being a glory, modern literature is narrow, world-weary, sick and unhappy, and desperate for alternatives. It is a cause for concern, and our critics and commentators have not failed us—they have been endlessly concerned for years, without suggesting a viable alternative.

Our literature is doomed to stagnate until there are radical changes in society, it is said. Or until there is a return to the secure confines of traditional religion. Or until we cease to experiment fruitlessly and imitate the successes of the giants of mimesis of the last century.

The problem with these solutions is that they are all determinedly mimetic. They suggest a return to past example, or more of the same—but better—rather than any true alternative, which is the sort of thing that mimetic thinking always does. It heals wounds with thorns.

It is the very particularities of the mimetic novel that are its chief limitation. Modern writers have an impressive array of technique at their command. They can *write*. But what is demanded of fictions today, technique alone can be no help for. It is to speak of the universal beyond the particular.

As long as fiction is limited to the surface of our society as its only possible subject, the best it will be able to do is speak of the dubious perfections of the world of practical men: the world of Stalin and Hitler, Lyndon Johnson and Richard Nixon. As long as the novel is limited to the sensible world as its single subject, its enforced vision, its totality, alternatives are out of the question. All it can do is become shriller, less relevant, and more frustrated.

As a single example among many of the limitations of the particular, let us look at legitimate tragedy, which seems to have disappeared as a literary possibility since the Elizabethans and the rise of the mimetic mode. As George Steiner says in *The Death of Tragedy*, "From antiquity until the age of Shakespeare and Racine, such accomplishment seemed within the reach of talent. Since then the tragic voice in drama is blurred or still."

It hasn't been for want of trying or good intention. Here is Arthur Miller writing in the 1949 *New York Times* on behalf of his new play, *Death of a Salesman*:

> In this age few tragedies are written. It has often been held that the lack is due to a paucity of heroes among us, or else that modern man has had the blood drawn out of his organs of belief by the skepticism of science, and the heroic attack on life cannot feed on an attitude of reserve and circumspection. For one reason or another, we are often held to be below tragedy—or tragedy above us. The inevitable conclusion is, of course, that the tragic mode is archaic, fit only for the very highly placed, the kings or the kingly, and where this admission is not made in so many words it is most often implied. I believe that the common man is as apt a subject for tragedy in its highest sense as kings were.

But *Death of a Salesman* is a failure as a tragedy. It is pathetic, not purgative. It is particular. It is mimetic.

Tragedy is compatible with these times. The problem is not in a lack of heroes or kings, or in the outmoded archaism of tragic perception, or in the skepticism of science. The problem is that tragedy is incompatible with the mimetic mode. Tragedy only remains an impossibility as long as all answers are assumed to be mimetic.

All literary works use selective emphasis to highlight and underline the workings of the world. In tragedy, irrelevant particularities are trimmed away to reveal the dynamics of the universe at their most concentrated and uncertain. The minutiae of daily life—jobs, meals, taxes and traffic—are the interfering irrelevancies that must be ignored if a tragedy is to be observed. Lear is possible on a removed moor. Lear is not possible in contemporary Chicago, any more than he would have been possible in the London of Shakespeare's day. Lear is not a mimetic king—he is larger than life allows. As Aristotle says in *The Poetics*: "The element of the wonderful is required in tragedy." The mimetic specifically excludes the wonderful.

But let us pause at this point for a moment. Let us go back over the ground we have covered.

We have been speaking as though fiction exists as an independent creature, serving its own purposes. It does not. It is a reflection, not a cause.

We have been talking of the Village and the World Beyond the Hill as though they had objective existence, as though they were real places with real populations in which real events occur, as though they were parts of the universe independent of ourselves. They are not—though the Village, in particular, is often mistaken for real. Both are equally places in our minds.

Fiction is a construct, a model of the universe made up of our perceptions, our feelings, and our ideas, and used to orient us in the real universe that we must live in but have such difficulty in understanding. The sway between the Village and the World Beyond the Hill that we have been describing is not an objectively existing struggle, with authors enlisted as generals and readers as armies. Changes in literary fashion are a reflection of changes in our minds and in the world we seek to understand. For this moment, then, let us look beyond the question of the fluctuations of literature to the history that necessarily lies behind them.

These are dangerous, frightening and uncertain times we live in, when all our oldest answers and institutions have failed us and even our continued existence as a nation, a species, and a planet seems more and more problematical to us. The failure of mimetic literature in our times is only the corollary of a general societal crisis.

The disestablishment of value that we feel so painfully is not unprecedented. At least twice before—when man changed from a hunter to a farmer, and again when man became a city dweller—his models of the universe have been shattered into fragments and had to be remade. These were historical moments as traumatic as our own.

In these last brief one hundred and fifty years of a new revolution in life style for mankind, far more disrupting than the fall of the

Roman Empire—which was a gradual event scarcely noticed in the mirror of fiction—all our old familiar sureties have again collapsed. Until we rebuild our minds, we will be in agony, unsure of anything, including our own survival.

We need to make new integrations. Our need is overwhelming. We need to move beyond the limited particularities of sensible perception and play again with the universals of feeling and idea, and there discover new life-giving alternatives.

With this as preface, we can look again at the seeming displacement of the World Beyond the Hill by the Village and read its true meaning:

All fiction offers answers to the eternal questions: Who am I? Where did I come from? What is my destiny? Mimetic fiction offers social answers. It is socially integrative, appearing only when society is in upheaval. Mimetic fiction is chiefly concerned with class, and with class's adjunct, sexual mores. It tells those men who might wonder—not every man—what society is about and how they fit within it. And when the time of upheaval is past, mimetic fiction disappears again.

In this way, New Comedy came into existence with the disintegration of the Hellenistic world. *The Satyricon* marked the crisis of the succession of the Roman Republic by the Empire—a more traumatic event than the end of the Empire because it involved sudden alterations in the style of daily life. And *The Decameron* was a product of the end of the Middle Ages and the coming of the Renaissance.

Non-mimetic fiction offers psychological answers to the same three questions of nature, origin and destiny. It is psychologically integrative, fitting us not merely into society, but into the universe. It shows us how to mature. It makes homes of our minds. It is more enduring than mimetic fiction because it does not wear social clothing, subject to sudden changes of fashion.

For as long as we can remember—the period of recorded history —non-mimetic answers have weathered social crises. After New Comedy, Homer still told men truths they could believe, and to some degree still does today. After *The Decameron*, the Bible still stood like a rock. And there has been nothing to keep new formulations of old truths from being written concurrently with mimetic fiction in the midst of social storm. *The Divine Comedy*, reaffirming the cosmic order in a time of social change, preceded *The Decameron* by only thirty years.

But our present social crisis is unprecedented in the four thousand years we can remember. The persistence of mimetic fiction since 1700 is a measure of the extent of the social crisis. Answers simply do not appear—and continue to appear—where there are no questions. These questions have continued for so long now that we have come to accept continuing social upheaval as a natural fact of life and social fiction as a natural and basic mode of expression.

The origin of the crisis came with the death of feudalism, the end of the old lord-and-peasant, land-based economic system. In England, the crisis, anticipated by Shakespeare, whose affirmations of natural order are a measure of his sense that natural order was in danger, may first have become generally visible with the seventeenth century inclosure of common land, gained violent expression in the Puritan Revolution, and was prolonged into the nineteenth century by the Industrial Revolution—the name we commonly give to the change, though industrialization itself is in part a response to the pre-existing crisis. This same revaluation of human life style spread slowly east through Europe after its appearance in England. It was the common cause of both the French and Russian Revolutions.

By 1900, the main force of the crisis was over. In America, its signs of passing may be seen in the Seventeenth and Nineteenth Amendments to the Constitution—those providing for popular election of senators and for woman suffrage. We live now amidst the fulfillment of the wildest utopian dreams of the nineteenth century. If this crisis had been of the same order as others in the period of recorded history, like a volcanic island suddenly thrusting up from the ocean floor and then disappearing again, the troubled waters would have been made calm again with its passing.

Instead, as we all know, the seas have become rougher in our century, not calmer. We live in utopia and we don't like it. We don't know what to make of it. We don't know how to live with it.

The problem is that the old religion and the old values that nurtured us so well through the centuries were integral pieces of a model of the universe directly connected to the vanished life style. The model did not survive the upheaval. Shakespeare's natural order of healthy men, existing in a healthy political state, within a healthy universe, no longer convinces and comforts us. The mechanistic universe of the eighteenth century Deists was the last attempt to hold the old world view together. But the attempt was not successful. The old world lies in pieces.

From social crisis, men have passed into a crisis of faith. As Yeats' 1921 poem, "The Second Coming," has it:

> Things fall apart; the centre cannot hold;
> Mere anarchy is loosed upon the world,
> The blood-dimmed tide is loosed, and everywhere
> The ceremony of innocence is drowned;
> The best lack all conviction, while the worst
> Are full of passionate intensity.

Or, in the words of Bertrand Russell:

> That Man is the product of causes which had no prevision of the end they were achieving; that his origin, his growth, his hopes and fears, his loves and his beliefs, are but the outcome of accidental collocations of atoms; that no fire, no heroism, no intensity of thought and feeling, can preserve an individual life beyond the grave; that all the labours of the ages, all the devotion, all the inspiration, all the noonday brightness of human genius, are destined to extinction in the vast death of the solar system, and that the whole temple of Man's achievement must inevitably be buried beneath the debris of a universe in ruins—all these things, if not quite beyond dispute, are yet so nearly certain, that no philosophy which rejects them can hope to stand. Only within the scaffolding of these truths, only on the firm foundation of unyielding despair, can the soul's habitation henceforth be safely built.

Firm foundation? Despair is killing us, and existentialism—the acceptance of the mimetic world raised to an ultimate principle—is not an answer for the generality of mankind. We need new integrations. We need our serious dreams again to speak of what we are and of what we may yet become. We need to remake our mental world.

With the shattering of the old world, it is the work of speculative fantasy to help to fit us into the new. But in the passing of the old world, all of the World Beyond the Hill's best metaphors were destroyed. Its countries and populations were taken away from it, and have had to be made new again. This is one more measure of the magnitude of the crisis through which we have passed.

In the nineteenth century, the sustaining metaphors of sf—non-mimetic fiction—were reconceived with the aid of science, the same science that Arthur Miller quails before today. New realms were posited—the future, outer space, and other dimensions. New beings were imagined—aliens and mechanical men. New wonders were conceived by the million. In this century, all of these metaphors were gathered under the name of science fiction and their nature and implications explored.

Now once again, we have the potential of a mature literature of psychological integration. And just in time. If we are to survive, the mental universe we inhabit must be remade. We must make new connections in our minds, new connections with each other, and new connections with the world. Now, as in times past, speculative fantasy will aid in the making.

Part II: SF in the Seventies

6/ FRAGMENTATION

[*Fantasy and Science Fiction*, June 1973]

These are desperately fragmented times. The Presidential campaign just past was most notably lacking in leadership—the winning candidate won by being less visible than the losing candidate. If a few years ago, Dylan and the Beatles were the two clear leaders of popular music, today there are no leaders but only factions. More than ever previously, the way to succeed in rock music is through Decadence and Contempt. We may yet see Alice Cooper and David Bowie surpassed by the ultimate in decadence and contempt—three young men with short hair and dressed in Kingston Trio candy-stripe shirts.

The fragmentation cuts all through our society. It affects sf, too. In the middle Sixties, science fiction fandom had a robust period. Today, fandom is a mass of small exclusive factions and the most vigorous fan magazines are not the large general interest creatures of yore, like *Science Fiction Review*, but small-circulation, Xeroxed, for-your-eyes-only personalzines whose names may not even be publicly mentioned—like *Egotismo* and *Cloaca*.

Five years ago, Roger Zelazny and Samuel R. Delany were the major talents in science fiction, the leaders of sentiment and fashion. The most that any aspiring sf writer could wish for then was to be numbered in their company. From 1965 through 1967, Zelazny won two Nebula Awards and two Hugos. From 1966 through 1969, Delany won four Nebulas and one Hugo. In more recent times, Zelazny has turned out one bad book after another, and Delany has been entirely silent.

Today, there is no clear leader. There is only fragmentation. Optimists in general have been curiously invisible. Those writers who have been able to write have written special answers for special audiences. The one major writer of the past several years—in fact, the one writer to establish himself as major during these past several years—has been Robert Silverberg, who previously was regarded as a hack or as a minor writer of sf. Silverberg is the rare writer who has been energized rather than sapped by the times. He has offered a barren, despairing worldview—if you like, one more special answer for a special audience.

But even Silverberg has been no leader of sf, even though some of his stories these past years have won prizes. It is not altogether an accident that the Hugo-winning novel this past year—Philip José Farmer's *To Your Scattered Bodies Go*—should have been written twenty years ago. The sf audience is so divided that in order to find an area of common agreement, it was necessary to look to a revenant. The winner of the Nebula Award, Silverberg's *A Time of Changes*, could do no better than fifth in the Hugo balloting.

Some of the tenor of these times may be glimpsed in the books present this month for review:

The Astounding-Analog Reader, Volume One, edited by Harry Harrison and Brian W. Aldiss, is a collection of fifteen stories published in *Astounding* between 1937 and 1946. It is, apparently, meant to serve an historical function. It is to be the first of several books that will give a sense of the course of what has been our strongest science fiction magazine as it has changed and developed through the years. This is a job eminently worth doing, and we asked specifically for the opportunity to read and review this book because we assumed we would be able to speak well of it. But, even though in terms of the stories it contains this is generally a strong and readable book, we can't speak well of it. In spite of the stories it contains, this book is not what it might have been or ought to have been. It is, in fact, a book of our times. It is aimed at a very narrow audience—or rather, at two narrow audiences—and it will be useless for practically anyone else.

If a book like this is to be done, the editors have the obligation of reading *Astounding* year by year from its beginnings in 1930. They ought to choose stories typical of the times and typical of the magazine. They might well look for forgotten masterpieces. Their commentary ought to set the material in a context that illuminates it for our time. This is the minimum that should be asked.

In actual fact, the editors have done a bad job. They have not edited historically. They have chosen to edit nostalgically. Both Harrison and Aldiss were born in 1925 and first began to read the magazine in the late Thirties. In consequence, they have honored the impressionable young people they were then at the expense of doing what needed to be done in this book.

Their commentary is less historical than it is an attempt to express their feelings in reading the magazine once upon a time. This means that they rely heavily on exclamation-pointed gush—broken occasionally by fits of condescension when their present adult selves momentarily reassert themselves.

It means also that they have relied on their memories in writing their commentary, and their memories have led them to make mistakes. For instance, they state that Isaac Asimov's *The Naked Sun* was not published in *Astounding*, the magazine they are honoring. In fact, it was. We know, because its serialization occurred during our own impressionable days, in 1956. Again, they ascribe the original publication of John Campbell's "Forgetfulness," which they reprint, to 1932, when in fact it was first published in 1937. Not a small mistake, and one that is no mere typo because it is repeated.

It means that they have ignored entirely all the issues of *Astounding* published between January 1930 and June 1937, one can only presume because they were not yet reading the magazine in those days and are not familiar with the stories. It means that instead of rereading *Astounding* issue by issue and making their selections on the basis of adult judgment, they have chosen to reprint stories that made the greatest impression on them when they were young. This has led them to make a few strange choices, like P. Schuyler Miller's

"Trouble on Tantalus," which they may have loved at age 15, but which were not respected by the readers of *Astounding* even when they were first published. And it has led them to make a great many over-familiar choices, like "Nightfall," "By His Bootstraps," "City," and "First Contact," that are readily available in other anthologies. These selections might have been more acceptable if the time scale of the book were smaller, but they won't do in a book that offers only fifteen stories from a ten-year period.

Let it be said that there are good stories here that have not been seen for a time, like an early Alfred Bester piece, "The Push of a Finger," and the Kuttners' "Vintage Season" and Fredric Brown's "Placet Is a Crazy Place." We do honor Harrison and Aldiss for the brilliant stroke of leading the stories with the original Campbell blurb lines. This, more than anything else in the book, does give some of the flavor that *Astounding* once had.

In the end, however, even young readers will be familiar with much of this book. And they will get small use from the commentary, which, we suspect, will seem nearly incoherent. Older readers, whose nostalgia might be touched, will find small use in this book either, unless their nostalgia happens to coincide exactly with that of Harrison and Aldiss in the few unfamiliar stories included.

Ultimately, then, *The Astounding-Analog Reader, Volume One* is designed for two audiences. One is librarians, who will buy anything if the premise sounds good enough. The premise in this case is a world-beater. The other audience is the editors themselves. They, more than anyone else, and almost exclusively, will enjoy this book fully.

But the major and important job of documenting the history of modern science fiction with anthologies chosen by an editor who has done his homework rather than relying on the recommendations of his fifteen-year-old self still remains to be done. The best solution might be retrospective best-of-the-year collections, fat volumes that do give a fair sense of the historical development of sf. Books like these will come, but apparently not this year.

Robert Silverberg's *New Dimensions II* is, on the face of it, a book of our times. It is an anthology of eleven original stories, and, as the editor points out, the authors—such as Tiptree, Malzberg, Bryant, Dozois, Effinger and Eklund—are writers of the Seventies. In terms of content, this is even more a book of our times. All of the stories but one—a conventional Isaac Asimov story of a complex scientific problem resolved by recourse to the simpler science of the twentieth century—are set in the present or near future. And the problems they recount are the problems of the present blown up to insoluble proportions.

The editor of the book says that these stories "represent the yield of a yearlong search for the best work currently being done in what is now one of literature's most exciting branches . . . Too long self-ghettoized as a simple-minded species of juvenile adventure fiction, science fiction has for some time now been struggling back towards the heights it reached in the hands of such masters as Wells, Huxley, Orwell, and Stapledon: we hope to extend and continue the present movement away from clichés and clumsiness, toward deeper insight, vision, and craftsmanship."

The actual result, however, as we see it here is exciting only if you find excitement in an emphasis of style over content and mature only if you find maturity in contemplation of frustration and madness. That is, this collection is aimed to satisfy one fraction of the sf audience, that part which actively enjoys being bummed out. These stories might be best summed by a quote from one of them, Gardner Dozois' "King Harvest":

> Now his fury had drained away, leaving only a scummy residue of futility. There was nothing he could do—it was too late for anything.

The Astounding-Analog Reader provides an interesting contrast with *New Dimensions*. The stories in *New Dimensions* are clearly better written. The level of writing skill has risen incredibly in the last thirty years. Frustration is not absent by any means in the stories of the early Forties. "By His Bootstraps" and "Nightfall" reach dead ends as final as any conceived in these new stories. But the fiction in *The Astounding-Analog Reader*, taken as a whole, has a vitality and a sweep of imagination that is altogether missing in the constricted and nihilistic stories in *New Dimensions*. An even better comparison might be drawn between these *New Dimensions* stories and the Bomb-haunted short stories that choked *Astounding* in the later Forties. Just as the writers of that day could not see beyond the compulsive vision of Atomic Doom, so these responsible writers of our day cannot see beyond the various dooms they perceive in embryo all about us. But we are willing to wager that these stories will seem as limited, one-sided and ultimately uninteresting twenty-five years from now as, say, Theodore Sturgeon's "Memorial" does today.

From the above, we suppose it should be obvious that we are not members of the audience for this book—though we would not doubt for a minute that there is one. For the record, however, let us say that we admired Joanna Russ's active symbol invention, even if we found her story, "Nobody's Home," deliberately obscure. We would have liked Barry Malzberg's "Out from Ganymede" even more than we did if we had not previously read what is effectively the same story by him twice before. We respected Gordon Eklund's "White Summer in Memphis." But the only story in this book that we actively enjoyed was R.A. Lafferty's "Eurema's Dam."

John Boyd published his first sf novel in 1968. *The I.Q. Merchant* is his seventh sf novel in five years. In reading this book, we made the off-hand guess that he was between fifty and fifty-five. In checking afterward, we discovered that he is fifty-three. That we could make that kind of guess, and that the guess was correct, may indicate that this book, too, will be satisfying only to a partial audience.

The I.Q. Merchant sets a problem. Like the stories in *New Dimensions*, the problem is of this moment, as the setting is the present. Unlike the stories in *New Dimensions*, *The I.Q. Merchant* does attempt a solution.

The protagonist of this story, the owner of a small California pharmaceutical corporation, injects his idiot son and himself with a drug that raises the intelligence of forty per cent of the lab animals it has been tested upon. It has killed another forty per cent and left twenty per cent unaltered. The drug turns the son into a superman, and leaves the protagonist unaltered. That is the nominal situation. What is actually being symbolized here, it soon becomes apparent, is the alteration in consciousness that we presently like to call the Generation Gap, even though it is clearly something more than that.

We were able to guess the author's age so closely because the story he writes is so patently the product of a man on the farther side of the gap who finds the change in consciousness horrifying. In fact, so horrifying that he is unable to deal with it honestly.

The son and other eventual supermen are painted as monsters. And they do act monstrously. They knowingly kill off forty per cent of the human race to turn another forty per cent into Things like themselves.

Boyd finds his solution to this problem by promoting the protagonist and a percentage of those others who do not seem to react to the drug to the status of double-superman. At the conclusion, they have plans to escape the Earth and split for the stars.

This is not a true solution for two reasons. One is that there is no real solution. The double-supermen avoid, evade and flim-flam the single-supermen. They never come to terms with them. They do not confront them. They have no true confidence in their own putative superiority. The other is that the protagonist himself is responsible for all the monstrousness we have been given leave by the author to condemn, but neither the author nor the protagonist is willing to accept responsibility. The author disguises the protagonist's true powers until the end of the book when they are brought out as a surprise. We then learn that certain episodes in the story that we took to mean one thing were disguised by the author and really meant something quite different. The result, however, is that taken the first way, the episodes mean that the protagonist is guilty of nothing more than turning his son into a superman and unleashing him upon the world. But if he was a super-superman all along, then unmistakably the protagonist himself is ultimately and knowingly responsible for the deaths of forty per cent of the human race, and responsible for turning another forty per cent into super-Things.

The protagonist never admits to knowing this. Boyd never admits to knowing this. The result is a pernicious book. This is not an adjective we use lightly, but we are quite serious in using it now. Boyd has fooled himself and is trying to fool the reader—and the result is morally objectionable.

If *New Dimensions* and *The I.Q. Merchant* are unable to deal with the problems they raise, or resort to trickery and false solution, Thomas Burnett Swann does present a problem and solve it honestly in *Wolfwinter*. But his book is no less special.

Swann is a poet and university professor with a love for the Greco-Roman. He has been turning out a series of delicate, pastoral Arcadian fantasies, filled with fauns and centaurs, for about the past ten years. If *New Dimensions* is like the Atomic Doom stories of the late Forties, *Wolfwinter* is like the other hallmark of those schizoid times, the romantic novels of remote futures and other dimensions that were being published in *Startling Stories*, of which Arthur C. Clarke's *Against the Fall of Night* can serve as an example.

Here is a taste of Swann's prose:

> How a Faun decorates his house is entirely up to him, and Fauns are not renowned for tasteful decorations or even comfort, since they like to live as close to the earth as possible and consider furniture, like clothes, an encumbrance. But every tree contains in its uppermost branches a railed platform, a kind of lookout nest with a chest of provisions, reached by a rope ladder, in case of attack by wolves ... Between the briar fence and the house is an area where the Faun grows his vegetables. He will eat practically anything, including leather sandals, but he prefers greenery. However, as in the case of Skimmer, he also relishes the meat of herbivorous animals like beavers, who feed on bark and roots. In his garden you are likely to find radishes, cabbages, turnips, onions, and other vegetables, as well as a covey of quail, whose wings have been clipped to prevent their escape, for they are much prized as pets and only eaten in case of a siege by wolves.

In order to find a problem that can be honestly solved, Swann must give us fauns, a young girl, and her half-faun son threatened by Death Wolves in an Etruscan wood twenty-five hundred years ago. That is a long way to retreat for a solvable problem, but if you badly need a book that isn't frustrated or dishonest, you might try this one. *Wolfwinter* is the strongest book by Swann that we have read.

If this column is a review of books that you don't want to read or are sorry that you did read; if you despair of fragmentation; if the times seem impossible; if sf seems to be dying—remember this. We have been here before and survived. Sf has had periods like this one before—there was one in the Thirties before Campbell became editor of *Astounding*; there was one in the late Forties after the advent of the Bomb; there was one in the late Fifties and early Sixties. This is another, and we will outlive it. Hang on. Good times are coming again. Good times will come.

7/ SCIENCE FICTION: NEW TRENDS AND OLD

[Science Fiction, Today and Tomorrow, ed.
by Reginald Bretnor, Harper & Row, 1974]

Our title—"Science Fiction: New Trends and Old"—was assigned to us by the editor of this volume, Mr. Bretnor. He tells us that our chapter is intended to be the opening salvo in a barrage of essays on the subject of "Science Fiction as Literature." But why the assumption that the most universalizing level on which sf can be discussed must be the level of trends?

What are trends? Perhaps we can say that trends are the small-scale movements, evolutions, progressions and fashions that are perceived by those living within one moment and stretching to anticipate the next. Trends are arbitrary. Their background interconnections are fuzzy. Trends are cosmic twitches.

There are people who have to anticipate trends, who have to be finely tuned to trends. Dress designers. Also boutique proprietors. Or, living on rock music, as so many of us do, we might be aware that rock has passed through a country-influenced phase, then an art song period, and now is experimenting with decadence. We might care about trends in rock music. Or those who are interested in publishing might care about the trends that affect *Life* and the trends that affect *Amazing*.

Is this the right scale? Do we agree that these are trends?

The assumption of the editor of this book is that sf criticism will operate at this level of awareness. And, if we look at what sf criticism has managed until now, we would have to admit that until now sf criticism has lived in the moment. It has questioned the meanings of individual books—as in Damon Knight's *In Search of Wonder*, the first major book of sf criticism. Or, as in James Blish's several books, it has questioned the professional competence presently apparent in sf. It has fitted shapes over the careers of various writers, as those careers have lengthened—as in several books by Sam Moskowitz, and in *Heinlein in Dimension*. It has begun to track its past, as in de Camp's *Science-Fiction Handbook*, and several other books by Sam Moskowitz. At its most universalizing, sf has attempted to make sense of the present in terms of the immediate past, as in Kingsley Amis's *New Maps of Hell*, which would have remade the sf of 1960 in the shape of the sf of 1954, only more so.

You would have to say, then, yes, sf criticism at its best has dealt in trend-snatching.

All right, if we are dealing in trends, what are the trends of the moment that seem significant?

In the past ten years, sf has played at the adaptation of myth to sf, as in stories by Roger Zelazny, Thomas Burnett Swann, Samuel R. Delany and Emil Petaja. In the late Sixties, the most notable sf seemed to be experiments in styles copied from mimetic models, as in stories by Brian Aldiss, John Brunner and Philip José Farmer. Most recently, the sf that demands attention is into decadence, as in stories by Robert Silverberg, Norman Spinrad and Barry Malzberg. Almost all sf stories at this moment are at least a bit into decadence.

If these are trends, how do we make sense of them, let alone predict what everybody will be expressing next year? Now that Robert Silverberg has slowed his writing pace, are we to assume that the phase of decadence will soon be over? Who is to be the next Writer of the Moment?

That's one kind of trend. Here's another: The often-declared and long-cherished division between science fiction and fantasy is becoming harder and harder to maintain. Independently of the year-to-year lurches of sf given above, the symbols of traditional fantasy are being accepted in modern sf stories.

Here's another: The audience for modern sf has grown ever since Hugo Gernsback founded *Amazing Stories* in 1926. In a time when the audience for mimetic fiction is becoming steadily smaller, sf is the one literature in the Western world whose audience is steadily growing.

Here's one last trend. Since 1926, the course of modern sf has never run smooth. Sf has had its good periods and its bad ones. As examples, sf was having a remarkably bad period when John Campbell assumed the editorship of *Astounding* in 1937, and sf was in another period of stagnation in 1960 when Earl Kemp won a Hugo for his fan publication, a symposium entitled *Who Killed Science Fiction?* But there have been other years when nobody would have been inclined to ask that question. For instance, the early years of the Forties, when Heinlein, van Vogt, de Camp, Sturgeon and Asimov were establishing themselves, were fruitful times. So were the middle Sixties. The 1967 year's best anthology edited by Donald Wollheim and Terry Carr is enough to make you smile. That isn't true of the work being written at the moment. We are getting ready to trot out the 1960 question again.

These are trends enough for anyone. If it were sufficient to talk about science fiction, new trends and old, we could pick these trends up one at a time and hash them out.

But if we did, we would not know any more than we do now. We would have a handful of well-analyzed trends, but still have no complete idea of the overall significance of science fiction.

Until now, we have always looked at sf in the most present and immediate way. We have wondered about books. We have judged contemporary standards of craftsmanship. We have added up careers as totals of and-then-he-wrote. We have taken the current temperature and pulse of the field. And we have marveled at how very marvelous and unpredictable science fiction has been.

If we try to understand trends in terms of trends, we will be unable to see the underlying unity that explains all the trends of sf that bewilder us. We suspect that until now sf criticism has been too much in the middle of an immense and radically changing thing to do more than take present bearings.

However, for the first time now it seems possible that one might view sf from a new plane and see how it can accommodate all these very different twitches, these trends. Since it seems possible, we want to try—with the editor's permission, and your indulgence of a bit of foolery.

Here is an assumption. Any unifying explanation of sf will lie in a dimension in which we are not used to looking when we think about sf. That is, any unifying explanation of sf will look *strange* at first. It will not be easy for some to accept at first, whatever it is, because it is strange.

With your indulgence, then, we will attempt a strange unifying answer. Take it as deadly serious, or take it as a joke—but consider that any unifying explanation of sf will look at least as strange as this.

Let us suppose:

It seems that if there is one conclusion made by modern psychology—Freud and all his legitimate and illegitimate heirs—that can stand as proven beyond challenge, it is this: we are in large part enigmas to ourselves.

Will we all accept this? It hasn't been a current idea for very long. The *Oxford Universal Dictionary* dates the first use of the word "unconscious"—meaning not available to the conscious mind—as an adjective to 1909, and as a noun to 1920. But it does seem indisputably true now that the unconscious exists.

None of us sees himself complete and whole. Whatever we may know about ourselves that others do not, none of us is able to see himself as others may. We may think that the way we are is just the natural way we are, and never realize that it is unusual. We may tick like a clock and never realize it. We may pulse visibly. We are able to see virtues and defects in others that we are blind to in ourselves. Ask us to explain ourselves, and we will rationalize as best we can. But some things we won't be able to talk about, and some we'll forget or leave out.

We know as much as we consciously know, but our unconscious knowledge is unavailable to us. This is not willful intent to ignore what is writ plain. At least, it is not merely that. We are separated from our unconscious and we don't know how to learn to know it better.

We may try to know ourselves by self-inspection, but it doesn't work. Conscious inspection inspects the conscious. We tote up what we know of our behavior. We find reasons for the behavior. We call the conscious and the reasons "I." But we are still separated from the unconscious. We cannot know the whole of our minds.

It may be that by means of education and training, it would be possible to circumvent our inability to know ourselves. But that kind of subtle instruction is not generally available. In spite of whatever hopes we might have had, it was missing for all of us in the schools and universities.

One of the ways in which we look to discover the full range of our minds is art. If we cannot discern our minds by direct inspection, we can see them indirectly—mirrored in art. Fiction is a form of the artistic mirror. In the symbol patterns of fiction we can see our minds reflected.

Our minds are the sum of our knowledge of the universe. In a story, knowledge is symbolized and committed to paper. The universe of any story is a symbol of the entire mind. Our conscious knowledge is symbolized by known things. Our unconscious is symbolized by unknown things.

This is an unusual construction of fiction. We are saying that a straight chair in a story is a symbol of consciously known things. And we are saying that an invading alien in a story who lands on the White House lawn and craves present audience with the administrator of the land is a symbol of the unconscious. If this is strange enough to move you to object, please hold your objections for a moment and see how the fit grows.

We may call the kind of story that insists on the primacy of known things "mimetic fiction." This is the product of writers like Jane Austen, Charles Dickens, Mark Twain, Norman Mailer, John D. MacDonald, and even James Joyce and Zane Grey. In these stories, everything, no matter how strange, can or should be reduced by confrontation to the status of known things. That is, no matter how strange Joyce may get, what happens can ultimately be explained as dream, or the flow of thought, or madness.

Mimetic fiction is explainable in daylight terms. It might equally be called social fiction, because it deals in the world of consensus, or rational fiction, because it deals in rational explanations. This is fiction of a conscious world. Its ultimate loyalties are to the power of the conscious mind, just as the loyalties of your conscious mind are to itself.

The purpose of mimetic fiction is consciousness-raising. Through inventory, the interconnections of the known are traced. The known gets to know itself. So might Charles Dickens acquaint you with society, Mark Twain with life on the Mississippi, and James Joyce with conscious phrasings of the existence of the unconscious.

On the other hand, the kind of story that insists on the primacy of symbols of the unknown is fantasy. Symbols of the unknown are such things as magics, or strange powerful spirits and beings, all that no ordinary power can successfully oppose. Magic can defeat an ordinary armed knight. It wouldn't be magic if it couldn't. Tele-kinesis can defeat an atomic bomb by mentally separating atoms.

Modern sf is fantasy. Its magics are various "scientific" powers that are stronger than any known to existing science. Its spirits and beings are robots and aliens.

Fantasy is fiction of the unconscious mind. It acts out unconscious knowledge. In the reflection of the universe presented in contemporary sf, our unconscious becomes more apparent than in any other fiction.

The purpose of fantasy is consciousness-expansion. The existence of unconsciousness, and the existence of unknown things in the world around us, forces us to expand the borders of the known. Consciousness expands itself by forays into the unconscious. Then consciousness makes a new inventory of itself—the act of consciousness-raising.

In the universe and in stories, the unconscious includes the conscious. Likewise, in the mind the unconscious includes the conscious. If we accept the similarity of the three—the universe of experience, the universe symbolized in stories, and the human mind—we can demonstrate this in terms of story symbols.

An sf story may include any known symbol. In the farthest reaches of time and space—in the World Beyond the Hill—an sf story may still refer to anything presently known. Moreover, any sf story may be set in the most familiar of familiar places—Greenwich Village, for instance. And into that familiar place, an unknown power or alien will be able to intrude. Such an sf story exists—Chester Anderson's *The Butterfly Kid*. The unknown includes the known. The unconscious includes the conscious.

If we take this contention in terms of mimetic fiction—fiction of the conscious mind and the known universe—we discover that mimetic fiction cannot set foot in the farthest reaches of time and space. That isn't the known universe—the experienced universe has only gotten as far as the Moon. And in a known place like Greenwich Village, the utmost unknown-like things that mimetic fiction can produce are a flock of Brazilian sailors, or a mad poet, or the gurgle of a stream of consciousness. But the sailors are reducible to fun-loving, sex-mad Brazilians; the poet is mad, but then Village poets are inclined to be like that, and we understand; and the stream of consciousness is the ear of the conscious listening for hints. The known excludes the unknown.

But if the unconscious were to break through into consciousness, if the truly unknown and possibly not knowable did appear in the heart of the known—if the Brazilians are from Betelgeuse, if the mad poet speaks words that take form and go capering down the streets of the Village to annoy us, if we are asked to take symbols of the unconscious as the most, not the least, serious thing—then our story must be sf. Mimetic fiction, conscious fiction, won't have it because an item in it has not been rationalized. In a mimetic story, a character might kiss a lamppost, the homeliest of known things, in gratitude that he does not have to take his fantasies seriously.

In order to write fully effective stories, stories of the whole mind, fantasists need two things. First, they need a conception of the universe in which the unknown includes the known. If the conception is compromised, the effectiveness of the stories is compromised. As in the universe of experience, so in the mind. As in the mind, so in the universe of a story. And the reverse, of course.

Second, fantasists must have a sensitive symbolic vocabulary that can be generally understood and that is capable of representing all aspects of the unconscious. Without this vocabulary, it would be difficult to represent some of what must be represented, and communication of it would be altogether impossible.

For a period of 5000 years or more, both necessary conditions existed. Representation of the whole mind was possible. In this assumed universe, the known world was Middle-earth. Middle-earth lay between the heavens, the unknown home of the gods above, and the underworld, the lower sky, the unknown home of the demons below. The juncture of worlds is the point where the two celestial hemispheres and the horizon meet. The known world is surrounded by the unknown.

In a universe like this, the unconscious and the full mind may be represented. Moreover, a sensitive symbolic vocabulary that could be read by anyone also existed. There were magics of every sort. There were strange gods, spirits and beings. There were endless countries.

The assumption of these stories was that in a past Golden Age, access between the known world and the unknown realms had been easy. The gods had visited Earth and men had visited the gods. But even in these later times, ghosts or spirits might wander onto our Earth in search of victims or at the call of sorcerers. Interconnections between the known and unknown worlds did exist. Subtleties could be expressed.

In this universe, of course, we do learn. The unknown lures the known. The known changes by accumulation. As the known world changes, our conception of the unknown world must change to contain it.

A shift in the conception of the universe must be traumatic for the people involved. As in the story universe, so in the mind. As in the mind, so in the world of experience.

In the 16th and 17th centuries, the shape of the known world changed. Copernicus, Galileo, Kepler and Newton revised the shape of the universe for us. They made the earth into a sphere in orbit about the sun. They made the planets into other spheres like the earth, also in orbit about the sun. They made the two celestial hemispheres into a single thing. They made the stars into other suns.

In this new universe, earth was no longer Middle-earth. At best, the underworld might be found in the vitals of the earth. And the heavens were to be found nowhere.

The known had changed so radically that a new universe had to be conceived. The unknown world was seemingly turned into the known, or the knowable. In a time like this, it would be impossible to express anything but rationality. It was no accident that the 18th century was self-proclaimedly rational. It was no accident that the 18th century should have invented the mimetic novel. They could not do else. They made a virtue out of a limitation.

In a time when the World Beyond the Hill seems untenable, you will see sunlit excuses for midnight acts. In a century like that it will be impossible to see the entirety of the mind. The unconscious will be feared, doubted and denied, as it has been since the 18th century.

In the time of disintegration of the old universe, fantasists suddenly began to live in a conscious world. This world allowed the World Beyond the Hill no place. If that were true, the end of the universe would truly be at hand. If the universe becomes totally conscious, all change will end. Stasis will have been achieved.

So fantasists reserved exception. One of the ways in which they did this was to conceive of a temporary corner of this earth in which the symbols of the unknown might claim to hold existence. The explorers of the 15th and 16th centuries had glimpsed a variety of strange countries. Fantasists placed the source of some of their unknowns in these countries, or in others like them beyond the present reach of exploration.

Exploration always proved these fairy lands false, but they were the described locations of many of the fantasies of the rational world —More's *Utopia* (1516), *Gulliver's Travels* (1726), and the lost race stories so common from 1870 to 1930. These stories were placed in the last crannies of the Global Village—in spring-heated valleys in the Antarctic, in subterranean caverns, in narrow wonderlands in the Himalayas. The last creditable example of this sort of compromise fantasy may have been James Hilton's *Lost Horizon* (1933). In this final statement of the relationship of the unknown to the known within the known world, we are told that when the immortals of the fabulous land of Shangri-La are exposed at last to the light of the mimetic world, they must wither and die of old age, dissolving "like all too lovely things, at the first touch of reality."

During these past centuries of exploration, men have demonstrated in very real terms just how far they can extend the bounds of the known. They have shown they can extinguish every possible preserve of the World Beyond the Hill on this earth. And if that were all there were to the universe, the end of the universe would be at hand: Consciousness is really very arrogant. It looms over the last delicate bit of unknown fluff in this world, and knowingly and brutally, it touches the thing, and *laughs* while the unknown fluff withers into a known thing.

Many fantasy symbols were never comfortable in this vulnerable unknown province in the hinterlands of earth. For instance, Gulliver may have found Lilliput at the ends of the earth, but no one ever found Witchland there. Many of the most powerful fantasy symbols took refuge in other unknown worlds—chiefly Never-Never Land.

Never-Never Land, in essence, is the old World Beyond the Hill. Because it was the old unknown, it could only include the old known. It must exclude much of the modern world, and hence no one was ever able to take it seriously, even in the hands of William Morris, Lord Dunsany or J.R.R. Tolkien.

However, during these same past centuries, fantasists did locate a new true home for the World Beyond the Hill that incorporates Never-Never Land. They have reconceived the universe. In order to do this, it was necessary that the known be extended to its fullest, as conscious busy-beavers, explorers, encyclopedists, novelists and scientists have seen that it has been in these past three centuries of consciousness-raising. We retire from the Moon. We strain at the limits of our conscious vision. The results of investment in monumental conscious projects like cyclotrons are less while our expense grows greater. Consciousness is such a burden that we are turning as much of it over to computers as we can. Our new conscious limits are now available to fantasists.

During the 19th century—or, shall we say more properly, in the bit more than a hundred years between *Frankenstein* (1818) and the founding of *Amazing Stories*—a new picture of the universe was adapted from science by writers like Poe, Verne, Wells, Burroughs and Merritt. They presented this picture in pieces, but it was complete and established by implication prior to Gernsback. The publication of *Amazing Stories* confirmed the new universe. The name of the new fantasy—"scientifiction" or "science fiction"—indicated its 19th century origin. *Amazing* assumed an audience that had made the conclusions of Poe, Verne and Wells their premises.

This new universe, as we have come to discover it, is one so vast that the Global Village, circling its little sun in the suburbs of its galaxy, lost among many galaxies, can easily be misplaced. And likewise, this new universe contains reaches of time so extended that Earth and all its works could be forgotten.

A universe like this has room for the unknown. Our known world is surrounded by unknowns again beyond our ability to explore.

In this new universe, the heavens and the underworld have become space and other dimensions. The Golden Age of the past has been replaced by a vision of future perfection. Spirits have become alien beings. Magic has been replaced by science-beyond-science. Sorcerers have become scientists.

The writers of the first hundred years of modern speculative fantasy established the existence of the new World Beyond the Hill. They demonstrated powers beyond the known. They showed that aliens might interact with us in a variety of ways. They showed that stories might be set in the future or on Mars, and that we might encounter the unknown there.

In the period since 1926, the period in which sf has been called "science fiction," modern fantasists have mentally explored the dimensions of their new universe. Science has played so much less a role in this process that apologists have had to strain to justify the name of science fiction. If speculative fantasy was "science fiction" prior to 1926, the sf from 1926 through the Fifties might be characterized as "idea fiction."

In these mental explorations can be found the meaning of some of the early "trends" of the field. For instance, inventors in stories built strange devices in their basements, including machines to travel in time and space. This was seen as a trend to gadget stories. Then, in the time-ships and space-machines, fictional explorers leaped to the planets, to the stars, outside the galaxy. They scouted, mapped and circumnavigated large portions of space and time. They saw the beginning and end of the universe. This was seen as a vogue for what the early Thirties called "thought variant" stories. Then, behind the explorers, came all conditions of men—space patrolmen, miners, pirates, pioneers—proving that men could survive in tents or domes here. That was a trend to adventure stories—space opera.

Behind them came the engineers, the planners, the bureaucrats, the empire-builders. In the Forties, space was structured into possible political units of every size, from Earth in the future, to Terra and her colonies, to Galactic Empire. Time was structured into epochs in which things could change and change again from the presently known.

It was a joy and a tumble to invent this. The void was filled consistently, vividly and plausibly with transportation, communication, government, economics and sociology. The arguments were made over and over. The best ones were rehearsed until they became accepted justifications. The worst ones were improved or discarded. So many arguments were made that it became clear that *any* situation could be plausibly justified in a variety of ways. And what we saw of all this was the Golden Age of *Astounding*. The surly little stories of the Fifties were merely the nit-picking end of all these arguments over symbols.

In other words, we suggest that most of the "trends" in science fiction from 1926 to 1957, including the stories and the careers of writers like E.E. Smith, Jack Williamson, John W. Campbell, Robert Heinlein, A.E. van Vogt and Isaac Asimov, may be explained as symbol invention, the defining and testing of a symbolic vocabulary. Or, if you like, these stories put in the plumbing and engineering of the new unknown universe. People can believe in a universe with these dimensions because of the stories of these men.

The writers of this period thought of this process of defining and testing symbolic vocabulary as "playing with ideas." James Blish, who began as an sf writer in 1940, has said, for instance:

Since at least about 1938, treatment has become steadily more important than springboard notion. Science-fiction writers borrow such notions from each other freely, to an extent that in other fields would sometimes be indistinguishable from plagiarism; this is almost never resented as long as direct quotation is avoided, and the resulting story is commonly welcomed as fresh if the borrowing writer succeeds in looking at the old idea in a new light—whether that light be dramatic, emotional, or even simply technological. Innovations of *this* kind, which are far more important in any literary field than any single germinal notion, are what make or break modern science fiction.

But what Blish is describing here is more fruitfully described as the defining and testing of symbols than as "looking at old ideas in a new light." By 1957, the symbols of sf were complete enough to sustain a wide range of imaginary activities—stories of invention, exploration, engineering, politics, economics; careers of various sorts; different life-styles. Activities as varied as the worlds of Smith, Sturgeon, Heinlein, van Vogt, Knight, Pohl and Kornbluth.

This range of symbols is now the common property of our culture. Children encounter the symbols of the sf of the Fifties from the time they are small. They know what a spaceship is. They know time machines. They know extra-terrestrials. All these are to be found on the backs of cereal boxes. The culture as a whole is sufficiently educated in the symbols of the new World Beyond the Hill that it was able to accept and understand the tv series *Star Trek* and the movie *2001: A Space Odyssey*, which were equivalent to the written sf of the Fifties. The shows had to assume an audience familiar with these symbols.

As the set of sf symbols has grown relatively complete, the symbols have been learned by a general audience. In a period when mimetic literature has been choking on its own desperation, sf has been the one consistently expanding literature in the Western world. The audience of sf has steadily grown since Gernsback. Sf has suddenly taken on interest as a subject in the academic community. The sense of this trend is apparent if we say again that a fantasist must have a sensitive symbolic vocabulary that can be generally understood and that is capable of representing all aspects of the unconscious. With the vocabulary that was established by the end of the Fifties, sf had become intelligible to a more general audience, and so attracted one.

We can assume that as these symbols continue to be used and acquire meanings and nuance through use—as our symbolic vocabulary grows more sensitive—the audience of speculative fantasy will continue to grow.

At the same time, it is clear that the symbolic vocabulary of the new redaction of the World Beyond the Hill is not yet as sensitive and flexible as the old vocabulary of fantasy was. Magic has subtleties that super-scientific power or even psi power do not have. Sorcerers have moral overtones that scientists do not have. There is a dimension in *Faust* that cannot be duplicated in the symbols available in *Frankenstein*.

A fantasy dragon has a wide and sensitive range of meanings as a symbol. Science fiction writers have attempted to write of alien beings that have dragonly qualities. De Camp has tried, and Jack Vance, and Robert Heinlein, and Anne McCaffrey, and Poul Anderson a number of times. All have caught at some of the essence of dragonness, but none has equaled or bettered the original.

The old symbols are useful. They were being saved in their preserve in Never-Never Land for a purpose. They are not going to be discarded. Instead, grounds are gradually being made for their existence in the new World Beyond the Hill.

As early as the Fifties, spacemen out on colonial survey set down on strange planets and discovered that the leprechauns had gotten there first. From that, we might have guessed that eventually it would be possible to discover all of the old symbols in the new World Beyond the Hill. If you like, the materials of our complete universe must include all that has ever been meaningful to us. Or, if you like otherwise, when the magical world discovered that the plumbing was in place, it moved into its new home.

So another trend is explained—the continuing merger of traditional fantasy into modern science fiction. The excursions into "mythology" by Zelazny, Swann and others that marked the middle Sixties were in fact a concentration on the accommodation of potent traditional symbols to modern sf and the new World Beyond the Hill. In *Lord of Light*, Zelazny was welcoming the symbol of Buddha to the future and a distant planet. If Buddha and leprechauns can exist in the new World Beyond the Hill, what can be denied access?

A prize-winning 1971 story by Poul Anderson, "The Queen of Air and Darkness," is addressed to this process. In this story, seeming fairyland is discovered on another planet, then denied and exposed. Now, James Blish might describe this story as an acceptable variant of an old idea. Anderson himself might say that it demonstrates the pain in the exposure of cherished illusion. But we would describe the story as one that tests the ability of traditional fantasy symbols to exist on far planets. And what is most interesting to us is that the fairyland was more convincing than its "exposure." In fact, Anderson's characters saw a true fairyland but were too rationalistic to accept it. It *was* true fairyland. There is no reason that it shouldn't have been.

The problem of sf now that its symbolic vocabulary is available is to learn to use the vocabulary, not just to extend it. To this point, we haven't found the handle on our invention. We writers haven't found our vocation yet. We don't know what we are good for. We do know that we are good for something serious, so for the past ten years we have tried our best to be serious.

We tried being mythological. But Roger Zelazny could not be serious about the Buddha. Being "mythological" didn't prove to be a serious enterprise.

Then we tried copying mimetic models. John Brunner tried writing like Dos Passos. And Brian Aldiss tried writing like the French anti-novelists and James Joyce. But the results did not justify continued serious attention after their considerable initial novelty. Aldiss's *Cryptozoic* will not be reprinted even as often as Zelazny's *The Dream Master*. We won't want to see the book again in years to come.

Most recently, like so much of the common stir in the world around us, we have been experimenting with decadence. Decadence is a very self-dramatizing way of being serious. We seem to feel serious in this way just now throughout the culture. The stories of

Robert Silverberg and Barry Malzberg may be the equivalent of Alice Cooper, David Bowie and the Rolling Stones. Or the equivalent of movies like *A Clockwork Orange* and *Last Tango in Paris*. Decadence is a mood that grips the entire culture, not just sf. It is a way of expressing frustration with the limitations of the conscious.

It isn't necessary for sf to express frustration with the limitations of the conscious. We might alternatively say that sf doesn't have to concern itself with crazy, frustrated Anglo-Saxon astronaut schleps in the shambles of some near-future version of the Apollo program. We are the authors of a story like this ourselves that expressed our feelings one winter, so Barry Malzberg, who specializes in these stories, is not alone. If we only knew where the handle on sf was, we should have much more to talk about.

When we have learned how to be serious with symbols like spaceships and ray guns and telepathy and alternate dimensions, then "serious" stories like *Cryptozoic* and *Beyond Apollo* will seem symptomatic of the 1970-mind, when we didn't know what was going on and were very frustrated. Anytime that we can write this narrowly and grant the possibility of only this little, while we sit amidst a wide availability of symbolic vocabulary, we must be frustrated in our seriousness.

This is true, of course, of us within our society, as well. We are living narrowly and granting the possibility of little while we sit amidst a wealth of tools that have never been properly used. And all we can do is watch our friends make sick nasty criticisms in parody before the eyes of the conscious world. As in our minds, so in the world of our experience. As in our stories, so in the world of our experience.

Because, you see, if you really *believed* in the unknown world that surrounds the known, which you will do if and when writers begin to find out how to write about it seriously again, then you would look around at the contemporary multiplicity—and isn't there a lot of it?—and you would put it together in new ways that you can't think of now, because your unconsciousness is unavailable to you now. Whatever television ultimately is, for instance, it isn't anything like the purposes for which it has been used up until now. But you haven't yet found the connective that makes sense of television and all the other trends of modern life. You will be more likely to as your unconscious becomes available to you.

We expect the next trend, when our period of acting out the end of the old line is over, after perhaps another two years, to be a period of fragmentation of a further three or four years—lasting to about 1978 or 1979. It will be a period of private search, private experimentation, and personal solution much more markedly than it is now behind the facade of decadence. Audiences will be smaller. Tastes will be more personal. But, particularly in retrospect, we will be able to see that among all the apparent experimentation for experimentation's sake, much of which will have seemed awfully god-damned frivolous, some was in fact serious. Truly serious.

In 1978 or 1979, we'll pause to think about this. Things will be less varied and lively for awhile. The experiments will seem to have come to an end. And we will have run the old stuff to its very last breath. But then, we will look back over the experiments of 1976 and decide that some of them look pretty good. And, if we were to take their conclusions as premises, what then?

What then will prove to be another creative explosion, beginning perhaps around 1980. This creative explosion will be much greater in impact than the creative explosions that occurred in 1939-1941 and again in 1964-1968.

Everything in this description should be true of sf as it is of the culture as a whole. Once again.

After 1980, traditional fantasy will have become comfortably integrated in modern sf—speculative fantasy. The audience for speculative fantasy will be multiply-larger than its present size. Speculative fantasy itself will be radically altered in character. It will be something new and truly serious, and more enjoyable than it has ever been.

—December 1972

8/ THE SPECIAL NATURE OF FANTASY

[*Fantasiae*, June 1974]

Fantasy is plainly an outmoded literature. In this modern world of interdependent nation states, computers and television satellites, fantasy speaks of mythical kingdoms and magic. Science fiction, at least, may pretend to have relevance to our future, and so capture our attention. Fantasy speaks only of a yesterday that is nowhere to be found in all our atlases and histories. The question we have always asked ourselves is, what is the difference between science fiction and fantasy? Perhaps the question we ought to have been asking is why fantasy should survive at all in our times.

The fact of the matter is that fantasy does continue to be read. Even more important, it continues to be written. These facts cannot be quarreled with. By their existence, they justify themselves. All that we may fairly do is try to understand why these facts exist.

Fantasy endures in our time in spite of its anachronistic superficial trappings because it has a special character that human beings need and seek which cannot be found in any other contemporary fiction. Not in ordinary mimetic literature. And not in science fiction.

In extraordinary moments, we may have the sudden conviction that the universe around us is not inert, fragmented and linear, but rather is a responsive whole. We may look into our past and realize that no simple chain of cause-and-effect can account for the miracles —the radical discontinuities—that have happened to us. We may even come to suspect that these miracles are more than accidental, that they are responses of the universe to our own moral conduct.

Fantasy is a reflection of these perceptions. The universe of fantasy stories is a responsive moral universe. In a fantasy universe, anything is possible. Any miracle may happen. Even the stones may speak. In a fantasy universe, all acts are significant. In our rush for personal power and success, there is no old man or little girl, no fox, no crow that we may safely ignore. All our acts must be morally pure. The whole universe is watching us and responding to what we do.

Mimetic literature does not reflect these perceptions. The universe of mimetic fiction excludes the transcendent, the miraculous. Only the accountable may happen. In consequence, whatever moral dimension there may be in a work of mimetic fiction will necessarily be constricted and rationalized. Mimetic fiction is social rather than moral in character. It is captivated by the superficial.

Science fiction, on the other hand, does permit miracles. In the sf of the last century, the miraculous was an invader of the rational cause-and-effect world. In the sf of our time, we have gone forth from our era and our familiar world to meet the miraculous. But the very fabric of the sf universe has not yet been demonstrated in story to be transcendent.

Moreover, in science fiction stories all acts are not yet perceived to be morally significant. In fantasy, magic is clearly white or black, moral or immoral. In science fiction, science-beyond-science—the contemporary equivalent of magic—is not so clearly defined. There are not white telepaths and black telepaths, even though telepathy does have a moral dimension.

Nonetheless, the trend of development in science fiction is toward the miraculous and the moral. Science fiction is striving to find contemporary terms which express the essential perceptions preserved for our time in fantasy stories. As this happens, science fiction and fantasy will tend to fuse. There will be less and less visible distinction between them. In our own lifetimes, pure re-creative fantasy will cease to be written. But sf will increasingly take on the character of fantasy.

9/ REFLECTIONS AND COMMENTARIES

[*Fantasy and Science Fiction*, March 1974]

Once upon a time, when the world was younger than it is today, speculative fantasy was a microcosm sufficient unto itself. Nobody outside its narrow borders noticed it or cared what happened to it. Sf was a literature confined to a handful of pulp paper magazines. An editor of a professional sf magazine could be nineteen. The attendance at a World Science Fiction Convention—so grandly named—could be one or two hundred people. Though there might be some argument as to what sf was, and further hairsplitting about the exact differences between science fiction and fantasy, these arguments could be settled by pointing.

Those times have passed now. Sf is changing and growing, and pointing no longer is sufficient to settle arguments as to its nature and purpose. There are quarters in which sf is taken as an oracle, a guide to *Future Shock* or *The Morning of the Magicians*. We are pushed forward as prophets. There is a more general feeling that sf has an importance for the times, though what that importance is, or should be, is hard for anyone to say.

When an editor like John Campbell or an author like J.R.R. Tolkien dies, the fact is noted in the *New York Times*. The attendance at science fiction conventions may number in the thousands, and the number of science fiction conventions grows yearly. Sf is a respectably large publishing category, and the only type of fiction whose

audience is consistently growing. Writers like Leslie Fiedler and John
Fowles announce themselves at work on science fiction novels. The
number of courses in sf in the schools and universities of the nation
is now 500 at a minimum, but no one knows the actual figure.

For those who grew up with sf, this is a moment long hoped for.
As sf is serious and respectable, so are we, at long last. But the moment is not a completely happy one. Important questions are being
raised by sf's success that demand answer.

Sf conventions have now reached an unwieldy size. There is a loss
of the old happy intimacy. Amateurs find it more and more difficult
to put on conventions, but what is to happen if they fall into the
hands of professionals?

Once sf provided a living for almost no one except a few publishers, who made their money by not paying their contributors.
Today, sf is an industry and people make money out of every bit of
the pig, including the squeal. There are editors, writers, tv and movie
producers, academics, anthologists, book dealers, hotel-keepers, psy-
chiatrists, hucksters of *Star Trek* marginalia, and magazine and paperback thieves who market publications with their covers torn off at
cut-rate prices. Not to mention book reviewers. All of these have
their own interests, their own angles, their own profits to make.
Some love speculative fantasy. Some couldn't care less, except for
immediate profit or advancement.

There are even editors and publishers of fan magazines, once purely amateur, who now make vacation money or better out of their
news-sheets or critical journals. Some of these now even pay their
contributors.

Is the pleasant happy insular sf microcosm to be ended by problems of size and questions of money? Are the amateur Hugo Awards
going to be mired in ugly questions of shamateurism? Is sf going to
be strip-mined by hustlers, careerists and profiteers?

Some of these questions may be beyond ready answer, but they
are all going to have to be confronted soon. They ought to be
thought about.

The changes in sf are reflected in the publications that we have on
hand for review this month. One of the changes is in the very fact

of these publications. Gone are the days when books of speculative fantasy were rare, and books about sf were nonexistent. For some twenty-five years, books of sf bibliography and criticism have been issued at the rate of one or two a year. But now change is upon us. All our publications this month are concerned with one facet or another of sf, and many more such are promised for the near future. We are going to content ourselves with only a bare few words about most of these items, pointing out how they illustrate the new times in sf, so that we can concentrate on one book in particular, Brian Aldiss's *Billion Year Spree: The True History of Science Fiction.*

Jack Williamson is a measure of both the changes of the twentieth century and the course of modern science fiction. Williamson was born in 1908, and as a young boy, in 1915, he moved with his family in a covered wagon from Texas to New Mexico. Williamson is the longest-active science fiction writer still at work. His first story, "The Metal Man," was published by Hugo Gernsback in the December 1928 issue of *Amazing Stories*, and he had a novel, *The Moon Children*, serialized in *Galaxy* in 1971. Williamson received his Ph.D. in English in 1964 and now teaches science fiction at Eastern New Mexico University.

H.G. Wells: Critic of Progress was Williamson's thesis for his doctorate. We had images of Jack reading Wells as he sat on the tailgate of that covered wagon, but no, it seems that he first encountered Wells in the pages of the early *Amazing*. This book is honest homage from an early master of science fiction to an earlier writer whom Williamson feels has not yet been surpassed. Take into account, however, the fact that it began as a thesis.

Marjorie M. Miller's *Isaac Asimov: A Checklist of Works Published in the United States, March 1939-May 1972* is a hardcover bibliography of the written works of the Good Doctor. It is a testimony to Asimov's industry and to the new legitimacy in academic circles of People Like Us.

Three Faces of Science Fiction by Robert A.W. Lowndes is an example of a new type of sf publication, the convention souvenir. This modest little book began life as a series of editorials in *Famous Science Fiction* in 1967 and 1968. Like *The Universe Makers* by Donald Wollheim, to whom this book is dedicated, it may be counted as an *apologia pro vita sua* by one who was a young sf fan in the Thirties and a young sf editor in the Forties. *Three Faces of Science Fiction* is genial, unrigorous and unpretentious, but it is unlikely to add to anyone's understanding of science fiction. It is also overpriced.

If the last item is over-priced, *From Elfland to Poughkeepsie* by Ursula K. Le Guin is a rip-off. This neatly-made pamphlet is a writers' workshop address that in former times would have been published as a commonplace fan magazine article. Its thesis is that the diction of fantasy stories should be appropriate. Agreed. But why $3 for a thirty-page pamphlet, and $5 for an autographed copy? Seemingly that is what the publishers feel the traffic will bear. Be warned.

The Science-Fiction Magazine Checklist 1961-1972, ed. by William H. Desmond, and *The N.E.S.F.A. Index: Science Fiction Magazines and Original Anthologies 1971-1972* are attempts to keep bibliographic control of sf. The *Checklist* is a small pamphlet that gives volume and issue numbers of sf magazines. Desmond intends to expand coverage to the years 1895-1975 and publish a complete checklist in September 1976. The *NESFA Index* is a continuation of previous magazine indexes, giving listings by contents, by story title and by author. It adds coverage of original sf anthologies, token of the shift in sf publishing from magazines to books.

The World of Fanzines: A Special Form of Communication by Fredric Wertham, M.D., is an example of notice from the outside world. Wertham is the author of *Seduction of the Innocent*, the book that was responsible for the laundering of the comic book industry some twenty years ago, and there were those who feared that Wertham might dislike fanzines. Indeed he does not. He likes them a lot. He finds them healthy and creative, and we dare say that he is right.

The fact remains that Wertham does not know or understand fanzines. He looks at them as a complete outsider, and his examination reveals the limitations of "objective study." To do a proper job would require someone who knows how fanzines are made, why they are made, and what the problems of making them are. But it might be better that such a study not be made lest it prove the death of its object of love. Let well enough be, and hope that *The World of Fanzines* is overlooked so that those who create fanzines may be left in peace.

Twenty years ago, Reginald Bretnor edited one of the early volumes of science fiction criticism, a symposium entitled *Modern Science Fiction: Its Meaning and Its Future*. Now he is issuing another collection of fifteen articles, *Science Fiction, Today and Tomorrow*. The chief difference that twenty years has made seems to be that the earlier volume was primarily concerned with explaining sf and justifying its existence, whereas the present book is more secure in its belief that sf has its own legitimacy. The contributors to the present volume are primarily concerned with the uncertain state of the world and how sf may affect it. Some few articles here, like Poul Anderson's "The Creation of Imaginary Worlds," may be of particular interest to those who read science fiction, but for the most part, this book seems directed more to those who don't read science fiction than to those who do. And, perhaps because these are temporarily inconclusive times, the sum and substance of these many articles seems ultimately inconclusive.

The most interesting item that we have for review is Brian W. Aldiss's *Billion Year Spree*, which is subtitled *The True History of Science Fiction*, and is, as Aldiss points out in his introduction, the first book-length history of sf. It seems incredible that it should be, but quite amazingly, it is. It is a timely book, and so is its intention of putting sf in perspective timely.

Close observers of this space may have noticed that on several

occasions in the past year or two we have taken exception to anthologies edited by Brian Aldiss. Because of this, and because we
are at work on our own history of science fiction, mutual friends of
ours and Aldiss have suggested that it might be better if we didn't
review *Billion Year Spree* lest our remarks be misunderstood.

However, it seems to us that if sf truly is to be put in perspective,
then perhaps *Billion Year Spree* is a book we should go out of our
way to comment on. Sf needs to be understood. Various theories
as to its nature and purpose are going to be offered now and in the
near future. They are going to contend for influence on the future
course of sf. Under these circumstances, the most direct commentary by us on Aldiss or Aldiss on us seems in order. The less misplaced hanging-back the better. Let us argue like friends.

First, the book itself. *Billion Year Spree* was apparently originally to have been a collaboration between Aldiss and Philip Strick.
Aldiss's part was to have been the 19th century, and Strick's the
modern history of sf, but Strick dropped out of the project because
of other commitments and Aldiss finished the whole history himself.
The result is that the 19th century chapters are the stronger part
of the book. They give an account of many works that will be unfamiliar to modern readers of sf and they touch on all of the works
that deserve commentary. The chapters on the 20th century are
more perfunctory, and too often they take refuge in alphabetical
catalogs like this (excerpt):

> Daniel Keyes' *Flowers for Algernon* was immediately hailed (and
> later filmed as *Charly*). Damon Knight, now too well known as critic
> and anthologist, was once a spirited and elegant short-story writer.
> Fritz Leiber, most celebrated for his fantasies set in imaginary
> worlds, was also capable of producing short sf as stunning as "A
> Pail of Air." J.T. McIntosh began with great promise in such novels
> as *One in Three Hundred*.

Etc., etc. This is either too much about these writers or it is surely
too little.

The other chief weakness of the book is that it has no consistent
narrative thread. In spite of its subtitle, it is not a coherent history.
It is not a systematic account of what has happened in the develop-

ment of science fiction, together with an analysis and explanation. Instead, it is a random grouping of books and authors, together with Aldiss's often strikingly insightful comments upon them. But a history it isn't.

What, then, is Aldiss writing, and why?

It seems to us that there are two Brian Aldisses. One is a person who received a good conventional high British education, and who accepted its values without question, in particular the prejudice that to be negative is to be more realistic and truthful about the universe than to be positive. The other is the boy who discovered science fiction around 1940, loved it wholeheartedly, and rebelled when he was told that it was trash.

The Aldiss who grew up to write science fiction attempted to make a consistency of his two selves. That is, he tried to write science fiction, which he valued, according to the standards of good literature that he had been taught and believed. The result has been stories of devolution like the Hothouse series. It has been novels modeled on James Joyce and the French anti-novelists. It has been stories with titles like ". . . And the Stagnation of the Heart." *Billion Year Spree* is Aldiss's attempt—ten years in the making, by his own account—to make an intellectual case for the virtues of his particular synthesis.

Aldiss offers this construction of science fiction:

> Science fiction is the search for a definition of man and his status in the universe which will stand in our advanced but confused state of knowledge (science), and is characteristically cast in the Gothic or post-Gothic mould.

It is the Aldiss who loved science fiction who would search for a definition of man and his status in the universe. But the other Aldiss has a mandarin certitude about the nature of man and his status that cuts the search short.

It is this Aldiss who writes:

> The evil that confronts the Poeian protagonist is not simply external; it is a part of his destiny, if not of himself. This is not an untruthful view of reality—later science fiction authors who change the terms of Poe's equation, making the protagonists gigantic and

heroic, and conquering the universe, or making the evil purely external—and so cast in opposition to an innocent mankind—falsify
disastrously.

It is this Aldiss who writes of the novels of Franz Kafka:

> And yet the baffling atmosphere, the paranoid complexities, the
> alien motives of others, make the novels a sort of *haute* sf.

And it is this Aldiss who baffles himself in this manner:

> Terms such as "pessimism" and "optimism" are loosely used in
> the science fiction debate. There was plenty of pessimism in *As-
> tounding*; that is a simple emotion. What it lacked was a natural
> and decent despair which has always characterized much of ordinary
> literature. But, even in 1972, editors in the sf field reject stories
> because they are "too down-beat"—a curious rejection, since sf has
> always been, on the whole, a gloomy literature.

If the nature of man and his status in the universe is still in question, then it is not yet time to declare ourselves for "a natural and
decent despair." Indeed, this despair does characterize ordinary
mimetic literature. If sf does not despair, it is because it has horizons
that are broader than those of mimetic literature.

Aldiss concludes *Billion Year Spree* by postulating

> ... that the sf field will undergo—is already undergoing—the
> same stratification already undergone in the general category, with
> high-brow novels and low-brow novels and several brows in between.

And he aims to increase this stratification:

> Sooner or later, the Prix Goncourts of the field will arrive, to be
> bestowed for works of genuine creation. We hope that the new John
> W. Campbell Memorial Award will be a step towards this end.

The John W. Campbell Memorial Award is the first political prize
to be offered in science fiction. Its politics are Brian Aldiss's politics.
In presenting the first award of the prize, Aldiss's statement reads, in
part:

> Until SF is allowed to be aware of corruption, and the fallen
> status of man on which most of the world's great writers have dwelt,
> then it will remain a nursery literature, as it largely has in even the
> best of the SF magazines.

Aldiss is certainly entitled to his own opinions. But it was an outright mistake to use John W. Campbell's name to further politics that he would have despised. It would have been more honest to name the award after Franz Kafka, or even after Brian Aldiss.

Brian Aldiss seems to hope and believe that his values will prevail, that science fiction will divide itself into a higher part and a lower part, and that the higher part will look very much like the kind of science fiction that Brian himself writes. But it is our belief that if Brian Aldiss pushes the distinction that he makes in *Billion Year Spree* and in his John W. Campbell Memorial Award, if he persists in perceiving the nature of man as fallen and his status as deserving nothing but despair, his will not be the high standard by which science fiction measures itself. Instead, he will separate himself from science fiction as J.G. Ballard before him has done.

Part III: Heinlein Reread

10/ READING HEINLEIN SUBJECTIVELY

[*The Alien Critic*, May 1974]

1

When Robert Heinlein's science fiction stories are read objectively —that is, as though they had primary relevance and reference to existing things and extrapolations of existing things—difficulties and contradictions arise. Heinlein becomes a controversial figure.

Immediately there are those who denounce him. An Austrian named Franz Rottensteiner has written an analysis of Heinlein entitled "Chewing Gum for the Vulgar." It describes Heinlein as naive, a fascist, a narcissist, a suppressed homosexual, an authoritarian and a savage.

Rottensteiner says:

> When an author makes a trivial error, such as writing of a Mars with a breathable air, almost all SF critics will jump at him (for that is something that any schoolboy knows), but blunders in more complex fields such as history, psychology, morals or politics will most likely remain unpunished.

This is the sort of pronunciamento that an objective reading of Heinlein brings out in a man. People argue heatedly over the meaning of his work. Imagine the argument when one of the apparent number who try to live by *Stranger in a Strange Land* encounters Mr. Rottensteiner who knows *Stranger* to be "a megalomaniac fascist fantasy."

Readers who take one of Heinlein's books as a bible must find others of his books bewildering. There are libertarians who have been persuaded to take *The Moon Is a Harsh Mistress* as an accurate map of the objective world. What happens to one such when he reads *I Will Fear No Evil*?

Critics faced with Heinlein throw up their hands, either because they have been psyched-out by the man, or because the objective contradictions are too much for them. We say psyched-out, because Heinlein has asked, demanded and pressured to be considered objectively.

Damon Knight's famous chapter on Heinlein in *In Search of Wonder*, "One Sane Man: Robert A. Heinlein," excuses Knight's inability to get a firm objective grip on Heinlein as a result of the supposed real multiplicity of Heinlein:

> Robert A. Heinlein has that attribute which the mathematician Hermann Weyl calls "the inexhaustibility of real things": whatever you say about him, I find, turns out to be only partly true.

That is the sound of a psyched-out critic.

Writing some years after Knight, with the advantage of acquaintance with a later and more blatant Heinlein, James Blish comments:

> Much of his major work gives the impression of being a vehicle for highly personal political and economic opinions, so that a critic who disagrees with these views may find himself reacting to the lectures rather than the fiction. A related danger is taking a firm stand on what Heinlein actually believes, for many of the apparent propaganda threads turn out to be in contradiction with one another.

But it is precisely the lectures that Heinlein wants his critics to react to. And inevitably the weighers of merit of argument bog down in discussions of the feasibility of the politics of *Starship Troopers* or the religion of *Stranger in a Strange Land*. Earnest people contend earnestly over Heinlein, and that is the way Heinlein wants it.

In a lecture delivered at the University of Chicago in 1957 and reprinted in *The Science Fiction Novel*, Heinlein defines science fiction several times. These definitions are Heinlein's self-estimate. They are the yardsticks by which Heinlein wishes his fiction to be judged.

First, Heinlein summarizes a definition by Reginald Bretnor which Heinlein calls "the most thoughtful, best reasoned, and most useful definition of science fiction." Science fiction, he says, is that sort of literature

> ... in which the author shows awareness of the nature and importance of the human activity known as the scientific method, shows equal awareness of the great body of human knowledge already collected through that activity, and takes into account in his stories the effects and possible future effects on human beings of scientific method and scientific fact.

Heinlein then asks, "If all fiction is imaginary, how is realistic fiction to be distinguished from fantasy?" And he answers,

> When I say "fantasy fiction" I shall mean "imaginary-and-not-possible" in the world as we know it; conversely all fiction which I regard as "imaginary-but-possible" I shall refer to as "realistic fiction," i.e. imaginary but could be real so far as we know the real universe. Science fiction is in the latter class. It is not fantasy.

Heinlein's argument is that science fiction is fiction that takes science and the facts into account. Science fiction is imaginary-but-possible. It is realistic fiction.

Heinlein then emphasizes his point. He draws up parallel tables:

REALISTIC FICTION

1. Historical Fiction
2. Contemporary-Scene Fiction
3. Realistic Future-Scene Fiction

FANTASY FICTION

I. Fantasy laid in the past
II. Fantasy laid in the present
III. Fantasy laid in the future

And he says,

> Class 3 contains only science fiction; a small amount of science fiction may also be found in class 1 and class 2.
>
> In the second division, good fantasy, consciously written and

skillfully executed, may be found in all three classes. But a great quantity of fake "science" fiction, actually pseudo-scientific fantasy, will be found there also, especially in class III, which is choked with it.

But the most significant fact shining out from the above method of classifying is that class 3, realistic future-scene fiction, contains nothing which is not science fiction and contains at least 90% of all science fiction in print. A handy short definition of almost all science fiction might read: realistic speculation about possible future events, based solidly on adequate knowledge of the real world, past and present, and on a thorough understanding of the nature and significance of the scientific method.

It becomes clear that Heinlein is confident of his ability to know the real world, past and present, adequately enough to write science fiction, realistic fiction of the future. And he separates his work, true science fiction, from the work of poseurs, who only pretend to know about the world and who write "pseudo-scientific fantasy," class III.

And, Heinlein further argues, the past is dead, the present fleetingly gone; only the future may be affected. Therefore, Heinlein says, "I must assert that speculative fiction is much more realistic than is most historical and contemporary-scene fiction and is superior to them both."

Quite plainly, Heinlein wishes to be taken as writing about factual objective matters. One of his book jacket photos shows him seated behind his typewriter working a slide rule, astronomical globe at his elbow. Damon Knight, speaking on Heinlein's behalf in the introduction to Heinlein's collected "Future History" stories, says,

Far more of Heinlein's work comes out of his own experience than most people realize. When he doesn't know something himself, he is too conscientious a workman to guess at it: he goes and finds out. His stories are full of precisely right details, the product of painstaking research.

Heinlein has declared himself willing to contradict theory, but not fact, and in his science fiction he has clearly stuck as close to the facts as he could. He has not hurled galaxies around like "Doc" Smith. He hasn't created galactic empires 50,000 years in the future like Isaac Asimov. He hasn't been an only child in an Art Deco city a billion years from now, like Arthur C. Clarke. He hasn't flown naked in space like A.E. van Vogt.

Heinlein hasn't displayed unheard-of powers to us, nor shown us incomprehensible alien creatures. He has only ventured as far afield as the lost starship in "Universe," and as far into the future as the empty palace 20,000 years from now in "By His Bootstraps." By the imaginative standards of the period in which Heinlein has been dean of the college of science fiction, Heinlein has been conservative.

However, in spite of Heinlein's arguments, science fiction is a form of fantasy. It is an act of the imagination. It deliberately projects itself outside the world of present existence.

It seems clear that if Heinlein really wanted to write about facts, about reality, about present existence, he would do so. Instead, he chooses to write imaginary projections that are studded with references to fact, with citations of authority, and with close analogy to present existence. His science fiction stories are none the less imaginary.

Realistic fiction speaks of the universe outside the human skin, about objectivity. Fantasy is subjective fiction. Imaginary settings, such as those found in science fiction, are representations of inner space, the country of dreams. For all Heinlein's claims of realism, Heinlein's fiction makes infinitely greater sense when taken subjectively than it does when taken objectively.

Heinlein has asked to be taken objectively. But taken objectively, Heinlein is ambiguous and contradictory. Heinlein has resisted subjective readings of his work. On two occasions he has withdrawn his gaze from informal magazines circulating among science fiction writers when the meaning of his work has come under discussion. And on yet another occasion, he did his best to discourage publication of a critical study of his work, not for its particular argument, but because it existed.

Nonetheless, it seems that Heinlein is responded to subjectively by the science fiction audience, which chiefly reads subjectively, to learn about itself, not about the world at large. Heinlein has always commanded an audience of science fiction readers exclusive of the special audiences, large and small, won for him by *Stranger in a Strange Land* or *The Moon Is a Harsh Mistress*. This constant audience, in the midst of hot objective argument, has given Heinlein the best novel of the year Hugo Awards for *Double Star*, *Starship Troopers*, *Stranger in a Strange Land* and *The Moon Is a Harsh Mistress*. What consistency of objective opinion can encompass these books?

Double Star: An actor is co-opted into the political process, assumes the place of a fallen statesman and watches paternally over the painful fortunes of common folk:

> But there is solemn satisfaction in doing the best you can for eight billion people.
> Perhaps their lives have no cosmic significance, but they have feelings. They can hurt.

Starship Troopers: War against an implacable group-minded alien race in a future in which only veterans of military service are qualified to hold office, to vote, and to teach courses in History and Moral Philosophy:

> A soldier accepts personal responsibility for the safety of the body politic of which he is a member, defending it, if need be, with his life. The civilian does not.

Stranger in a Strange Land: A young man raised by Martians returns to Earth to turn things topsy-turvy, in particular founding a new religion. He is martyred and takes over responsibility for us in his new role as God's favorite son.

In this story, Jubal Harshaw, the philosophical fount of the novel, says:

> "My dear, I used to think I was serving humanity . . . and I pleasured in the thought. Then I discovered that humanity does not want to be served; on the contrary it resents any attempt to serve it. So now I do what pleases Jubal Harshaw."

The Moon Is a Harsh Mistress: A former penal colony on the Moon establishes its independence from an overpopulated sinkhole Earth. The novel culminates with a speech by the philosopher of the revolution:

> He stopped for cheers, then went on, "But that lies in the future.

Today— Oh, happy day! At last the world acknowledges Luna's sovereignty. Free! You have won your freedom—"

And he drops dead.

What consistent politics can encompass these books?
Add this small treasury of Heinlein, always speaking with evident conviction:

> "It's neither your business, nor the business of this damn paternalistic government, to tell a man not to risk his life doing what he really wants to do."

> When any government, or any church for that matter, undertakes to say to its subjects, "This you may not read, this you must not see, this you are forbidden to know," the end result is tyranny and oppression, no matter how holy the motives.

> Those who refuse to support and defend a state have no claim to protection by that state. Killing an anarchist or a pacifist should not be defined as "murder" in a legalistic sense. The offense against the state, if any, should be "Using deadly weapons inside city limits," or "Creating a traffic hazard," or "Endangering bystanders," or other misdemeanor.
> However, the state may reasonably place a closed season on these exotic asocial animals whenever they are in danger of becoming extinct. An authentic buck pacifist has rarely been seen off Earth, and it is doubtful that any have survived the trouble there . . . regrettable, as they had the biggest mouths and the smallest brains of any of the primates.
> The small-mouthed variety of anarchist has spread through the Galaxy at the very wave front of the Diaspora; there is no need to protect them. But they often shoot back.

> ". . . But your psychometrical tests show that you believe yourself capable of judging morally your fellow citizens and feel justified in personally correcting and punishing their lapses . . . From a social standpoint, your delusion makes you mad as the March Hare."

> "Democracy can't work. Mathematicians, peasants and animals, that's all there is—so democracy, a theory based on the assumption that mathematicians and peasants are equal, can never work. Wis-

dom is not additive; its maximum is that of the wisest man in a given group."

"The private life and free action of every individual must be scrupulously respected."

What objective reality can make these sentiments into a consistency? None that we know of. Taken subjectively, however, the apparent inconsistencies of Heinlein's fiction fall into intelligible order. Heinlein's fiction forms an emotional, not a logical whole.

In one unguarded moment, Robert Heinlein described the subjective basis of his stories. This was in an essay entitled "On the Writing of Speculative Fiction" in a small 1947 symposium of early and naive science fiction criticism entitled *Of Worlds Beyond*.

In this essay, Heinlein defined both "story" and the kind of story that he wished to write. "A story," he said, "is an account which is not necessarily true but which is interesting to read." And he said:

> A story of the sort I want to write is still further limited to this recipe: a man finds himself in circumstances which create a problem for him. In coping with this problem, the man is changed in some fashion inside himself. The story is over when the inner change is complete—the external incidents may go on indefinitely.

It is precisely that which Heinlein calls the "recipe" of his fiction that we take to be the key to subjective readings of science fiction. That is, we believe that all stories are about growth experiences. Mimetic fiction—what Heinlein calls "realistic fiction"—describes how growth experiences are acted out in our society. Fantasy, including science fiction, presents literal actings out of the objectively hidden inner processes of the act of growth. Fantasy stories are subjective models—which is why adolescent readers are so notoriously fond of science fiction. They read it for subjective guidance.

A science fiction writer sets forth a theoretical growth problem. This consists of a set of invented circumstances which provide a character, a nation, a planet, or the universe with a problem.

This problem is "not necessarily true." In fact, it is imaginary. But it is interesting. The reason that it is interesting is that it is a symbolization of human growth experiences, and growth is the natural personal business of the human being. Animals are fixed in their individual growth and grow chiefly as species. Humans are distinguished from animals precisely by the fact that we are never arrested in personal development and may evolve all our lives. Whenever we say that something is interesting or entertaining, we are, more precisely, saying that it has relevance to our chief business: personal growth, evolution, higher development, self-improvement, inner refinement.

Science fiction proposes symbolic problems. These problems are either solved or not solved. In the successes and failures symbolized in science fiction stories, the reader finds lessons in the means of changing himself.

Heinlein says of the stories he would write: "In coping with this problem, the man is changed in some fashion inside himself."

But the change is not the result of coping with the problem. The change is the *means* of coping with the problem. Science fiction stories act out lessons in how it feels to change, and how one must feel in order to change.

Our premise is that the imaginary problems that Robert Heinlein poses, the solutions that he envisions, the facts he invents, and the models he presents in his fiction, that all these reveal more about Heinlein's subjectivity, his personal relationship with the universe, than they do about the objective realistic factual universe that Heinlein lays claim to writing about. If we look at Heinlein's imaginary problems and solutions, we will learn what Heinlein believes the universe to be like. Read subjectively, Heinlein is consistent. However, before we look more closely at Heinlein's fiction, we must establish a basis for subjective understanding of science fiction.

2

We are born possessing three means of knowledge about the universe and ourselves within the universe. These means are instinct, intuition and intelligence.

Intelligence is the ability to learn new details about the universe. In simpler animals, intelligence is altogether missing. In more complex animals, intelligence is a highly limited quality. It is, of course, more highly-developed intelligence that seems to distinguish humanity from other animals.

However, not only human intelligence, but the very capacity for intelligence is not fully developed at birth. The new-born human infant must rely for his knowledge on instinct and intuition. In contrast to intelligence, these older and more established means—the legacy of man's long evolutionary history—are fully developed at birth, as they are in lesser animals.

Instinct is a form of knowledge that is built into living beings. The goal of instinct is self-preservation—the maintenance of the integrity of the individual being against the corrosive and homogenizing effects of entropy. To instinct, the individual—the Self—is primary. To instinct, the Other—the rest of the universe—is secondary to the Self.

Instinct is selfish and divisive. It promotes the good of the individual, or, at most wide-ranging, the species, at the cost of all else that exists. But instinct is necessary to the survival of individuals and species. It prompts frogs to snag flying insects. It drives new-born kittens to seek their mother's nipples. It sends chickens that have never seen a hawk running for cover at their first glimpse of a flying shadow. It urges young salmon to seek the sea, and then to return to the streams of their birth to spawn.

Intuition, the other and more basic form of in-born knowledge, offsets the selfishness and special interest of instinct. To instinct, the individual is primary, and the universe secondary. By contrast, intuition is a knowledge that informs us that the universe as a whole is primary, and that individual beings within that universe are secondary.

Intuition yields a sense of the underlying unity and harmony of the universe. As we are taught in school with diagrams of food-chains, with charts of nitrogen cycles, with tables of atoms, we are all made of common stuff. The individual matrix that is a tree or a human being may remain continuously in existence for an extended period of time while interchangeable atoms fill that matrix for a shorter time and are then replaced.

Intuition informs us that divisiveness is not all there is to existence. It tells us that Self and Other are in some fundamental sense One. The condition that embraces an apparently discrete Self and Other, and links them as One, human beings call "love."

The human infant, of course, knows nothing of abstract theorization. He has no memories, no developed sensory perceptions, none of the complex symbolic vocabulary that adult human beings traffic in. He has no objectivity. Necessarily, he must take everything that happens to him personally.

The thought of the infant is immediate and subjective. All that exists is sentience, like himself. Sentience interacts with him in dramatic personal terms—as it were, story.

The infant, of course, is the Self. At the outset, the rest of the universe is the Other—a single sentient being like the Self. Everything that occurs to the infant is taken to be motivated. That is, the Other is taken to have its own self-preserving motivations that cause it to act either benignly or hostilely to the Self. However, beyond any specific behavior of the Other, the infant has the intuitive conviction that Self and Other are linked by love.

The human infant is born in a peculiarly helpless state. The oversized human brain that permits our intelligence is too large to develop within the womb. In consequence, we humans are born only partially developed, and even that partial development strains the pelvic equipment of the human female.

But because we are born in such an unfinished state, we are more helpless at birth than the young of other species. Fish can swim at birth, and know how to feed themselves. A colt can stand shortly after birth, walk and run. A baby baboon can cling to its mother's fur.

A human baby can only lie in utter helplessness. It cannot cling. It cannot run. It cannot even hold its head up to take its mother's nipple. The most that it can do is cry in hope and fear.

Like other animals, the human infant has instincts which urge it to preserve and protect itself. They make constant suggestion to the infant. But the infant is helpless to act upon its instincts. When these instincts are not responded to, they signal louder. And louder. This is a process of feedback. The signals of instinct become so over-whelming that the fainter and less immediate underlying signals of intuition are blotted out.

When contact with intuition is lost, so is the awareness of loving and being loved. At the times when instinct overwhelms intuition, the infant is confronted by a crueler, lonelier subjective environment. The infant personifies this loveless environment as another character in its mental playlet. This character is the Demonic.

The infant Self assumes that the Demonic has willed the disappear-ance of the Other—that which can be loved. The Demonic is taken to be an unnatural monster of pure evilness which has intruded itself from outside the universe of Oneness perceived through intuition. The Demonic is the outsider—that which is excluded from the bond of love that united Self and Other. In its pain, the Demonic has sought to destroy the love of Self and Other and isolate the infant Self in its own condition of permanent lovelessness.

The one recourse available to the infant is to repress its awareness, to block out the now-unendurable signals of instinct. In story terms, this is taken as the casting-down of the Demonic into the Pit.

But the infant does not merely block out the Demonic. The infant is not able to repress selectively. It cannot merely block out the over-amplified instinctive signals that disrupt intuition. In repressing the over-amplified signals that it takes to be evil, hostile, intrusive and loveless, it also blocks the more moderate stimuli it takes as pro-ceeding from the good, protective and loving Other.

The infant Self must conclude that the Demonic has been brought under control—but only after the Demonic had successfully driven away from the Other. The infant must at all cost continue to repress the Demonic lest it break free from the Pit and destroy the Self as well.

At this point, both intuition and instinct are crippled as means of knowledge. The infant comes to rely on his developing intelligence. Intelligence presents factual knowledge. It informs the infant of a multiplicity of detail without preconception as to its nature.

The age we are speaking of is 4-6 months, which is the age when scientific observers are first able to detect the operations of intelligence and the age when the infant's skull, which has been soft and plastic to allow the continued growth of the brain after birth, grows firm. From this age, the human being is primarily aware of the universe as a multiplicity. It is in the world of multiplicity that we learn to talk, to walk, to interact, form friendships, go to school, establish opinions, grow up and live our daily lives.

We judge the world of multiplicity by our instinctual habits of thought. That is, we make sense of facts by relating them to our goal of self-preservation. The facts we encounter are variously pigeon-holed by us as good things (to which we are attached) and bad things (which we avoid).

Our basis of action in this world of multiplicity is intelligent self-interest. We try to maximize that which we categorize as good and minimize that which we categorize as bad.

Fact and multiplicity, we conclude, are subject to rules. The world of multiplicity includes human society, which is based on rules. We find there are rules for talking and walking and interacting and forming friendships and going to school and establishing opinions and growing up and living our daily lives.

These rules tell us how we are "properly" to order the multiplicity we find ourselves surrounded by. The rules tell us how to maximize the good and minimize the bad. We do our best to follow the rules. We bargain and game-play our way through the universe of multiplicity.

There are, of course, problems inherent in game-playing. There are situations where we don't know the rules, or where different sets of rules conflict. However, the universe of multiplicity is distinctly less trying than the previous universe of instinct and intuition. A child may have temporary difficulties learning new sets of rules when he goes off to school or moves to a new neighborhood, but the rules, once learned, will continue to serve him. He does not have to cope with an ambivalent unity, both benign and hostile, which insists on being accepted as a whole. That is, as children, we can deal with the universe of multiplicity without having to reconcile its contradictions through love.

As we grow, the universe of instinct and intuition is consciously forgotten. But it is not gone from our minds entirely. It is merely repressed, banished to the unconscious.

Sometimes, however, without ever being clearly and explicitly remembered, our earliest experiences well up into consciousness and color our perceptions of situations. There are times when we may have vague, nostalgic intimations of a lost dream-world from which we were forcibly exiled. As we grow up, for instance, we may recall our childhood as a time of purity and joy which has somehow ended, and regret our lost innocence—without, of course, being able to specifically remember what made it all so wonderful. Or we may discover a perfect Golden Age somewhere in human history—Eden, Augustinian Rome, pioneer America—which was destroyed by a Fall from Grace.

Or we may fear the Demonic as a still-present menace lurking just beyond perception to snatch us up if we lose our grip on the factual universe—that is, if we try to evade the rules. This fear is the source of irrational behavior which alters and interferes with logical rational self-interest. As children, if our family relationships suggest it, we may perceive our mother as the Other, and our father as the Demonic who tore us away from the nurturing breast. We may be warned by our parents that if we are not good the Bogey-man will get us. We may bully or be bullied—that is, we may interact with irrational aggressiveness or irrational timidity with what we take to be symbols of the Demonic. The Nazi misperception of the Jews as the Demonic, the cause of the Fall that was Germany's defeat in World War I, most certainly caused them to act against their rational self-interest.

So it is that for the most part we live whole-heartedly in the world of facts and rules and society. But sometimes an event or a set of circumstances may remind us of something we think we may once have known in some other time and place—joys beyond telling and dreads beyond endurance.

The capacity of intelligence continues to grow until about the age of fourteen. We become able to handle more and more facts in an ever more sophisticated manner. But by fourteen we have become as adept in the manipulation of facts as we will ever be.

In our adolescent years, with our full intellectual command and whatever facts we have accumulated, we review the situation in which we find ourselves. We try to relate ourselves to the universe by separating the essential from the contingent. We try to decide for ourselves in the course of endless bull sessions and in private rumination what is real and what is not.

We have two major problems to settle. One is the problem of society. Are the rules and games of society mere accident or are they necessary? Are they creations of the human mind, subject to doubt and change, or are they real and absolute? The other is the problem of evil. Is evil a fact of existence or is it a mere seeming?

Both these problems are the inheritance of our instincts. It is instinct that informs us of the Demonic. And it is instinct that first sets us to bargaining and game-playing to maximize our self-interest. The question for the adolescent is whether or not there is a basis in the world of multiplicity—a factual basis—for our conviction that evil and society have essential existence.

The adolescent may decide to believe in one or both or neither. We might call those who decide that both evil and society are real "conservatives." Those who believe in society, but not evil, we might call "liberals." Those who believe in evil, but not society, we might call "nihilists." And those who believe in neither evil nor society we might call subjective "anarchists."

Human childhood—the period of care and protection by family or society—extends through the adolescent years. This, like the immaturity of other higher animals, is a period of flexible growth—though far more extended than for any other animal.

At the end of childhood, we leave our shelter and face the universe with our own developed resources, as ones who are responsible for our own direction, goals and fate. We have been educated. Our intellect has been developed. We have, that is, a sense of the objective interrelations of the universe around us. And we have, as well, a developed subjective position—conservative, liberal, nihilist or anarchist—which suggests how we and the universe are related.

It is only now that our mature development begins. While it does seem to be our highly-developed intelligence that separates humanity from the lesser animals, the true separation between humanity and other animals is not in intelligence alone, but rather in the human ability to evolve in quantum leaps as mature adults.

Children, with their constant looking forward to "when I grow up," have an appreciation of the fact that the real business of being human begins with adulthood. For the child, life is one long postponement until he is an adult.

And then the true business of life for human beings does begin. The first quantum leap that we are called upon to make is the leap from childhood to adulthood. From the child's point of view, this jump looks impossible. And in fact it is—for a child. To complete the jump successfully, the child must reject his former limited self, stake his life on a new identity, and remake himself in larger scale.

The child is essentially a selfish being. He is a Self in a world of multiplicity. In repressing the Demonic as an infant, he has cut himself off from the Other, from love, and from Oneness. As a child, he has been sufficient unto himself. If he could remain a protected, childish Self, he would not grow, he would not change on reaching maturity.

Instead, however, he is thrust into the universe to make his way. And it is then that he discovers that his childish Self is insufficient, no matter what he may have thought in his ignorance. In order to deal with the universe, he must expand his Self.

This is only possible by incorporating some part of the universe into the Self. And that sort of incorporation is possible only through a recognition of the Other, a confrontation with the Demonic, and a binding of Self and Other through love into a Oneness. The result is a new and larger Self who is capable of separation from parents, of employment in an adult occupation, of marriage—in short, of all those responsibilities and independences that the childhood Self is incapable of.

The recognition of the Other, confrontation with the Demonic, and the binding of Self and Other through love into a Oneness is a subjective process. From the objective point of view, the late adolescent may seem to fumble, to wander in circles, to lie around in a stupor, to strike off in blind directions, and to be unable to explain himself. And then suddenly "to find himself." That is, to make a commitment—or decision to love—which he thereafter pursues. And about time, too.

But it is not only in the leap from childhood to adulthood that we undertake the subjective adventure that leads past the Demonic to Oneness, the result of which is personal evolution, the expansion of Self. At various moments in our adult lives, we are certain to be faced with circumstances that the resources of our present Self are inadequate to deal with. We find that our conscious dedications are cut too small. We are not large enough persons to deal with the crises we face.

If we are to surmount these crises, we must personally evolve. We must exchange our old limited Self with our particular problems for a new larger Self that is larger than the problems that confront us. And the means is love, the linkage of Self and Other as One.

Are these crises biologically rooted? Though they may differ in their individual details from one person to another and may be resolved in very different outward terms, they seem to happen to most of us at the same times of life. There is the crisis of the late adolescent striving to be an adult. There is another crisis at about the age of 26 to 28, and yet another in the early thirties, say age 32 to 35. Again, we find life asking us to redefine ourselves in the later forties, and further crises follow. Each is a potential quantum leap.

It is the successful subjective monomythic journey within oneself to re-contact the wellsprings of intuition that, for example, befits a man who was once an unsuccessful hat salesman to become a more than usually competent President of the United States. It is precisely the subjective quest that is the stuff of science fiction stories and other fantasies.

Or—in Heinlein's words:

> A story of the sort I want to write is still further limited to this recipe: a man finds himself in circumstances which create a problem for him. In coping with this problem, the man is changed in some fashion inside himself. The story is over when the inner change is complete—the external incidents may go on indefinitely.

3

In the first section of this essay, we pointed out that although Robert Heinlein, for his own reasons, has demanded to be read objectively, when he has been, it has led to controversy. And not surprisingly. Heinlein is the author of many strongly-phrased but seemingly objectively inconsistent opinions. We offered as an example a number of Heinlein statements that appear to apply to politics. There does not appear to be objective consistency in these statements. Read subjectively, however, we believe they are consistent and intelligible.

In the second section of this essay, we have presented a simple version of a theory of subjective growth in the human being. We believe this theory indicates the nature, value and subject matter of science fiction and other fantasy stories.

There is much more to be said about Robert Heinlein's subjectivity than we can possibly say here. Throughout his long and prolific writing career, Heinlein has made himself subjectively explicit in his work to a degree unmatched by any other science fiction writer. He has reserved nothing of himself.

Since we cannot be complete, we will concentrate on Heinlein's earliest stories, and, to a lesser extent, his other fiction written before World War II, when Heinlein stopped writing to devote himself to defense work. We will only make small reference to his later stories by way of example.

These early stories do not make an objective whole. They do not make an objective whole even though a conceptual framework—the "Future History"—was imposed on many of them.*

They do, however, make a subjective whole. They return again and again to the same fundamental questions of Robert Heinlein's relationship to the universe—and, by extension, our own.

In this section, we mean to demonstrate the fruitfulness of a subjective reading of these early Heinlein stories, and to show that there is in a subjective reading none of the ambiguity that leads a critic like

---

* See, by way of argument on the objective inconsistency of the Future History, *Heinlein in Dimension*, pp. 121-124.

Mr. Rottensteiner to fire his barrage of negative judgments, or a critic like Damon Knight to throw up his hands in surrender. And, as a by-product of our investigation, we hope to suggest the consistent basis for Heinlein's apparently inconsistent imaginary politics.

An early biographical note describes Robert Heinlein's first 32 years:

> Born in Butler, Missouri, in 1907, he received his early schooling in the public schools of Kansas City. He learned to play chess before he learned to read, and it is his intention to take up chess again when his eyes play out. Originally the stars were his goal; he planned to be an astronomer. But something slipped and he landed in the U.S. Naval Academy instead. He spent not quite ten years in the Navy, was disabled, and retired. Thereafter he tried a number of things— silver mining, real estate, politics, and some graduate study in physics and math. Finally, more or less by accident, he wrote a science fiction story, calling it "Life-Line." It sold and was published in *Astounding Science Fiction* in 1939. He sold his next effort, and, in his own words, he "was hooked, having discovered a pleasant way to live without working."

At the age of 32, Heinlein had negotiated his first two subjective crises successfully. He had made his adolescent decisions. He had passed from adolescence to adulthood. And he had passed again from being a young one-dimensional adult-in-uniform to be a multi-faceted man of many skills and abilities.

In July 1939, when his first story, "Life-Line," was published in *Astounding*, Heinlein was just turning 32 and entering into his third crisis of adulthood. At that moment, Robert Heinlein must have been in an extremely uncertain state of mind.

The question that he was being asked by circumstance to consider was this: Is it enough to be a competent man among other adult men, or is there more to life? If a man can do anything he sets his hand to in a competent way—silver mining, real estate, politics, graduate studies—what, among all the things that he can do or might do competently, is worth the devotion of a lifetime? What occupation or dedication can justify a life?

This is a subjective question. It asks nothing about the facts of the universe. Instead, it is a question of meaning. How can I find meaning in my life? How can I meaningfully relate to the universe around me? Robert Heinlein's fiction was his best attempt to define his problem and to arrive at a solution.

From an objective viewpoint, Heinlein was as lazy and undirected as any adolescent self-locked in his room. Heinlein calls his story writing "a pleasant way to live without working." But of course it was far more than that. Between 1939 and 1942, Heinlein produced a torrent of stories—meaningful self-questioning.

Heinlein attempted two lines of attack on his problem. On the one hand, he recapitulated his earlier crises in story form. These were models of how crises are successfully negotiated. On the other hand, he projected his present problems and perceptions in symbolic form, and attempted to find theoretical solutions for them.

Heinlein's fourth story and first novel, *"If This Goes On—"* (*Astounding*, February-March 1940), was one recapitulation of a past crisis. The personal relevance of this first Heinlein novel is apparent. It was his first work longer than a short story. It was the first of his stories to be told in the first person. And his protagonist, his narrator, quite significantly bears Heinlein's mother's maiden name: Lyle.

The story takes place late in the next century after a rabble-rousing evangelist, Nehemiah Scudder, and his successor "Prophets Incarnate," have assumed control of the United States and run it for generations as a religious-military dictatorship. John Lyle is a member of the personal guard of the current Prophet Incarnate. At birth, he was consecrated by his mother to the Church. He is a West Point graduate who has been assigned to the holiest regiment of the Prophet's hosts, primarily on the basis of top grades in piety.

The home of the Prophet is a strange and paranoid palace, filled with intrigue and corruption. Lyle is an innocent. He only becomes alienated from the Prophet through his forbidden desire for one of the Prophet's handmaidens, who are called Virgins. Lyle's eyes then become open to the corruption around him. With the help of friendly outside forces, he escapes from the palace to join the underground that opposes the Prophet.

Lyle is re-educated. He learns to smoke and to unbend a trifle from his state of stiff rectitude. At the climax of the story, Lyle directs vital elements of the forces of revolution. But he never directly confronts the Prophet himself. Instead, when the forces of revolution reach the Prophet, they find that the Virgins "had left him barely something to identify at an inquest."

We might analyze this story subjectively as follows: An idealistic young man, who believes in both society and evil, discovers that his own society is corrupt. He recognizes the Other in the form of a band of kindred spirits, dedicated revolutionaries. As one of these, he confronts the Demonic and overcomes its tyranny. He becomes free of his former bondage by his identification with the Other.

It is this crisis that is the template for all of Heinlein's many stories of justified revolt against an intolerable domestic tyranny. Examples are *Between Planets* and *The Moon Is a Harsh Mistress*.

One of the significant factors in Heinlein's representations of this crisis is that the Demonic is confronted only distantly. That is, Heinlein has declared himself reluctant to write of the model of the Prophet: "I probably never will write the story of Nehemiah Scudder; I dislike him too thoroughly." And although John Lyle is a member of the Prophet's personal guard and the story itself begins directly outside the Prophet's apartments, the only glimpse we are allowed of the Prophet Incarnate is late in the story on television. Even so, Lyle is awestruck:

> He turned his head, letting his gaze rove from side to side, then looked right at me, his eyes staring right into mine. I wanted to hide. I gasped and said involuntarily, "You mean we can duplicate *that*?"

Similarly, *Between Planets* and *The Moon Is a Harsh Mistress* are both settled by confrontations with the Demonic at arm's length. In the first of these novels, colonial Venus wins its freedom by placing a sphere of force around the Federation capital at Bermuda. But this is not shown. It happens by implication after the novel is over. In the second novel, the Moon wins its freedom from a tyrannical Earth by chucking rocks at the Earth until it gives up.

We take the crisis represented in *"If This Goes On—"* to be Heinlein's first, that which comes at the end of adolescence and the beginning of adulthood, because the objective bases of the major symbols are rooted in the family. The troops of the Prophet are addressed as "Brother." The Virgins are called "Sister." Lyle—who bears Heinlein's mother's name—makes frequent emotional reference to his mother, but none whatever to his father. It is his mother who consecrates Lyle to the Church at birth. The Prophet is both a father figure and Demonic. In other words, *"If This Goes On—"* is most intelligible if read as a symbolic representation of Heinlein's subjective quest which resulted in his escape from the narrow confines of his family.

Heinlein's second story, "Misfit" (*Astounding*, November 1939), also seems to be a recapitulation of a successfully passed crisis— Heinlein's second, that which comes during the twenties. If the question posed in Heinlein's first crisis was: What is an idealistic young man to do when he discovers that the society to which he is committed is corrupt—the question posed by Heinlein's second crisis was: How does a bright but maladjusted young man manage to find a place in society for himself?

In "Misfit," an asteroid is to be jockeyed into orbit between the Earth and Mars and turned into an emergency space station by a work crew of asocial young men. Heinlein's protagonist, Andrew Jackson Libby, is maladjusted through no fault of his own—his father, now dead, had rejected society. At exactly the right wrong moment, a ballistic calculator fails. Libby, who is able to do high-order mathematical integrations instantly in his head, fills in for the calculator, thereby establishing his place in society, and earning dinner with the Admiral.

In this crisis, evil is remote—or at least exterior to society. The concern is to establish a place for the Self within a good society. The Self is an outsider who recognizes society as the Other. He confronts the Demonic in the form of natural forces, as in "Misfit," or in the form of evil enemies of society, as in *Starship Troopers*. The courage and dedication of the Self are recognized. The Self, in Heinlein stories that reflect this crisis, is often, like Libby, the indispensable man. And, like Libby, is welcomed into society.

Another early Heinlein story, "Coventry" (*Astounding*, July 1940), draws a neat distinction between the first and second crises. This story takes place some fifty years after *"If This Goes On—"*. A good society—the best society that Heinlein could then imagine—has been established. But Heinlein's protagonist has rebelled against it. He has violated its canons. He has struck another man who insulted him, and he refuses re-education. In consequence, he is exiled to Coventry where the remnants of the Prophet's hosts, fascists and other evil people live. This is the true Demonic, as David MacKinnon quickly comes to realize. What is more, the Demonic means to break free and conquer the good society. MacKinnon hurries to warn society—and thereby re-earns his place within it.

And why did MacKinnon make his error of rebellion in the first place? Because he projected onto society his hatred of his father:

> Dave's father was one of the nastiest little tyrants that ever domi-
> nated a household under the guise of loving-kindness . . . The boy's
> natural independence, crushed at home, rebelled blindly at every
> sort of discipline, authority, or criticism which he encountered else-
> where and subconsciously identified with the not-to-be-criticized pa-
> ternal authority.

Heinlein's most symbolically sophisticated presentation of his second subjective crisis is to be found in the short novel "Waldo." Waldo is a sick misanthropic genius who lives by himself in an artificial satellite. His only contacts with the Earth are via remote-control devices. At the risk of death, Waldo comes to Earth, recognizes a symbol of the Other in the form of an ancient Pennsylvania hex doctor, and as a result solves both society's problems and his own, healing his body and turning himself into a masterful ballet-tap dancer and brain surgeon.

While Heinlein's recapitulations of his earlier crises in "Misfit" and *"If This Goes On—"* were of aid in telling him where he had been, they were not solutions to his present crisis. They did not answer the question that can only be asked after Libby has earned his place in society, after Waldo has made himself a dancer and surgeon: Is it enough to be a competent man among other adult men, or is there more to life? What dedication is worth the devotion of a lifetime?

In order to complete the monomythic journey successfully, a

death is indicated—the death, that is, of the old limited Self. As token of this death, Libby faints in the midst of his calculations. Waldo surrenders himself in all his frailty to the overwhelming gravity of Earth, which may kill him. MacKinnon, in escaping with his warning, dives under a deadly force Barrier, even though to do so may kill him—and is hurt so badly that he is taken for dead.

However, the thought of the death of the Self with which the 32-year-old Heinlein was faced did not come easily to him. This may have been because he had come near to physical death in the illness —tuberculosis—that had ended his Navy career. And it may have been because Heinlein was consciously satisfied with his present familiar Self, as he had not been when he lived under the spell of the tyrant, and again as he had not been when he was an outsider to society.

Of Heinlein's first five published stories, two—"Misfit," his second, and *"If This Goes On—"*, his fourth—were recapitulations. The other three addressed themselves to this question of the death of the ego.

Heinlein's first story, "Life-Line," poses the question: What sort of man can bear the knowledge of the absolute certainty of his own death? The answer that Heinlein arrives at is: A man not very like the present Robert Heinlein. Some kind of queer, stoical foreigner, perhaps.

In "Life-Line," Hugo Pinero, a gross, fat, white, foreign-born man, appears with a machine that can accurately predict the date of any man's death. We are shown examples of its accuracy—both a reporter and a young bride die as inevitably as we are told they must. Pinero is opposed by members of the Academy of Science, who refuse to examine the evidence, and opposed by a corrupt insurance industry, which is losing money because of the accuracy of his predictions. The insurance industry has Pinero assassinated. When he is dead, it is discovered that he knew the time of his own death, and that he met death calmly. Those who discover this fact are not as calm. They destroy the sealed envelopes that contain the dates on which they will die. And so the story ends—inconclusively.

Heinlein's third story, "Requiem" (*Astounding*, January 1940), returns to this question again. "Requiem" asks: What conditions would make it possible for a man like me to die? Answer: You might willingly die to gain your heart's desire, but only when you are very very old, and only if given outside aid in the crucial moment.

"Requiem" is the story of Delos D. Harriman, a man born *c*. 1907, the year that Heinlein was born. Harriman has wanted all his life to reach the Moon. He has dedicated himself to this end single-mindedly. He is the man who made travel to the Moon possible. But because of a heart condition, he has been forbidden to travel in space.

The story opens at a county fair in Butler, Missouri—the town where Heinlein was born. Harriman approaches a pair of outcasts from society—men who have worked in space and then been excluded from it for cause—and suggests they fit a rocket out and take him to the Moon. Eventually they agree. However, at the crucial moment, Harriman collapses and must be carried on board the spaceship.

But he does gain his heart's desire. He reaches the Moon. The cost is his death.

However, this death is blissful: "He lay back still while a bath of content flowed over him like a tide at flood, and soaked to his very marrow." Though this was but Heinlein's third story, there is no happier moment to be found anywhere in all his fiction.

There is a failure of realization in this story. Heinlein does not seem to know that the death in question is not a permanent physical death, but only a death of the old limited Self, followed by rebirth. Such a realization, however, is implicit in Heinlein's fifth story, " 'Let There Be Light' " (*Super Science*, May 1940).

As a story, " 'Let There Be Light' " is not totally successful. It is an attempt to strike a light note after the model of Stanley Weinbaum's stories of five years earlier. But the story is over-compressed, even sketchy in crucial detail. And Heinlein is clumsy and heavy-handed in his attempted lightness. It is these defects that account for the story being published in *Super Science*, a secondary market, rather than in *Astounding*. However, the story is successful at striking to the heart of Heinlein's greatest problem.

The subjective question the story poses is: How is death-in-life to be achieved? By what means is the Demonic to be faced?

The answer: Relax. That is, become as helpless and hopeless as the infant who is in touch with his intuitive knowledge of Oneness.

In " 'Let There Be Light'," the central characters are two young scientists, a male physicist and a female biologist, who set out to discover an efficient light source. They discover not only light, but power. They are opposed by corrupt power companies—much like the corrupt insurance companies which oppose Pinero in "Life-Line." They are faced with law suits, labor troubles, and fire bombing, and are shadowed wherever they go by goons. The young physicist takes to carrying a gun. An end like Pinero's seems imminent.

But then, the biologist asks:

> "Archie, do you know the ancient Chinese advice to young ladies about to undergo criminal assault?"
> "No, what is it?"
> "Just one word: 'Relax.' That's what we've got to do."

She suggests that they should give their secret of light and power to the world-at-large. They do so, and their antagonists are nonplussed. And the story ends with marriage and the prospect of happiness.

The Other in this story is knowledge—which is, indeed, a higher dedication than mere worldly competence. Knowledge is symbolized as "light" and "power" and it is described in near-mystical terms:

> The screen glowed brilliantly, but not dazzlingly, and exhibited a mother-of-pearl iridescence. The room was illuminated by strong white light without noticeable glare.

The symbol of the Demonic is the corrupt power companies. The threat of the Demonic is met by relaxation—the death of what had seemed to be Self-interest. By giving knowledge away rather than keeping it selfishly, the two young scientists completely defeat the Demonic which had threatened to kill them and suppress their knowledge.

Here is Heinlein's answer to his thirties crisis. However, he was never able to apply this answer again in any more serious fiction than " 'Let There Be Light'." Heinlein had the answer he was seeking in hand, but was not able to trust it.

Heinlein had lost his faith in society, but was not able to perceive a new Other to which he could commit himself. If he and his protagonists were all right, their surroundings clearly were not. Society may once have seemed good and right and sufficient to Heinlein. But in "Life-Line," society is infected by the evil of corrupt life insurance companies. In "Requiem," society does all that it can to prevent D.D. Harriman from doing what he most wants to do. And in " 'Let There Be Light'," society is corrupted by self-seeking power companies.

In these stories, society as a whole is not evil—as in *"If This Goes On—"*. But the society that Heinlein had once seen as good and right was no longer so. He no longer perceived it as the Other—but rather as the society of multiplicity, dominated by the short-sighted interests of businessmen, bureaucrats and unionists. There was in society a susceptibility to corruption and disintegration. Since the appearance of Heinlein's first story, World War II had begun. Under the cracking of society, there lurked the Demonic. With no new perception by Heinlein of the Other—no higher dedication to knowledge, to mankind, to the ends of evolution, or some other love with which to replace the failed dedication to society—he could see nothing to prevent the onslaught of the Demonic.

These were the perceptions of four further Heinlein stories published in 1940 and 1941, which attempted to preserve the dedication to society. These four stories were "The Roads Must Roll" (*Astounding*, June 1940), "Blowups Happen" (*Astounding*, September 1940), "Logic of Empire" (*Astounding*, March 1941), and "Solution Unsatisfactory" (*Astounding*, May 1941).

"The Roads Must Roll" asks: How can a socially dedicated man avert ultimate social catastrophe?

"The Roads Must Roll" postulates a 1965 America in which the American economy is totally dependent on moving roadways—strips that move at speeds from five to one hundred miles an hour between large cities. Factories and businesses line the roads. The bulk of the population lives in the countryside beyond.

The system is incredibly vulnerable because any disruption means social disaster. No breakdowns must occur. No strikes may be permitted.

The roads are so vital that the men who run them, the transport engineers, are a semi-military officer corps, graduated from the United States Academy of Transport.

> We try to turn out graduate engineers imbued with the same loyalty, the same iron self-discipline, and determination to perform their duty to the community at any cost, that Annapolis and West Point and Goddard are so successful in inculcating in their graduates.

The weak spot is the common workers on the roadways, the technicians. They lack the dedication to society of the engineers. And even though they "are indoctrinated constantly with the idea that their job is a sacred trust," as the story opens they are being led out on strike by a renegade engineer with an inferiority complex.

Gaines, Heinlein's protagonist, is Chief Engineer of the roadway that is struck. He is an unhappy, pain-wracked man. His emotions are "a torturing storm of self reproach." He is "heartsick." And we are told: "He had carried too long the superhuman burden of kingship—which no sane mind can carry light-heartedly . . ."

When the strike occurs, Gaines faces his renegade subordinate and destroys his rebellion by telling him that people are aware of his inferiority. Gaines is taught a lesson by his experience:

> Supervision and inspection, check and re-check, was the answer.
> It would be cumbersome and inefficient, but it seemed that adequate safeguards always involved some loss of efficiency.

And "The Roads Must Roll" ends with Gaines whistling "Anywhere you go, you are bound to know, that your roadways are rolling along!"

Heinlein has declared that he wants to write stories of men who are changed in the course of coping with a problem. However, Gaines is not changed in the course of coping with his problem. Instead, he re-dedicates himself to society. But "check and re-check" is not "the answer." At the conclusion of the story society remains as vulnerable, as susceptible to corruption and disintegration as at the beginning. The Demonic still lurks. If Gaines breaks down under "the superhuman burden of kingship" or a traitor with greater will reveals himself, the result will be social disaster.

In "Blowups Happen," society is again at ransom. This story, too, is projected to occur around the year 1965. The sun-screens that power the rolling roads are not sufficient to the needs of society. We are dependent on a single gigantic atomic power plant, vital to society. The plant—called "the bomb"—is delicate and requires constant tuning. It is "a self-perpetuating sequence of nuclear spliting, *just under the level of complete explosion.*"

The strains of duty are unbearably intense:

> Sensitive men were needed—men who could fully appreciate the importance of the charge entrusted to them; no other sort would do. But the burden of responsibility was too great to be borne indefinitely by a sensitive man. It was, of necessity, a psychologically unstable condition. Insanity was an occupational disease.

There are six central characters in this story. Three are young engineers—men yet to pass through their second crisis. Three are older, more competent men. The experiences of the story provide opportunities for growth to all six characters. The three young characters all grow—like Libby, they act as indispensable men when they are needed and bind themselves to society. But the three older characters do not grow. One cracks under the strain and tries deliberately to explode the Demonic bomb. The other two come to the very edge of cracking.

And the solution of the story is no solution. The bomb is thrust away into space. But it remains as Demonic at the end as at the beginning. It will still drive men crazy—just fewer of them. And it is still as certain to explode. The effects of the explosion will merely affect the peripheries of society rather than the heart of society. But society remains vulnerable.

By his own standards, Heinlein set himself a fair problem in "The Roads Must Roll" and again in "Blowups Happen." But in both stories, the dedication to society—re-asserted—is merely enough to inhibit the Demonic. The problems Heinlein sets are not solved but rather postponed or thrust away.

In "Logic of Empire," Heinlein tried a new tack. In this story, he recapitulated both of his first two crises, and then drew an extrapolation, as though he felt that by telling coherently where he had been, he could determine where he was to go. But all that Heinlein is able to do is to carry his character smoothly through two crises and then run him into a brick wall.

Humphrey Wingate, Heinlein's protagonist, finds himself an abused slave on Venus, working in the swamps and drowning his miseries in a soporific drink. He rebels against the tyranny and faces the prospect of a worse fate. Instead, he is given aid to escape the power of his owner. Thus a recapitulation of Heinlein's first crisis.

Wingate then finds himself in a perfect society of free men ruled in an off-hand manner by a competent man. Wingate takes his place in this society by filling an indispensable function—he operates the radio and improves the radio system. Thus a recapitulation of Heinlein's second crisis.

But then abruptly Wingate is rescued from Venus. He returns to Earth and writes a book telling of his experiences. But no one will listen. The last note in the story is a mention of Nehemiah Scudder, soon to become the First Prophet of America. There is no way, we are told, to change the slavery that Heinlein hates. And there is no way, we know, to prevent the Demonic Nehemiah Scudder from overwhelming society.

The story ends:

> "What can we *do* about it?"
> "Nothing. Things are bound to get a whole lot worse before they can get any better. Let's have a drink."

"Solution Unsatisfactory" was Heinlein's last attempt to retain his societal dedication. It provides evidence that Heinlein was perceiving society as disintegrating around him. "Solution Unsatisfactory" does not take place in 1965, like "The Roads Must Roll" and "Blowups Happen." This story, published in 1941, is an account of the development of a deadly atomic weapon during World War II, and it is projected as taking place in 1943, 1944, and immediately thereafter.

This ultimate weapon is described as ending World War II. But it is so horrible and final that it cannot be allowed to be used again. As in "The Roads Must Roll" and "Blowups Happen," we have a situation in which supreme dedication and vigilance is necessary if society is to be preserved from the Demonic.

Heinlein describes his dedicated man as a "liberal." But this dedicated man, Col. Manning, decides that the only way to preserve society is to suspend the freedom of everyone. He and a few other dedicated men save society from the Demonic weapon. How? By bullying the nations of the world with a threat to explode the Demonic weapon.

Col. Manning, the competent man, can trust himself, but he cannot trust society. But Col. Manning has an uncertain heart condition and he may keel over dead tomorrow.

The narrator concludes:

> For myself, I can't be happy in a world where any man, or group of men, has the power of death over you and me, our neighbors, every human, every animal, every living thing. I don't like anyone to have that kind of power.
> And neither does Manning.

But Heinlein cannot see any alternative to the inevitable disintegration of the society to which he has dedicated himself. The story is clearly titled "Solution Unsatisfactory."

And it is an unsatisfactory solution in Heinlein's own terms. Once again, a character has not changed. Once again, a problem has not been solved.

After this, Heinlein began to look beyond society for his answers. For instance, in the story "They" (*Unknown*, April 1941), our familiar societal multiplicity is doubted and called an insanity:

> "I saw all around me this enormous plant, cities, farms, factories, churches, schools, homes, railroads, luggage, roller coasters, trees, saxophones, libraries, people and animals. People that looked like me and who should have felt very much like me, if what I was told was the truth. But what did they appear to be doing? 'They went to work to earn the money to buy the food to get the strength to go to work to earn the money to buy the food to get the strength to go to work to get the strength to buy the food to earn the money to go to—' until they fell over dead. Any slight variation in the basic pattern did not matter, for they always fell over dead. And everybody tried to tell me that I should be doing the same thing. I knew better!"

And Heinlein doubted society again in "Universe" (*Astounding*,

May 1941)—a story published in the same magazine issue as "Solution Unsatisfactory." In "Universe," society is likened to a starship that has forgotten its purposes, and which now wanders blindly through the galaxy. Those aboard are satisfied with their narrow little game-playing lives. They are oblivious to the wider world outside. Heinlein's protagonist is a bright and able young man who discovers that his teachers have lied to him in their ignorance. There exists a universe that is larger than society.

In three further stories published in 1941 and 1942, Heinlein searched outside society for the answer to his subjective quest. In these stories, his protagonists approached symbols of the Demonic in the form of strange transcendent creatures. But in each case, his protagonists lacked the recognition of the Other, the new love, the new dedication, that makes a successful confrontation, death, and re-birth possible.

In the first story, *Methuselah's Children* (*Astounding*, July-September 1941), Heinlein's protagonist, Lazarus Long, escapes from a disintegrating society, travels to the stars, almost encounters transcendence (he waits outside while another enters), and returns unchanged by his experience, hoping to find society essentially unchanged. In the second story, "By His Bootstraps" (*Astounding*, October 1941), Heinlein's protagonist—like Heinlein named Bob—leaves American society of 1942 without regret, travels to the future where he rules a placid society, becomes bored, and searches for transcendence. He finds it, but a mere glimpse is enough to age him prematurely, to kill his curiosity and to ruin his sleep. In the third story, "Goldfish Bowl" (*Astounding*, March 1942), two scientists follow their curiosity beyond contemporary society, up giant anomalous pillars of water, into the clouds, where they are captured by strange transcendent intelligences. But the scientists have nothing to say to their captors. The intelligences are never seen. All that Heinlein can think to do is to return the dead bodies of the scientists to society bearing messages of warning.

This is not the end of Heinlein's subjective progress. It has continued—always intelligible—from 1941 and 1942 until the present, including Heinlein's most recent novel, *Time Enough for Love*. We have not space to follow this progress further, but the distance we have traveled is sufficient to establish the viability of subjective readings of Heinlein and science fiction.

We have also traveled far enough to make sense of Heinlein's objectively inconsistent "politics." Read subjectively, the inconsistency vanishes.

Essentially, Heinlein's political statements fall into three kinds, corresponding to his first three crises. Statements endorsing liberty at all costs derive from Heinlein's first crisis. Statements endorsing society derive from Heinlein's second crisis. Statements in which society is found wanting, but not evil, derive from Heinlein's third crisis.

Thus, for instance, these statements apply to Heinlein's first crisis attitudes:

> When any government, or any church for that matter, undertakes to say to its subjects, "This you may not read, this you must not see, this you are forbidden to know," the end result is tyranny and oppression, no matter how holy the motives." [*"If This Goes On—"*]

and

> "Today— Oh, happy day! At last the world acknowledges Luna's sovereignty. Free! You have won your freedom—" [*The Moon Is a Harsh Mistress*]

These apply to Heinlein's second crisis:

> But there is solemn satisfaction in doing the best you can for eight billion people.
> Perhaps their lives have no cosmic significance, but they have feelings. They can hurt. [*Double Star*]

and

> ". . . But your psychometrical tests show that you believe yourself capable of judging morally your fellow citizens and feel justified in personally correcting and punishing their lapses . . . From a social standpoint, your delusion makes you mad as the March Hare." ["Coventry"]

And these apply to Heinlein's third crisis attitudes:

> "My dear, I used to think I was serving humanity . . . and I plea-

sured in the thought. Then I discovered that humanity does not want to be served; on the contrary it resents any attempt to serve it. So now I do what pleases Jubal Harshaw." [*Stranger in a Strange Land*]

and

"Democracy can't work. Mathematicians, peasants and animals, that's all there is—so democracy, a theory based on the assumption that mathematicians and peasants are equal, can never work. Wisdom is not additive; its maximum is that of the wisest man in a given group." [*Glory Road*]

Objectivity cannot encompass these statements.
Only Heinlein's subjectivity can.

11/ TIME ENOUGH FOR LOVE

[*Apollo*, Summer 1976]

The unfortunate one is he who averts his head from this door.
For he will not find another door.

—Saadi of Shiraz

1. Time Enough for Love

We have just seen an announcement that a new Robert Heinlein novel is to be published in May [1973], his first book since *I Will Fear No Evil* in 1970. That's an event that calls for comment.

The book is to be called *Time Enough for Love: The Lives of Lazarus Long*. The publishers have been quoted as calling it "a profound and prophetic story that ranges over twenty-three centuries and countless light years of space." It is to be 640 pages long, half again as long as *Stranger in a Strange Land*, Heinlein's previous scale-breaker.

We know no more of the book than this.

Time Enough for Love may prove to be a greater embarrassment than *I Will Fear No Evil*. On the other hand, it might be the true masterpiece that Heinlein has never written. A true sf masterpiece is going to be written soon—this year, next year—and it would be appropriate if Heinlein wrote it. He has always followed a secret star. He has earned the right to grasp it. Whether or not it is successful, *Time Enough for Love* unquestionably must be his best attempt.

Robert Heinlein is an uncomfortable subject for many people nowadays. Damon Knight has called Heinlein "the nearest thing to a great writer the science fiction field has yet produced," and James Blish has written that Heinlein is "plainly the best all-around science-fiction writer of the modern (post-1926) era." Both of the statements are true beyond argument.

The problem is to maintain our respect in view of the dismaying public spectacle Heinlein has made of himself from " 'All You Zombies—' " and *Starship Troopers* on. It's all the worse from a man so dignified, so private, and so self-conscious. It's like watching a Supreme Court Justice spit up on himself.

Heinlein's public breakdown has been so bizarre and dangerous that we have each found our own reasons not to look. Heinlein has been wrestling with demons and he has been bent in the struggle. He has uttered perniciousness. Like Philoctetes, Heinlein has oozed from poisoned wounds, and the stink has been unbearable. But to look away from the agony is to refuse to treat Heinlein with the respect he has earned and earned and earned again.

If we are to judge *Time Enough for Love* with anything that approaches true justice, we need to reconsider science fiction and Robert Heinlein's place in its development.

2. The Meaning of Science Fiction

Fiction is an analog of life. This is obviously true of mimetic fiction like the Bobbsey Twins and *The Naked and the Dead*. But it is even more true of science fiction.

Mimetic fiction presents a universe that is totally known. In mimetic fiction, chairs behave like chairs, Tibet behaves like East Overshoe, Massachusetts, and humans do what humans have always done. And those to whom everything is always different are mad, and are locked up until they see the world like everyone else.

Science fiction presents a universe that is partly known and partly unknown. Because the unknown is unknown, science fiction represents it with symbols like nothing any of us has ever seen: powers that can trisect the atom; unpredictable sentient robots; alien beings like clouds or firestorms or pure intelligence; worlds beyond.

Science fiction presents a truer analog of life. For much in our world is unknown to us. Our American reality begins to seem a parochial consensus. Modern technology upsets balances it knows not of. Gross expensive atom smashers flail at invisible motes with less and less result. If it is the mad who reject the social consensus, we are all secret madmen. Drugs and mysticism tell us of alternatives unknown to our educators and public oracles. Our vaunted world history proves to be a partial account of the public relations announcements of the latest fraction of human existence—5000 years out of 100,000? 5000 years out of 1,000,000? What do we know of ourselves? We live, as science fiction tells us, on a dirt speck traveling around a commonplace sun in the suburbs of a commonplace galaxy in an unbelievably vast hall of matter.

Science fiction isn't queerer than that. Science fiction is just exactly as queer as that.

Anything science fiction can tell us, *anything*, is no less than an analog of the truly true.

All fiction is nothing less than a dramatic presentation of one lesson. Fiction demonstrates over and over that it is possible to solve seemingly insurmountable problems, problems that could not be solved by any pattern of conduct within a person's previous range. These problems are solved not by direct attack, but by change within the person that makes his problem no longer a problem.

A mimetic writer, an author of paperback Westerns, gave out one version of the lesson in an article in *Writer's Yearbook*, and they did up a poster version for the back cover of the magazine: "A strong character struggles against overwhelming odds to achieve a worthwhile goal."

In a science fiction story, a character comes to face a totally unknown aspect of the universe, both frightening and desirable. If the character does not surmount fear and desire, he will be wounded or even eaten alive by monsters. But if he is able to surrender attachments to his accustomed behaviors, if he meets the unknown with courage, love and unselfish purpose, then he will receive a necessary new power from the universe and be such a one as never was before.

This is the true pattern of human growth. Anyone who has owned a cat must know that when it is a kitten it can learn a variety of responses to the world, but that when it grows up, it is, to a heart-breaking extent, condemned to the small range of behaviors it learned while it was free. We humans have a tendency to do the same. Few of us are as flexible as adults as we were as children. But still it is possible for us to evolve in a way not known to other animals.

Over and over through our adult lives, we are called upon to face the unknown squarely, surrender attachments and become new people. One of these moments comes at 17 or so, when we are called upon to put our childhoods behind us and become apprentices: college students, brides, privates, hod carriers—all these being what we could not be before.

Another common moment comes in the mid-twenties, when we have learned our tools well enough to practice a craft and become journeymen. Students graduate. Wives become mothers. Privates become sergeants. People become known by their occupation.

It takes personal evolution to live as a journeyman. It takes personal evolution to become more than a journeyman. Another crisis of identity commonly comes in the early thirties. This is a crisis of dedication, a crisis of prodigious evolutions. Mere journeyman skill is no longer enough. Abilities must be applied to a higher end. The journeyman must become a master.

At 17 or 19, the child finally saw himself as an "adult," that mysterious state of being he had been growing to become. And at last he has become a man among children. At 25, he realized that he could stop practicing and fulfill an adult role. He became a man among men. During his twenties, he has inventoried his abilities in one occupation or in a variety of occupations. Now, however, mere journeyman skill is no longer enough. Abilities must be applied to a higher end. The journeyman must become a master.

Masters do not produce their work as their ends, but as means to higher ends. They produce byproduct rather than product. This is the difference between masters and journeymen.

At the crisis of dedication, Jesus ceased to be a carpenter and became something more. Luther nailed his ninety-five theses to the door of the church in Wittenberg. Albert Schweitzer, who had been a musician and theologian, began the study of medicine so as to apply his music and theology to the world.

This is the age when people like Robert Heinlein and Ursula Le Guin turned to writing science fiction. And it is the age when other writers like Philip K. Dick, Robert Silverberg and Poul Anderson, who in their twenties wrote and sold every story they thought of, took pause to discover which stories were worth writing. The results of the questionings of these men were respectively entitled *The Man in the High Castle*, *A Time of Changes* and *The Man Who Counts*.

Mimetic fiction represents the exterior of adult growth experiences. It shows how people do one thing or another, how people become one thing or another. It is a report of behavior and the behavior all looks much the same.

But mimetic representations must omit the unknown interior of the personal adventure of growth. That which is truly humanly unknown cannot be represented in mimetic fiction. Powerful extraterrestrials, for instance, are not part of the vocabulary of mimetic fiction. In mimetic fiction, those who encounter alien beings are mad or drunk.

Science fiction reveals the heart, the interior of the private adventure. Monomythic quests into unknown outer space are the truest way that exists of representing the experiences we undergo in inner space.

How far we each evolve and what we become in the course of our evolution depends on the purposes we bring with us into the unknown and the courage with which we pursue them. Or, as Tom Lehrer once said: "Life is like a sewer. What you get out of it depends on what you put into it." Life is like life. What you get out of it depends on what you put into it.

If Heinlein's life were the subject of a mimetic novel, all that would be revealed would be behavior—the life of another writer. But Heinlein has given us a truer record of his life in his science fiction stories—and it has been a magnificent and harrowing adventure. No sf writer has left a clearer record of his quest than Heinlein. As the nearest thing to a true master that sf has produced, his work has been his adventure, and his stories the byproduct of his search. He has left a permanent record of his questions and his answers. If we are willing to look, he has laid himself bare.

3. Heinlein at 32

The August 1939 issue of *Astounding* containing Robert Heinlein's first story, "Life-Line," came into his hands in early July, just in time for his thirty-second birthday. Judged by the common yardstick of society, he was overdue to find himself. In his twenties, he had been a naval officer, an engineer who had graduated high in his class at Annapolis. Then he caught tuberculosis, at that time still an often fatal disease, and retired from the Navy. He had been an invalid, a graduate student, a mine-owner, a real estate salesman, an architect and a losing politician. He explored the bounds of low life: he has said that he knew a number of murderers socially and once failed to sell a silver mine because the prospective buyer was tommy-gunned the night before. It may be rumor or it may be truth, but there are stories that he shilled in a carnival and that he flacked for an L.A. holy man. He was five years into a first marriage.

But he had no dedication.

Suddenly, instantly, he became a science fiction writer. Suddenly, instantly, he became the best science fiction writer in *Astounding*, the best science fiction magazine in America. It was a sudden complete transformation, as dramatic as any evolutionary leap.

Heinlein began with a charming verbal facility, a natural narrative instinct, and the wide-ranging knowledge he had acquired as a journeyman. But at the outset he was a clumsy and untutored writer. Most of his stories were badly made. To this day, the largest number of Heinlein's stories are badly made. Heinlein has not succeeded on his skills as a craftsman. His education and goals were never in fiction writing. Nonetheless, since 1939, Robert Heinlein has been the best science fiction writer in the business and he has been well-rewarded for his work. Two years after Heinlein began to write, he was Guest of Honor at the Third World Science Fiction Convention in Denver. His novels have won more awards than his wife has patience to give houseroom. He has made good, steady money. More recently, he has made big money.

The reason for Heinlein's instant and continuing success as a writer lies elsewhere than skill, a head for ideas, a nose for the trends of the moment, a hunger for money, for fame, for Being a Writer. Heinlein was successful as a writer to a degree undreamed by other science fiction writers in 1939 and never approached by anyone in the years since precisely because science fiction writing was never his primary object.

In 1939, Robert Heinlein was the most able and competent man he knew. And life was a puzzle to him. He did not know what his ability and competence were *for*. He wanted to know the meaning of life. He wanted to know why Robert Heinlein existed.

This is the stuff of a life crisis. These are the questions that everybody asks himself, though we may not phrase them exactly this way. We answer them as best we can, and we become the answer we give.

If Heinlein had concluded that the meaning of life was to be a science fiction writer, after great struggle he would have become a science fiction writer somewhat better than Randall Garrett but perhaps not as good as Robert Silverberg. But Heinlein could not see any satisfactory answer anywhere. He read widely beyond the fringes of respectable knowledge. He entertained his wildest thoughts. And the conclusion that he came to was this: For social respectability, he would pass himself off as a science fiction writer, but he would not commit himself to a true new identity. He would wear one as a cloak. And he would write science fiction stories.

Yes, he would write science fiction stories, but for his own purposes. Heinlein realized that he could use science fiction stories to ask his questions and test his answers, and that he could earn a living doing it. Science fiction was a means to Heinlein from the first. It is not altogether surprising that he has considered discussion of his stories an invasion of privacy.

Robert Heinlein has passed himself off as a science fiction writer for more than half his life. And because his true purposes have been ultimately serious, his byproduct has been recognized as the True Stuff, sought out, identified with, loved, hated, bought and read. Success as a science fiction writer has never been a problem to Heinlein because he has never recognized succeeding as an sf writer to be a problem to be taken seriously. That isn't true for other sf writers, except now for a few like Ursula K. Le Guin and R.A. Lafferty. And neither of these, nor nobody else, has been as reckless or as ruthless in his pursuit of the riddle of life as Heinlein has.

His search is announced in the title of his first story, "Life-Line." The life-line is the shadow of mortality we carry in the flesh of our palms. What is existence for? In Heinlein's story, the inventor of a machine that accurately measures the length of any man's life foresees his own murder. He knows his mortality and is helpless before it. Without the life-line of a certain knowledge of meaningfulness, life is a pointless dead end. And nobody throws a life-line to Pinero the inventor. He dies, and other men burn the records of their deaths-to-come without looking at them.

The quest begins with an averting of the eyes.

4. The Future History

Heinlein published two short stories in *Astounding* in 1939 and a third in the January 1940 issue: "Life-Line," "Misfit," and "Requiem." These were all superficially conventional neo-Gernsbackian stories of the near future. "Misfit" proved that a bright and competent boy can make a place for himself in society if he calculates fast enough, a point of which Heinlein has always been certain. But "Requiem" said that if you try to reach for the moon, you will be prevented, and if you grasp the moon, you will die.

Then Heinlein's first novel was serialized. His 32-year piece. The novel was short, awkward, and fuzzily romantic. It was entitled *"If*

This Goes On—", a clutch of words that imply the greatest hopes and the greatest fears, grand prospects and no prospects at all.

As much as his other early stories, *"If This Goes On—"* was typical of sf as Heinlein found it. There was, at the time, a dichotomy between stories of invention and adventure in a future not radically strange, and stories of farther futures and distant places without connection to now. Stories of the farther future on Earth were all set in a single place—a misty nebulous thing called The Future, recognizable by its medieval feel. Heinlein's first three short stories fall into the first category. *"If This Goes On—"*, just as clearly, is set in a palace in The Future.

Clumsy though it was, *"If This Goes On—"* was second in popularity and impact only to *Slan* among the stories published in *Astounding* in 1940. (Or perhaps third to L. Ron Hubbard's nightmare of eternal World War II, *Final Blackout*, which made a great impact at the time and is almost unreadable now.) The reason is clear—the high degree of involvement in Heinlein's story.

His main character, John Lyle, wears Heinlein's mother's maiden name. He is bright and able and serves loyally in the home of the Prophet who rules America. But he has not been Told All. He has been duped and deluded. When he discovers the truth, he rebels. And in a crucial moment in the climactic battle, he, a lieutenant, assumes control of the forces of rebellion and sweeps the Prophet aside.

If there is a major flaw in this story, it is not that it is concerned with an evolutionary moment that comes early in life when it is discovered that the father does not know all there is to be known. The flaw is that Heinlein proposes this answer, which he knew by experience was partial, for a character in his mid-twenties. And the Prophet is a poor excuse for an unknown. He has no strange power except the ability to cast shadows over other people's minds and he is lightly put down.

Heinlein published five more stories in 1940, three of them near-future stories of invention, one a short sequel to *"If This Goes On—"*, and the last a light fantasy entitled "The Devil Makes the Law" in *Unknown*.

In the February 1941 issue of *Astounding*, John Campbell said:

> I'd like to mention something that may or may not have been
> noticed by the regular readers of *Astounding*: all Heinlein's science-
> fiction is laid against a common background of a proposed future
> history of the world and of the United States. Heinlein's worked
> the thing out in detail that grows with each story; he has an outlined
> and graphed history of the future with characters, dates of major
> discoveries, et cetera, plotted in. I'm trying to get him to let me
> have a photostat of that history chart; if I lay hands on it, I'm going
> to publish it.

Campbell did publish the chart in the May issue, and it demonstrates the prodigious investment Heinlein was making in his stories
as a vehicle for his search. His imaginary future is described by dates,
by stories, by the space in time his story characters occupy, by the
modes of power, communication and travel at different times to
come, by inventions, by social data, and by general remarks.

In his initial conception, *"If This Goes On—"* must have assumed
a central position. Opposite it on the page, standing alone, is the
final social datum: THE FIRST HUMAN CIVILIZATION.

Heinlein's conception of Future History was a major event in the
development of science fiction. It imposed structure on the future
universe and united near-future stories of adventure and invention
with stories of The Future. No more could stories take place outside
time and change. When pinpointed in time, *"If This Goes On—"*,
romantic and medieval, proved to take place in the year 2070.

If science fiction fruitfully combines the known and the unknown,
Heinlein's Future History chart was significant for bringing the unknown into common scale with the known, for rendering the unknown world accessible. Heinlein's Future History chart made stories like those he had been writing obsolete. That is, no longer was it
necessary either to write constipated stories of the near and known or
to write wild romances of the distant unknown. Now the two could
be combined—known and unknown together in the same story.

At the time the chart was published, not all the stories it proposed
had been written. There was one group of stories of the relatively
near—1950-1990. And there were two stories set after 2070. Actually, three—for the chart proved to show that "Misfit" with its neo-

CCC—the "Cosmic Construction Corps"—was set fifty years *after* *"If This Goes On—"*.

Heinlein had not then written the stories set in the gap from 1990 to 2070—the stories between "Requiem" and the death of Harriman on the moon, and the fall of the Prophet in *"If This Goes On—"*. He had not written the stories of the rise of the Prophet that reconciled the two worlds—the known or knowable, and the unknown.

These proposed stories—"The Sound of His Wings," "Eclipse," and "The Stone Pillow"—must have been difficult for Heinlein to consider. Stories of the most awful bondage. Heinlein once wrote: "I probably never will write the story of Nehemiah Scudder; I dislike him too thoroughly." In a sense, the publication of the chart rendered these stories unnecessary, or avoidable, and Heinlein never did write them.

In fact, by the time the Future History chart was published, Heinlein was seemingly nearly ready to abandon the project as having served its purpose. After World War II, before Heinlein prepared the series for book publication, he added a handful of *Saturday Evening Post* stories to the near future before 1990. But before the war —and specifically in 1941—Heinlein published just four Future History stories. Afterthoughts.

There was, first, a novelet called "Logic of Empire," Heinlein's token gesture at filling the hole in his chart. "Logic of Empire" is set on an exploited colonial Venus around 2000. An heir again learns —like John Lyle—that his inheritance of known fact is tainted. Distant rumor only is made of Nehemiah Scudder, the rabble-rousing political preacher who became the First Prophet.

The other three stories are set later than *"If This Goes On—"*. Heinlein had realized that there was more yet to come in the search for meaning. And a more mature seeker was required than John Lyle.

One was presented in the novel *Methuselah's Children*, which was serialized in *Astounding* in the summer of 1941. The seeker is a man who has chosen the name Lazarus Long, though he was born Woodrow Wilson Smith about the time that Heinlein was born. He is an immortal, or if he isn't, he doesn't know the fact. He is the heart of the Future History, for he binds the chart together. He was born before it starts. Pinero failed to see the end of his life-line. And Lazarus Long still lives when the Future History chart ends.

We must be particularly interested in *Methuselah's Children* because Lazarus Long is the central character of *Time Enough for Love*, Heinlein's new novel. And it is a very interesting book because it is highly inconclusive.

In this story, some humans have been carefully bred for longevity, beginning at the end of the Nineteenth Century. Some time after the setting aside of the Prophet and the establishment of "The First Human Civilization," ordinary men discover the existence of the long-lived Families. Their rage for the secret of long life knows no bounds. The Families are forced to hijack a starship, and flee.

They find a pleasant planet elsewhere to settle on. But this planet is ruled by creatures far more advanced than we. They call the leader of the ship for examination. He goes into "the temple of Kreel" while Lazarus Long waits outside. A veil is drawn over the confrontation. The confrontation is failed. These god-like creatures cannot be rid of the Earthmen too fast. They lift them through the air and into space. They stuff them into their ship. They hurl the ship away from them—thirty-two light years away to a specific destination. The new planet the ship reaches is ruled by a group mind.

Here is Heinlein's commentary:

> The hegira of the Families had been a mistake. It would have been a more human, a more mature and manly thing, to have stayed and fought for their rights, even if they had died insisting on them. Instead they had fled across half a universe (Lazarus was reckless about his magnitudes) looking for a place to light. They had found one, a good one—but already occupied by beings so superior as to make them intolerable for man . . . yet so supremely indifferent in their superiority to men that they had not even bothered to wipe them out, but had whisked them away to this—this overmanicured country club.
>
> And that in itself was the unbearable humiliation. The *New Frontiers* was the culmination of five hundred years of human scientific research, the best that men could do—but it had been flicked across the depths of space as casually as a man might restore a baby bird to its nest.

The Little People did not seem to want to kick them out but the Little People, in their own way, were as demoralizing to men as were the gods of the Jockaira. One at a time they might be morons but taken as groups each rapport group was a genius that threw the best minds that men could offer into the shade . . . Human beings could not hope to compete with that type of organization any more than a back-room shop could compete with an automated cybernated factory. Yet to form any such group identities, even if they could which he doubted, would be, Lazarus felt very sure, to give up whatever it was that made them *men*.

And Lazarus muses to himself: " 'What shall it profit a man . . .' " That is, what shall it profit a man to gain the world and lose his soul?

And, immediately, important things happen. Word is brought to Lazarus that Mary Sperling, the chief female character of the book, has joined the group mind.

"She's gone over to the Little People. 'Married' into one of their groups."

"*What?* But that's impossible!"

Lazarus was wrong. There was no faint possibility of interbreeding between Earthmen and natives but there was no barrier, if sympathy existed, to a human merging into one of their rapport groups, drowning his personality in the ego of the many.

Mary Sperling, moved by conviction of her own impending death, saw in the deathless group egos a way out. Faced with the eternal problem of life and death, she had escaped the problem by choosing neither . . . selflessness. She had found a group willing to receive her, she had crossed over. . . .

A short distance outside the camp he ran across a native. He skidded to a stop.

"Where is Mary Sperling?"

". . . I am Mary Sperling . . ."

"For the love of— You *can't* be."

". . . I am Mary Sperling and Mary Sperling is myself . . . do you not know me, Lazarus? . . . I know you . . ."

That is the first important happening. The second is that a human baby has been born which has been "improved" by the Little People. The Families cannot accept the prospect of merger into the group mind. They cannot accept the prospect of alterations in the human body-as-it-is. They flee back to Earth.

When they arrive, they discover that the normal human beings of

Heinlein's "First Human Civilization" whom they have left behind have themselves achieved great longevity through self-confidence and vitamins, so that they, too, may have all the time they need to find their answers to the purpose of life. In the margin of his Future History chart, Heinlein remarks: "Civil disorder, followed by the end of human adolescence, and beginning of first mature culture."

But has true maturity been won in this story? Not at all. At the outset, the long-lived people run from known problems into the unknown. There they encounter wonders and marvels that they are not prepared to deal with. Lazarus Long, Heinlein's surrogate self, stands on the sidelines throughout. He is on the outside when another man enters the temple of Kreel. He is on the outside when Mary Sperling joins the group mind. His great importance is that he proposes the retreat to Earth. When they arrive on Earth, they discover their original problem has evaporated. The final note is Lazarus Long's intention to look up a chili house in Dallas—that is, the hope that things have *not* been changed by his adventure.

This is a very strange and meaningful story.

The final contribution that Heinlein made to his Future History in those days before World War II was a pair of connected novelets, "Universe" and "Common Sense." These stories are even more strange and meaningful than *Methuselah's Children*. These were the sort of stories that Heinlein had remade science fiction in order to be able to write. One proposes the problem of life in very explicit terms, and the other offers a solution. The story that proposes the problem is brilliant. The story that proposes the solution is both longer and less convincing.

Though "Universe" and "Common Sense" are nominally set in the Future History universe, they are completely separated from the rest of the series. They take place long after the other stories, in 2600, on a starship that is a twin of the ship in *Methuselah's Children*, lost somewhere in the galaxy. Any solutions these stories offer cannot be applied to the rest of the Future History.

In "Universe"—Heinlein has never been coy about his preoccupations—a bright, able young man discovers that he has been lied to. The universe (the starship he lives in) is not what his teachers have taught him that it is. It is not what his society has thought. In fact, the world of his experience is but a pebble in the void, a speck in a larger universe that he is permitted to glimpse, a ship that has lost its way on its voyage and forgotten its purposes. Like the ship of history, like Heinlein. Heinlein's seeker after truth discovers his vision from freakish outcasts of society—a dwarf and a two-headed man—whom he has served as something between a slave and a disciple. The seeker is energized. He is confident that if he reports the true state of affairs to society, they will quickly set to work to remember their true nature and the destination of the ship. But when he tries to speak of his knowledge, he is called a mad heretic who would destroy society. He has not reckoned with the blindness of men committed to trivial purposes and petty games of advantage and disadvantage, men too attached to their limited natures to evolve.

In "Common Sense," Heinlein's seeker is betrayed by one who pretended to be convinced of the truth. He must flee the universe of society. He sets out with a few companions in a little ship and by virtue of what Heinlein says no less than ten times is luck, they land on the paradise of a planet:

> Our own planet, under our feet, is of the "There ain't no such animal!" variety. It is a ridiculous improbability.
> Hugh's luck was a ridiculous improbability.

Luck is not the way the search is successfully concluded, but it is all that Heinlein can think of

One more story is listed on the Future History chart after "Universe" and "Common Sense." Its title is "Da Capo," a musical term for a theme to be repeated.

Rebirth and a new evolutionary quest? Or merely one more time around the park?

Heinlein has never written the story.

5. Heinlein Speaks

In 1939 and 1940, all of Heinlein's stories but "The Devil Makes the Law" ("Magic, Inc.") were Future History stories. They were published under his own name and were the basis on which he was chosen to be Guest of Honor at the World Science Fiction Convention in Denver in 1941: his thirty-fourth birthday present.

He gave his Guest of Honor speech on the Fourth of July, 1941. He said, "I'm tired and confused and nervous and quite frankly considerably stirred up by the fact that I was selected as Guest of Honor here. It embarrasses me and at the same time I enjoy it."

Heinlein used the opportunity to speak to say all that was most important to him. "I'm preaching—sure; I know that," he said. "I could have filled up a speech with wisecracks and with stories and anecdotes; but I feel very deeply serious about this. I mean it."

He proceeded to speak in a rambling fashion and what he said has the greatest bearing on the fiction he published in 1939 and 1940, the other fiction he wrote before World War II, and what he has done with his life and his writing since that time.

He said:

> I myself have been reading science fiction oh, I don't know, when did Gernsback start putting them in *Electrical Experimenter*? ["1913" from floor] —well, I've been reading about that long. And then I used to read it in *Argosy* and I dug up all that I could of that sort of thing out of the Kansas City Public Library . . . And, never had any particular notion of writing it until about two years ago when a concatenation of peculiar circumstances started me writing it, and happened to hit the jackpot on the first one, so I continued writing. It amazed me to discover people gave money away for doing things like that—it beats working.

Heinlein began his talk by speaking of the particular virtues of science fiction, which he called time-binding:

> The operation of time-binding consists of making use of the multitudinous records that we have of the past and on the basis of those records, on the basis of the data that we have collected directly and the data that we get from others by means of our time-binding techniques, including reading and writing, sound movies . . . by means of those techniques, figuring out something about the way the universe looks and making predictions on which we can plan our future con-

duct. And it means that we have lived mentally in the past, and in the future as well as in the present.

This, effectively, is a description of where Heinlein had been. It is a description of the Future History. And Heinlein spent some time elaborating on the anticipation of change that time-binding permits. This from a man who desperately needed to change, desperately desired to change, but who could not change.

Heinlein then said that science fiction

—even the corniest of it, even the most outlandish of it, no matter how badly it's written—has a distinct therapeutic value because *all* of it has as its primary postulate that the world *does* change, and I cannot overemphasize the importance of that idea in these days. Unless you believe in that, unless you are prepared for it—as I know all of you are—you can't retain your sanity these days; it's an impossibility. When a man makes predictions and they keep failing to come out, time and again, things don't come out the way he wants to, he goes insane, functionally insane—it's been proved in the laboratories time and again. It's been proved with respect to men . . .

Heinlein then went on to predict that a large portion of the world, large portions of the human race, will be in a condition of insanity for years to come:

Five years, ten years, it may go twenty years, it may go fifty years—you and I may not live to see the end of it. I personally have hopes—wishful thinking—I have hopes it will terminate quickly enough so that I can pass the rest of my lifetime in comparative peace and comfort. But I'm not optimistic about it. And during such a period it is really a difficult thing to keep a grip, to keep a grip on yourself . . .

Heinlein saw but one way to survive this period:

There's a way out, there's a way out, there's something that we can do to protect ourselves, something that would protect the rest of the human race from the sort of things that are happening to them and are going to happen to them. It's very simple and it's right down our alley: the use of the *scientific method*.

I'm not talking about the scientific method in the laboratory. The scientific method can be used to protect our sanity, to protect ourselves from serious difficulties of other sorts—gettin' our teeth smashed in, and things like that—in our everyday life, 24 hours of the day.

> I should say what I mean by the scientific method. Since I have
> to make the definition in terms of words, I can't be as clear as I
> otherwise might be, if I were able to make an extensional definition
> on it. But I mean a comparatively simple thing by the scientific
> method: the ability to look at what goes on around you . . . listen to
> what you hear . . . observe . . . note facts . . . delay your judgment
> . . . and make your own predictions. That's all, really all there is to
> the scientific method: To be able to distinguish facts from non-facts.

And Heinlein concluded with this thought:

> I don't suppose I'll be writing very much longer. Things shaping
> up the way they are, I'll probably have other things that I'll have to
> do. A lot of us here will have other things that we're going to have
> to do, whether we like it or not. And I may not come back to it.
> But I hope to be a fan of science fiction for at least another fifty
> years, if I can hold myself together that long and keep from getting
> my teeth kicked in.

6. The Freakiest One, the Seeker

The self-portrait that Heinlein painted in his 1941 Guest of Honor
speech was of a man who had turned to writing science fiction only
for a time and for limited urgent purposes. In July 1941, two years
into the Second World War, it was clear to Heinlein that his time was
growing short. He had to use his time to best advantage while he had
it, to say his say, to solve his problem. He had, at best, until the end
of that year.

As it proved, he had a little longer than that—he continued to
publish stories through 1942. The stories he published were not
Future History. They were too strange to fit in any framework.
They were the purest statements that Heinlein could conceive of his
problem, in symbolic terms, and the soundest symbolic solutions.
They were the stories that the Future History had made possible—
stories that mixed the known and the unknown in potent combination. They were the truest, freakiest stories that science fiction
has ever seen. Heinlein only had a limited final time in which to
work, and he searched deeply within himself. Heinlein, the notorious
rational man, then showed himself to be freakier than Phil Dick has
ever dreamed of being.

This was not realized at the time, and it has never been noticed since. The reason is this: of Heinlein's eight major stories published in 1941 and 1942 outside the Future History series, only the earliest and shortest, "They" (*Unknown*, April 1941), appeared under Heinlein's own name. Four were by Anson MacDonald. One was by Caleb Saunders. One by Lyle Monroe. One by John Riverside. The cumulative effect of these stories was lost in the confusion of pseudonyms.

These stories finally appeared in book form in the late Forties, in the early Fifties, as late as 1959—scattered, lost in collections, lost among newer and more restrained Heinlein stories. Never placed. Never truly noticed.

Here are the eight:

"They" is a statement of the situation. A brilliant and able man whose chief haunts are New York City and Harvard University is being treated in a mental institution. He believes that he is not like other people. Other people never do or talk about things of importance. They have no interest in the meaning of existence. The protagonist claims to be able to see through the sham that surrounds him:

> "I saw all around me this enormous plant, cities, farms, factories, churches, schools, homes, railroads, luggage, roller coasters, trees, saxophones, libraries, people and animals. People that looked like me and who should have felt very much like me, if what I was told was the truth. But what did they appear to be doing? 'They went to work to earn the money to buy the food to get the strength to go to work to earn the money to buy the food to get the strength to go to work to get the strength to buy the food to earn the money to go to—' until they fell over dead. Any slight variation in the basic pattern did not matter, for they always fell over dead. And everybody tried to tell me that I should be doing the same thing. I knew better!"
>
> The doctor gave him a look apparently intended to denote helpless surrender and laughed. "I can't argue with you. Life does look like that, and maybe it is just that futile. But it is the only life we have. Why not make up your mind to enjoy it as much as possible?"
>
> "Oh, no!" He looked both sulky and stubborn. "You can't peddle nonsense to me by claiming to be fresh out of sense. How do I know? Because all this complex stage setting, all these swarms of actors, could not have been put here just to make idiot noises at each other. Some other explanation, but not that one. An insanity

as enormous, as complex, as the one around me had to be planned.
I've found the plan!"

"Which is?"

He noticed that the doctor's eyes were again averted.

"It is a play intended to divert me, to occupy my mind and con-
fuse me, to keep me so busy with details that I will not have time
to think about the meaning. You are all in it, every one of you."
He shook his finger in the doctor's face. "Most of them may be
helpless automatons, but you're not. You are one of the conspirators. You've been sent in as a troubleshooter to try to force me to
go back to playing the role assigned to me!"

The character is alerted to the hollowness of ordinary reality one
day when he notices that it is not raining out of the back of the
house when it is raining in front. On this slim evidence, he rejects
conventional reality. If this were a mimetic story, the character
would be mad. But this is an sf story, and the character is not mad.

Notice that his situation is the same as the situation of the seeker
in "Universe." Hugh Hoyland, who is called a "scientist" and who
unknowingly echoes Galileo when he maintains his truth of a larger
universe, is only different from the protagonist of "They" in being
called a heretic rather than a madman, and in not taking his situation
personally.

But the character in "They" is right to take his situation personally. He has caught them out, the conspirators. They fear that he
will remember the truth, so they "adjourn this sequence." In the
next sequence he may be given the Taj Mahal, which he values for
reasons the conspirators cannot understand.

This is a first-rate statement of the problem, but the solution is
not a true solution. In his own quest, Heinlein cannot see through
the sham, call the conspirators to book, and end the game. The
universe Heinlein knows may be a sham, but he is still stuck.

Around and around we go again in "By His Bootstraps," a story
by Anson MacDonald in the October 1941 issue of *Astounding*.
Again a statement of the problem without a solution. This time,
the problem is stated in terms of the dynamics of a character rather
than as a societal situation, and consequently the failure of Heinlein's
protagonist is more agonizing and painful than ever previously.

The central character of "By His Bootstraps" begins as a student in our own time, unhappy, confused and dissatisfied with life. He is writing a thesis entitled: "An Investigation into Certain Mathematical Aspects of a Rigor of Metaphysics." The thesis denies the possibility of time travel.

As he types, a time gate opens in the air behind him. Through it come variously ignorant older versions of himself. The gate signifies the opportunity to evolve, to escape this stale world and pass through into an unknown future. His older selves debate whether or not he should actually pass through the gate. The question is settled by an accidental blow.

The protagonist wakes 20,000 years from now in an all-but-empty palace. Palace and time machine, he is told, are the relics of mythic High Ones who came and ruled the human race for a time and then went away again.

The seeker is in the hands of an old and unpleasant man named Diktor, who hustles him along and speaks glib words of a great future. At Diktor's direction, the seeker inevitably recapitulates the older states of himself that he has already met, passing back and forth through the time gate, arguing and fighting futilely with himself, from this experience learning only to fear Diktor. He steals a notebook from Diktor with information about this future and flees into its near past. There the seeker is the most competent of competent men and effortlessly rules a human culture that has forgotten its drive. These people of the future regret the loss of the High Ones, but they have no curiosity about the meaning of life. They are children to him.

Heinlein says: "His was a mixed nature, half hustler, half philosopher." His hustle has carried him to the top of this meaningless society that at first had seemed full of promise. Now his philosophical curiosity leads him to look beyond his society for the High Ones, the unknown makers.

He searches time with a viewer, seeking the mysterious Builders of the palace and the time machine. And at last he is rewarded with a glimpse of what he has longed to find. But he hasn't the courage to face what he sees. He cannot confront the High One. He can only scream and run away:

He saw it.

It was moving toward the Gate.

When he pulled himself together he was halfway down the passageway leading from the Hall. He realized that he had been screaming. He still had an attack of the shakes.

Somewhat later he forced himself to return to the Hall, and, with eyes averted, enter the control booth and return the spheres to zero. He backed out hastily and left the Hall for his apartment. He did not touch the controls nor enter the Hall for more than two years.

It had not been fear of physical menace that had shaken his reason, nor the appearance of the creature—he could recall nothing of *how* it looked. It had been a feeling of sadness infinitely compounded which had flooded through him at the instant, a sense of tragedy, of grief insupportable and unescapable, of infinite weariness. He had been flicked with emotion many times too strong for his spiritual fiber and which he was no more fitted to experience than an oyster is to play a violin.

He felt that he had learned all about the High Ones a man could learn and still endure. He was no longer curious. The shadow of that vicarious emotion ruined his sleep, brought him sweating out of dreams.

Heinlein has penetrated close to the truth that he seeks. He has provoked a confrontation with a true representative of the unknown, but the confrontation, as we have just seen, is a failure. Why?

The reason is this: when we confront transcendence, a true symbol of the unknown, we only get the successes we can visualize. It is Heinlein's problem that he cannot yet visualize what true success might be. The only success his protagonist can conceive is to become Diktor, the horrifying older man from whom he has escaped. Thus, because he has not prepared himself for the confrontation with transcendence, the seeker must scream and flee.

There is confirmation of failure of perception in a mistake made by Heinlein and Bob Wilson. High emotions are afoot in the experience, which Wilson and Heinlein feel are "too strong for his spiritual fiber and which he was no more fitted to experience than an oyster is to play a violin." These emotions are mistaken for the stuff of a higher evolutionary state. But they are not. They are evidence of the character's own self-limitation. The emotions that scar him are nothing less than his own emotions, highly amplified. It is the seeker himself who is held fast in the sticky net of tragedy, who is sad, grieving and weary.

And no wonder. Because he has no other image of evolution, because he does not seize his opportunity to evolve, the protagonist is doomed to become Diktor. As a result of his view of the High One, his hair turns gray and his face grave and lined, like Diktor's. The character has modeled himself on Diktor in order to usurp his place. Now all that he can do is copy his worn-out stolen notebook so that it will be fresh for its purpose. And then he fishes back through time for his younger self, to entrap him as he has been entrapped in the futile round of existence. Only then does he realize that he is Diktor. No one else is.

Because he could not be the philosopher, the protagonist must act the hustler. He must hustle himself as once he was hustled by himself. He smiles and says: " 'There is a great future in store for you and me, my boy—a great future!' "

And as his final, sad, weary, grieving, tragic narrative comment, Heinlein must echo ironically: "A great future!"

"By His Bootstraps" is a truly meaningful and important story. Heinlein was able to assemble the materials for a successful quest in this story, which he has seldom been able to do, but he was unable to make a success of them. His character must fall back into the maze of ego, a maze self-made, unable to evolve. How might it have been otherwise?

For one thing, Diktor and his younger self both assume that the High Ones—the higher evolutionary state—are unapproachable. They assume without evidence that the relationship of the High Ones to the human race was lacking in love. But only true confrontation could have settled the point. Heinlein's protagonist could not bring himself to that test.

And Heinlein could not write it.

Second, there are only two real and continuing things in this story: the protagonist and the mysterious notebook without origin. In that notebook are many secrets which have been given to the seeker for his use. When he first comes to the future, he finds it "indispensable." He has copied the notebook, but has he read it with a mature eye? The answer is no. He carefully copies it over prior to his confrontation but "to refresh his memory of English rather than from any need for it as a guide." But Bob Wilson misuses the notebook. He uses it to cling to the past rather than to prepare himself for evolution. If Heinlein had been prepared for success, his protagonist would have found significant clues in that notebook.

Finally, if there is one thing that "By His Bootstraps" demonstrates, it is that attachment to the ego—the "Bob Wilson-ness of things," or the "Bob Heinlein-ness of things" is a delusion. The confusing profusion of "selves," quarreling and fighting, are a comedy play. The student does not inevitably have to be Diktor. He is not doomed. He can reject the necessity of becoming Diktor at any moment—not only by confronting the High Ones, but simply by choosing to use the time machine to go and be someone else somewhere else. He is trapped only by ego games. He fails and becomes Diktor because he chooses to fail and become Diktor.

"By His Bootstraps" by Anson MacDonald, in which confrontation with the unknown is evaded and no evolution occurs, and "Common Sense" by Robert Heinlein, in which no true confrontation with the unknown occurs and evolution is achieved by luck, both these two long stories were published in the same October 1941 issue of *Astounding*. Heinlein's time was getting urgently short. Consequently, in two other long stories that autumn—"Elsewhere" by Caleb Saunders in the September issue of *Astounding*, and "Lost Legion" by Lyle Monroe in the November issue of *Super Science Stories*—Heinlein attempted to skip past confrontation and get to the heart of the matter. He wrote directly of what he knew and he hoped about the far side of the evolutionary leap.

Both stories are fascinating botches. They are necessarily botches because fiction is about nothing but confrontations, failed confrontations, evolution and failure to evolve. Fiction is not about new securities of a higher order. Fiction tells about departures and arrivals, not about happy tours in other pleasant countries. But these "stories" are fascinating for what they tell of Heinlein's knowledge and hopes.

"Elsewhere," later "Elsewhen" in a Heinlein story collection, sets a group of philosophy students loose in eternity, which their savant calls "two-dimensional time":

> "I must explain the theory of time I was forced to evolve in order to account for my experience. Most people think of time as a track that they run on from birth to death as inexorably as a train follows its rails—they feel instinctively that time follows a straight line, the past lying behind, the future lying in front. Now I have reason to believe—to know—that time is analogous to a surface rather than a line, and a rolling hilly surface at that. Think of this track we follow over the surface as a winding road cut through hills. Every little way the road branches and the branches follow side canyons. At these branches the crucial decisions of your life take place. You can turn right or left into entirely different futures. Occasionally there is a switchback where one can scramble up or down a bank and skip over a few thousand or million years—if you don't have your eyes so fixed on the road that you miss the short cut.

> "Once in a while another road crosses yours. Neither its past nor its future has any connection whatsoever with the world we know. If you happened to take that turn you might find yourself on another planet in another space-time with nothing left of you or your world but the continuity of your ego.

> "Or, if you have the necessary intellectual strength and courage, you may leave the roads, or paths of high probability, and strike out over the hills of possible time, cutting through the roads as you come to them, following them for a little way, even following them backwards, with the past *ahead* of you and the future *behind* you. Or you might roam around the hilltops doing nothing but the extremely improbable. I can not imagine what that would be like— perhaps a bit like Alice-through-the-Looking-Glass."

And,

> "To one who believes in Bishop Berkeley's philosophy the infinite possibilities of two-dimensional time offer proof that the mind creates its own world, but a Spencerian determinist, such as good friend Howard Jenkins, would never leave the road of maximum probability. To him the world would be mechanistic and real. An orthodox free-will Christian, such as Miss Ross, would have her choice of several of the side roads, but would probably remain in a physical environment similar to Howard's. I have perfected a technique which will enable others to travel about in the pattern of times as I have done. I have the apparatus ready and any who wish can try it."

All of the students volunteer to go, led by one named Robert

Monroe—Robert like Heinlein and Bob Wilson, Monroe like Heinlein's alter ego Lyle Monroe. All of the students find limited alternatives cut to the measure of the intentions they carry with them into the unknown. One becomes an angel. One becomes a temple prostitute. One becomes a mindless soldier. Robert Monroe becomes a gnomish engineer:

> He had been short and slender before, but was now barely five feet tall, and stocky, with powerful shoulder muscles. The brown costume with its peaked hood, or helmet, gave him a strong resemblance to the popular notion of a gnome.

Only one of the students and the teacher are able to treat eternity as eternity, rather than as a new kind of limitation, and move about at will. The failure of the story is that the ability to travel through eternity is granted to teacher and pupils by fiat.

And, at some level, Heinlein realizes the fact. At the end of the story, the teacher is left in the uncertain state between wakefulness and sleep, musing of unfinished business:

> Time enough for a little nap before lunch. Time enough . . .
> Time.

The other story, "Lost Legion"—reprinted by Heinlein as "Lost Legacy"—places three attractive young people, a doctor on a medical faculty, an instructor in psychology and a psychology student, in the hands of a community of Perfect Masters somewhere on the slopes of Mt. Shasta, where they are given instruction in the development of super-powers. These powers are the legacy of long-vanished High Ones, whom we remember as the gods of ancient legend, who left their records in various of the high places of the world. Again, the transition to a more evolved state is rendered trivial by being given rather than earned.

What is interesting in this story is the acts of the young people in their new state of perfection. First, they return with good news to their society, but like Hugh Hoyland in "Universe" they are discounted, disbelieved, ignored, opposed, and threatened with arrest, even when they are prepared to demonstrate their abilities. Second, they identify and dispose of the evil and benighted elements of society:

> . . . the antagonists of human liberty, of human dignity—the
> racketeers, the crooked political figures, the shysters, the dealers in
> phony religions, the sweat-shoppers, the petty authoritarians, all of
> the key figures among the traffickers in human misery and human
> oppression, themselves somewhat adept in the arts of the mind, and
> acutely aware of the danger of free knowledge—all of this unholy
> breed . . .

Third, they take the children of the world, those uncorrupted by
their environment, and teach them the ancient arts. And, in time,
there is the promise that humanity has escaped this Earth in pursuit
of the vanished High Ones.

"Lost Legacy" is notable for this brief potent glimpse of the
nature of self-limitation:

> Jove's eyes rested thoughtfully on Vulcan's crooked leg. "You
> should let me heal that twisted limb, my son."
> "No one can heal my limb!"
> "No. No one but yourself. And until you heal the twist in your
> mind, you can not heal the twist in your limb."
> "There is no twist in my mind!"
> "Then heal your limb."

And "Lost Legacy" is notable for this brief potent glimpse of the
nature of Heinlein's self-limitation:

> "We see the history of the world as a series of crises in a conflict
> between two opposing philosophies. Ours is based on the notion
> that life, consciousness, intelligence, ego is the important thing in
> the world."

The attachment to ego is the twist in Heinlein's limb. The nuclear
"I" is that thing that makes the "unholy breed" unholy. The confusion of ego with life and consciousness flaws the symbology of
"Lost Legacy." And, at the end of the story, with man flown elsewhere, a great ape "with a brain too big for his need and a spirit that
troubled him" must climb to a high place and be disturbed by the
records of the High Ones. If "Lost Legacy" were as true as Heinlein's
hopes, then Heinlein would not need to have this particular evolutionary jump repeated.

In December 1941, the United States entered World War II, as

Heinlein had foreseen. In the pages of *Astounding*, John W. Campbell announced the departure for war of a number of science fiction writers, led by Robert Heinlein and Anson MacDonald. They would, he said, likely not be writing again until the war was over.

In fact, however, in the space before he went to war, Anson MacDonald found world enough and time to write three final stories. "Goldfish Bowl" (*Astounding*, March 1942), the first of these, was the least important of the various freaky stories that Heinlein published in 1941 and 1942.

In this story, a variety of odd phenomena have been correlated with the appearance of gigantic twin waterspouts that have been named the Pillars of Hawaii. These are five hundred feet thick and eleven thousand feet high, their tops lost in clouds. Water goes up one spout and eventually comes down the other.

It is proposed that two men go up the rising pillar in a bathyscaphe to learn what may be learned in the unknown world at the top. Before that can happen, one of them is carried away to that world by a fireball. The other ascends the pillar in his machine and they are reunited at the top. They spend time captive there, never seeing their captors, never confronting them. Again, the seekers lack higher goals and fail to evolve. All that they can do is eventually die and be dumped into the other waterspout, the refuse drain.

The longer-lived of the two carries a message back with him, self-tattooed on his body: "BEWARE—CREATION TOOK EIGHT DAYS." But this message that higher beings and higher states of evolution exist is not understood by men who cannot step outside the assumptions of their society. A final ironic comparison is made by Heinlein between us and goldfish with bored keepers.

This is a deadend. As final a deadend as the one that Pinero ran into, or the one encountered by Bob Wilson. As hard as he may try, Heinlein cannot conceive a higher role than those that society offers, roles he has already rejected as too limited. Without a conception of a higher state, Heinlein cannot trust those unknown High Ones from whom the boon of evolution is derived. He must imagine them in Gloucester's despairing terms:

> As flies to wanton boys, are we to the gods;
> They kill us for their sport.

"Goldfish Bowl" is a minor story. The other two Anson Mac-
Donald stories published in 1942 were not minor. They were in fact
the centerpieces of his early writing career, the very best statements
that he could manage, the soundest generalizations, of problem and
solution.

Beyond This Horizon appeared directly after "Goldfish Bowl" in
the April and May issues of *Astounding*. Like so many Heinlein
titles, this one again signifies the enclosed universe and the necessity
of evolution.

The central character, Hamilton Felix, is a genius, a man of overwhelming competence, the heir of the star line in a future where
mankind is trying to breed the best possible race of man by selecting
each man and woman's most fruitful characteristics for their children. Hamilton is told by one who knows, the District Moderator
for Genetics:

> "I could set you down on an island peopled by howling savages
> and dangerous animals—in two weeks you would own the place . . .
> You've got the physique and the mentality and the temperament."

This is a future in which conduct must be defended by a willingness to instantly fight with hand weapons. This insures politesse and
eliminates the unfit.

Like so many Heinlein characters, Hamilton looks at his society
and finds its best opportunities unworthy. He employs himself, and
earns his living, by amusing people. He builds games machines of
which he is contemptuous—he diverts himself by building diversions.

The District Moderator for Genetics, Mordan Claude, seeks to en-
list Hamilton's cooperation in the breeding program. He is, after all,
the best of humanity, the star line. But Hamilton refuses. Life is a
charade and he sees no point in assisting it to continue:

> "I know of no reason why the human race *should* survive . . .
> other than the fact that their make-up insures that they will. But
> there's no sense to the whole bloody show. There's no point to
> being alive at all. I'm damned if I'll contribute to the comedy . . . .
> You can probably eliminate my misgivings [in my children] and pro-
> duce a line that will go on happily breeding for the next ten million

years. That still doesn't make it make sense. Survival! What for?
Until you can give me some convincing explanation of why the
human race should go on at all, my answer is 'no'."

Hamilton lives in a world with no High Ones that he can recognize
to whom he might present his best answer to the riddle of life, and
from whom he might receive his appropriate evolution. The nearest
thing to the unknown that he encounters to confront is a half-assed
revolution led by dilettantes, evil and banal, seeking personal power.
This is easily put down, though nearly at the cost of Hamilton's life.
There are interesting results:

When he and the District Moderator for Genetics, whom he has
unselfishly come to warn and protect, are under fire and death seems
close, Hamilton has an insight:

> "Damn it—I don't want to die. Not just yet. Claude, I've
> thought of another joke."
> "Let's have it."
> "What's the one thing that could give life point to it—*real*
> point?"
> "That," Mordan pointed out, "is the question I've been trying
> to answer for you all along."
> "No, no. The question itself."
> "You state it," Mordan parried cautiously.
> "I will. The one thing that could give us some real basis for our
> living is to know *for sure* whether or not anything happens after we
> die. When we die, do we die all over—or don't we?"
> "Hmm . . . granting your point, what's the joke?"
> "The joke is on me. Or rather on my kid. In a few minutes I'll
> probably know the answer. But *he* won't. He's sitting back there
> right now—in a way—sleeping in one of those freezers. And there
> is no way on earth for me to let him know the answer. *But he's the
> one that will need to know.* Isn't that funny?"
> "Hmm . . . If that's your idea of a joke, Felix, I suggest that you
> stick to parlor tricks."

But of course it is no joke. In the face of death, it is the most
serious thing Hamilton can think of, the best expression of what he
has on his mind.

And, *immediately*, he is presented with an answer, the whole answer to everything that Heinlein and Hamilton care about. The quest

that Heinlein and the various surrogate Heinleins of his stories have undertaken is to understand the meaning of life, and to discover what, if anything, in life is a worthwhile occupation. Anything less Heinlein has rejected as rendering life a joke. Any of us who ask this question ourselves may possibly be content with any of a variety of solutions, any of a variety of occupations within the purview of society. But Heinlein has consistently rejected all temporal and partial answers. Nothing that society has to offer is enough to content Hugh Hoyland, or the unnamed protagonist of "They," or Bob Wilson, or the professor in "Elsewhen," or the various seekers in "Lost Legacy." Heinlein requires nothing short of ultimate answers and total certainty. He desires to know *for sure*, for once and for all, and the intensity of his desire is what makes him so fascinating a writer.

There is only one such answer that humanity has ever been able to present, and it is this answer that Robert Heinlein has approached in his fiction time and time again, only to shy away. And no wonder. The answer is an answer that society has never liked—because it denies the ultimate validity of society. The answer is one that men of strong ego have never liked—because it denies the ultimate valid ity of the ego. Nonetheless, if there is any answer that will satisfy Robert Heinlein, that could satisfy Robert Heinlein, it is this:

Call it the Mystical Solution. This solution says that all that exists is God. And the only way out of the illusion of less-than-Godliness is to identify completely with one's Godly nature and occupy oneself in love and service of One's Own True Purpose. At first inspection, this solution seems to be a rejection of existence in favor of solitary contemplation of one's own navel. In practice, however, sitting on a mountain top staring at one's own navel is *not* the true Mystical Solution, but an aberration. Because, if all that exists is God, including the individual human being, then true contemplation of One's Own Navel in love and service means engagement with Existence.

Here we have the solution that Heinlein seems to be aiming for, but never quite able to seize. Whether or not it is our own personal solution is irrelevant. It is the stuff of Heinlein's fiction and if we are to understand Heinlein, we must understand mysticism.

Following Hamilton Felix's serious joke, something very strange happens. Objectively, within the story, Hamilton is gassed and wakes in the hospital. The gas is deadly unless an antidote is given immediately. The various conspirators do not receive the antidote, but Hamilton, of course, more than qualifies. In the meantime, however, he has been treading in unknown places beyond the reach of consciousness, and there he has encountered the Highest of all possible High Ones.

The sequence is not easy to follow because it involves Hamilton's true mind flitting lightly from viewpoint to viewpoint. This true mind begins with Hamilton's view. Mordan, Hamilton's fiancee, and another character named Monroe-Alpha Clifford, a mathematician, are referred to in the third person. But then, suddenly, in the second paragraph, the true mind sees itself successively as Monroe-Alpha, as Hamilton, and as Mordan—who have each been viewpoint characters in the story. And on and on we go until the true mind wakes—as Hamilton Felix.

This passage deserves extremely close reading because it is so central to the problem of understanding and assessing Heinlein's fiction:

> It was pleasant to be dead. Pleasant and peaceful, not monotonous. But a little bit lonely. He missed those others—serene Mordan, the dauntless gallantry of Phyllis, Cliff and his frozen face. And there was that funny little man, pathetic little man who ran the *Milky Way Bar*—what had he named him? He could see his face, but what had he named him? Herbie, Herbert, something like that —names didn't taste the same when words were gone. Why had he named him Herbert?
>
> Never mind, The next time he would not choose to be a mathematician. Dull, tasteless stuff, mathematics—quite likely to give the game away before it was played out. No fun in the game if you knew the outcome. He had designed a game like that once, and called it *Futility*—no matter how you played, you had to win. No, that wasn't himself, that was a player called Hamilton. Himself wasn't Hamilton—not this game. He was a geneticist—that was a good one!—a game within a game. Change the rules as you go along. Move the players around. Play tricks on yourself.
>
> "Don't you peek and close your eyes,
> "And I'll give you something to make a s'prise!"
>
> That was the essence of the game—surprise. You locked up your memory, and promised not to look, then played through the

part you had picked with just the rules assigned to that player. Sometimes the surprises were pretty ghastly, though—he didn't like having his fingers burned off.

No! He hadn't played that position at all. That piece was an automatic, some of the pieces had to be. Himself had burned off that piece's fingers, though it seemed real at the time.

It was always like this on first waking up. It was always a little hard to remember which position Himself had played, forgetting that he had played all of the parts. Well, that was the game; it was the only game in town, and there was nothing else to do. Could he help it if the game was crooked? Even if he had made it up and played all the parts.

But he would think up another game the next time. Next time . . .

And Hamilton Felix wakes.

Mordan is awake before him, and immediately Hamilton turns toward him—not surprising in view of the places his head has just been. One would think he would urgently need to know what Claude feels the world is like. But—he forgets the question. "There was something he wanted to ask Mordan, but it escaped him."

Or, as he knew in his dream state: "You locked up your memory, and promised not to look, then played through the part you had picked with just the rules assigned to that player."

Heinlein never refers to this nightmare passage again. His characters pick up the story where they had left it and proceed as though nothing has happened.

But much has happened, and if we look at it closely in view of our knowledge of the Mystical Solution, we can understand it. We said at the outset that in a science fiction story, a character comes to face a totally unknown aspect of the universe, both frightening and desirable. If the character does not surmount fear and desire, he will be cruelly wounded (like Bob Wilson) or eaten alive by monsters (as the characters of "Goldfish Bowl" effectively are). But if he is able to surrender attachment to his accustomed behaviors, if he meets the unknown with courage, love and unselfish purpose, then he will receive a necessary new power from the universe. That is to say, science fiction tells us that our personal evolutions at various times in our lives are achieved by a fractional version of the Mystical

Solution. We enlarge ourselves by trading a lesser identification for a greater one.

Hamilton Felix has faced death unselfishly for purposes larger than himself. He has earned the right to ask his boon. He asks, and as is always the case, his answer is implicit in his question.

At the point of death, Hamilton Felix says: "The one thing that could give us some real basis for our living is to know *for sure* whether or not anything happens after we die. When we die, do we die all over—or don't we?"

And immediately he is given the answer. The answer that he is given is that we don't. The universe is Himself, under various names, in various aspects, appearing as one partialness or another. Hamilton Felix learns this, but after he has learned it, he cannot hold on to the information.

Because of this, he must continue his search. At Mordan Claude's suggestion, his society determines to invest great resources in the attempt to scientifically investigate the serious metaphysical questions, including survival after death. And Hamilton Felix is enlisted in the investigation.

Hamilton Felix has one advantage that Robert Heinlein lacked in 1942 in his own similar investigation. Hamilton has time, all the time until he dies, in which to conduct his search. This opportunity to search is enough to satisfy him. It was the boon he asked for at the point of death, and it is enough to satisfy. He has the children society wants him to have. And after five years of slow earnest investigation, he is presented with an intimation that keeps him happy —the strong likelihood of reincarnation.

Hamilton's final thought is: "It was a good world, he assured himself, filled with interesting things." But the thought rings hollow to anyone who remembers the protagonist of "They." The assurance is not reassuring to anyone who remembers the experience that Hamilton and Heinlein have forgotten.

In effect, Hamilton has made the same compromise that Heinlein made in 1939 when he began writing science fiction. And the compromise has not been satisfying to Heinlein—not completely satisfying, which is what he must have.

Why isn't Hamilton truly successful? He has a larger answer—the very largest—and then must labor to recover the shadow of a fraction of it. Why?

The reason is this: Hamilton Felix's unselfishness is compromised by his attachment to Hamilton Felix, that partial aspect of the true reality—Himself. (Himself, who links the three viewpoint characters of the story: Hamilton, Mordan, and frozen-faced Cliff, whose significant name in full is Monroe-Alpha Clifford.) When Hamilton asks "do we die all over?" he is not asking about the true reality, Himself. He is asking about that temporary matrix filled by Himself—Hamilton Felix, who must perish.

Now, early in the story, Hamilton Felix sees through mere survival. "Survival! What for?" Survival for its own sake seems futile to him. But when the crunch comes, all that he knows to ask for is survival—survival in order to do more investigation of the reason for life. That is what he asks for and that is what he gets.

Hamilton's and Heinlein's attachment to the ego—which blinds them to their Himselfness—is apparent in the central scene. In this scene, Heinlein doubts the Himselfness of some human beings: "That piece was an automatic, some of the pieces had to be." But there are no automatic pieces. All that exists is Himself. And all humans have the potential to recognize that fact. It is what makes us human.

Hamilton Felix is given the opportunity to recognize that fact as consequence of his unselfishness. But he cannot hold on to it. No one can who believes that his ego is ultimate. Hamilton's selfishness is his limitation.

As the Mystical Solution, truly recognized, has it: If one remembers one's true nature and can be continuingly above ego, constantly unselfish, there is no limit to what can be requested of the universe and received. But if one forgets one's Himselfness and clutches the ego, then necessarily memory will be locked away and one will be doomed to play through "the part you had picked with just the rules assigned to that player."

The sad, grieving, weary, tragic quality that infects Hamilton's central and soon forgotten vision is not accidental. *Beyond This Horizon* is ultimately as much a story of unnecessary failure as "By

His Bootstraps."

The final Anson MacDonald story, "Waldo" (*Astounding*, August 1942), uniquely among Heinlein's pre-war stories, is not a story of failure, or a story of success by luck or fiat. It is an honest success. At the same time, it is not a solution of Heinlein's problem. How can this be?

Here is the story of "Waldo":

A future society powers itself by general wireless broadcast of radiation. This radiation is making everyone sick. Everyone who does not wear a lead-lined overcoat—and only one doctor who realizes the situation does—suffers from fatigue and malaise. No one has energy enough to exercise. More and more children are "bookish." Athletic records are not being extended or even matched.

At the same time, the air cars that draw on the generally broadcast power are failing. The great conglomerate, North American Power-Air, is distressed and worried that the great underground cities that draw on the broadcast power will inexplicably fail next.

They believe that only one man can possibly solve their problem, Waldo Farthingwaite-Jones. Waldo is a sick genius. He suffers from myasthenia gravis. He has no muscular strength at all. Waldo has invented remote-control hands to do his work for him. He has removed himself from the home of his wealthy parents to an isolated space station, which he calls "Freehold" and others call "Wheelchair." There, no strain is put on his muscles. He lives there alone with his pets, communicating with others remotely, touching things on Earth only through his mechanical hands, which are called "waldoes" after him. Waldo fancies himself independent of Earth.

Waldo is in personal contact with only one man, the doctor worried about the rise of general myasthenia in the population. North American Power-Air contacts Waldo through the doctor to solve their problem for them. Waldo at first refuses, but is convinced by the doctor who demonstrates his dependence on society to him. Moreover, the doctor insists that any solution to the failure of the air cars also eliminate the broadcast radiation.

Here we have an unprecedented double problem. Nothing that Waldo knows leads him to believe that they can be solved by a com-

mon answer. They do not seem to be problems of the same order.
And, in fact, he is unable to solve either by any means with which he
is familiar. Eventually he must admit—to himself if no one else—
that his resources are insufficient. He, Waldo-as-he-is, can simply not
solve what must be solved.

But Waldo hears of someone who seemingly can solve the problem
of the failed air cars. This man is an ancient Pennsylvania hex doctor.
He has repaired the engine of an air car by making it operate in an
unprecedented manner. No one else can repair an air car engine. No
one else can tell Waldo how the altered engine works—though one
rational man has learned how to duplicate the hex doctor's effect
by going mad:

> "Hens will crow and cocks will lay. You are here and I am there.
> Or maybe not. Nothing is certain. Nothing, *nothing*, NOTHING is
> certain! Around and around the little ball goes, and where it stops
> nobody knows. Only I've learned how to do it."
> "How to do what?"
> "How to make the little ball stop where I want it to."

Waldo needs the aid of the hex doctor, Gramps Schneider, but
Schneider will not come to him, will not even speak to him on a
tv-phone. If Waldo wants to approach this particular Master, he must
go to Earth, which means grave risk to his life and perhaps his sanity.
But for a greater good than himself, Waldo goes to visit Gramps
Schneider.

He is flown to Earth in a supportive water bed/iron lung and carried in to see Schneider. Waldo is ordinarily a nasty and abusive
egotist, but in Schneider's presence he is mild as milk. Schneider
settles him down, feeds him coffee and cake, and tells Waldo what
he wants to know:

Schneider says that to fix the machines (and to repair Waldo's
flabby body), it is necessary to reach into "the Other World" for
power.

> "One of the ancients said that everything either *is* or *is not*. That
> is less than true, for a thing can both *be* and *not be*. With practice
> one can see it both ways. Sometimes a thing which *is* for this world
> is a thing which *is not* for the Other World. Which is important,
> since we live in the Other World."

This advice sounds very like the teaching that Carlos Castaneda received from his mentor, the Yaqui sorcerer, don Juan, as reported in a series of recent books. Schneider tells Waldo that the air cars have failed because of the doubt and weakness of their pilots.

> "Hugh Donald," Schneider went on, "was tired and fretting. He found one of the bad truths."
> "Do you mean," Waldo said slowly, "that McLeod's ship failed because he was worried about it?"
> "How else?"

Waldo comes away from his encounter with Schneider with the power he has asked for, the power to alter the ships to draw on the Other World's energy. But this conflicts with everything he thinks he knows. Eventually, to keep his sanity, he must conclude that the world is as it is because we believe it is so. "The world was flat before geographers decided to think of it otherwise."

And: "Orderly Cosmos, created out of Chaos—by Mind!"

This is a purely mystical conclusion.

Waldo determines that he can make the Other World, whatever it is, behave as he wants by impressing his picture of it on everyone else. He says:

> "I think of it as about the size and shape of an ostrich egg, but nevertheless a whole universe, existing side by side with our own, from here to the farthest star."

And:

> To its inhabitants, if any, it might seem to be hundreds of millions of light years around; to him it was an ostrich egg, turgid to bursting with power.

And with this concept in mind, Waldo is not only able to solve both his society's problems at a stroke by trading the power of the Other World for the conventional power that is making men weary, sick and doubtful, but he is able as well to heal himself. He makes himself slim and trim, and turns himself into an exquisite professional dancer and masterful brain surgeon.

Here is a problem honestly solved. Waldo confronts a higher one than himself, unselfishly, at the risk of death. He evolves. He solves his society's problems and his own problem. All as it should be. But this solution is not Heinlein's solution.

It is not Heinlein's solution because Waldo starts as something less than the all-around competent man that Heinlein is and at the end is willing to settle for being a dancer and surgeon—societal roles like the one of "science fiction writer" that Heinlein has assumed. But Waldo is content and Heinlein is not.

In fact, what we see in "Waldo" is a process that Heinlein himself has already undergone. When Heinlein was a naval officer, he was something like Waldo—aloof, semi-independent of society, a stranger to the variety of society. Like Waldo, Heinlein was carried out of his state of separation on a stretcher, so to speak, when he developed tuberculosis and was retired from the Navy. Like Waldo, Heinlein survived his state of helplessness and approach to death and thereafter expanded himself to assume a variety of societal roles. The air of morbidity that surrounds "Waldo" may be a reflection of Heinlein's own past.

There is confirmation that this is a version of the mid-twenties crisis that Heinlein has successfully passed in the confrontation scene. When Heinlein writes of the evolution he has not made but earnestly desires to make, he evades confrontation. His characters avoid their High Ones, as in "By His Bootstraps" and *Methuselah's Children*. And Heinlein must doubt the good will of the High Ones, as he does again and again. In writing of this earlier evolution that Heinlein has successfully made, he has no doubt or fear. Gramps Schneider is totally unfearsome. He invites Waldo into his home, pats him on the shoulder, serves him coffee and cake and tells him everything he wants to know.

Everything that Waldo wants to know—and more. And that more is what Heinlein wants to know, but cannot recognize even when he tells it to himself. Waldo is content to draw on the power of the Other World to make himself a human being like other human beings, an above-average dancer and surgeon. But that is only a partial use of the power of the Other World. It is merely all that Waldo feels impelled by necessity to demand.

But he doesn't have to settle for being merely a dancer and surgeon. He could be *anything*. He could be someone like Gramps

Schneider—he could be a Perfect Master, or perhaps even a High One, himself. But neither Waldo nor Heinlein is quite ready for that. Even though Schneider's last words in a letter to Waldo are:

"The power of the Other World is his who would claim it—"

And there is further confirmation of the inadequacy for Heinlein of the "solutions" offered by *Beyond This Horizon* and "Waldo" in the contrast between these stories and those of 1941. "Universe"/"Common Sense" looks for the largest symbolic answer to the meaning of life that it can, an answer completely outside the bounds of society and the given world. It forces that answer, but the answer itself is not a compromise. "Elsewhen" and "Lost Legacy" are answers of the same order, given by fiat. "They" and "By His Bootstraps" are stories of what we must take to be outright failure, but there is no compromise in them. They are small tragedies.

On the other hand, *Beyond This Horizon* is a compromise. It asks the same questions as before—"What is the meaning and purpose of life?"—but it settles for its answer. It offers the dubious proposition that continuing search for the meaning of life, in this incarnation and in the next, if there is one, is enough in itself to give life meaning. "Waldo" compromises on both question and answer. It asks: "How can a misanthropic invalid genius find happiness?" And its answer, dubious and desperate, is: "Tap dance-ballet, brain surgery, fame and friendship are sufficient to give life meaning."

Heinlein knew better than this. That he knew better is plain in the final story he published before he was claimed by World War II, the short novel "The Unpleasant Profession of Jonathan Hoag" by John Riverside (*Unknown Worlds*, October 1942).

"Jonathan Hoag" is an incoherent shambles of a story, and not accidentally. *Beyond This Horizon* and "Waldo" are Heinlein's attempts to be sound and sensible about life and the search for meaning. And they are sound and sensible—but only at the cost of excluding important and essential meaning. "Jonathan Hoag" is the expression of what these sound stories exclude. It is not at all sensible, but it is intensely meaningful. It is a story of terror.

It has been Heinlein's practice to make his heroes the smartest, swiftest, most gifted and able all-around competent men that he can imagine. He has armed them for their encounters with the unknown with the best weapons that he can give them, and he has allowed them to be contemptuous of ordinary folk who are not smart, swift, gifted and competent and able to work a slipstick. Hamilton Felix, with his ability to rule wild islands instantly, might serve as the exemplar. Their greatest weaknesses have tended to be ignorance and naiveté, both correctable.

Uniquely, in "The Unpleasant Profession of Jonathan Hoag," Heinlein's protagonist, a detective named Edward Randall, is not smart, gifted or even competent. He is a very ordinary man, a small-timer.

Throughout the story, for no reason that bears examination, Randall is threatened, frightened, terrorized, toyed with, lied to, hypnotized and confused. He is dragged into the mysterious world that lurks behind mirrors by cruel, ugly sneering monsters who put him on a large table, sit around it and haze him unmercifully. His only ally is his wife, and she is treated similarly. In fact, their love and fear for each other is exploited without shame or limit.

The world becomes a very uncertain place for Edward Randall. Nothing whatsoever can be counted upon.

He is offered two mutually exclusive "explanations" for the state of the world and the nature of life. The monsters say this:

> "In the Beginning," Stoles stated, "there was the Bird." He suddenly covered his face with his hand; all the others gathered around the table did likewise.
>
> The Bird—Randall felt a sudden vision of what those two simple words meant when mouthed by this repulsive fat man; no soft and downy chick, but a bird of prey, strong-winged and rapacious—unwinking eyes, whey-colored and staring—purple wattles—but most especially he saw its feet, bird feet, covered with yellow scales, fleshless and taloned and foul from use. Obscene and terrible—
>
> Stoles uncovered his face. "The Bird was alone. Its great wings beat the empty depths of space where there was none to see. But deep within It was the Power and the Power was Life. It looked to the north when there was no north; It looked to the south when there was no south; east and west It looked, and up and down. Then out of the nothingness and out of Its Will It wove the nest.
>
> "The nest was broad and deep and strong. In the nest It laid one

hundred eggs. It stayed on the nest and brooded the eggs, thinking Its thoughts, for ten thousand thousand years. When the time was ripe It left the nest and hung it about with lights that the fledglings might see. It watched and waited.

"From each of the hundred eggs a hundred Sons of the Bird were hatched—ten thousand strong. Yet so wide and deep was the nest there was room and to spare for each of them—a kingdom apiece and each was a king—king over the things that creep and crawl and swim and fly and go on all fours, things that had been born from the crevices of the nest, out of the warmth and the waiting.

"Wise and cruel was the Bird, and wise and cruel were the Sons of the Bird. For twice ten thousand thousand years they fought and ruled and the Bird was pleased. Then there were some who decided that they were as wise and strong as the Bird Itself. Out of the stuff of the nest they created creatures like unto themselves and breathed in their nostrils, that they might have sons to serve them and fight for them. But the sons of the Sons were not wise and strong and cruel, but weak and soft and stupid. The Bird was not pleased.

"Down It cast Its Own Sons and let them be chained by the softly stupid— Stop fidgeting, Mr. Randall! I know this is difficult for your little mind, but for once you really must think about something longer than your nose and wider than your mouth, believe me!

"The stupid and the weak could not hold the Sons of the Bird; therefore, the Bird placed among them, here and there, others more powerful, more cruel, and more shrewd, who by craft and cruelty and deceit could circumvent the attempts of the Sons to break free. Then the Bird sat back, well content, and waited for the game to play itself out.

"The game is being played."

If this were not enough, the *other* explanation is this:

"Once there was a race, quite unlike the human race—quite. I have no way of describing to you what they looked like or how they lived, but they had one characteristic you can understand: they were creative. The creating and enjoying of works of art was their occupation and their reason for being. I say "art" advisedly, for art is undefined, undefinable, and without limits. I can use the word without fear of misusing it, for it has no exact meaning. There are as many meanings as there are artists. But remember that these artists are not human and their art is not human.

"Think of one of this race, in your terms—young. He creates a work of art, under the eye and the guidance of his teacher. He has talent, this one, and his creation has many curious and amusing features. The teacher encourages him to go on with it and prepare it for the judging . . . The Sons of the Bird were the dominant feature of the world, at first . . . .

"The teacher did not approve of the Sons of the Bird and suggested certain improvements in the creation. But the Artist was hasty or careless; instead of removing them entirely he merely— painted over them, made them appear to be some of the new creations with which He peopled His world.

"All of which might not have mattered if the work had not been selected for judging. Inevitably the critics noticed them; they were —bad art, and they disfigured the final work. There was some doubt in their minds as to whether or not the creation was worth preserving. That is why I am here."

It must be evident that this is not Heinlein's usual sort of thing. Not sensible. In no sense reassuring. But intensely meaningful, especially for this particular man, this writer, at this time.

For Edward Randall, of course, it is hellish. He is offered two mutually exclusive explanations of the world. Neither allows that life has much point for ordinary human beings. Either we live in the Bird's nest and are the creation of the Sons of the Bird, or we are the creations of a beginning Artist and the only points in our favor are that we eat and copulate—amusing idiosyncrasies. And either way, our future is uncertain. The Sons of the Bird, if they are right, are on the point of bursting their bonds and doing all sorts of filthy and hideous things to us. And if Jonathan Hoag is right, the art critics may judge us wanting and wipe us out at any moment.

A great future!

All Edward Randall can do is retire from Chicago, the not altogether inappropriate setting of this story, to a place in the country and wait for The End, whichever and whatever. He and his wife eliminate mirrors from their house, and every night when they go to sleep they handcuff their wrists together and hope they won't be parted.

And, on this note, Robert Heinlein turned to the business of World War II.

7. The Man Who Survived

Robert Heinlein survived the war, but only at great personal cost. Like Robert Monroe, the most anxious of the students in "Elsewhen" to explore the possibilities of eternity, he had been turned into a gnomish engineer and put to work developing airplanes to defend his attacked nation—a remarkable instance of prescience. Another cost—for this work must be reckoned a cost—was Heinlein's first marriage. In 1942 it had been reported by a magazine editor that Heinlein's alter ego, Lyle Monroe, and his wife believed themselves to have an almost telepathic rapport. But during World War II, the bonds — or the handcuffs — that united them were broken, and after the war they were soon divorced.

Heinlein had been expecting his crisis to be settled by World War II, one way or another. This is clear in the stories from 1941 and 1942, particularly in their increasing desperation as the war approached. And, as his 1941 Guest of Honor speech had made clear, he had not really expected to be a writer after his crisis:

> I don't suppose I'll be writing very much longer. Things shaping up the way they are, I'll probably have other things that I'll have to do . . . and I may not come back to it . . .

The greatest cost to Heinlein of World War II may simply have been that his expected evolution never occurred. His preparation was for nothing. He did not come away from World War II with something better to be than a science fiction writer.

What a missing stair!

After the war, he was slow to return to writing. And when he did return, at last. in 1947, it was not with stories of search in *Astounding*, but with simple (even simplistic) Future History stories of the near future in *The Saturday Evening Post*. And it was with a series of juvenile novels published by Scribners at the rate of one a year from 1947 through 1958. And it was with the script of the movie *Destination Moon* in 1950.

The post-war Heinlein had largely abandoned his search, and with it he abandoned the almost magical quality that had so clearly separated him from all other science fiction writers before the war. The post-war Heinlein wrote, in large part, to make money. And he was, at best, in the years of the Scribners juveniles, chief among equals among science fiction writers rather than without peer.

The twelve juvenile books for Scribners were effectively forecast in the 1941 speech in Denver. These books do not involve themselves in the search for the meaning of life. Instead, they concentrate on the problems of growing up and holding onto one's sanity in the face of trouble.

The means of holding onto one's sanity, Heinlein had said, is to learn to distinguish between facts and non-facts. In these books, Heinlein presents fact after fact from a secure position of omniscience.

In the 1941 speech, Heinlein had said:

> So far as astronomy is concerned, I've never seen anything that surpassed, for a popular notion of the broad outlines of the kind of physical world that we live in, than John Campbell's series that appeared in *Astounding*. When did they start?—Julie Unger can tell us, I think [from floor: "1936"]—ran on for 15, 16 issues, something of the sort, his articles on the solar system. I've always been sorry that Campbell didn't go on from there and cover stellar astronomy, galactic astronomy, and some of the other side fields. But even at that, anybody that's read through that series by Campbell on the solar system will never again have a flat-world attitude— which most people do have.

In his Scribners juveniles, Heinlein concentrated on solar, stellar and galactic astronomy, gradually expanding his scope from the moon in the first book to other galaxies in the last. He gave a generation a useful education, doing fictively and rather better, what Campbell had once done in factual articles. Anybody who has read them will never again have a flat-world attitude.

But the chief lesson of these books is survival. As one of them, *Farmer in the Sky*, has it:

> I was thinking about the Schultzes and how good it was to find them alive, as we trudged over to our place. I told Dad that it was a miracle.
>
> He shook his head. "Not a miracle. They are survivor types."
>
> "What type is a survivor type?" I asked.
>
> He took a long time to answer that one. Finally he said, "Sur-

vivors survive. I guess that is the only way to tell the survivor type
for certain."

I said, "We're survivor types, too, in that case."

"Could be," he admitted. "At least we've come through this
one."

The last of the Scribners juveniles is the most successful. It is as
solid and sturdy a story as Heinlein has ever written. *Have Space
Suit—Will Travel* (1958) begins in a backyard in the near future with
a boy who does not know how to be a man. It proceeds to the
moon, to Pluto, to a planet of the star Vega, and to a place somewhere in the Lesser Magellanic Cloud, one of our companion galaxies.
In that unknown place, the hero is judged as a representative of the
human race. If he is found wanting, the human race will be destroyed. But he defends the human race unselfishly, thinking not
of himself at all. He concludes:

> "Mr. Moderator—if the verdict is against us—can you hold off
> your hangmen long enough to let us *go home*? We know that you
> can send us home in only a few minutes."
>
> The voice did not answer quickly. "Why do you wish this? As I
> have explained, you are not personally on trial. It has been arranged
> to let you live."
>
> "We know. We'd rather be home, that's all—with our people."
> Again a tiny hesitation. "It shall be done."

But the verdict is not against us. The hero is sent home to Earth
with great gifts—the information that will allow us to damp out nuclear reactions at a distance, anti-gravity, time travel, new approaches
to matter conversion. More than enough to keep us occupied.

What is most interesting, and indicative that it is subjective growth
experiences that are being symbolized, is that all of the hero's adventures have taken place in no time at all. Effectively, he has never
been away. But in that no time at all, his problems and society's
problems have both been solved. The book concludes with the hero
demonstrating his new manhood in action. He is no longer a boy.

Heinlein did not simply abandon his search. He made an attempt
after the war to pick it up again in the novel *Stranger in a Strange
Land*, which is closely related to the central scene in *Beyond This
Horizon*.

Heinlein has said that his purpose in writing *Stranger*

> ... was to examine every major axiom of Western culture, ... throw doubt on it—and, if possible—to make the antithesis of each axiom appear a possible and perhaps desirable thing—rather than unthinkable.

That is clearly an attempt to step outside the bounds and limitations of inherited assumption—just as in the stories before the war.

In *Stranger*, the key perception is: "Thou art God." And that is truly a key perception, as we have seen.

But again, in *Stranger* as in *Beyond This Horizon*, the perception is qualified. "Thou art God"—except for those people who aren't, and there seem to be quite a few of them. These empty counters may be treated roughly or worse than roughly—like Edward Randall—without those who are God taking second thought. In other words, Heinlein's search again founders on the rocky shoal of ego.

And this is confirmed by the silly destiny of Heinlein's chief character, Valentine Michael Smith. When he dies—"discorporates"— Smith goes somewhere to Heaven where he is the chief and favored son of the Boss. He is equipped with wings and a halo—hardly a rejection of the axioms of Western culture—and put in charge of us and the pointless play that is our lives. No ultimate meaning here, but only exaltation of ego.

But what is most interesting about *Stranger in a Strange Land* is that Heinlein could not finish the book in the late Forties when he began it. He had to set it aside—incorporating material from its background in his third juvenile novel, *Red Planet* (1949)—and only eventually was able to finish it for publication in 1961.

In the late Forties and through the Fifties, Heinlein wrote only six significant adult stories. His primary energies were invested in the juvenile novels. But those few adult stories, three short novels and three novels, are worth a brief look for their bearing on his search:

In "Jerry Is a Man" (*Thrilling Wonder Stories*, October 1947), Heinlein admitted a selectively bred anthropoid slave — a "neo-chimpanzee" worker with cataracts, splay feet, a limited ability to reason and speak, and a love for music—to the ranks of humanity, chiefly on the basis of his small musical talents. But Heinlein, as we have seen, was unable to sustain this admission of general worthiness in *Stranger in a Strange Land*.

"Gulf" (November-December 1949) was Heinlein's only story in *Astounding* between 1942 and 1956. It was written as a favor to fit a given title. "Gulf" might have been about anything, but Heinlein chose to make it about the gap between normal men and superior men: "*homo novis*, who must displace *homo sapiens*—*is* displacing him—because he is better able to survive than is homo sap."

Heinlein's hero is granted to be *homo novis*, New Man, a superman among supermen, and is given training to develop his abilities. This training for personal evolution occupies the largest part of the story. Then the hero and his chief tutor are sent out on a dangerous mission and are successful, but immediately killed. Heinlein tries to portray these deaths as a glorious sacrifice:

> The letters on the metal marker read: TO THE MEMORY OF MR. AND MRS. JOSEPH GREENE WHO, NEAR THIS SPOT, DIED FOR ALL THEIR FELLOW MEN.

But we may ask—fellow men of which kind? In fact, the conclusion of the story is evidence that Greene is not a superman, that his training was a waste. He does not survive—as a New Man would. He does not evolve.

"Year of the Jackpot" (*Galaxy*, March 1952) presents us as the helpless victims of various cycles, driven by the dictates of cycles into mad behavior of one sort or another. At the end of the story, we are caught in the crunch of one last super-cycle. The sun, it seems, is about to go nova. Humanity does not evolve in the face of this crisis, and the conclusion of the story is: "THE END."

These are the short novels. Here are the novels:

The Puppet Masters (1951) is about a young man, a secret agent, whose remote manipulative boss is his father. Earth is invaded by demonic aliens, slugs that attach themselves to humans and direct them against their will. In the climactic confrontation, slugs and father are allied—no, united. The hero faces the issue squarely, evolves, and survives. So does the father, no longer demonic. At the end of the story, however, the protagonist is setting out on a twelve-year journey (without his father) to track down the slugs and exterminate them:

> I feel exhilarated. Puppet masters—the free men are coming to kill you! *Death and Destruction!*

This is the same transition as that presented in Heinlein's first novel, *"If This Goes On—"*, much more effectively stated. But it is no final solution. What is particularly interesting about this story is that the attractive horror that the slugs bring to humanity, for which the hero means to exterminate them, is loss of ego, submersion in a group mind.

Double Star (1956) is about a man in an impasse. It begins with him drowning his sorrows in a bar. The man is an actor without prospects. He is hired to impersonate a politician who has been kidnapped by his enemies, and when the politician dies from the mistreatment he has received, the actor assumes his place permanently. This story says that evolution is possible, but only a very temporal evolution and only by usurping someone else's place. Even to the end of the story, the actor is still only acting.

What makes the impersonation necessary in the first place is that the politician is scheduled to be adopted by Martians (whom the actor fears and loathes) and the Martians would not understand if no one showed up for the ceremony—to the point that human beings would be killed for the slight, "maybe every human on Mars." The Martians accept the substitution without apparently noticing it, and in the guise of the politician, the actor is adopted—and thereafter is able to "evolve" into the politician who loves and cares for all humanity:

> No, I do not regret it, even though I was happier then—at least I slept better. But there is solemn satisfaction in doing the best you can for eight billion people.
>
> Perhaps their lives have no cosmic significance, but they have feelings. They can hurt.

But this "evolution" is a shuck. Heinlein is unable to visualize the central confrontation with the unknown. He draws a veil over the crucial Martian adoption ceremony. Moreover, true evolution, particularly one that permits you to watch over the feelings of eight billion people, is not achieved by usurping what another has earned.

The Door Into Summer (1956) is yet again about the search for the door that Heinlein cannot find, the door from which he averts his gaze. Like *Double Star*, *The Door Into Summer* begins with a man in an impasse, drowning his sorrows in a bar. This man, an inventor, does not like his own time, which is 1970. In search of something better, he skips ahead to the end of the century—past the time of trouble and insanity that Heinlein foresaw in 1941.

Things aren't perfect when he gets there, so the man slips back in time to 1970 via a time machine to make a few necessary adjustments. He picks up his cat, Pete, whom he had left behind, and he arranges with a little girl he knows to come and look for him when she has grown up. Then back he goes to the end of the century via cold sleep, where all is just as he would like it to be:

> . . . I don't worry about philosophy any more than Pete does. Whatever the truth about this world, I like it. I've found my Door Into Summer and I would not time-travel again for fear of getting off at the wrong station. Maybe my son will, but if he does I will urge him to go forward, not back. "Back" is for emergencies; the future is better than the past. Despite the crapehangers, romanticists, and anti-intellectuals, the world steadily grows better because the human mind, applying itself to environment, *makes* it better. With hands . . . with tools . . . with horse sense and science and engineering.
>
> Most of these long-haired belittlers can't drive a nail nor use a slide rule. I'd like to invite them into Dr. Twitchell's cage and ship them back to the twelfth century—then let them enjoy it.
>
> But I am not mad at anybody and I like now.

So Heinlein says, but this is whistling in the dark. We know that he does worry about philosophy. We know that he does wonder about the truth of the world. And we know from what the character says that there are indeed people he is mad at—if no others, at least crapehangers, romanticists, anti-intellectuals, and long-haired belittlers who can't drive a nail or use a slide rule. We may very well doubt that he will be any more content with the future that he has found than Bob Wilson of "By His Bootstraps" was.

One last story closes this period of Heinlein's avoidance of his problem. It is the book version of *Methuselah's Children*. The first three books of the Future History—*The Man Who Sold the Moon, The Green Hills of Earth*, and *Revolt in 2100*—were published in 1950, 1951, and 1953. *Methuselah's Children* languished from 1941, when it was serialized in *Astounding*, until 1958, when it was finally published as a book.

When at last it did appear, however, quite significantly, it was with a new conclusion. The original had Lazarus Long speculating about a chili parlor in Dallas that he had known seventy-five years before. This conclusion is avoidance of the implications of mankind's odd lurch into the unknown world. Lazarus Long wants to forget that he was ever gone. It was a mistake that he wishes to write off.

This Lazarus Long has much in common with the Robert Heinlein of the post-war period.

But in 1958, avoidance no longer seemed a viable answer to Heinlein. In republishing *Methuselah's Children*, Heinlein puts the Dallas chili house aside. Instead, he ends on a philosophical note with a conversation between Lazarus Long and a friend. Long says:

> "Someday, about a thousand years from now, I intend to march straight into the temple of Kreel, look him in the eye, and say, 'Howdy, bub—what do *you* know that I don't know?' "
>
> "It might not be healthy."
>
> "We'll have a showdown, anyway. I've never been satisfied with the outcome there. There ought not to be anything in the whole universe that man can't poke his nose into—that's the way we're built and I assume that there's some reason for it."
>
> "Maybe there aren't any reasons."
>
> "Yes, maybe it's just one colossal big joke, with no point to it." Lazarus stood up and stretched and scratched his ribs. "But I can tell you this, Andy, whatever the answers are, here's one monkey that's going to keep on climbing, and looking around him to see what he can see, as long as the tree holds out."

An interesting alteration.

8. The Man Who Feared Evil

The work that Heinlein did following World War II, the juvenile novels and the adult novels with their unconvincing solutions, was essentially predictable from Heinlein's 1941 World Science Fiction Convention speech.

Heinlein had said:

> When a man makes predictions and they keep failing to come out, time and again, things don't come out the way he wants to, he goes insane . . .

He had said that for a period of up to fifty years large portions of the human race would be in a condition of insanity.

> And during such a period it is really a difficult thing to keep a grip, to keep a grip on yourself . . .

He saw but one mode of self-protection. The scientific method—the ability to "distinguish facts from non-facts." He said:

> The scientific method can be used to protect our sanity, to protect ourselves from serious difficulties of other sorts—gettin' our teeth smashed in, and things like that—in our everyday life, 24 hours of the day.

In the juvenile novels, he had done his best to educate a younger generation to factual matters to give them the means to survive. In *Double Star*, there is envisioned a period of insanity and trouble and the protagonist evolves into a political figure in order to tip the scale toward survival. In *The Door Into Summer*, the protagonist is so freaked by the time of trouble that he abandons the present entirely in order to find a sunnier time of "comparative peace and comfort" —in Heinlein's 1941 phrase. Survival. At all costs, survival.

Survival was the solution that Heinlein found when he suffered from tuberculosis in the Thirties. Time and again, survival is the answer he has settled for in lieu of a larger answer to the meaning of life.

But the 1941 speech holds even more pertinence for our understanding. Heinlein had said that when a man makes predictions for himself and they keep failing to come out, time and again, he goes insane. That when the world is insane, it becomes difficult for a man to keep a grip—"to keep a grip on yourself." We may read this as "difficult to keep a grip on *your self*"—which is to say, to retain the continuity of the ego, which is what survival means to Heinlein.

The one method of survival is to distinguish between facts and non-facts. And since the war, Heinlein had done his best to distinguish between facts and non-facts. He had written the most rational stories that he could conceive. He had compromised.

But at cost, just as there was cost in the compromises of *Beyond This Horizon* and "Waldo." For fifteen years, Heinlein had denied the search for larger meaning in favor of preaching the benefits of fact and survival.

Finally, in the March 1959 issue of *The Magazine of Fantasy and Science Fiction*, Heinlein published a story that, like "The Unpleasant Profession of Jonathan Hoag," expressed what he had been holding locked so tightly within himself. In this story, " 'All You Zombies—'," nothing is real but the protagonist. Heinlein's character, by means of time travel and a sex-change operation, has become father and mother of herself/himself and recruited that self into a time travel police corps. It is not a happy story. It ends like this:

> I *know* where *I* came from—but *where did all you zombies come from?*
> I felt a headache coming on, but a headache powder is one thing I do not take. I did once—and you all went away.
> So I crawled into bed and whistled out the light.
> *You* aren't really there at all. There isn't anybody but me—Jane—here alone in the dark.
> I miss you dreadfully!

This is all the greatest doubts expressed by "They," "By His Bootstraps," the key scene of *Beyond This Horizon*, and "Jonathan Hoag" all together in one short, succinct, nightmare package.

This short story was the first expression of a new facet of Heinlein and his search. In this new phase of his career, Heinlein has been led into overstatement, philosophic pontification, and seemingly dangerous opinion. His books have been less and less carefully crafted as they have grown longer and longer. If, in his first phase, Heinlein was without peer, and in the second he was chief among equals, in the third he has been as solitary as the singular character of " 'All You Zombies—'."

Heinlein began his third phase with an inflation of his long-cherished concern for survival, and for facts as the means of survival. Survival he saw as a thing that might be purchased only at the risk of a glorious death. He expressed his opinions not only in his fiction, but in a second World Science Fiction Convention Guest of Honor speech, this one at Seattle in 1961, twenty years after the first.

This is what Heinlein saw as "fact" rather than "non-fact" in 1961: He claimed that the wars and mass insanity that he had predicted twenty years earlier had actually come to pass. He divided the possible futures that he now foresaw—which was to say, his own future, too—into two groups. One group, assigned a ten per cent probability, was a collection of improbables, on the order of the sun becoming a nova, as in "Year of the Jackpot," Khrushchev becoming a Christian, or there being peace in the world. The more likely group, assigned a ninety per cent probability, contained just three possibilities: Russia destroys us in a war; we collapse internally and give up to Russia; or we and Russia destroy each other and China wins. In any case, no matter which of these three possibilities should come to pass, one-third of us would die. Heinlein's attitude was that since we were going to lose, no matter which of the three occurred, we ought to go down fighting. We ought to stock bomb shelters, as Heinlein did. We ought to acquire unregistered weapons. And we ought to die as gloriously as we could.

It is not beyond understanding why opinions like these, pressed as hard as Heinlein has pressed them, must seem pernicious. They are a projection into the world at large of Heinlein's own fears and uncertainties, and if they were strictly lived by, then indeed, Heinlein's likely ninety per cent of possible futures might already have come to pass.

The first novel to press these opinions—to shout these opinions—was *Starship Troopers* (1959). In this story, we are faced with alien enemies even more vicious, implacable and impossible to deal with than those in *The Puppet Masters*. Nothing can be learned from them. They can only be fought.

The central philosophic conceit of the novel is this:

Morals—*all* correct moral rules—derive from the instinct to survive; moral behavior is survival behavior above the individual level—as in a father who dies to save his children. But since population pressure results from the process of surviving through others, then war, because it results from population pressure, derives from the same inherited instinct which produces all moral rules suitable for human beings.

Check of proof: Is it possible to abolish war by relieving population pressure (and thus do away with the all-too-evident evils of war) through constructing a moral code under which population is limited to resources?

Without debating the usefulness or morality of planned parenthood, it may be verified by observation that any breed which stops its own increase gets crowded out by breeds which expand. Some human populations did so, in Terran history, and other breeds moved in and engulfed them.

Nevertheless, let's assume that the human race manages to balance birth and death, just right to fit its own planets, and thereby becomes peaceful. What happens?

Soon (about next Wednesday) the Bugs move in, kill off this breed which "ain'ta gonna study war no more" and the universe forgets us. Which still may happen. Either we spread and wipe out the Bugs, or they spread and wipe us out—because both races are tough and smart and want the same real estate.

Do you know how fast population pressure could cause us to fill the entire universe shoulder to shoulder? The answer will astound you, just the flicker of an eye in terms of the age of our race.

Try it—it's a compound-interest expansion.

But does Man have any "right" to spread through the universe?

Man is what he is, a wild animal with the will to survive, and (so far) the ability, against all competition. Unless one accepts that, anything one says about morals, war, politics—you name it—is nonsense. Correct morals arise from knowing what Man *is*—not what do-gooders and well-meaning old Aunt Nellies would like him to be.

The universe will let us know—later—whether or not Man has any "right" to expand through it.

These opinions, of course, do not properly belong to the nominal narrator of the novel—a boy hardly twenty. They belong to Heinlein. They are the natural product of Heinlein's special and personal history. They are not the opinions that he would have expressed in 1939 or in 1942, or even in *The Puppet Masters* in 1951.

Starship Troopers was originally submitted to Scribners to be the thirteenth in the series of juvenile novels that Heinlein had been writing for them, but the opinions expressed were too extreme for them and the book was issued by another publisher—as a juvenile.

Heinlein's next novel was *Stranger in a Strange Land*, finally completed now that he had let go his death grip on calm rationality. The novel succeeding *Stranger* was *Glory Road* (1963). In this story, a young Vietnam veteran, unhappy with our world, takes an opportunity to become an adventurer in parallel universes. He meets a transcendent alien enemy in single combat and defeats it. But he returns to our world with no new gifts except the right to leave again, and as the book ends the character is as unhappy as he was when he began.

Glory Road rejects democracy:

> "Democracy can't work. Mathematicians, peasants, and animals, that's all there is—so democracy, a theory based on the assumption that mathematicians and peasants are equal, can never work.

And the novel endorses the philosophy of survival equalling harmony-with-the-universe: The Empress of the Twenty Universes is *right* and is instantly obeyed until she is dead. When an assassin finally gets to her, she won't be *right* anymore.

Since 1963, Heinlein has published but three novels, strange and desperate wrestlings with the questions of survival and purpose: *Farnham's Freehold* (1964); *The Moon Is a Harsh Mistress* (1966); and *I Will Fear No Evil* (1970).

Farnham's Freehold has characters thrown through time by an atomic bomb blast into a future no more palatable than the present. In this future, the black race rules and Heinlein's protagonist, Hugh Farnham, and his party are taken as slaves. Farnham and his wife escape from this future back into our own time. They flee from the atomic war and take refuge in an enclave in the hills:

> They lived through the missiles, they lived through the bombs, they lived through the fires, they lived through the epidemics— which were not extreme and may not have been weapons; both

sides disclaimed them—and they lived through the long period of disorders while civil government writhed like a snake with a broken back. They lived. They went on.

The Farnhams give those who approach fair warning:

> WARNING!!! Ring Bell. Wait. Advance with your Hands *Up*. Stay on path, avoid mines. We lost three customers last week. We can't afford to lose YOU. No sales tax . . .
> High above their sign their homemade starry flag is flying—and they are *still* going on.

In this novel, Farnham is able to bring back but one boon from the unknown country of the future into which he penetrates. That boon is personal survival. Without the penetration into the future, Farnham must necessarily have died. But survival is all that he asks for and survival is all that he gets. What is gained from life is no more than what is offered to life.

Farnham's "Freehold" must inevitably serve as a reminder of that other place in a Heinlein story that is called "Freehold"—Waldo Farthingwaite-Jones's lonely space station home, which more objective men than he call "Wheelchair." This "Freehold" is as independent of the outside world as Waldo's was. Farnham's possession of his "Freehold" is exactly as much of a triumph as Waldo's possession of "Wheelchair." What is sad is that we are asked to cheer for Farnham.

The Moon Is a Harsh Mistress is a bloated novel of the successful Lunar Revolution of 2076, in which Earth's first colony frees itself from the tyranny of a troubled and decaying planet that can no longer feed its teeming billions. The revolution is planned, directed and largely executed by a sentient super-computer named Mike.

At the end of the story, after the revolution is won, the computer falls silent. It has been bombed. Speculation is made as to whether it has lost its sense of self-awareness.

> Why doesn't he wake up? Can a machine be so frightened and hurt that it will go into catatonia and refuse to respond? While ego crouches inside, aware but never willing to risk it?

But the only explanation of the novel that makes sense—an explanation never suggested by Heinlein, but convincing in terms of the structure of the novel, and even more convincing in view of Heinlein's convictions and preoccupations—is that the machine has done what it set out to do in the first place, insure its own survival, and now has chosen to fall silent. "Mathematicians, peasants, and animals, that's all there is . . ." Why should the best mathematician in existence choose to communicate with peasants and animals unless there is a specific reason?

Heinlein's last novel, *I Will Fear No Evil*, is an unpleasant place to visit. No one, to our knowledge, except its publishers, has had a good word to say for it. It is even more bloated than *The Moon Is a Harsh Mistress*, and stands next in length among Heinlein's published work to *Stranger in a Strange Land*.

I Will Fear No Evil is about a dying 95-year-old billionaire who has his brain transplanted into the body of his 28-year-old female secretary. Her mind remains behind—somehow—and the two spend the rest of the book agreeing with each other interminably. The character gets himself/herself pregnant by a sperm bank deposit that the billionaire has put away in better days. After a year, they marry their 72-year-old lawyer and lover. The lawyer dies of a stroke and his mind joins the other two.

In this story, set in the early years of the next century, Earth is an unredeemed sinkhole. There are seven billion people in the world. Illiteracy is more common than literacy. Armed guards are necessary everywhere. City centers are officially "Abandoned Areas" where the law no longer applies.

None of this is described directly. In fact, in this long long book, very little at all is described directly. Eyes are averted throughout to avoid looking at the hell. Instead, we are given our information in conversation, monolog and dialog, and in collages at the beginnings of chapters. Here is one small excerpt from one long example of many:

> Peace Negotiations, both in Paris and Montevideo, continued as before. Fighting continued on a token basis, and the dead did not complain. Harvard's new president was dismissed by the student government, which then adjourned without appointing a successor. The Secretary of H.E.W. announced a plan to increase the water content

of San Francisco Bay to 37%; the Rivers & Harbors Commission denied that H.E.W. had jurisdiction.

Etc., etc., etc., to the point of pain and nausea.

The lawyer says this about the state of the world:

> "We've reached an impasse; we can't go on the way we're headed —and we can't go back—and we're dying in our own poisons. That's why that little Lunar colony has *got* to survive. Because *we* can't. It isn't the threat of war, or crime in the streets, or corruption in high places, or pesticides or smog, or 'education' that doesn't teach; those things are just symptoms of the underlying cancer. It's too many people."

The billionaire, too, has given up on the world. He says that forty years before—which is to say, in our recent past—he ran for office and lost:

> "They *clobbered* me, Jake!—and I've never been tempted to save the world since. Maybe someone can save this addled planet but *I* don't know how and now I *know* that I don't know."

All that he/they are prepared to do now is survive. They have a billion dollars, and that has bought the billionaire his brain transplant. Now they use their dollars to take them to the moon and the hope of safety.

However, when they have reached the moon, the body dies in childbirth. And this is how the book ends:

> (Jake? Eunice?) (Here, Boss! Grab on! There! We've got you.) (Is it a boy or a girl?) (Who cares, Johann—it's a baby! 'One for all and all for one!')
> An old world vanished and then there was none.

9. The Ultimate Confrontation

Now, at last, we are prepared to look at the possibilities suggested by the news of Robert Heinlein's new novel, *Time Enough for Love: The Lives of Lazarus Long.* His longest book ever. His first new book since *I Will Fear No Evil.* "A profound and prophetic story that ranges over twenty-three centuries and countless light years of space."

The question is whether *Time Enough for Love* will prove to be as bad a book as *Farnham's Freehold* or *I Will Fear No Evil*, or whether it will be the true success that Heinlein approached again and again in his pre-war stories but was unable to achieve then. Will *Time Enough for Love* be one more saddening disaster or will it be a triumph? Heinlein has been evading a vital confrontation all these many years —in his fiction, a confrontation by his characters of frightening High Ones; in his life, a confrontation with the deepest and truest sources of his inner being. If the confrontation is present in *Time Enough for Love*, the book will be a success. If it is not, the book will be 640 pages of sadness, grief, weariness and tragedy.

But, first, let us try to determine if true success is possible at all. Is it possible to know the true meaning of life? Does life have a point? Has Heinlein been wasting his time all these years in a fruitless and futile quest?

It is impossible to prove whatever answers we give to these questions to the final satisfaction of anyone who has not himself set out on Heinlein's quest and returned with *knowledge* of the matter. But, perhaps, an indication is possible in the posing and the answering of three central questions. Not proof, but indication.

First, are things in our world as finally desperate and without hope as Heinlein has painted them in *Farnham's Freehold*, *The Moon Is a Harsh Mistress*, and *I Will Fear No Evil*? Is life without meaning except for temporary survival? Are we as doomed as the helpless characters in "The Year of the Jackpot"?

Second, is the fictional solution that Heinlein has never been able to bring himself to write possible for anyone to write?

Third, can a man of Heinlein's age, who has been trapped as long as Heinlein has been trapped, who has been as desperate and hopeless as Heinlein has been, make a successful evolution to a happier state and the certain knowledge that Heinlein has never had?

Let us answer these, one by one.

First, the objective situation of our world. This is a thorny problem. Things are not well with us. Only a few years ago, we ourselves were every bit as uncertain as Heinlein. It seemed to us then that if we continued as we have been headed, that no more than twenty-five years remained to us before we ran into a brick wall.

That still might be said. If we do not change, we will die. But this is the state that precedes any moment of evolution: Change, or die. The situation is only hopeless if the possibility of evolution is denied.

For whatever confirmation they lend, here are some remarks by the professor of electrical engineering, Leonard Lewin, in the introduction to his recent anthology *The Diffusion of Sufi Ideas in the West*:

> In the incredibly complicated and ever more rapidly changing setting which is today's world, many traditional values are now seriously under challenge, while new ones vie for support. To most observers it is far from clear what it is that is taking place: what fresh patterns of human thought and activity may be emerging from the matrix of mankind's vast evolutionary past. When the present upheaval which is beginning to manifest in social and cultural unrest, both national and international, has finally disclosed the true nature of the world of tomorrow, we can all then participate in that knowledge of the further evolution of the human state . . .
>
> What does the caterpillar know of the destiny of the butterfly? . . . A butterfly does not look at all like a caterpillar, yet it is, in some sense, the inevitable eventual form that it must take. Mankind is now preparing to emerge from the chrysalis. Not his physical form, but the quality of his consciousness is about to undergo a transformation to a new condition long latent within. The protective casing which must be breached is a mental prison-shell compounded of vanity, self-love, self-deceit, greed, mental arrogance, prejudice, selfishness, and years and years of conditioning.
>
> In all cultures, and at all times, a few, a very few, individuals have been able to free themselves and have helped others also to escape. Now this opportunity is being made available to all who are able to perceive its reality. The social turmoil of our times can be seen as an external manifestation of this process. The analogy to the caterpillar's transformation is a weak one because it is too *superficial*.

This certainly opens the possibility of an alternative to Heinlein's unhappy conviction.

Second, the possibility of the fictional solution that Heinlein has not been able to write. Here is one such that seems appropriate.

It is a confrontation from Ursula Le Guin's 1968 novel, *A Wizard of Earthsea*, in which a young man's worst demons prove to be himself and are conquered by the surrender of attachment to ego:

> At first it was shapeless, but as it drew nearer it took on the look of a man. An old man it seemed, grey and grim, coming towards Ged; but even as Ged saw his father the smith in that figure, he saw that it was not an old man but a young one. It was Jasper: Jasper's insolent handsome young face, and silver-clasped grey cloak, and stiff stride. Hateful was the look he fixed on Ged across the dark intervening air. Ged did not stop, but slowed his pace, and as he went forward he raised his staff up a little higher. It brightened, and in its light the look of Jasper fell from the figure that approached, and it became Pechvarry. But Pechvarry's face was all bloated and pallid like the face of a drowned man, and he reached out his hand strangely as if beckoning. Still Ged did not stop, but went forward, though there were only a few yards left between them now. Then the thing that faced him changed utterly, spreading out to either side as if it opened enormous thin wings, and it writhed, and swelled, and shrank again. Ged saw in it for an instant Skiorh's white face, and then a pair of clouded, staring eyes, and then suddenly a fearful face he did not know, man or monster, with writhing lips and eyes that were like pits going back into black emptiness.
>
> At that Ged lifted up the staff high, and the radiance of it brightened intolerably, burning with so white and great a light that it compelled and harrowed even that ancient darkness. In that light all form of man sloughed off the thing that came towards Ged. It drew together and shrank and blackened, crawling on four short taloned legs upon the sand. But still it came forward, lifting up to him a blind unformed snout without lips or ears or eyes. As they came right together it became utterly black in the white mage-radiance that burned about it, and it heaved itself upright. In silence, man and shadow met face to face, and stopped.
>
> Aloud and clearly, breaking that old silence, Ged spoke the shadow's name, and in the same moment the shadow spoke without lips or tongue, saying the same word: "Ged." And the two voices were one voice.
>
> Ged reached out his hands, dropping his staff, and took hold of his shadow, of the black self that reached out to him. Light and darkness met, and joined, and were one.

In the immediate next moment, as confirmation of the success of this confrontation, the sands drop away from beneath Ged's very feet and he finds himself afloat in the living sea. He is reborn from this confrontation as a man who is more than a man, as a wizard, eventually the master wizard of his world.

Thus, we do have the result that Heinlein has never been able to honestly achieve in any story.

Now to address our third question: Is it possible for a man of Heinlein's age to successfully achieve the evolution that Heinlein has so long deferred?

We may look, for our example, at a man not altogether unlike Robert Heinlein, a man who was at the outset of his career the premier writer of science fiction in his own day—H.G. Wells. When he died in 1946, H.G. Wells had been famous for fifty years. His first fame came with science fiction novels like *The Time Machine* and *The War of the Worlds*.

Thereafter, Wells wrote utopias and dystopias, contemporary novels, *The Outline of History* and *The Work, Wealth and Happiness of Mankind*. Wells raised himself from a poor excluded Cockney boy by means of education and he made his mature dedication to education of others—not altogether unlike Heinlein. Therefore the utopias and dystopias that he wrote—visions and warnings. Therefore the novels of people rising or falling in society. Therefore *The Outline of History*. Therefore *The Work, Wealth and Happiness of Mankind*.

But before he died so many years later in 1946, Wells had ceased to be listened to. Everyone knew by then what he had to say, and no one was reading him closely. Conventional wisdom says that as he grew old, Wells necessarily realized that the situation of mankind had become more desperate while he was futilely attempting to point the way. He had aimed at changing all mankind, and he had failed. Again, not unlike Heinlein.

Wells became more and more bitter, and less and less relevant. At last, nearly eighty, he wrote a final book entitled *Mind at the End of Its Tether*, a notorious book, the last senile ravings of a man whose work and world had failed. And then he died.

Everyone who mentions *Mind at the End of Its Tether* speaks slightingly of it. Lewis Mumford has described it in this fashion:

"Written when Wells's mind was itself collapsing and projecting its own situation into the world; but significantly fulfilling Chesterton's prediction that Wells's philosophy must end in despair."

That's a futile end for a man famous for fifty years. But it takes account of only half the truth, and not the best half. There is a better story in Wells than this one.

It is true that by 1946, Wells was more honored than respected. He was dismissed by reviewers who filtered blurred and hasty readings through their own preconceptions. Wells was read by few and understood by nobody.

Mind at the End of Its Tether is not a bulky book. It is a pamphlet of 34 pages bound with a companion pamphlet, *The Happy Turning: A Dream of Life*. These pamphlets are short and loosely printed, and written in a simple and idiomatic English. Yet, somehow, the true nature of *Mind at the End of Its Tether* has never been recognized by anyone who has ever mentioned it, and *The Happy Turning* is never ever mentioned.

H.G. Wells was a remarkable man. He continued to grow at an age when most men have abandoned growth. At an age when book reviewers no longer expect growth. At an age when only the best among us continue to grow—those with the perception, the imagination, the self-knowledge, the honor and the courage to pursue the possibilities of being human all their lives. If Wells did not change all mankind, he did change himself.

Mind at the End of Its Tether and *The Happy Turning* are H.G. Wells's announcement of his own evolution. They are, perhaps, an early glimpse of the same change in the human state to which Leonard Lewin refers in the passages we have quoted from *The Diffusion of Sufi Ideas in the West*. Wells, who had been seeking his own evolution as diligently as Heinlein, was among the first to announce the new vision. And *then* he died. This is a very different story from the conventional one.

Mind at the End of Its Tether begins by expressing total despair with man as he is, that poor doomed futile creature. His present troubles, says Wells, are only a sample of those that will end the race of man-as-he-is. This is what was taken for senile collapse by Wells's critics. But the essay then predicts a better race of man to come, a quantum jump, as man made a quantum jump to become man, or life to become life. The best of us will make that jump.

Mind at the End of Its Tether is an objective argument—man is doomed. He will only survive by changing radically. *The Happy Turning* is an account of a mystical dream of the farther side of the quantum jump. It concludes:

> So we found ourselves in agreement that the human mind may be in a phase of transition to a new fearless, clear-headed way of living in which understanding will be the supreme interest in life, and beauty a mere smile of approval. So it is in any rate in the Dreamland to which my particular Happy Turning takes me. There shines a world "beyond good and evil," and there, in a universe completely conscious of itself, Being achieves its end.

In his final days, Wells made a quantum jump of his own, a final successful identification of himself with the evolutionary course of all Being.

And so we have our indications. Yes, an alternative vision of man's future is possible. Yes, a successful fictional confrontation with the hatefulness and limitation of the human ego is possible. Yes, a final personal identification of oneself with the evolutionary course of all Being is possible.

Heinlein is not damned.

Time Enough for Love: The Lives of Lazarus Long may be the completely successful personal adventure that Heinlein has never been able to envision.

Time Enough for Love may be a wretched book. It will be if it is a picaresque, episodic novel, filled with heavy-handed philosophic pronunciamentos in place of honest confrontation. If its great size is bloat. If "time enough" means continuance rather than evolution. If love is confused with sex. In that case, it will not be profound. It will be a desperately bad book.

Time Enough for Love will be a good book only if the confrontation that Heinlein has always avoided is made, if it is made on the right grounds, with the right question asked and answered in the right way. But what evidence do we have that such a happy conclusion may occur? What reason do we have to think that *now*, after all that has occurred, Robert Heinlein may be ready to make his move, to come to terms with life and the universe? What grounds do we have for hope?

In part, the hope of a successful confrontation is dependent on *I Will Fear No Evil* and its conclusion. But that conclusion, at least for us, is enigmatic.

The three minds in the single body survive in some sense, even though the body died. That is clear. Jake and Eunice reach through from some safe place and grab hold of Johann. But from where? Do they all three pass into the body of the new-born baby? That is not clear. Reincarnation would be an avoidance, but is what we are reading an instance of reincarnation? We are not sure.

The last line of the book is:

"An old world vanished and then there was none."

No replacement of the old world. Perhaps not reincarnation, then. Perhaps, just perhaps, the intimation of life after death, but not the survival of the ego. All this approached in a long long book in which, throughout, almost nothing is seen. The narrator's eyes are pinched tight. Perhaps to make the approach to the conclusion easier.

Perhaps. And perhaps not.

So let us pass on.

Since *I Will Fear No Evil* was finished, Robert Heinlein has suffered a major illness. He was gravely ill with peritonitis. He underwent major surgery and he was on the order of a year or more in recovery. Once again, as in the Thirties, Heinlein has walked through the valley of the shadow of death. And he survived. The question is, on what terms? The title of his previous book—and titles have always been extremely significant in Heinlein's work—was a promise that though he might walk in death's shadow, Heinlein would fear no evil.

For Heinlein to fear no evil from death means, it would seem, a willingness to surrender ego—that which fears death. Since Heinlein did survive, it seems possible that he has let go his grip on himself. That he did surrender ego.

The size of *Time Enough for Love* is of interest. To be sure, it is possible to have a fiction with a successful confrontation with the demonic that is quite short. "By His Bootstraps" might have been such a story, for instance. But for Heinlein, it is quite possible that an honest conclusion took much circling, much building up to. Certainly, a book of this great size coming now is at least evidence of Heinlein's intense seriousness.

The range of this new large book is also of interest: "twenty-three centuries and countless light years of space." Recent Heinlein novels have taken place in much more constricted areas—freeholds, and the surrounds of a computer, and the inside of a head crowded with people. We might say, too, that these novels have been constricted by the limits of Heinlein's fears. In *Farnham's Freehold*, *The Moon Is a Harsh Mistress*, and *I Will Fear No Evil*, nothing but fear, trouble and insanity have been given leave to exist. It hardly seems possible that the entire span of twenty-three centuries and countless light years of space can be a time of trouble. We seem to have the promise of new horizons. A freeing of the spirit to roam widely again.

Time Enough for Love is also a return to the Future History, so long laid aside. Lazarus Long, Heinlein's protagonist, is the very meat of the Future History. In spite of the shadow cast upon it by Nehemiah Scudder, the Future History was the story of a happier future than any Heinlein has been able to envision lately. Would Heinlein now do violence to his own conceptions? Or is his return to the Future History a fulfillment of what could not be fulfilled thirty years ago?

Lazarus Long, even more than most Heinlein protagonists, was obviously a Heinlein surrogate. He was born about Heinlein's time, and he promised to continue forever until he discovered what life was for. In this story, he continues for at least twenty-three centuries. Has he indeed discovered what Heinlein needs for him to discover? Has Heinlein brought him back to life because he can finally put period to him?

The original conclusion of *Methuselah's Children* was clearly unsatisfactory. Turning away from the search and coming home for dinner is not an answer.

But neither was the altered conclusion of the 1958 book version of *Methuselah's Children* satisfactory. Confrontation is recognized to be necessary, but confrontation is postponed. Perhaps for a thousand years:

> "Someday, about a thousand years from now, I intend to march straight into the temple of Kreel, look him in the eye, and say, 'Howdy, bub—what do *you* know that I don't know?' "

The question is, on what grounds might Lazarus Long successfully walk into the temple of Kreel? Or to put it another way, what went wrong the first time? What *really* happened on the first voyage of the starship *New Frontiers*?

Lazarus Long fears, resents and envies the gods of the Jockaira, these creatures he would confront. He finds their indifference intolerable, and he would make them notice him and acknowledge him as an equal.

But in fact, the gods of the Jockaira are not indifferent at all. In fact, as Heinlein says without noticing, they treat mankind as man might treat a baby bird, placing it tenderly (and casually) where it belongs.

These gods reject man as unfit for the blessing that Heinlein seeks. The problem of Heinlein and Lazarus Long is ego. The gods of the Jockaira, doing what is needful rather than what is flattering, send Long and the others where they need to go in order to learn to lose their egos. This is the planet of the Little People.

The Little People adopt one adult human into their group mind. They make genetic improvements in one human baby. These portents of loss of ego and evolution—of merger and alteration—are too much for Lazarus Long to contemplate and he must flee back to the safety of Earth. Either for a bowl of chili or for the thought of another confrontation in a thousand years.

Again and again, the prospect of loss of ego has been too much for Heinlein to accept. But again and again, he has been forced by its attractions into making it his subject. Even to the point that he must portray it as an ever more awful evil in "Lost Legacy," and in *The Puppet Masters*, and in *Starship Troopers*.

It is his attachment to his ego that is the twist in Heinlein's limb.

The road of Lazarus Long to the temple of Kreel and his confrontation with the gods of the Jockaira lies through the planet of the Little People.

Time Enough for Love will be a true and honest success only if that road is finally taken.

Love has never been a Heinlein theme. That is because love is the absence of ego.

It is past time for Heinlein to love.

The title *Time Enough for Love* is intensely meaningful. But does this book merely request even yet more time—as *Methuselah's Children* did? Or does it mean that the time for love is now?

Is *Time Enough for Love* to be merely *"If This Goes On—"* one more time? Or are we finally to have the unwritten story, "Da Capo," that Heinlein promised so long ago?

By all means, let the time be *now*.

Let time lose its finitude, its horror, its finality now. Let there be an infinity of time. Let there be eternity, honestly won.

Because the door that Heinlein has sought, the door from which his gaze has been averted, the door to which ego has blinded him, is this:

Love is the source of evolution.

Love is the power that lifts the human heart.

Love is the secret of the universe, revealed at last.

And where love is, time is eternity.

—February 1973

12/ "FOUND IN SPACE," by R. MONROE WEEMS

[*Amazing*, April 1974]

Once upon a time, there was a community of giant mutant chipmunks, furry and blue, living in an abandoned basement in a great spaceship lost between the stars. One day, without any explanation that they could think of, they found a human baby in their midst. Pinned to his diaper was a note that said: "Cheep-cheep 3:16—'The wider world awaits,' " which was a quotation from the sacred scriptures in which they no longer believed.

They marveled at this miracle. For as they used to say to each other, giving the main bulkhead a rap with their furry knuckles: "What could be more solid? We know what we know."

However, they were generous folk and more than a little afraid of this infant creature they could not understand, with his absurd message, so they determined to raise the misfit foundling as one of their own, and never to tell him how ugly he was. They named him Francis X. Cheep-cheep, after the evangelist, and they put him in the good hands of a sweet old mom and dad who raised him as though he were one of their own litter. His legacy was lost, thrown into the nearest wastepaper basket.

Frank was given the best education his society had to offer. He was taken on field trips to the ends of the universe. He was made acquainted with all the dimensions of the world. He was a bright and able lad, and he prospered.

Oh, he had the usual troubles in growing up. He yearned for his mom and resented his dad, who was a bit heavy-handed. And once he fought with young Meeper Blue, who told him he was adopted. But boys will be boys, his bites soon healed, as did Meeper's, and they were friends thereafter. Once he called nasty old Mrs. Snidely names and had to be punished. And finally there was the period when he had his problems in confronting his father and leaving home.

But when he did grow up, he rose to the top. He invented a mechanical currycomb. He invented a superior new waste-disposal system that *blooped* junk, trash and other crap into nowhere in particular. He invented other machines and made millions. On the side, he was a mean fighter, a cool jiver, a sweet singer, and a bad dude. But in his success, he remembered his friends like Meeper Blue, and he paid honor to his mom and his dad.

But with all this success, money and fame, Francis X. Cheep-cheep wasn't happy. He ought to have been. Everyone told him that if *they* had what *he* had, *they'd* be happy.

But he wasn't. He kept feeling that there was something else he ought to be doing, if only he could remember what it was. He felt threatened by nameless terrors. He slept badly. That doesn't sound like much, but it was awful. Every time he started to feel good, really good, along would come a nameless terror and wipe him out.

Part of it was that there was nothing left to do, nothing that was worth doing. Life was as confining as a goldfish bowl. He looked around him at his society and it seemed a shuck. Anything anybody else could do, he could do, and he knew it. Life seemed pointless, a cosmic joke.

"There has to be more than this, beyond this limited horizon," he said. "If life has any meaning—and if it doesn't, why live?—there has to be more to it than this."

But he looked around him and there was nothing more. After all, *rap*, *rap*, what could be more solid?

He let his mind wander in search of an answer, but the places his mind wandered were bad places, and in those bad places he found only more nameless terrors. Wow, bad!—stuff like falling through space forever and ever, never fetching up against a bulkhead.

Something had to give way. The situation was intolerable. And, one day, something did give way.

Frank was visiting his dear old mom and dad, and he happened to look in a mirror. He looked in the mirror. He looked at mom and dad. He looked back into the mirror again.

Something was clearly wrong.

"Aargh," he cried, leaped upon his dad and bit him severely on the thigh. It was something he had always longed to do.

They came and took him away to an institution for bewildered chipmunks like himself so that he could do no one harm until he recovered his senses. Meeper Blue was his doctor. They felt an important person like Francis X. Cheep-cheep would feel more comfortable in the capable hands of someone he knew.

"I see through it all now," Frank said. "None of this is real but me. You can end the sequence at any time. Wrap it up and put a ribbon around it and put it in the disposal! None of this is real. None of this is reasonable."

"Hmm . ." said Dr. Meeper Blue, in a serious and professional way. "Why do you say that, Frank?"

Frank leaped up and flicked on the water tap next to the disposal system. "Is *this* reasonable?" he asked. "Why should water spring forth out of the wall at a touch? It isn't natural."

Meeper noted his words, wrote them down, read them over, and then nodded to himself. Then he looked up at Frank.

"Why not?" he asked judiciously. "Water has always come out of a tap, just like that. Why should it be any different now just because you aren't feeling yourself?"

Frank snorted. "I knew you'd say that. It's *plausible*, and you want me to believe in plausibility. But I won't. I refuse to believe in plausibility any longer. It violates common sense."

"Hmm . ." said Meeper, and noted it all down.

"Or how about this? All around me I see this elaborate facade— bulkheads, schools, nuts, currycombs, chipmunks. What is it for? What is life for? All I can see is chipmunks working to live, living to work, working to live, living to work, ad infinitum. That's pointless ninnygaggle."

"Shucks, Frank. I have bad days when it looks like that to me, too. You're going to die someday. Get fun out of life while you can. You'll feel a lot better when you go back to work."

"You'd better be careful how you talk to me, or I'll bite you on the thigh, too!"

"Sorry, Frank."

"You're just saying that, but you don't mean it. I can tell. I know the truth now. All this spigglemorphing nonsense exists for just one reason. To keep me distracted so I won't be able to remember. But the truth is that *I'm not like you!*"

At these words, Meeper Blue averted his eyes.

"Yes. Ha. Gotcha. You're more or less real. You're one of *them.* Most of you aren't even that much. I know that now. Empty counters, automatons, automatic pieces, zombies. But you, you were assigned to me at the outset to see that I didn't remember."

"It isn't that way, Frank. Really. It isn't that way at all."

"That's what you say," Frank scored triumphantly.

Meeper sighed and set down his notebook.

"Now, Frank, it is true that you are ugly, and we've all done our best not to rub it in. But it's natural. I mean, you were *adopted.* But you can be helped. New surgical techniques have been developed since you were a squeaker. If it bothers you so much—and we've all gotten used to it—we'll fix you up. Heaven knows, you're rich enough. You should be happy . . . And you can afford this kind of work if anyone can.

"Your sweet old mom and dad have signed the papers. We weren't going to tell you. We were going to let the fur and tail transplants be a surprise. But probably it's better that you should know now."

Frank looked at Meeper Blue and chittered in wonderment. He was two feet taller than Meeper or any other chipmunk. He was furless (except for lank drapings on his head and fuzzy patches elsewhere). He had no tail. He wasn't blue.

There was an unbridgeable gulf between them. How had he accepted it for so long? How had he ever accepted it?

They had told him that he was like them. They had seemed not to notice how ugly he was. They . . . And he had craved popularity and social acceptance.

He had been a fool. He felt like a stranger alone in a strange land.

Frank said: "You mean you aren't going to dismantle the sequence?"

"No, Frank."

"But I've seen through you now."

"No, Frank."

Dr. Meeper Blue stood. "I think that's enough for now. We're making real progress, Frank. Real progress. We'll see how things look to you after the operation. *I* think we'll have you out of here in no time at all. The nurse will be here in a few minutes, swinging her bushy little tail behind her, to give you your shot. You'll like her. She's a real—*chht, chht*—sweetiepie."

He winked. "And when you wake, you won't be ugly anymore."

Meeper went out of the room. Frank didn't bother to say goodbye.

Instead, he occupied himself with his thoughts. The prime datum of existence was himself, Francis X. Cheep-cheep. He was sure of that. They had told him clumsy lies, that he had but a few short years of life behind him, a few short years to anticipate. But that was wrong, and he knew it. This space of time was but a tiny phase in his experience. He was sure of his continuity.

"I'm not going to die. I may be a closed curve, but closed or open, I neither have a beginning nor an end," he said aloud to himself. "That for you, Meeper Blue."

But the prospect of the operations frightened him. What if they made him forget? What if he had to start all over again to work out the truth?

There was a discreet tap at the door.

"Yoo-hoo, Mr. Cheep-cheep," came the voice of a real sweetiepie. "Are you decent?"

He heard the words as "you who?" and they struck him to the heart. He was galvanized into action.

"I am Francis X. Cheep-cheep," he said. "And I will not forget!"

He crossed the room in a bound, fed himself into the disposal system of his own invention, pressed the handle, and *blooped* elsewhere. It gave him great joy to do it.

He landed on a great pile of crap, trash, and other miscellaneous junk. As he strove to get his bearings, a nutshell materialized in the air above him, plinked him sharply on the noggin, and bounced away down the slope.

He followed its progress with his eye. He was in the largest room he had ever seen, spherical, well-lit, fully two hundred feet across. The surface of the sphere was frosted gold. Through the center of the sphere ran a roadway of metal latticework. At the very heart of the sphere, a band of something encircled the roadway.

The heap of trash he sat upon rested on the roadway not far from the central ring—that part of the trash that had not spilled over and fallen far far to the surface of the sphere below. The nutshell fell down down down to join the garbage below. It was the greatest unbroken distance he had ever seen, and it made him giddy to look.

And it was then that Frank realized an incredible fact. He had traveled *outside the universe*—and he still lived!

He brimmed over. He nearly fainted.

But there was something somehow familiar, elusively familiar, about this place. He scrambled down the slope of trash as carefully as possible, sending only a few small avalanches of this and that careening over the edge and down to the golden surface below. At last he reached the roadway.

He was drawn to the central ring around the roadway. The frame of the ring was some transparent material. A variety of dials and gauges were inset into the framework so that they might be read by one standing on the roadway. And in front of Frank's eyes there was a red button asking to be pressed.

Insisting to be pressed.

Demanding to be pressed.

He had to press it. He could not help himself. He must. He must. He was governed by irresistible impulse.

He pressed the button.

Instantly, the light around him failed. The surface of the golden globe became transparent (except where the pile of trash, junk and random crap rested).

Frank saw the larger universe outside the ship!

He hung alone in nothingness. He was surrounded by deepness. He saw the stars! (Except where the garbage impeded the view.) It was too much. It was too much!

This vision was one of those nameless terrors that had haunted him all his life. It had been terrifying in dreams, and it was terrifying now.

He screamed and stabbed at the button to turn the vision off.

He fell to his knees and cried with the agony of it all. He grokked wrongness.

Then he heard a sigh. Not his own sigh, but a sigh like the tolling of a bell.

"Garbage," a voice said. "Garbage all over my frosted golden globe. That will really be a mess to clean up. You really screwed up this time, didn't you? Garbage isn't what the machine is for."

Frank looked up, but the radiant glory of the figure standing before him was too much for him and he had to look away again. He felt stabbed with the sharp knife of emotions that were too powerful for him, emotions he was no more fitted to experience than a clam to play a tuba. Waves of weariness, tragedy and grief swept over him like a shitstorm.

With eyes averted, he said, "W-who are you?"

"R. Monroe Weems. Who do you think you are?"

"I'm Francis X. Cheep-cheep."

"Wrong, Bob," said the great glorious personage. "You've forgotten yourself again. You are not Francis X. Cheep-cheep."

"But it's all I know. It's the one thing I'm certain of."

The figure sighed once more, a sigh that rang in the ears of Francis X. Cheep-cheep like the sound of doom.

"You haven't done what you were assigned to do. You are supposed to use the Machine to lead those chipmunks out of that blasted basement they huddle in and show them the stars. Not for a *garbage disposal*. Not just to pop about by yourself like a silly tourist. You have a job to do and you still haven't done it. Will you never learn?

"Well, you'll just have to go all the way back to the beginning one more time and try to do it over. My boy, you *know* you have a great future in front of you if you can only forget this Francis X. Cheep-cheep nonsense and *remember* yourself."

A great future.

A great future!

So Francis X. Cheep-cheep had his answer. He was a closed curve. (Or was he?)

But a lot of good it did him to know it.

When the chipmunks found the baby boy in their midst, there was a note pinned to his diaper.

It said:

"Cheep-cheep 3:16—'The wider world awaits.' (Save this note for future reference.)"

Part IV: The Renewal of SF

13/ RETROSPECTION

[*Fantasy and Science Fiction*, December 1974]

We are passing through a time of retrospection. An era is ending and we are looking again at our recent past as though it were a mirror in which we could see both what we have been and what we are about to be.

Speaking specifically, it is possible to buy Shirley Temple dolls and Mickey Mouse watches. Pulp magazines like *Black Mask* and *Weird Tales* are available again, as though this were 1939. The June 1938 issue of *Action Comics* and the May 1939 issue of *Detective Comics*, which presented the first appearances of Superman and Batman, are available in over-size reprint editions. Also available in reprint are EC comics from the early Fifties like *The Haunt of Fear* No. 12 and *Weird Science* No. 15.

Bette Davis, John Garfield and Mae West movies are being shown on television. We are offered records containing the best work of the Andrews Sisters, Cab Calloway and Elvis Presley.

Suddenly, as though the Earth had swung into a time-node of retrospection, the movies, comic books, music and stories which are the fossil record of where our minds have been these past forty-five years are being made available to us, and we are paying attention to them.

This great re-examination includes science fiction. We are now seeing histories of science fiction appear in England, France and the United States. Terry Carr is embarked on a project to place the best stories of various years in the past of science fiction in appropriate volumes so that they may be seen in context.

It is no mere random coincidence that the four books under review here—one book of bibliography and three collections of science fiction stories from the Thirties—should all have been published in the spring of 1974. Their appearance is timely.

The good work of establishing the foundations of science fiction bibliography and reference has been most effectively carried out up to the present moment by fan compilers and fan publishers. One of the best such works has been Donald H. Tuck's *A Handbook of Science Fiction and Fantasy*, self-published in Hobart, Tasmania. The most recent edition appeared in 1959 in two legal-size mimeographed paper-bound volumes.

Now the first volume of a new edition has appeared from Advent, calling itself *The Encyclopedia of Science Fiction and Fantasy*, and deserving the title. It is a large hardcover book, handsomely bound and printed in double columns. More information is contained in the new first volume than in the entirety of the previous edition.

The *Encyclopedia* presents biographical and bibliographical entries for authors of science fiction. Also for authors of single works of science fiction and materials of related interest.

There are entries for Asimov and Heinlein. There are entries for Dickens, for Aldous Huxley, for Julian Huxley and for L. Frank Baum. Italo Calvino, Truman Capote and Al Capp are all here. So are Lafferty and Le Guin, Geis and Gernsback.

This book is both a culmination and a first step. It is easily the broadest, most ambitious and most professionally conceived and executed work of science fiction scholarship and publishing that we have ever seen. It will necessarily become a standard library reference tool. It is an epitome of fan publishing, so significant that we wonder if Advent will be able to publish it and remain the same Sunday-afternoon publisher they have been.

At the same time, it is partial and incomplete. We have here only the first of three volumes—covering work only through 1968. More recent work is ignored and more recent writers omitted.

Even in its evident incompleteness, however, the *Encyclopedia* is a treasure. If you have an interest in sf, you will find it well worth its price of $20. Buy it, or ask your library to buy it.

When the first science fiction anthologies were published after World War II, they tended to concentrate on work from the Campbell Era—stories by writers like Heinlein, van Vogt, Padgett and Asimov. The earliest anthologies contained a few stories from the Thirties, but by comparison with later work these seemed crude, unrigorous and verbose. When it was possible to offer "By His Bootstraps" and "Nightfall" for the first time to a book-reading audience, there seemed no point in presenting "Tumithak of the Corridors" or "The Brain Stealers of Mars."

The anthologies that followed concentrated increasingly on contemporary material. Through the Sixties, only a handful of musty stories and novels from the Thirties saw republication.

A young reader coming to science fiction could be totally ignorant of the special qualities of the sf of the Thirties. He could only imagine the "sense of wonder" that older readers like Sam Moskowitz claimed was missing from more recent work.

Now we have before us a book edited by Isaac Asimov, *Before the Golden Age*—twenty-five stories from the Thirties. Because the sf of the Thirties was, in fact, crude, unrigorous and verbose, this is one of the longest science fiction anthologies ever published.

It is a mark of the change of attitude toward science fiction and of the personal prestige of Asimov that this book could be published now. It could not have been published earlier.

Before the Golden Age came into being in a flash of intuition. Asimov, who says that he almost never remembers his dreams, awoke on the morning of April 3, 1973 from a dream in which he had made up an anthology of all the good old sf stories he had read and loved as a kid:

> Simply talking about it filled me, quite suddenly, with a burning urge to do it. I've had these burning urges before, and I know it means I will have to do it at once regardless of any commitments I may have.

Asimov did well to follow his burning urge. *Before the Golden Age* is a book that needed doing, and only a man like Asimov—or perhaps Heinlein—could have the clout and the personal investment of love necessary to produce an anthology like this.

Before the Golden Age is presented as autobiography. There are thirty thousand words of Asimov and his youth to serve as a context for presenting these stories. They cover the period from 1931, when Asimov was eleven and reading the science fiction magazines on the newsstand in his father's Brooklyn candy store, to 1939, when he was a senior at Columbia and had himself begun to write and sell sf.

This book is Asimov's life. These are the stories that impressed him. There is no second-guessing. He has not included stories, like those of Campbell in his Don A. Stuart guise, that Asimov was too young and unformed to appreciate at the time. He has not included classics like Weinbaum's "A Martian Odyssey" that he happened to miss or overlook at 14. And he has not denied the impact of stories that a more mature Asimov recognizes as morally and stylistically imperfect.

Before the Golden Age is warts-and-all autobiography. It is personal and partial. A similar volume edited by Heinlein would be very different.

The great virtue of this book is that it presents a large representative sample of the sf of the Thirties in chronological order. It allows us to see for ourselves the visible evolution of the genre through the decade. The earliest stories that Asimov presents, like "The Man Who Evolved" by Edmond Hamilton and "Awlo of Ulm" by Captain S.P. Meek, have much the flavor of Burroughs and Merritt and Cummings. They are work left over from an earlier day. On the other hand, later stories like "Minus Planet" by John D. Clark and "The Men and the Mirror" by Ross Rocklynne are harbingers of the rigorous, closely-textured, scientifically-oriented work that Asimov himself came to write.

Some of the work is surprisingly good fun—like Charles R. Tanner's Tumithak stories. Some, like Murray Leinster's "Sidewise in Time" and "Proxima Centauri," present ideas, now old, in their first fresh appearance. Some stories are almost unbearably bad, like Leslie Stone's "The Human Pets of Mars."

The book as a whole is slow going. It is long, almost 1000 pages. The world of mind that it presents is not our contemporary world— the stories talk of another time and place.

In this sense, *Before the Golden Age* is a relic. It will not have much to offer to the reader who picks up science fiction for excitement and casual entertainment.

Readers interested in Isaac Asimov will find more here. So will readers who care about the origin and development of science fiction sufficiently to do their homework. Work it will be, but readers will find themselves rewarded for their trouble.

One small group of readers will find more here—those who would write science fiction. Recent sf has been narrow, pessimistic and unimaginative. *Before the Golden Age* offers an alternative example. This volume illustrates an element that existed in Thirties science fiction and was later misplaced.

There is pessimism here—the last forty-five years as a whole have been one of the most dourly pessimistic periods in the history of civilization. But these stories from the Thirties, for all their limitations in detail, in rigor, in style, for all their chauvinism and xenophobia, for all their fear of devolution, are neither narrow nor unimaginative.

Before the Golden Age shows us men penetrating alien realms and other dimensions in spite of all fear. In contemporary sf the universe is seen as limited and men as victims. A new vision of possibility is in order. *Before the Golden Age* offers significant clues toward imagining new possibility. It is a book that can be learned from.

The Best of Stanley G. Weinbaum offers a different approach to science fiction of the Thirties. It presents twelve short stories by an early master who died in December 1935, only a year and a half after the appearance of his first story.

To readers in the Thirties, Weinbaum was a revelation. He was a Campbell writer before Campbell became editor of *Astounding*. In fact, he was an influence on Campbell, as a comparison of "A Martian Odyssey," the story that first won Weinbaum his high reputation, and Campbell's "The Brain Stealers of Mars," in *Before the Golden Age*, will show. He was witty, a master of style, a sophisticate. Like Zelazny in the Sixties, he was a demonstrator of new possibility.

Heretofore, most modern readers have had no opportunity to perceive Weinbaum for themselves. Nothing by him appeared in the large early anthologies of science fiction. At best we may have seen "A Martian Odyssey" and Weinbaum's novel, *The Black Flame*.

Now, at last, we are given the chance to see Weinbaum in context with this major collection of his short work. It is a revelation. Time has swallowed what were once Weinbaum's particular virtues. What is left seems quaint and quirky.

In the Thirties, Weinbaum was light, compressed, fast. Since his time, standards of lightness, subtlety and speed have been raised to such a point that Weinbaum is no longer a positive model. He has been superseded.

In the Thirties, Weinbaum was enjoyed for his sophisticated handling of male-female relations. At this distance, it now appears that he was deeply ambivalent toward women. In every one of these stories, they appear—compulsively, it seems—as either unobtainable ideal or as the Demonic. In "A Martian Odyssey" a black, writhing, rope-armed horror—the dream-beast—projects an appearance of the narrator's dream girl, Fanny Long, to lure him to destruction. This episode turns out to be more typical of Weinbaum than one could ever have imagined in reading "A Martian Odyssey" alone.

Even in his own time, Weinbaum was a comparatively constricted and mimetic writer. His stories tended to be either contemporary gadget stories with café society characters or nearly plotless romps with alien playfellows on one or another of the planets of our solar system. He was a consolidator rather than an explorer of strange realms or stranger ideas. Read today, Weinbaum seems both frivolous and dated. He does not strain the imagination, as cruder writers like Jack Williamson and Don A. Stuart still do.

Seen in contrast to *Before the Golden Age*, we can see that Weinbaum lacks the expansive, visionary, exploratory quality that is for us the greatest virtue of the period. It is sad to say, but when Asimov introduces "The Parasite Planet" by saying that it hit him with the force of a pile driver and turned him instantly into a Weinbaum idolater, we can only wonder why. The special power to command that Weinbaum once had no longer exists. What is left is, at best, no more than occasionally and tepidly amusing.

Like *Before the Golden Age*, Jacques Sadoul's *Les meilleurs récits de Astounding Stories 1934/37* is a general anthology of Thirties science fiction—eight stories to Asimov's twenty-five. What is most significant about this collection is that Sadoul has not depended on childhood memory for his selections. He has read the magazines of the period with a mature eye and in consequence has mined gold. He has picked over the Tremaine *Astounding* in the years that have been called "the first Golden Era" and found stories typical of the Thirties that still have truth and excitement for a contemporary audience.

The stories Sadoul reprints include "Old Faithful" by Raymond Z. Gallun, also reprinted by Asimov, and "The Lotus Eaters" by Weinbaum. Sadoul also includes one of Williamson's best, "The Galactic Circle," in which a space ship goes far enough and fast enough to leave our universe entirely and enter a larger cosmos, emerging from an atom of a flower in time to see itself originally taking off on its voyage—a startling vision of Oneness. Also included here are "Tryst in Time" by C. L. Moore and "Night" by Don A. Stuart, stories an adolescent Asimov would be unlikely to appreciate.

The translations vary in quality. Clumsy stories are rendered more graceful. Workmanlike prose is adequately served. But the special and idiosyncratic flavor of "Night" is entirely lost.

Sadoul's love for science fiction is apparent and deserves high respect. In the last year, he has published a more extensive history of science fiction than has so far appeared in English and a book of science fiction illustration that is to be republished in this country. The present anthology is the first in a projected series that will include volumes of the best stories from *Amazing* 1926-32, *Wonder Stories* 1929-35, and *Weird Tales* 1930-40.

The present moment of retrospection is apparently not confined to the United States.

We will be both lucky and well-served if an American editor produces a volume as tight and heavy as this neat little collection of stories from *Astounding*.

14/ FICTION AND HUMAN DEVELOPMENT

Like all art, fiction exists as a reminder from ourselves to ourselves of the possibility and the necessity of personal evolution. If we need to be reminded loudly and often that growth is our business, it is because we find it easy to forget when living in the midst of the immediate demands and claims of society. We divert ourselves. We distract ourselves. We cling to what we are and what we have, greedy to keep, afraid to lose. And yet, not quite knowing what we do, we return again and again to fiction to be reminded of true order, value and purpose.

And to the extent that true order, value and purpose are to be found in fiction—found in the very structure of fiction regardless of its particular content and recommendations—fiction serves as a practical guide to life. To serve as a practical education, it is not necessary that fiction should be about familiar circumstances, or even about people, places or things that have ever existed or are ever likely to exist. Fairy tales are not read to children as reportage of existing fact. They are read to children as essential practical education in the moral order of the universe—as truth.

We trap and cheat ourselves if we assume that fiction, in order to be taken seriously, should reflect familiar circumstance, current behavior and present possibility. What we cannot imagine . . . we shall be that. Next to what we cannot imagine, all present social demands and claims must stand revealed as petty and impractical. The true practicality revealed by fiction is evolution, not attachment.

As an analogy, we might consider our human use of fossil fuel supplies. To many men, it has seemed the height of practicality to use these supplies of fuel as though they were endless, to use fuel to find more fuel to make more machines to use more fuel to make more profit to buy more machines to use more fuel . . . We might say instead that it would be true practicality to use our fossil fuel supplies as the means by which to develop self-renewing sources of power, even though these sources do not presently exist, and that it is false "practicality" to use these supplies as final ends in themselves. This set of alternatives might even make the basis of a novel, as similar sets of alternatives have made the bases of a hundred novels.

It is the mistaken, if not wholly unnatural assumption of a child that the condition of adulthood to which he aspires is a single thing, permanent and complete. For all that he knows, his parents were born to be his parents, his teachers were destined to be his teachers, and the policeman who helps him across the street has always been a policeman and always will be. If he is given a biography of a great scientist to read, it will be an account of a far-sighted youngster just waiting for the proper hour to utter his equation of moment and receive the applause of the world.

In fact, however, as adults know, adults are not born, but made, and re-made and re-made again. Over and over through adult life we are faced with critical situations which are too large, complex and difficult to be resolved by the resources of our present selves. The only way these life crises may be successfully met is by personal evolution—that is, by a sudden spurt of growth, by a wild quantum jump in ability that reduces what was previously impossibly difficult to a mere triviality.

In our society, these crises occur with statistical regularity. A man's particular problem may be his own. His particular solutions may be his own. But the same crises seem to happen to most men at the same approximate moments in life, and if successfully surmounted are surmounted in the same way—by an evolutionary leap, a quantum jump.

The first of these crises generally occurs at the age of seventeen to nineteen when childhood ends and adulthood begins. From the child's point of view, the jump to adulthood looks impossible. In fact, the jump is impossible—for a child. To complete the jump successfully, the child must reject his former limited self, stake his life on a new identity, and remake himself and his universe in larger scale. When the child does identify himself with some end beyond the horizon of the childhood world, and loves it wholeheartedly, suddenly what was impossible to children becomes possible to him. He may separate himself from the shelter of his parents. He may take a full-time job. He may join the army. He may marry. He may become a university student.

A second crisis generally occurs in the mid-twenties. Society has encouraged the child to assume a new adult identity—has, indeed, held adulthood out as an end. But, by the mid-twenties, life usually reveals new and larger ends that cannot be contained within the new adult identity of the nineteen-year-old. That is to say, for the student, graduation approaches. For the husband or wife, parenthood. For the worker or soldier, promotion. In order to solve these problems—for their immediate prospect looms as problems of desperate proportion—the person must again expand his horizons. Again, he must change and become someone new. Again, he must evolve by rejecting his former limited self, by identifying himself with higher purposes, remaking himself and his universe to larger scale.

The person then ceases to be an apprentice adult, a mere man among children, and becomes a journeyman, a man accepted among men. He who passes this crisis generally is not only able to encompass the entire basic range of adult behaviors with which he formerly struggled, but has also qualified himself in some profession or other. If apprentices are known by the training they are engaged in, journeymen are known by their occupations.

And so it continues through life. Again and again, the pressure of societal demand, or ambition, or aspiration makes the limitations of present self-definition inescapably apparent. Again and again, we children must take a reckless plunge into the unknown and stake our lives on a new larger identity. This is how journeymen become masters. This is how university professors become deans, politicians become senators, businessmen become company presidents.

In our society, crises tend to come in the early thirties, again at the end of the forties, in the mid-sixties, and at the close of life. Each of these is an identity crisis. Each can only be solved by a quantum jump, by an evolutionary leap, by an expansion of personal universe, by an identification with a new and higher object of love. Each new identification opens new horizons of possibility and makes formerly unsolvable problems as nothing.

Fiction is a dramatic description of personal crises and their resolutions. This is the common structure of all fiction. There is, in fact, only one eternal Story, of which the thousands upon millions of individual stories that men have told through the centuries are but variations or fragments.

The Story begins with a protagonist ripe for change. This protagonist may be a single character, or several, or a community. The protagonist may be restless. He may have unfulfilled potential. He may be troubled by dreams. He may feel hedged about by inappropriate rules. But in one way or another, his ripeness for change is apparent.

The character makes a transition from his familiar, safe-but-limited environment into a larger and more dangerous world in which there is room to grow. The transition may occur voluntarily or under the pressure of events. It may be an accident or it may be deliberately sought.

In the larger world of unknown things, the character encounters perils and problems such as he has never faced before. The more that he attempts to deal with these in his previous terms, the more dangerous and threatening the perils and problems become. Ultimately, the protagonist has three choices. He may refuse the challenge of the unknown and retreat to the tight confines of his former situation. This is the way of stagnation. Or he may remain in the unknown world, fail to change, and be devoured by its perils. This is the way of attachment. Or he may surrender his former attachments and grow. This is the way of evolution.

It is the way of evolution that is the true way. A version of the Story might, for instance, present us with three brothers and a challenge from the unknown. Perhaps a giant on the rampage. Perhaps men with legal documents. One brother might preserve his present state, but would clearly not be the better for it. One might die for the sake of his limitations. But the third, whom we would be invited to admire, would certainly evolve.

This is the way of evolution in stories: The character must perceive the necessity for change. Whatever it was that formerly he identified himself with in this universe—and counted his chief strength—must seem, either sooner or later, to be evidently inadequate to deal with the perils and problems of the larger world of unknown things. What seemed to him his strength must be revealed to him as his limitation.

In a very real kind of death, he must surrender his old identity. This surrender is only possible if the character has and holds clearly in mind a higher aspiration—some new and higher object of worthy identification. The character then tests his new identification on the problems and perils that have threatened him. And if re-birth has taken place, if there has been evolution, the new identification gives him such power that the problems and perils fall before him as though by magic.

Fiction not only tells us that personal evolution is possible. It tells us that evolution is identification with higher aspiration, and that such larger love renders overwhelming problems trivial.

These lessons of fiction are borne out in life. They explain, as nothing else can, the differences in ability that separate the apprentice from the journeyman, and the journeyman from the master. These differences are so marked that to the apprentice the abilities of even a journeyman seem magical—and the abilities of the master are beyond his ability to accurately reckon.

The apprentice loves a craft. That is his higher identification. But what he loves is appearance—mere surface. The apprentice serves his love by imitating the acts of his betters. But because he has identified himself with appearance, essence eludes him, and in every act he stumbles.

The journeyman differs from the apprentice in recognizing the existence of art-beyond-mere-craft. He has dedicated himself to a higher love—the art of the master, unsuspected by the apprentice. And the craft that is a problem to the apprentice in every detail comes effortlessly to the hand of the journeyman. The journeyman is accomplished in craft, but a bumbling imitator in art.

The master may accomplish what the journeyman only dreams because art is the higher love of the journeyman, while art is not the end of the master but merely the means to even higher ends. In consequence, art is no problem to the master, but his natural tool.

A man may be a true creative artist in any human endeavor if his ends are high enough. This is as true of janitors as of musicians, as true of pizza makers as of physicists.

Fiction tells us that there is a hierarchy of purpose in the universe. If this is true, proper occupation can be nothing less than devotion of oneself to the ultimate purpose of the universe by all available means. If one were able to identify oneself with this purpose, then all personal problems would be as nothing and much would be possible that is impossible to the ordinary apprentice, journeyman, or even master.

This is the self-justification of all organizations. It is the promise of advertising, of political movements, of the various religions that seek to claim our allegiance, and of low art and high. All these appeal to us through the vehicle of the Story. All present us with candidates for the ultimate purpose. Under test, however, these supposed ultimate strengths generally prove to be limitations of one kind or another. If there is an index of true human adulthood, it is not the attainment of legal majority or of full physical growth, but the ability to distinguish lesser purpose from ultimate purpose.

—March 1973

15/ THE UNICORN AND THE MIRROR

[*Fantasy and Science Fiction*, August 1975]

We are used to understanding speculative fantasies as rational predictions of what might be. Or as entertainments, accidents thrown up by the imagination, mere dismissable merenesses.

Sf is better understood as a mirror.

Sf offers its writers unlimited possibilities to choose among. An sf writer may define his settings, his characters, his stories as he pleases and as he is able.

But given the vast reaches of time and space in which any possibility may be considered true, which states of mind does a writer present in dramatic form? What situations does he imagine? Who does he imagine himself to be? What does he imagine himself doing?

The choices a writer makes are an elaborate self-definition, both of himself and of the times of which he is a product. In the mirror of a science fiction story may be seen a reflection of the author. In the mirror of science fiction stories may be seen a reflection of an era. And in our reading of science fiction—the stories we choose and what we make of them—may be seen a reflection of ourselves. We read science fiction to know ourselves better.

Sf is a potent and important literature still in process of being born. Even its best practitioners do not yet know its full dimension. Even its most insightful critics can not yet conceive of what it will become.

Some months ago, Joanna Russ began a column in this space by saying, "The reviewer's hardest task is to define standards." We know the standards of mimetic fiction do not stretch to encompass the virtues and limitations of existing sf, let alone the sf that is to come.

What broader and apter standards are we to apply? By what standards are we to judge science fiction when we understand neither science fiction nor ourselves?

Our best course is to look into the mirror and see what the mirror reveals. We look for ourselves—for the complete actions we might perform and the whole people we might be. The better a science fiction story is, the deeper and wider and clearer we will see.

This standard, at least, has a chance of revealing to us the virtues that we always sensed in science fiction, those virtues that mimetic standards denied. It tells us why, for instance, Robert Heinlein has been the most consistently interesting of modern science fiction authors. He has been a deeper and more revealing mirror for more of us than any other writer of our time. It also suggests how Robert Heinlein, in his partial people, in his incomplete actions, in his cloudiness and obfuscation, and in his allegiance to the prejudices of a particular time, might be superseded.

The books on hand for review this month are deep and subtle mirrors. They are among the very best of what science fiction currently offers. All are partial and incomplete, but even in their partialness and incompleteness they are revealing.

Paul Linebarger, who was born in 1913 and died in 1966, was a strange austere man, intellectually brilliant, emotionally repressed, raised abroad, removed from the mainstream of America. Linebarger was a psychologist and military man, a specialist in the Far East and in psychological warfare. Throughout his life, he carried on a series of literary careers under various pseudonyms, eventually and chiefly as the science fiction writer, Cordwainer Smith.

The bulk of Cordwainer Smith's work is not large—five books. Most of this science fiction is set against a common far-future background, a huge incomplete tapestry, the largest piece of which is

Norstrilia, the only novel by Cordwainer Smith. *Norstrilia* was originally written in 1960. Cut in half, and unsuccessfully prettied to look like two novels, it was published as two paperbacks, *The Planet Buyer* (1964) and *The Underpeople* (1968). It is only now, however, fifteen years after it was written, that we have the opportunity to see *Norstrilia* in its complete and original form—if we ignore the many proofreading errors that disfigure the book.

It is a strange, static, hierarchic universe that Smith shows us. It is a world of underpeople—animals formed into simulacra of humanity —of men, and of men elevated into rulers of the universe, the Lords of the Instrumentality. This vastly changed world allows no change. Signs of difference, breaches of custom, and unauthorized opinions are all answered with instant death. The open pastoral world of Norstrilia is as static, hierarchic and intolerant as the closed urban world of Earth. One is equivalent to the other.

Against this background, men struggle and plot for the means of vastly extended life—the drug stroon, extracted from gigantic sick sheep by the farmers of Norstrilia. But men lack all sense of purpose. The men of Earth play desultorily at games derived from the life styles of our own time as a substitute for purpose. The men of Norstrilia live to produce stroon, so that they may live longer to produce more stroon.

For what reasons did Smith invent this bizarre half-mad situation? Quite clearly, it seems, the static universe and the rigid hierarchy of beings within it were an intertwined problem that Smith felt the need to sort out and solve.

Norstrilia, this long, serious and inventive novel, is Smith's best attempt to state and resolve his problem. But the novel, even in its complete and restored form, is not successful.

In a "Theme and Prologue" at the outset of *Norstrilia*, Smith describes the story to come. He tells us that all that remains are the details. But the details don't match the original description. We are promised a hero who knows his own mind. We are promised adventures and consequence.

What we are given is Roderick Frederick Ronald Arnold William MacArthur McBan the 151st, who when asked his purposes is helpless to answer. He is the epitome of ignorance. His experiences are a blur to him. Throughout the story, he is the tool of others. He has no power over his own wealth, the nominal motive center of the novel. He is not responsible for its original acquisition. He is not responsible for its ultimate disposal. Quite simply, he has no active part to play in what is given as his story.

We have two problems in *Norstrilia*. One is the problem of the static hierarchic universe. The other is Rod's problem of bewilderment and repression. If the novel were a success, both would be solved in common terms.

In fact, neither is solved. Rod falls into the hands of a "clinical psychologist" who gives him the gift of being ordinary. Rod's money falls into the hands of a foundation dedicated to providing fun, games and easy hatreds to occupy a motiveless mankind. But nothing whatsoever is changed by the events recounted in *Norstrilia*. At the conclusion, the world remains as static and hierarchic as it was at the outset. And Rod McBan the 152nd is brought on in the last paragraph to demand of his father, our hero, why the world is as it is and why he is who he is—the central questions of the book. How many more times must they be doomed to be Rod McBan? And there is no answer.

The aristocratic and unhappy world of the Lords of the Instrumentality is a better mirror of Smith, with his special and peculiar upbringing, than a mirror of our times. This may explain why Smith has never been widely popular, but rather has appealed to the elite few who can identify with the situation Smith presented. Presented, but never resolved.

Michael Bishop is a new writer to watch. He is twenty-nine and has been writing science fiction since 1970. In the last year, several of his novellas have been nominated for awards. *A Funeral for the Eyes of Fire* is his first novel.

A Funeral for the Eyes of Fire shows an interest in the anthropological comparable to Ursula Le Guin and a sense of the alien comparable to James Tiptree, Jr. But it is an individual work, Bishop's own and no one else's. *A Funeral for the Eyes of Fire* is highly imperfect. It is a pied mirror, everywhere reflecting brilliantly bright, everywhere cloudy. It leads the eyes inward, and ultimately reveals nothing clearly. Even so, it is the most impressive first novel so far seen in the Seventies.

Bishop is one of the new and still rare breed of science fiction writer attempting to produce art without rejecting the pulp vigor that is science fiction's continuing strength. If the cover blurbs of his book are to be believed, *A Funeral for the Eyes of Fire* is just so much more pulp trash. But the blurbs are a lie. Bishop is attempting to use undiluted science fiction to present a tragic action of Shakespearean dimension, a disintegrating situation comparable in its mindless destructiveness and pain to our conduct of the Vietnamese War.

Two Earthmen—brothers—have fled one hundred light years from the claustrophobic confines of the Urban Nucleus of Atlanta to seek haven on the planet of Glaparcus. In company with two Glaparcan envoys, they have traveled a further six light years on a mission to the planet Trope. If successful in their mission, the Earthmen will earn themselves a home on Glaparcus. Nominally, they are successful. In actual fact, their mission is a farrago of lies, betrayals, misunderstandings, bloodshed and death.

Our comparison of *A Funeral for the Eyes of Fire* to Shakespeare was fully intended. Bishop clearly has Shakespeare in mind in his construction, and sometimes even in his diction. The result is not successful, but the failure is not laughable.

In part, Bishop fails because his situation is not plausible. Early in the book, a character calls it ludicrous, and it is. It is a set-up, a situation designed to disintegrate as spectacularly and painfully as possible, existing for no other reason.

In larger part, Bishop fails because of his choice of narrator. In function, Gunnar Balduin is Rosencrantz and Fortinbras in one, a tool and petty villain, and a mopper of blood and burier of bodies. But as Bishop presents him, he is a character without knowledge, sincerity, history or personal characteristics. He is a cypher whose eloquence and special vision are not his own, but Bishop's.

Here is Bishop's voice:

> Its orchid glow made the sky seem to be in a state of lush, organic
> rot . . . like a crisply burning fuse down the indigo sky . . . like a
> piece of crisp paper burning at the edges . . . like a purple intoxicant
> . . . like a shiny black placenta.

These words fit unconvincingly in Gunnar Balduin's mouth.
Bishop might have come closer to fulfilling his ambitions if he had
foregone the safety and ease of first-person narrative, reserved his
voice to himself the author, and observed his protagonist from outside.

A Funeral for the Eyes of Fire is an awkward and discordant
book, easy to resist, easy to reject. But if its implausible situation
and characterless narrator are set aside, it has a rare power. Its
wealth of detail, its special vision, and its inexorable progress suggest
that when Michael Bishop has his voice and tools under firm disci-
pline, he will be a force to be reckoned with.

In her book, *The Female Man*, Joanna Russ attempts to disarm
criticism by anticipating it. She fills a page with dismissive phrases
and indicts all those who might use any of them as benighted and
lightless.

One of the phrases is "this pretense at a novel," and we are
tempted to use it. *The Female Man* is advertised as a science fiction
novel, but it is not one. It is not a story. It is not an action. There
is no narrative thread. Instead, one might more fairly call *The Female Man* a meditation or an exercise in self-revelation that uses
some of the devices of science fiction.

In *The Female Man*, the author divides herself into four fragments.
Joanna, from what might be our own world, is most like the author.
Jeannine is the product of a variant universe in which the Depression
world of the author's childhood has lingered and lingered. Janet is
an emissary from the all-female world of Whileaway—stated to be
another planet in the author's award-winning short story, "When It
Changed," but here given as a possible future Earth. Jael is from an
alternate universe in which men and women are at war, the possible
seed from which Janet's Whileaway grows.

These characters meet again and again in varying combinations and situations to demonstrate the author's convictions and confusions. It's all a grand kaleidoscopic interior monolog, well-written, passionate and intense. But it is not a novel. Nothing is visualized, nothing happens.

If there is a conclusion to be drawn from the book, it is that the author feels that men are not altogether human, but that women without men are or might be.

Here are the males of our species:

> Burned any bras lately har har twinkle twinkle A pretty girl like you doesn't need to be liberated twinkle har Don't listen to those hysterical bitches twinkle twinkle twinkle I never take a woman's advice about two things: love and automobiles twinkle twinkle har May I kiss your little hand twinkle twinkle twinkle. Har. Twinkle.

On a certain level, the author's dismissal of criticism is correct and inarguable. These are her feelings, sufficient in themselves by their very existence. If you share these feelings, *The Female Man* is a perfect emotional mirror. If you don't share these feelings, go fuck yourself.

But *The Female Man* is also an exercise in self-indulgence. Fiction in general, and science fiction in particular, exists as a device by which our attitudes may be challenged and altered. *The Female Man* is solipsistic—a crime Russ tells us is punishable by death on her planet of Whileaway because it is such a tempting attitude. Cordwainer Smith's *Norstrilia* and Michael Bishop's *A Funeral for the Eyes of Fire* both fail because they allow no internal challenge to themselves. In *Norstrilia*, Smith lacks the nerve to imagine a larger power than the rigid and self-satisfied Lords of the Instrumentality. In *A Funeral for the Eyes of Fire*, Bishop is so determined to be tragic that he falls into implausibility. In the same way, *The Female Man* does not dare to be a novel, to challenge its own certainties and test them in the crucible of character and action.

A few years ago, Joanna Russ delivered a number of talks at science fiction conventions complaining that the heroes in sf stories were all too like the male in the quote given above and that sf offered no place for complete women. She had a point. But the answer is not *The Female Man*. The answer is sf stories in which whole women —not female children as in *Rite of Passage* or female cyborgs as in *The Ship Who Sang*—are imagined. That is the best contribution to the cause of female liberation and human liberation that Joanna Russ or any other writer could make. Because we will never be whole until we imagine ourselves whole, and live what we imagine.

There was a time in the Sixties, from the publication of "A Rose for Ecclesiastes" in 1963 to the publication of *Lord of Light* in 1967, when Roger Zelazny was the most stimulating and adventure-some of the writers of science fiction. In a remarkable series of splendid novellas and imperfect novels, Zelazny demonstrated that many of the limitations of science fiction that we had suffered without question were unnecessary. He transcended them in a single bound, leaving us to follow him.

But then the magic died. When the Sixties ended and Zelazny's nearest peer, Samuel R. Delany, and other writers of their common generation fell silent, Zelazny continued to write one novel after another. One bad novel after another. Hasty books. Books without the surge and sweep of language that had made Zelazny a delight. Books in which the only reality was power and the only motive revenge. Books in which comic-book gods contended, hurling mean-ingless lightning at each other. It became possible to wonder if Zelazny was a burnt-out case or whether there had ever been merit in his work.

Among these books were *Nine Princes in Amber* and *The Guns of Avalon*, the first two novels in a projected series. Their narrator was Corwin, one of the royal family of the alternate universe of Amber—true reality—all other worlds, including our own, being but shadows of Amber. At the outset of *Nine Princes in Amber*, Corwin awakes in our world to a realization of his own amnesia and sets out on a quest to remember himself and seize power in Amber. For two books, through harrowing adventures, imprisonment and mutilation, he does not pause until at last he has succeeded in feeding his appetite for power. He does not think. He does not reflect.

He moves ahead, hating and hungering, destroying everything that crosses his path.

Nine Princes in Amber is morally sleazy and solipsistic. *The Guns of Avalon* is self-hating. Both of these facts are somewhat disguised by the immediate egotistical hypnotic power of first-person narration, and Zelazny offers no evidence to his readers that he is aware of them. Both books badly need second drafting. Zelazny cannot seem to remember from one end of a book to the other even the simplest postulated facts—like the number of Corwin's brothers and sisters and the names and identities of their mothers. Seemingly, the kindest thing that could be said of these books is that certain symbols, certain scenes, certain moments, contain hints and flashes of the old Zelazny power.

Now the third book in the series, *Sign of the Unicorn*, has been published, and all is changed. Oh, some things are the same. Inconsistencies remain. *Sign of the Unicorn*, like the two books before it, could stand a second draft. But oh what a difference the differences make. Having attained power at last, for the first time Corwin stands still to ask some of the necessary questions that were ignored in the earlier books. Characters, previously without definition, begin to take on form and weight and individuality.

Perhaps the true turning point is a scene that takes place in our world. Corwin has retreated there when wounded, in a sudden unconscious flash. He waits there, without power, without help, without hope—and aid comes to him, a neighbor of whom we have heard previously not a word. This man's acceptance of Corwin, complete, selfless and unquestioning, is a redemption.

The last two chapters in the book are brilliant. They toss away all the certainties and self-protections that Zelazny has bounded himself with—that crucial move that Smith and Bishop and Russ could not make. They reveal Amber as less than the truest reality. Solipsism as a way of life is explicitly brought up and finally discarded. New levels of meaning are achieved. At the conclusion of the book, Corwin-the-solitary is left with boon companions in a stranger and realer place than he has ever known before, a realm of magic where his own familiar magics have become questionable, following the unicorn, symbol of innocence, in pursuit of truth.

Sign of the Unicorn redeems *Nine Princes in Amber* and *The Guns of Avalon*. It takes what was Nothing and makes it into Something. We can now understand the first-draft crudity of this series. Zelazny has started on a True Quest from a basis in amnesia equivalent to the blankness of a newborn baby. He has launched himself into a life-or-death improvisation. He is in honest pursuit of true reality—of whole nature and worthwhile action. He has probed his old familiar too-ready answers of solipsism and the exercise of pure power, and seen beyond them. This is what science fiction is for. In view of the daring and magnificence of the undertaking, clumsiness and crudity become secondary. The pursuit is all.

Sign of the Unicorn is Zelazny's best book since *Lord of Light*. Zelazny is back! Hooray! Hooray!

May he pursue his quest in the Amber books to come. May he find what he seeks.

16/ FAREWELL TO YESTERDAY'S TOMORROW

[*Galaxy*, June 1974]

All our lives we have assumed that the near future would hold one of two likely possibilities. One possibility was atomic war between us and the Commies. We used to practice huddling under our desks in school and guarding our eyes against the bomb flash, but in our hearts we knew that our chances of survival were slim and that those who survived would wish they were dead. The other possibility of our times was that America would rule the world on the strength of its superior morality, politics, economics, power, and knowledge.

It is a new year now. In 1974 the two possibilities that have ruled our lives for so long have become wild unlikelihoods. American and Russian generals may still thumb-wrestle for hypothetical advantage, but there will not be an atomic war. Neither will there be a New American Empire imposing democracy and California on the world. The planet is aswarm with independent forces that do not accept the superiority of America and who will not have control imposed on them by anybody. Some of these forces are older and wiser than we yet recognize.

In this new year it is clear that we are entering a new era. What its shape will be, we cannot yet tell. But the old era is over.

The old era ruled our lives and our thinking for thirty years. All its factors were established by the end of World War II:

Computers. Plastics. Television. Rocket ships. Atomic weapons and atomic power plants. The United Nations. Russian-American antagonism. The arms race. Technological superfluity.

All of us whose years of awareness have come since 1945 have grown up in a world dominated by these factors. It was as though we had been handed a particular situation and it was our fate to play its permutations out to their conclusion—atomic disaster or American triumph. We had no choice other than these. Like it or lump it. Love it or else.

The protest of the 1960's was an objection to the American Dream Machine, but it was doomed to fail. When an era has crystalized, alternatives are unimaginable. Hate their two choices as they might, the protesters of the Sixties could not imagine any others. They still believed that their most likely futures were nuclear hell or America squatting on the face of the world.

The imagined universe of science fiction during these same years was a reflection of the hopes and fears of the new era. The great fear was Atomic Armageddon. The great hope was that the men of Earth might stride forth to conquer the stars.

These hopes were first expressed in the pages of the Golden Age *Astounding*—in exactly the same period of time in which our modern world crystalized itself. They were the basic assumptions of the superman stories of A.E. van Vogt, of the Future History stories of Robert Heinlein, and of the Foundation stories of Isaac Asimov. If no sf writers during the past thirty years have matched these three in importance, it is because Asimov, Heinlein, and van Vogt have held the patents within which a generation of science-fiction writers have labored.

The writers of the Campbell *Astounding* set forth the outline of our future. We would establish colonies among the stars. We would dominate alien races. We would found galactic empires. And we would explode through the entire universe. The heroes of this world to come were technocrats, secret agents, and team players—the analogs of all the bright young Americans who expected to rule the postwar world.

By the end of the 1950's this sf scenario of the future had become gray, trivial, and unpromising. Heroes revealed fatal fallibility. The virtues of human rule of the universe seemed questionable.

In the 1960's, just as there was reaction to the assumptions of American life, so was there reaction to its science-fictional image. Writers sought color. They wrote of lost colonies and of the drop-outs of Galactic Empire. They wrote, too, of the exotic landscapes that might survive the nuclear firestorm, of holocaust as the well-spring of magic. But like the political and cultural protest move-ments of the time, the science fiction of the 1960's was an evasion rather than a true alternative to the mainline future that had been set out in the Golden Age *Astounding*.

When an era has crystalized, there are no alternatives. This can be seen in the stories that J. G. Ballard wrote during the 1960's. His inert inner landscapes of the imagination are an expression of Ballard's hatred of the postwar universe of sterile plastic. But his stories offer no alternative to the Future History of Heinlein and the others. They offer only exaggeration of sterility, ennui, and death.

All the abortive revolutions of the 1960's failed at the end of the decade. Rock music heroes discredited themselves or died squalidly. Weathermen went underground. Dissenters were prosecuted in pub-lic show trials. The counterculture went into seclusion. The Ameri-can Monster won a final victory in the election of Richard Nixon, who is the living symbol of the postwar era and all its assumptions.

Since 1969 the typical science fiction story has been able to en-vision little besides disaster. The common story of the period is an account of final extinction in the near future resulting from a willful abuse of technology.

The most successful writer of the past few years in science fiction has been Barry Malzberg. Malzberg has been overheard to say, in the spirit of these years, "Paranoia *is* science fiction." And in his stories of insane astronauts, such as his novel *Beyond Apollo*, Cape Canav-eral and Future History meet in some ultimate disaster of the spirit.

But science fiction is not inevitably paranoid. Not all writers have succumbed to the fear and loathing that result from being trapped by a choice between the unsurvivable and the unendurable. There have been some few stories in these past years that see a new and wholly different world lying just before us.

Examples of these new stories are R.A. Lafferty's "When All the

Lands Pour Out Again" and Fred Pohl's "The Gold at the Starbow's End"; Jack Dann's "Junction" and our own "When the Vertical World Becomes Horizontal." Listen to the titles of these stories. They are portents. They bid farewell to yesterday's tomorrow.

They speak of the new time that we have now entered. For here it is 1974 and suddenly all our long-held assumptions no longer obtain. It is a new springtime season.

The old crystalization that held us in thrall has been shattered. We have entered a new era. Change is upon us once again.

For who could have dreamed that the American economy of abundance would now be plagued by scarcity? Who would ever have suspected that a crisis in the supply of energy would already be transforming the great American machine? Who would have thought only a few years ago that the political trials of the Nixon Era would all fail, every one, and that Richard Nixon would himself be on trial? All the discredited young men of the Nixon Administration—technocrats, secret agents, team players—are our former heroes in discard.

All is fluid now. The old situation, the old era, is no more. The new era has not yet become fully apparent.

In a period of fluidity there are opportunities for all those who can perceive them. For those who strive to cling to the hopes and fears of yesterday, the times will be profoundly disturbing. But for those who can grow, these will be times of unparalleled adventure.

Revolutions are now under way throughout the sciences—in astronomy and physics, geology, anthropology, archaeology, and psychology. The details are unclear, but it is already certain that when the revolutions are complete, we will have completely revised our ideas about the nature and history of the universe, about the emergence of life on this earth, about the origins of man and the length of his existence, about the intellectual abilities and achievements of prehistoric man, and about the nature and capacity of the human mind.

We are likewise entering a period of radical international readjustments. The bases of world finance and of world trade will be redefined. The arms race will be abandoned as an expensive anachronism. World controls on population growth will be established. It will be demonstrated that the United Nations is no longer an instrument of American foreign policy. The UN will grow in effectiveness and change in function.

Within fifteen years we will all be living in ways that are presently unimaginable to us. All the priorities of American life will be altered. There will be new goals in education, new styles of life. We will become masters of the American machine rather than cogs within it.

This new season of change might be likened to the 1860's, the decade that saw the rise of corporate capitalism and of European imperialism, the decade that set the crystal that was the early twentieth century. It is also like the 1930's, the period of the Depression and the New Deal, the time in which American values were last rearranged.

Science fiction, the ideal reflection of the world around us, will also change. All our former assumptions, the assumptions of the 1940 *Astounding*, will be abandoned. We can no longer write seriously of Nuclear Cataclysm or of Terran Empire.

We might take note of the fact that we are living now in the days that were imagined as the beginning of Future History. That future is now, this very moment. But when we look about us, we do not see Heinlein's rolling roads. We do not see van Vogt's Slans. We do not see Asimov's positronic robots. The future of 1940 is now, but this now is not the world that was dreamed in 1940.

The last period in science fiction that was like the one we are now entering came during the 1930's. Hugo Gernsback had founded *Amazing Stories* in 1926, in the last days of the crystalization of the 1860's. *Amazing* reflected that world. It was a sister magazine to popular science magazines. The future it expected was populated by young Tom Edisons. Its heaven was a utopia of backyard invention. Its hell was devolution—the collapse of civilization and return to skin-clad barbarism. The other planets of our solar system were envisioned as being likewise utopic or barbaric. Their populations were either just like us, or they were monsters with a taste for human flesh. This sf world was laid down by Jules Verne and given its classic expression by H.G. Wells.

After 1930, however, all was different. There were new magazines. With the appearance of *Astounding* in 1930, sf took on the racier style and size of the pulp magazines. It no longer seriously pretended to be popular science. During the 1930's the number of science fiction magazines grew. As late as 1937 there were only three. By 1940 there were seventeen.

There were new editors—in particular, F. Orlin Tremaine and John W. Campbell. With their encouragement new writers entered the field. The assumptions and matter of sf changed radically. Before 1930 there was "scientifiction." After 1930 there was "science fiction."

Such writers as E.E. Smith, John W. Campbell, Jack Williamson, and Stanley Weinbaum began producing stories with strange premises and stranger conclusions. They provided the basis from which Heinlein, van Vogt, and Asimov eventually elaborated a new conception of the future. With Smith and Campbell we traveled to the stars and beyond the bounds of our own galaxy. With Williamson we penetrated new dimensions. The planets of our solar system were colonized. With Weinbaum we discovered that aliens need not be either humanlike or monstrous.

With all this exciting possibility there was no point to writing the familiar old-fashioned style of story about wearing a sweater and bow tie and living in a utopia of chuff-chuffing inventions. It was more creative and exciting to imagine being an explorer of alien realms, or an asteroid miner, or an outlaw of the spaceways.

Just so, as of this springtime of the mid-seventies that we are entering, will sf once again be made wholly new. Just as E.E. Smith's *Skylark* once went forth to discover the universe, so we need to send new starships of the imagination forth to take account of a new world. These ships will not find an empty universe to be stripmined and subjugated. Instead, they will find a universe filled to the brim with the new, rare, and different. It will contain standards by which to measure ourselves—alien races with different abilities, some less advanced than we, some more advanced. This universe will be the ideal reflection of the new multiplex Earth we are now awakening to.

The key words of this new time are *synergy* and *ecology* and *evo-*

lution. The era will be a time of liberation, unfolding, maturation, creativity, and growth.

What the actualities that wait locked in these words may be we do not yet know. We must discover these things for ourselves, and it is an exciting prospect.

The new sf will help us to understand and direct our new lives in the years immediately ahead. It will be more popular in appeal than it has ever been. There will be new magazines and new forms of magazines. There will be new editors and new writers. Sf will excite you as it has never excited you in all your years within the Great American Machine. It will amaze, astound and delight you as you never dreamed possible. It will scratch forgotten itches and satisfy unrecognized thirsts. It will aid in the remaking of your minds and your lives.

It is time to say good-bye to yesterday's tomorrow and put it out of mind.

Good-bye. Good-bye.

The goodbys are now all said.

A new tomorrow is waiting.

17/ INTUITION AND MYSTERY

[*Fantasy and Science Fiction*, July 1976]

In *Alternate Worlds*, the second full-length attempt in English at a historical consideration of science fiction, James Gunn says:

> One problem with trying to define such an amorphous field as science fiction is that every definition tends to include stories which any panel of critics would agree were not science fiction or to exclude stories that the same panel would insist were science fiction; historically, science fiction has been defined as "what I mean when I point at it, or write it, or publish it."

SF is a great mystery. Gunn gives us some sense of the mystery by quoting consecutively no less than ten definitions or impressions of science fiction. In the middle, he pauses to call these definitions a sea: "a sea from which we will extract ourselves only with great difficulty and almost certainly without what we came to seek."

What did we come seeking? A pearl, an elusive treasure. Many have seen it, or think they have, but no one can capture it with words. A wonderful and powerful mystery.

Gunn rightly calls *Alternate Worlds* "a consensus history of science fiction." He closes his flurry of inadequate definitions with a definition of his own, which might serve as a fair consensus description of what science fiction has tried to be about in his time. He says: "My own definition has, if nothing else, brevity: 'In science fiction a fantastic event or development is considered rationally'." Ever since Gernsback founded *Amazing*, emphasis has been put on the rational aspects of science fiction.

But Gunn recognizes the inadequacy of these definitions. The "science fiction" treated in *Alternate Worlds* is nothing like his definition. It is, in fact, that larger SF that we all implicitly recognize and which we cannot define. SF is a broad tent. It covers science fiction and structural fabulation, sci-fi and stf, speculative fiction and science fantasy. It is all of these and more besides.

Gunn's standard is ultimately his sense of work inhabited by the spirit of SF, not work which conforms to the letter of his definition. That is, he behaves as irrationally as a fan.

Rational definitions are inadequate not merely because they would kick the likes of van Vogt and Zelazny out of the tent. They take no account of mystery. They exclude the most important part of SF.

Among the impressions that Gunn quotes is this one by Isaac Asimov: "Social science fiction is that branch of literature which is concerned with the impact of scientific advance upon human beings."

However, at the outset of *Alternate Worlds* there is an introduction by Asimov entitled "Science Fiction, I Love You" that presents a very different picture of SF. He says that forty years ago:

> I was only a kid, reading science fiction and experiencing in it an extreme of joy beyond description. I envy that kid, for I have never known such joy since and I never expect to. I have known other joys—the sales of stories, the discovery of sexual love, the earning of advanced degrees, the sight of my newborn children—but none has been as unalloyed, as all-pervasive, as *through and through*, as reaching out for a new issue of a science fiction magazine, grasping it, holding it, opening it, reading it, reading it, reading it . . .

It was not science and rationality that we sought so joyfully. It was the pearl. It was SF.

Irrationality was a dirty word in the era that is now closing. Science fiction could not then admit itself to be irrational. But the time has now come when the leading edge of contemporary science has specifically disavowed rationality. It is possible now for SF to come out of the closet and admit to its own irrationality.

The fact is that science fiction writers have always been led by their intuition like sleepwalkers off in a dream. SF stories mean more than their authors necessarily know.

And how could it be otherwise? SF not only cannot be rationally defined, but there is no common language by which one SF writer can talk to another about his work. Lafferty cannot talk to Le Guin. Le Guin cannot talk to Heinlein. Heinlein cannot talk to Panshin. Panshin cannot talk to Zelazny. The *SFWA Forum*, the inner journal of the guild of stf writers, is not a forum for the discussion of SF.

The writer of SF has only his intuition to guide him, his sense of the mystery. In SF stories, those things that are realest and matter most are mysteries, transcendent powers and beings that lead and elude understanding like a will-o'-the-wisp. These mysteries yield knowledge and exceed expectation. They shimmer when they walk.

SF is like the things it portrays. It is a transcendent mystery.

The old rational standards by which we attempted to judge science fiction have been shown to be inadequate. New standards vie for attention. One standard we might apply to books presented for consideration is their relationship to the mystery of SF.

Alternate Worlds: The Illustrated History of Science Fiction is a minor mystery all in itself. It is a large, handsome, and expensive tablebook. It is a miracle that it should have been published in a depression. To what audience of millionaires is it addressed?

The text of the book is James Gunn's consensus history of science fiction. He has mined the work of previous commentators and homogenized it. He has added his own store of personal knowledge and experience of SF as a reader and writer and teacher. His account of science fiction may fairly be taken as the Sound Opinion of his day, crystalized Essence of 1953.

In addition to Gunn's consensus, *Alternate Worlds* contains pictures. There are book covers, balloons, a Model T, Hugo Gernsback, Homer, Raymond Z. Gallun, Harlan Ellison, Larry Niven, Dean R. Koontz and David Gerrold. There is a picture here of almost anyone you might want to see except Ursula Le Guin. More than anything else, however, there are pictures of magazine covers.

These are just the black-and-white and sepia-tinted pictures. There are, besides, five sections of color plates, 32 pages in all. Two of these pages are of photos from the 1971 World Science Fiction Convention in Boston, including a picture of Poul Anderson's daughter Astrid in the guise of a mermaid. The other thirty pages are of more SF magazine covers. As though the sight of the covers might reawaken some suburbanite's remnant memories of the joy he once felt when he was a boy and first bought, yes, that very issue of *Astounding*.

What a strange time this Fall of 1975 is! In one sudden burst we have been presented by different publishers with not only *Alternate Worlds*, but no less than four collections of SF illustration—one of them by Lester del Rey, two from England including one by Brian Aldiss, one translated from the French. Not to mention a collection of the art of Frank Frazetta. Eight or ten years ago, the proposal of a collection of SF illustration was not considered to be of interest. In the ripeness of this moment, however, publishers seem to be convinced that we want to see the face of yesterday's tomorrow once again.

Probably we do. But why now? Why is it SF illustration time *now*? It's a mystery.

It is also SF history time *now*. Aldiss was first. Gunn is second. There will certainly be more.

Aldiss's *Billion Year Spree* and Gunn's *Alternate Worlds* shed light on each other. According to Aldiss:

> Science fiction is the search for a definition of man and his status in the universe which will stand in our advanced but confused state of knowledge (science), and is characteristically cast in the Gothic or post-Gothic mould.

But Aldiss's account of SF is exclusive. He values literary excellence and appreciation of the fallen state of man, and he is not in sympathy with pulp SF.

By comparison, Gunn's book is loosely and offhandedly written, unoriginal and generally superficial. Even so, his sense of the true mystery of SF has produced a book that makes *Billion Year Spree* seem sterile, narrow and ungenerous. It is not by accident that the first comment on the nature of science fiction that Gunn prints should be this one by that closet irrational, John W. Campbell:

> Fiction is simply dreams written out. Science fiction consists of
> the hopes and dreams and fears (for some dreams are nightmares) of
> a technically based society.

Gunn's formal argument in *Alternate Worlds* is narrow and outmoded, but he doesn't fully believe in it anyway. The book is
broader than its arguments. A youthful Asimov might look on it
with wonder.

You might want to glance through this book at your library.
Or catch it when the price comes down.

The science fiction of the Thirties is almost unknown to contemporary readers and writers. It was the immediate predecessor of the
Campbell-era SF that is so familiar to us all. But in the years since
1946, the years of SF book publishing, Thirties' science fiction has
remained largely unreprinted. We only know of it what we have
been told. What we have been told is what Damon Knight tells us
at the outset of his anthology, *Science Fiction of the 30's*:

> The earliest science fiction anthologists, surveying the field as
> they knew it, found most of the s.f. of the thirties inferior in style
> and content to the new science fiction pioneered by John Campbell
> in the forties.

But is it true that the SF of the Thirties was so unworthy as not
to deserve reprinting? These were the stories that thrilled Isaac Asimov beyond any joy he has encountered since or hopes to encounter.
These were the stories of a time in which SF rapidly metamorphosed,
in the space of a decade changing from Burroughs and Merritt to
Heinlein and van Vogt. But the actual fiction of the Thirties is hidden to us. We know it only as strange titles by forgotten names in
the Day *Index*. How are we to reconcile Asimov's childhood perception with what we have been told about the patent inferiority
of these stories?

Science Fiction of the 30's is another product of this moment.
Suddenly, after thirty years of SF book publishing, we are being presented with multiple glimpses of Thirties SF: *The Best of Stanley G.
Weinbaum*; *The Early Williamson*; *Before the Golden Age*; *Les meilleurs récits de Astounding Stories, 1934/37*. Now there is another

large anthology of Thirties SF. Damon Knight's *Science Fiction of the 30's* presents us with eighteen stories in roughly chronological order. And, as a further example of synchronicity, Knight has thought to include an original magazine illustration with each story he has exhumed.

If *Science Fiction of the 30's* were all the evidence available to us, we could quickly agree that Thirties SF was inferior and of no interest and let the matter drop. This anthology is a museum of futility and failure. There are no lost treasures here to make a young reader of today giddy with delight. Everywhere there is desiccation and dust, everywhere empty husks from which the spirit has flown.

Are we who seek to find traces of light in the SF of the Thirties inevitably to be disappointed? Not necessarily. Not inevitably. There was some light to be found in Asimov's anthology, *Before the Golden Age*, and considerably more in Jacques Sadoul's collection of stories from *Astounding*.

One crucial difference between Asimov and Knight seems apparent. Asimov selected his stories from those he had loved as a child. He remembered his sense of the spirit of SF and honored it— and his selections still manage to hold some mystery and wonder for us.

On the other hand, Knight, compiler of avant-garde *Orbit* volumes and author of *In Search of Wonder*, has edited *Science Fiction of the 30's* as though he were Hugo Gernsback. His stories are those that demonstrate stock SF ideas for the first time or which anticipate later and superior stories. Or they are stories which seem to prevision the science or the facts of today. There are stories here of star voyagers bollixed by the time contraction paradox, stories of bee language and mammals breathing water, stories of energy crisis and urban disorder. But Knight's stories are dead, whatever their precedence may have been. If Knight had remembered himself and sought wonder in the Thirties instead of pseudo-science, he would have served SF and our needs better.

In 1953, the best understanding of SF to be found was L. Sprague de Camp's *Science-Fiction Handbook*, a marvelous and ungainly book issued in a how-to-write series. It was a stewpot of everything de Camp could imagine a writer of SF needing to know. Practical advice. Basic tips on writing. Inside anecdotes. Biographies of writers. Contemporary market reports. The first major historical account of imaginative fiction, original scholarship on which Gunn's consensus merely expands today.

The book was de Camp's farewell to science fiction writing. Like the Gunn, but even more so, it was successful in spite of its faults. It served the mystery. Almost by accident, *Science-Fiction Handbook* caught some sense of the dynamic multiplicity of SF at one particular moment in time. A generation of readers used it to consolidate their impressions of SF. A generation of aspiring SF writers learned from it, found clues in it, used it as an oracle.

Science-Fiction Handbook reflected the spirit of SF in 1953, but more than twenty years have passed now and the old book does not display the spirit as brightly as it once did. And yet, here it is reissued in 1975 as *Science Fiction Handbook, Revised* by L. Sprague de Camp and Catherine Crook de Camp.

And how, pray, has it been revised? By abridgment. A ruthless hand has passed through the original book and taken away from it all that was particular of 1953. A venerable classic has been consistently simplified, softened and trivialized. De Camp's once-original scholarship now reads as though it were someone else's work that the de Camps were dimly repeating. All that is left intact, more or less, is the practical advice of a man who ceased to write science fiction twenty years ago. The advice is not adequate to the problems of writing contemporary SF.

A knife was raised over *Science-Fiction Handbook*. With the first stroke, the spirit flew. Another husk.

Along with Robert Heinlein and Isaac Asimov, A.E. van Vogt must be counted one of the three major SF writers of the Forties. Even though van Vogt ceased to write science fiction through much of the Fifties and Sixties, and has not made much impression with his recent work, he remains, along with Heinlein and Asimov, one of the three major SF writers of the whole era that is now passing.

Van Vogt is a problem that the new historians of SF like Gunn and Aldiss must surely come to terms with. Those like Aldiss who value literary excellence cannot approve of van Vogt. He is foggy, semi-literate, pulpish and dumb. Those like Gunn who value rationality must admit, as Gunn does, that "van Vogt's stories did not attempt to present a rational picture of the world." And yet, anyone with any sense of SF must acknowledge the true power of van Vogt's work. A power that the present critical understanding of SF is totally inadequate to deal with.

We are now privileged to have a small paperback autobiography entitled *Reflections of A.E. van Vogt*, published by Fictioneer Books, Lakemont, Georgia. It is based on twelve hours of interview conducted for three universities in 1961, but altered, rewritten and brought up to date by van Vogt.

It is a strange and disconcerting book. If you believe van Vogt, he had a normal childhood in Canada and grew up to write confession stories. By chance he saw the August 1938 issue of *Astounding* with John Campbell's "Who Goes There?" and was hooked. Within less than a year, his own fiction was appearing in *Astounding*. In another two years, John Campbell was willing to commit himself to buying two to three hundred dollars worth of work a month from van Vogt. And, as though caught in some bizarre dream, van Vogt found himself writing science fiction stories "from the time I got up until about eleven o'clock at night, every day, seven days a week, for years." For years, van Vogt says, he had no idea why he was writing science fiction.

And yet, van Vogt considers himself a thoughtful and rational man, a practical person without much imagination in everyday affairs, a writer whose proper place was *Astounding* and not *Unknown*, for which he could not comfortably write. Van Vogt even says, "Other writers may be able to work on intuition, but I can't."

But this same man says, "I dream my story ideas in my sleep." He doesn't plot his stories consciously. Instead, he programs his dreams and writes down the results. His consciously plotted stories never sell.

Van Vogt prizes his special ability to write what he calls "fictional sentences." Like a transcendent power, this ability comes and goes, but it animates and legitimizes van Vogt's fiction: "Every once in awhile I realize, 'Oh, I'd better describe something in fictional sentences. I need some enduring reality'."

Van Vogt gives an example of his method. He says, "What leads up to this passage is that the protagonist suddenly realizes he's been poisoned by something that he's touched while lowering himself on a rope."

> A pang went through his body and was followed instantly by a feeling of rigidity. With a gasp he clutched at his blaster intending to kill himself. His hand froze in mid air. He toppled stiffly unable to break his fall. There was the sharp contact with the hard ground. Then, unconsciousness.
>
> The will to death is in all life. Every organic cell ecphorizes the inherited engrams of the inorganic origin. The pulse of life is a squamous film superimposed on an underlying matter so intricate in its delicate balancing of different energies that life itself is but a brief vain straining against that balance. For an instant of eternity a pattern is attempted. It takes many forms but these are apparent. The real shape is a time and not a space shape, and that shape is a curve up and then down. Up from the darkness into the light, then down again into the blackness. The male salmon sprays his mist of milk onto the eggs of the female and instantly he is seized with a mortal melancholy. The male bee collapses from the embrace of the queen he has won, back into that inorganic mold from which he climbed for one single moment of ecstacy. In man, the fateful pattern is impressed time and again into numberless ephemeral cells but only the pattern endures.

It is not by accident that van Vogt writes like this. It is a matter of deliberate choice. "I believe that the reality resulting from this and similar passages in my work, has made my science fiction more enduring than that of most sf writers," says van Vogt.

> My work has been somewhat invalidated by critics who are determined to force mainstream techniques on science fiction; but we'll just have to wait and see who wins in the long run.
>
> My wager is on my method of presenting science by way of fictional sentences, and on the timeless reality that must underlie the dreaming process, when it is used consistently as I have done.

Wrestle with *that*, ye Gunns and Aldisses. It's a challenge that must be answered.

18/ A NEW WORLDVIEW

1

How strange and flat and lifeless these Seventies have been! Lacking in leadership. Lacking in direction. All creative impulses inherited from the Sixties—but now grown stale and meaningless.

In these days, for instance, it would seem a wild unlikelihood to hear of a youngster being expelled from school for refusing to cut his hair. That old battle has long been won. The signs of rebellion in the Sixties—long hair, marijuana, and rock music—have become the cultural commonplace of the Seventies, but the Seventies have been without any positive character of their own.

In times to come, 1975 may well seem a central year of transition in our culture, the end of one moment and the beginning of another.

A ballot has just been received by the membership of the Science Fiction Writers of America, nominating some eighteen novels for consideration for the Nebula Award. Among the eighteen are *Guernica Night* by Barry N. Malzberg and *The Stochastic Man* by Robert Silverberg. Malzberg and Silverberg have been those two writers of science fiction who have best expressed the mood of the first half of the Seventies, a mood compounded of despair, desolation, decadence and doom. Most interestingly, both of these writers have recently made repeated public declarations of their intention to cease writing science fiction. If their resolution holds, these novels may be their last major contributions to the genre.

Also among the eighteen novels nominated for the Nebula Award are *Dhalgren* by Samuel R. Delany and *Doorways in the Sand* by Roger Zelazny. If Malzberg and Silverberg have been the writers most typical of the early Seventies, it was Delany and Zelazny who best caught the rebellious, expansive mood of the Sixties.

The last time these two writers appeared together on a Nebula novel ballot was 1968, eight years ago. Between them that year, Zelazny and Delany received no less than six separate Nebula award nominations and five Hugo nominations for their 1967 work. Delany won the Nebula for Best Novel in 1968 for *The Einstein Intersection*, while Zelazny won the Hugo award for Best Novel for *Lord of Light*.

In the dismal Seventies, however, Zelazny and Delany have been in eclipse. Delany has written little or nothing, while Zelazny's work has not been thought worthy of consideration for awards.

So here we have an apparent moment of transition. The dominant writers of the early Seventies, masters of negative expression, are taking their bows and making their farewells. And simultaneously, the two major new writers of the glory days of the Sixties are taking this moment to make their reappearance.

By a coincidence that may be no mere coincidence, but rather further evidence of a significant shift in cultural mood, 1975 was also a year in which the makers of Sixties rock music re-emerged from obscurity and began to catch the public ear once more. Group after group, like Quicksilver Messenger Service and Iron Butterfly— hear the now old-fashioned ring of those names—have reformed after having been disbanded through these years of fragmentation. Jefferson Airplane, now evolved into the Jefferson Starship, is back in prominence. Laura Nyro is back, and Janis Ian. Simon and Garfunkel have recorded together again.

Perhaps the most interesting of all these resurrections is the record *The Basement Tapes* by Bob Dylan and The Band. This music was originally laid down on primitive recording equipment in 1967. It was thought of then as nothing more than home music intended for the artists and their friends. In a year when the Beatles' *Sgt. Pepper* was setting new standards of technical multiplexity and sophistication, this music was certainly never considered for general release.

However, when *The Basement Tapes* was finally issued as a double album in 1975, it was a surprise best seller, cited by *The New York Times* as well as *Rolling Stone* as one of the most important albums of the year. Obviously, this was not for its technical merits. It could only have been for its content.

Are the Sixties in some sense upon us once more? For all those who remember the Sixties as a time of great positive expression, there must surely be as many who remember them as the moment when the stability that our society had enjoyed since World War II came to an end and our time of troubles began. The Sixties were a time of maximum polarization—a time of generation gaps and distrust of those over thirty. A time of hippies and flower-children. A time of marches, riots, sit-ins, be-ins, and protest. A time of menace to society that President Nixon and Vice-President Agnew were elected to combat in 1968.

In these middle Seventies, the polarization is gone. The flower-children are gone. Nixon and Agnew are gone. And the creativity is gone, too.

What does remain is trouble, but the trouble has changed character. The troubles of the Sixties consisted of oppositions to society. The troubles of the Seventies have been society itself disintegrating.

If those who were the positive and creative forces of the Sixties —long absent—are returning now, what can we expect of them? What messages might they have for us?

It may be possible to answer these questions by looking at the last twenty years of science fiction. Science fiction is a subtle and sensitive mirror of our internal states. If we can discover the origins and meaning of Sixties' sf, we may be able to come to a clearer understanding of the present moment.

2

At the end of the Fifties, science fiction seemed caught in the grip of stagnation, reflecting a general state of stagnation within society-at-large. Like the rock-n-roll music of the period, science fiction had become tame, slick and unimaginative. In what was thought of at the time as a reaction to the greater realism of Sputnik, science fiction magazines were disappearing. Many of the brightest young talents of science fiction were ceasing to write. And in 1960, Earl Kemp published a Hugo Award-winning symposium, *Who Killed Science Fiction?*

These were the days of gray flannel reality—organization men, commuters, Miltown-gobblers, cogs in the wheel of big business and big government. President Eisenhower set the tone of the day, a tone of bland and smothering conformity. This corporate reality seemed all-pervasive. The bright young college graduate of the Fifties had to fit himself into the box of this worldview if he wished to be a useful, successful member of society.

The science fictional parallel to this all-encompassing worldview was the Future History framework established in the Forties by Heinlein and Asimov. In 1957, Heinlein definitively categorized 90% of all science fiction as "Realistic Future-Scene Fiction"—and all true science fiction as respectful of fact. Anything else was dismissable as "pseudo-scientific fantasy." Serious science fiction must fit within the parameters of the-way-things-would-be—and the way things *would* be was Future History, a corporate universe rationally operated by engineers and technocrats.

The demands of the moment in science fiction were for realism, facts, and linear, rational extrapolation from fact. The speculative and fanciful were excluded. The most successful writer of the period was Poul Anderson. Three of his stories may give a hint of the spirit of the times.

In *The Man Who Counts* (*War of the Wing-Men*) (1958), Anderson wrote of men surviving a wreck on an alien planet through a rational appreciation of fact. The "man who counts" is a fat, greedy, conscienceless entrepreneur, who is described as bribing, blustering, lying, cheating, politicking and slaying his way to survival and profit.

In *We Have Fed Our Sea* (*The Enemy Stars*) (1958), Anderson's heroes are engineers doing grim, boring, necessary labor in a lonely outpost at risk of their lives—because this is their job and because this is the nature of man. Except for its extrapolative elements, this might as easily have been the story of men on an oil-rig in the Atlantic, rather than men on a spaceship bound for the stars.

As a final example, there is the Hugo-winning novelet, "The Longest Voyage" (1960). In this story, Anderson imagined an analog of Sir Francis Drake, embarked on a voyage in his sailing ship, *Golden Leaper*, to circumnavigate his planet in the name of his Queen. When this character discovers that his planet is a lost colony, he forgoes the unknown possibilities of the wider stellar universe in order to continue living out his atavistic adventure: " 'We'll sail the seas of this earth, and walk its mountains, and chart and subdue and come to understand it.' "

Much implicit assumption is wrapped up in that word "subdue." Employed so offhandedly in 1960, it has an alien ring in 1976.

As the Sixties opened, a few writers began to offer a reaction to the airless "realism" of contemporary science fiction. This reaction was not a fundamental challenge, but a change in style and attitude —just as Kennedy did not challenge Eisenhower's assumptions so much as he presented them in a more dashing and adventurous form. The new style was one of romantic adventure. The shift is visible in the differences between Anderson's "The Longest Voyage" and his stories of two years earlier.

An example of this new direction in sf was Jack Vance's Hugo-winning novella, "The Dragon Masters" (1962). Like "The Longest Voyage," it is a story set on a lost colony planet. However, instead of close analogs of our past, it presents men and alien beings mutated into grotesque and fantastic forms through deliberate breeding.

As another example, Cordwainer Smith, who was increasingly prolific after 1960, presented stories that in other hands might have been mere space opera. But Smith cloaked them in colorful trappings and told them in a high mythic voice, and transformed simple sf conventions into something new and different.

Some of the new romanticism became possible through the willingness of writers not to be taken seriously. Sword-and-sorcery fantasy, for instance, was a type of story long out of style. But in 1959, Fritz Leiber resumed his long-abandoned series of Fafhrd and the Gray Mouser stories, set in the land of Nehwon—"no-when" spelled backwards. At first the stories were clearly tongue-in-cheek, but as Leiber continued the series in the Sixties, they became more un-apologetically romantic.

The first sf stories of Roger Zelazny and Samuel R. Delany, who would be the major new talents of Sixties' science fiction, appeared in 1962—the same year that Bob Dylan and the Beatles made their first recordings. Zelazny's first stories appeared in *Fantastic* and *Amazing*, the least serious but most open magazines of the period. Delany's first novel, *The Jewels of Aptor* (1962), was half of an Ace Double-Book, the least common denominator of sf book publishing.

The work of both writers fell into the new vein of romantic adventure. Their stories were space opera, sword-and-sorcery, and post-atomic-disaster adventure. Both *The Jewels of Aptor* by Delany, and Zelazny's Hugo-winning novel, . . . *And Call Me Conrad* (*This Immortal*) (1965), were after-the-bomb stories. In the Fifties, novels set after the holocaust, like John Wyndham's *Re-Birth* (1955) and Walter M. Miller, Jr.'s *A Canticle for Leibowitz* (1959), pictured a grim scrabble for existence in barren lands. Delany and Zelazny saw instead a world transformed, a landscape filled with magical mutation.

The back cover blurb of the single-volume edition of Delany's 1963-65 trilogy, *The Fall of the Towers*, promised a world filled with:

> Acrobats and urchins, criminals and courtiers, fishermen and factory-workers, madmen and mind-readers, dwarves and duchesses, giants and geniuses, merchants and mathematicians, soldiers and scholars, pirates and poets, and a gallery of aliens who fly, crawl, burrow, or swim.

It now can be seen that all of this prodigious inventiveness did not exist merely for the sake of color, thrills and casual entertainment. It was an attempt to express meaning. It was an attempt to challenge the premises of the ruling worldview. Zelazny and Delany were not alone in this attempt. They were only two among a number of writers who were suggesting strange and disconcerting alternatives during the mid-Sixties.

This new work was appearing at the same time that freedom-riders and draft-card-burners were challenging the established premises of the social sphere of American life. What was happening in both cases was no mere petty rebellion, no mere generation gap. Just as there were Viola Liuzzos and David Dellingers among the social protesters, so were there writers much older than Zelazny and Delany, like Frank Herbert and Philip José Farmer, involved in the new science fictional expression.

Underlying the old worldview, in both cases, was a conception of the universe as rigid, lifeless, linear, discrete, mechanistic, predictable and purposeless. What was being opposed to it was an emerging worldview that suggested a very different universe. Some of the outlines of the new universe can be glimpsed in the science fiction of the period.

In the new universe, nothing was fixed, nothing was final, nothing was beyond challenge or question. Zelazny's heroes were magnificently defiant outlaws challenging every structure and establishment they encountered, from the Galactic Federation to God. In "King Solomon's Ring" (1963), for instance, Earth is seen as a corrupter of simpler worlds. The hero, once an agent of the establishment, has his consciousness fused with that of a space pirate and is converted to an enemy of Earth. In the Hugo-winning *Lord of Light* (1967), the protagonist is a renegade god who brings his old comrades down in the name of an oppressed ordinary mankind.

If Zelazny's characters were opposed to all external establishments, Delany's attempted to break down internalized structures. Psychic flexibility was the hallmark. Delany's characters alter their bodies, shift from one form to another, change their personas. In *Empire Star* (1966), Delany presented people who metamorphose into higher crystalline form. In his Nebula-winning novel, *The Einstein Intersection* (1967), Delany suggested that what look like men in his story are not mankind as we know it, but the outward husks inhabited by a new spirit.

One of his characters explains:

> "We have taken over their abandoned world, and something new is happening to the fragments, something we can't even define with mankind's leftover vocabulary. You must take its importance exactly as that: it is indefinable; you are involved in it; it is wonderful,

> fearful, deep, ineffable to your explanations, opaque to your efforts
> to see through it . . ."

And, but a little distance further on, the same character says:

> "There are an infinite number of true things in the world with
> no way of ascertaining their truth. Einstein defined the extent of
> the rational. Goedel stuck a pin into the irrational and fixed it to
> the wall of the universe so that it held still long enough for people to
> know it was there. And the world and humanity began to change."

Frank Herbert's *Dune* (1965), a winner of both the Hugo and
Nebula awards, is important for its ecological characterization of
the new universe. Not only is the planet Dune a whole in which
everything is interconnected and all life mutually dependent, but the
old-fashioned Galactic Empire of which the planet is a part is shown
to be dependent on Dune for its cohesion and insight.

But not only was the new universe interdependent, it was infinitely mutable and plastic. In the series of novels that began with *Maker
of Universes* (1965), and in the Riverworld magazine stories that
appeared from 1965 to 1967, Philip José Farmer presented a variety
of strange, artificial *ad hoc* realities—thereby calling into question
our confidence in the organic necessity of our own assumed reality
structure. Philip K. Dick, in novels like the Hugo-winning *The Man
in the High Castle* (1962) and *The Three Stigmata of Palmer Eldritch*
(1964), and Robert Sheckley in *Mindswap* (1966), raised doubt that
there was any fixed reality of any kind.

Mindswap presented a character who passes through a succession
of bodies on different planets, and finally travels into an area of
fundamental chaos called the Twisted World. At the end of the
story, Marvin finds himself back on Earth without knowing how he
got there:

> He realized that nothing is impossible in the Twisted World, and
> that nothing is even improbable. There is causality in the Twisted
> World, but there is also noncausality. Nothing *must* be; nothing is
> *necessary*. Because of this, it was quite conceivable that the Twisted
> World had flung him back to Earth, showing its power by relinquish-
> ing its power over Marvin.
> That indeed seemed to be what had happened. But there was
> another, less pleasant alternative.

This was expressed in the Doormhan Propositions as follows: "Among the kingdoms of probability that the Twisted World sets forth, one must be exactly like our world, and another must be exactly like our world except for one detail, and another exactly like our world except for two details, and so forth."

Which meant that he might still be on the Twisted World, and that this Earth which he perceived might be no more than a passing emanation, a fleeting moment of order in the fundamental chaos, destined to be dissolved at any moment back into the fundamental senselessness of the Twisted World.

Fundamental chaos—that is the essence of what was offered by the new science fiction of the Sixties. Chaos set in opposition to an Order identified with the most rigid and reprehensible aspects of our own society. Chaos—in which neither reality nor personal nature was fixed, in which anything might change into anything, and anybody might evolve into Anybody. Chaos embraced.

3

The first occasional hints and tentative expressions of the new emerging worldview appeared in science fiction between 1953 and 1957, a time of relative openness before the extremes of inflexibility and materialism that marked the end of the decade. By significant coincidence, this speculative moment in sf was exactly that time in which rock-n-roll music made its appearance in our culture, a wild, raucous, disturbing outlaw presence that sane and settled adult America viewed as a threat to all civilized values.

The early Fifties were also the moment for the beginnings of a significant shift in scientific perception. During the first half of the century, the acknowledged Queen of the Sciences was physics, which of all science seemed the truest because it was the most systematizable and reducible to laws. Physics was taken as a basic model of reality. It was assumed that everything that existed, even consciousness, could ultimately be reduced to the movements of a few fundamental particles.

These billiard-ball assumptions about the nature of reality can be seen in a 1950 Isaac Asimov story, significantly titled "Darwinian Poolroom." This story suggested that we humans might destroy ourselves with our atomic inventions and be replaced by evolved thinking machines. The implication of the title was that evolution and consciousness were a result of simple, mechanical permutations.

Since 1950, however, physics has discovered a vast number of "fundamental" particles with no promise of an end or limit to the process of discovery, and no unifying theory to make sense of the profusion. Moreover, the laws of physics have become riddled with anomalies.

In 1975, an article appeared in *Science News* under the title "Kafkaphysik." The article reports:

> A reputable mathematical physicist tells us that if we apply the traditional ideas of communication to our notions of space and time, we reach the dilemma that either determinism, the ability to predict the physical future, becomes meaningless or the laws of physics need radical revision. Another, equally reputable, gleefully tells us that causality, the principle that gives order to physics, collapses in the weird realm of a naked space-time singularity.

And the article as a whole is described in these terms:

> Modern physics seems to be presiding over the death throes of objectivity. In the end solipsism may be the only philosophy and the fabulous the only reality.

The disciplines that have been emerging since the early Fifties to replace physics as the model sciences of the day have been biology and psychology, the life sciences, which are comparatively non-materialistic, non-linear, multiplex and holistic in their understanding of the universe. While physics has been wandering in bewilderment, biology has gone from strength to strength. The central event in the emergence of biology was the discovery of the structure of DNA, the molecule of genetic inheritance, a discovery that was made —again, by significant coincidence—in 1953.

The first presentiments of the advent of radical newness appeared in science fiction in that same year, 1953. There was promise of a new mankind in Theodore Sturgeon's *More Than Human* and Arthur C. Clarke's *Childhood's End*. Previous representations of superior man in sf pictured the odd sport or mutant who was just like us, only stronger and gifted with a higher I.Q. These two novels saw conventional mankind's children joined together to become something better, and the species on the brink of a general evolutionary leap.

Childhood's End contributed another new suggestion. To the extent that science fiction had taken account of science, that science had almost without exception been physics, or been imagined as physics-like. Clarke anticipated the dethroning of physics. Speaking in the voice of an alien visitor to our planet, he gave this account of our science and understanding:

> "In the centuries before our coming, your scientists uncovered the secrets of the physical world and led you from the energy of steam to the energy of the atom. You had put superstition behind you: Science was the only real religion of mankind. It was the gift of the western minority to the remainder of mankind, and it had destroyed all other faiths. Those that still existed when we came were already dying. Science, it was felt, could explain everything: there were no forces which did not come within its scope, no events for which it could not ultimately account. The origin of the universe might be forever unknown, but all that had happened since obeyed the laws of physics.
>
> "Yet your mystics, though they were lost in their own delusions, had seen part of the truth. There are powers of the mind, and powers beyond the mind, which your science could never have brought within its framework without shattering it entirely."

The terms in which the science-shattering powers of the mind are imagined in *Childhood's End* are very interesting. In earlier science fiction, the tendency had been to present telepathy as though it were mental radio, communication by means of a form of physical energy akin to electromagnetism. In this novel, the psi powers are psychological and biological, the result of the collective unconscious mind of the race.

If Clarke laid challenge to the primacy of physics, Philip Dick, in his first novel, *Solar Lottery* (1955), questioned the absolute power of cause and effect. In his mature Sixties' novels, it was the stability of underlying reality itself that Dick doubted. In this first attempted

expression, Dick presented his theme in a more outward, social form
—the mood of a population:

> The disintegration of the social and economic system had been
> slow, gradual, and profound. It went so deep that people lost faith
> in natural law itself. Nothing seemed stable or fixed; the universe
> was a sliding flux. Nobody knew what came next. Nobody could
> count on anything. Statistical prediction became popular . . . the
> very concept of cause and effect died out. People lost faith in the
> belief that they could control their environment; all that remained
> was probable sequence: good odds in a universe of random chance.

Perhaps the most brilliant early expression of the coming fluid,
evolutionary worldview can be found in "The God Business" (1954),
a novelet by Philip José Farmer, another major contributor to the
work of the Sixties. In this story, the authorities are called in to
deal with an area of disorder in which the rivers run with beer and
men are transformed into representations of their animal natures.
The protagonist survives by letting go, by going with the flow, by
dying to his old self and being re-born. The most striking thing
about this story is its suggestion that effective behavior within the
circle of Chaos must be based on symbolic and poetic thinking rather
than rigidly causal scientific logic.

Not all of those few sf writers who wrote about Chaos in the
Fifties were as comfortable with it as Farmer. It was Poul Anderson
who first identified fluidity as Chaos in his novel *Three Hearts and
Three Lions*, serialized in *F&SF* in 1953. Anderson took an engineer
from our world and threw him into the legendary Carolingian universe of magic and romance. But in the story, Anderson suggested
that the attractions of Chaos in the guise of Faerie and magic were
a dangerous evil, to be identified with the entropic breakdown of
the universe and the horrors of Nazi-ism. His protagonist muses:

> This business of Chaos versus Law, for example, turned out to
> be more than religious dogma. It was a practical fact of existence,
> here. He was reminded of the second law of thermodynamics, the
> tendency of the physical universe toward disorder and level entropy.
> Perhaps here, that tendency found a more . . . animistic . . . expres-
> sion. Or, wait a minute, didn't it in his own world, too? What had
> he been fighting when he fought the Nazis but a resurgence of an-

cient horrors that civilized men had once believed were safely dead?

In this universe the wild folk of the Middle World might be trying to break down a corresponding painfully established order: to restore some primeval state where anything could happen. Decent humanity would, on the other hand, always want to strengthen and extend Law, safety, predictability.

There was a vision of a state where anything can happen in another novel of the period, Damon Knight's *Hell's Pavement* (*Analogue Men*) (1955). Knight imagined a future United States broken up into small separate areas, each with its own "reality" enforced by machine conditioning. However, in one strange area, the Blank, ordinary reality as we know it is suspended and the analogue machines, instead of conditioning men, invest them with strange powers. Knight did not react to his vision with Anderson's cry of indecency and horror, but his character does shy away from the possibilities of personal evolution:

Arthur turned, and saw the other Guard frowning slightly, concentrating. After a moment a hair-thin golden halo glowed into being over his head. It hung unsupported and unsubstantial. It pulsed rhythmically, like a Store sign.

"Oh, no!" said Arthur.

"Oh, yes," said the ex-Guard solemnly.

A large mountain lion dropped to the ground from nothingness, strolled past the Guard, and lay down. It was followed by a small woolly lamb, which curled up against the lion. Both of them stared offensively at Arthur.

"Glory!" said the ex-Guard. *"Mirabilia, mirabile dictu.* We can do anything we believe in *and we can believe in anything!"* He strolled off, followed by the lion and the lamb.

"Now then, your turn!" said the little man cheerfully, standing beside one of the empty couches.

"I'd rather not," said Arthur desperately. Whatever happened to people under that antique analogue helmet, it broke all the rules he knew, and he wanted no part of it.

The partial and tentative nature of this first emergence of the new worldview in the Fifties should be emphasized. It was presented in only a very few stories, widely scattered. A suggestion here, a fragmentary statement there. Chaos was imagined as confined to limited areas, as in the Farmer and Knight stories. Or it appeared for a time

and then disappeared again. And, as we have seen, even those authors who did admit the strange new possibilities could be wary
and uncertain of them.

Chaos in the sf of the Fifties was as peripheral to the general
preoccupations as, say, the Beatniks of the period were peripheral
to ordinary society. Likewise, the new Chaos-embracing sf of the
Sixties, like the hippies and flower-children of that era, was far more
widespread and had much greater impact.

Nonetheless, in the course of the period of relative openness, 1953
to 1957, all of the elements that would be gathered and concentrated
in the Sixties made their initial appearance. Rogue heroes, as in Jack
Vance's *To Live Forever* (1956) and Frederik Pohl and C.M. Kornbluth's *Wolfbane*, serialized in 1957. Strange rebel societies, as in
Kornbluth's *The Syndic* (1953). And, as we have just seen, denials
of the supremacy of Western science, denials of cause and effect,
and suggestions of coming radical evolution.

But the harbingers of the new worldview in the Fifties only
appeared for a time. One of the last expressions of the decade came
in Jack Vance's 1957 short story, "The Men Return." In this story,
as in Dick's *Solar Lottery*, cause and effect are explicitly suspended.
But the suspension is carried beyond the mere perceptions of society
and is suggested to be part of the nature of the universe:

> Man had dominated Earth by virtue of a single assumption: that
> an effect could be traced to a cause, itself the effect of a previous
> cause.
>
> Manipulation of this basic law yielded rich results; there seemed
> no need for any other tool or instrumentality. Man congratulated
> himself on his generalized structure. He could live on desert, on
> plain or ice, in forest or in city; Nature had not shaped him to a
> special environment.
>
> He was unaware of his vulnerability. Logic was the special en-
> vironment; the brain was the special tool.
>
> Then came the terrible hour when Earth swam into a pocket of
> non-causality, and all the ordered tensions of cause-effect dissolved.
> The special tool was useless; it had no purchase on reality. From
> the two billions of men, only a few survived—the mad. They were
> now the Organisms, lords of the era, their discords so exactly equiva-
> lent to the vagaries of the land as to constitute a peculiar wild wis-

dom. Or perhaps the disorganized matter of the world, loose from the old organization, was peculiarly sensitive to psycho-kinesis.

The suspension of cause and effect in "The Men Return" is limited and temporary. It obtains only so long as Earth remains within that "pocket" of non-causality. At the conclusion of the story, Earth leaves this area in which logical understanding and order are suspended. Business as usual is resumed, a character taking account of the new situation with these words:

> "But once more the sun rises and sets, once more rock has weight and air has none. Once more water falls as rain and flows to the sea." He stepped forward over the fallen Organism. "Let us make plans."

Indeed, it was the end of a brief era of strangeness. Order was restored. By the next year in science fiction, Poul Anderson's entrepreneurs and engineers were doing normal business as though the encounter with Chaos had never happened . . .

Until science fiction and our society entered a new and larger pocket of non-causality in the Sixties.

4

For all its flamboyance, creativity and impact on society, however, the expression of the new worldview in the Sixties was still limited in extent and duration, a mere pocket of exception in the old order. If in Fifties' science fiction the areas of Chaos in the universe were county-sized patches, in Sixties' sf they were lost colonies and alternate universes. The main-line future was still felt to be the legitimate property of the old Galactic Empire/Future History.

In Sixties' sf, this future was challenged and rebelled against. But the challenges and rebellions were subject to the same essential criticism that was leveled against the societal protesters of the Sixties— they did not offer a comprehensive, positive alternative to the existing state of affairs. Like middle-class flower-children living in Haight-Ashbury on the conventionally-won earnings of their parents, lost colonies of would-be psionic supermen still derived their origins from the efforts of Poul Anderson's Future History-centered engineers and entrepreneurs. That fact was inescapable.

Even more inescapable was a natural consequence of the new worldview. If we live in an ecological universe in which everything is connected, then we are responsible for humanity's violations of the eco-system. If we are free to do and be Anything, then we are responsible for what we have done and what we have become. The action of protest against racial injustice and against U.S. interference in Vietnam could not absolve the protesters from their personal responsibility for the ills of American society. Lost interstellar colonies, no matter how seemingly far removed from the muscle-flexers of Galactic Empire, must still bear responsibility for the moral failures of Future History.

In the last years of the Sixties, science fiction increasingly reflected a sense of guilt and fears of retribution. Both Delany's *The Einstein Intersection* and Zelazny's *Lord of Light* end with guilt-wounded heroes removing themselves from the scene, even after hard-won victory and self-sacrifice.

In Harlan Ellison's Hugo-winning story, "I Have No Mouth, and I Must Scream" (1967), a handful of humans, including a conscientious objector and peace marcher, are trapped inside a giant computer which has killed all other humanity. The computer tortures these people endlessly and informs them—the author says "politely"— in capital letters:

> HATE. LET ME TELL
> YOU HOW MUCH I'VE
> COME TO HATE YOU
> SINCE I BEGAN TO
> LIVE. THERE ARE
> 387.44 MILLION MILES
> OF PRINTED CIRCUITS
> IN WAFER THIN
> LAYERS THAT FILL
> MY COMPLEX. IF THE
> WORD HATE WAS
> ENGRAVED ON EACH
> NANOANGSTROM OF
> THOSE HUNDREDS OF

MILLION MILES IT
WOULD NOT EQUAL
ONE ONE-BILLIONTH
OF THE HATE I FEEL
FOR HUMANS AT THIS
MICRO-INSTANT FOR
YOU. HATE. HATE.

In Robert Silverberg's *Nightwings* (1969), a novel which includes the 1968 Hugo-winning novelet of the same title, Earth is presented as a one-time master of the galaxy which felt free to abuse lesser races and tamper with its own eco-system in the name of science. Now Earth is a wasteland and weak and impoverished remnants of mankind search the skies, waiting for retribution, which indeed soon comes.

The devastation of Earth is a common note in novels of this period. Several of the prestigious Ace Science Fiction Specials, which carried the glories of Sixties' sf up to the threshold of the Seventies, touch on it.

In Alexei Panshin's Nebula-winning novel, *Rite of Passage* (1968), mankind's attainment of the stars is a direct consequence of the self-destruction of Earth. And the giant Ships which are the home of the remaining scientific elite of humanity continue to exploit and destroy the relatively-backward colony planets without concern or restraint.

In R.A. Lafferty's *Fourth Mansions*, published in the last month of the Sixties, we are left at the end to wonder whether our society will be destroyed by wildness and suffer a crash to a regressive state, or whether wildness will be the means through which we attain a new and more glorified condition of being. Similarly, the Ace Special published the following month, Joanna Russ's significantly-titled *And Chaos Died* (1970), concludes with the fate of a morally-questionable Earth being weighed in the balance. No clear outcome is given.

In the late Sixties, as romanticism faded, a new mode of realistic science fiction made its appearance. In these stories, the sins of our society were extended into the near future and made overwhelming. Thus, in Norman Spinrad's *Bug Jack Barron* (1968), immortality for the powerful few is the result of subjecting children, mainly black, to deadly radiation. In Thomas M. Disch's *Camp Concentration* (1967), a jump in intelligence is the result of scientific experiments with mutated syphilis germs on war resisters. And in John Brunner's Hugo-winning *Stand on Zanzibar* (1968), we are shown a horrifying vision of an overpopulated near future. One character is permitted to offer the possibility of salvation—but another character assassinates the one person capable of implementing the possibility:

> "Isn't it *typical*? We train one man—one ordinary, inoffensive, retiring little man—to be an efficient killing machine and he kills the one person who stood a chance of saving us from ourselves!"

As the Sixties ended, the creativity, the rebelliousness, the expansiveness that marked the decade deserted the new voices of science fiction, just as it deserted the hippies and flower-children of the social counter-culture. After publishing nine novels between 1962 and 1968, Samuel Delany issued a few short stories at the end of the decade and then dropped out of sight. What happened to Roger Zelazny was worse—he continued to write. But his brilliant way with language, which had made him the marvel and inspiration of the Sixties, failed him. In the face of the new realism, he continued to write fantastic novels in which near-immortals sought vengeance on one another, but in the chilly climate of the Seventies, and without his former eloquence, these novels seemed increasingly irrelevant and juvenile.

The creative moment of the Sixties ended, but unlike the similar moment at the end of the Fifties, there could be no simple reassertion of the old deterministic worldview. The impact of the rebels had been too great. But the rebels themselves, the vanguard of the Sixties, were overwhelmed and silenced, their strength sapped by too many battles. It was a moment of supreme ambivalence, marked by fear of the self-confrontations demanded by the new worldview, and nausea and horror at the thought of being trapped in the old.

This was true of the culture at large as much as it was true of the writers of science fiction. In society, the creative rebels disappeared from view, but their impact continued. In the Seventies, the marijuana and long hair of the hippies were adopted by the young, by the hippies' straight contemporaries, and by the middle-aged middle class—all those people who had stood removed from the wearying confrontations of the Sixties.

In the same way, in science fiction the attitudes of the new world-view—and the ambivalent horror of the moment—were left to be expressed in stories by beginning writers, by writers who had stood outside the creative ferment of the Sixties, and by long-absent middle-aged writers returning to the genre.

The series of *Clarion* anthologies, showcases for the work of talented new writers like Vonda McIntyre and Geo. Alec Effinger, were dominated by engulfing visions of near-future sterility, madness and doom. A story by Gardner Dozois, "King Harvest" (1972), speaks for many of the beginning writers of the Seventies. This piece is a vision of a man tottering through the hellish disintegration of a near-future American city, seeking the sea to die. The man dreams of speaking to his parents:

> *I killed the world, Mama. Papa. It's true. I did. So did you, Mama. So did you, Papa. We all did.*

Barry Malzberg, a writer of the same age as Zelazny, came into his own in the Seventies, most notably with a cycle of stories that included "Notes for a Novel About the First Ship Ever to Venus" (1971), "Out from Ganymede" (1972), and the award-winning novel, *Beyond Apollo* (1972). In these stories, Malzberg attacked the very roots of Future History and modern science fiction, portraying the space program as an empty façade and the astronauts as lunatics.

The two most prolific writers of the Seventies were Malzberg and Robert Silverberg. Silverberg had been one of the youngest of the new sf writers of the Fifties. After a few years of prolific hackwork, he had left science fiction along with so many others at the end of the Fifties. Silverberg finally established himself as a major voice with "Nightwings" in 1968, and in the Seventies published novel after novel, a series of bleak visions. In *Dying Inside* (1972), for instance, Silverberg showed a contemporary telepath whose talent is inescapably fading. And in *The World Inside*, also 1972, Silverberg depicted the Urban Monads, vast human warrens in a super-overpopulated, static future. In this story, all the activity that is left to mankind is to ignore circumstances and fuck. Those characters who might hope for better are eliminated as menaces to society, or inevitably commit suicide.

Among the old masters returning to science fiction in the Seventies, Robert Heinlein, the inventor of Future History, was also overwhelmed by visions of inescapable near-future awfulness. In *I Will Fear No Evil* (1970), Heinlein wrote of a billionaire, a very old man, trapped in an early Twenty-First Century so squalid and repulsive that Heinlein could not bear to describe it directly. Because of his age and because of his wealth, one would think that this character, if anyone, would bear responsibility for the nature of his times, which are the consequence of the deterministic, materialistic worldview. But all that Heinlein could imagine was an attempted avoidance of death and emigration from Earth.

Two of the other old masters returned to science fiction in the Seventies with novels that won both the Hugo and Nebula awards, Isaac Asimov with *The Gods Themselves* (1972) and Arthur C. Clarke with *Rendezvous with Rama* (1973). Both of these books presented the guise of the old science fiction, while implying the new, but both avoided the consequences of their own implications. In *The Gods Themselves*, our universe is shown as inextricably linked with another populated by sexually-strange aliens of a less material nature than our own—but Asimov did not permit passage or even direct communication between the two worlds. In *Rendezvous with Rama*, our solar system is invaded by a strange object that proves to be a gigantic spaceship, the property of superior aliens. These beings might well be our teachers—but they are never seen, never encountered. All that Clarke could do was have his conventional spacemen board the object, discover its nature, nod and depart, while the ship passes on as mysteriously as it arrived.

The one writer who dealt best with the ambivalence of the Seventies, the feeling of being caught between old and new, was Poul Anderson, who had continued to write throughout the Sixties, but had seemed irredeemably out of touch with the times. In some sense, Anderson had always spun on his heel between realism and romance, between the rational and the magical, between Law and Chaos. Now his personal ambivalence matched the ambivalence of the moment, particularly in two prize-winning novelets.

In the first of these Hugo-and-Nebula award winners, "The Queen of Air and Darkness" (1971), Anderson posed the same quarrel between Law and Chaos that had preoccupied him nearly twenty years earlier in *Three Hearts and Three Lions*, and, as before, came down on the side of the safely predictable. In this story, Anderson describes a beautiful Fairyland in the twilight regions of a planet lately settled and half-known by humans. This Mystery is investigated by an implied descendant and near analog of that arch-logician, Sherlock Holmes, who is in search of a kidnapped human child, a changeling. This rational detective exposes Fairyland as a dream, an illusion, the mere thought projection of ordinary, mortal, fallible, lean, scaly, long-tailed, long-beaked aliens native to the planet.

The detective explains how he engaged the aid of a human changeling, Mistherd, by demonstrating the fact of the illusion to him:

> "I turned off the mindshield," he said. "I let their band get close, in full splendor of illusion. Then I turned the shield back on, and we both saw them in their true shapes. As we went northward, I explained to Mistherd how he and his kind had been hoodwinked, used, made to live in a world that was never really there. I asked him if he wanted himself and whomever he cared about to go on till they died as domestic animals—yes, running in limited freedom on solid hills, but always called back to the dream-kennel." His pipe fumed furiously. "May I never see such bitterness again. He had been taught to believe he was free."

But such was Anderson's skill as a purveyor of illusions that his Fairyland seemed truer than its ultimate exposure as a sham and a delusion. All that his detective ever actually "proved" were his own initial assumptions about the naturalistic origins of the phenomena. But, if ordinary aliens could project the illusion of Fairyland to charm and entrap the gullible among humankind, then certainly it might as easily be the case that Fairyland could project the guise of ordinary aliens to sooth the fears of hyper-rational men. Mistherd might well have been right to be bitter—but not with the good Fairy folk. With the detective.

The second of these double-prizewinning stories, "Goat Song" (1972), was far more convincing and powerful, arguably the best piece of work that Anderson has ever done. The story was a highly-effective sf version of the Orpheus legend. The protagonist of "Goat Song" is a poet and madman, a singer of powerful songs in a computer-ruled future, who eventually shatters the rule of the machine, SUM, and sets men free. The defiant eloquence of the story was such that one could think that Anderson had been reading the Zelazny of the Sixties and been sufficiently touched to throw the balance of his feelings this one time to the side of Chaos.

The Harper, Anderson's hero, cries out:

> What is man? Why is man? We have buried such questions; we have sworn they are dead—that they never really existed, being devoid of empirical meaning—and we have dreaded that they might raise the stones we heaped on them, rise and walk the world again of nights. Alone, I summon them to me. They cannot hurt their fellow dead, among whom I now number myself.

And again he asks:

> But what, then, is our proper reality? And how shall we attain to it?

And he answers himself:

> Man is older than SUM: wiser, I swear; his myths hold more truth than Its mathematics.

And the Harper goes forth and speaks to men:

> I tell them how sick and starved their lives are; how they have made themselves slaves; how the enslavement is not even to a conscious mind, but to an insensate inanimate thing which their own ancestors began; how that thing is not the centrum of existence, but a few scraps of metal and bleats of energy, a few sad stupid patterns, adrift in unbounded space-time. Put not your faith in SUM, I tell them. SUM is doomed, even as you and I. Seek out mystery; what else is the whole cosmos but mystery? Live bravely, die and be done, and you will be more than any machine. You may perhaps be God.

Anderson's Harper is challenged by the agent of SUM, the Dark Queen—strange analog of the alien Queen of Air and Darkness in his earlier story, but this time the symbol of Law rather than the symbol of Chaos:

> "What is this freedom you rant about?" She demands.
>
> "To feel," I say. "To venture. To wonder. To become men again."
>
> "To become beasts, you mean. Would you demolish the machines that keep us alive?"
>
> "Yes. We must. Once they were good and useful, but we let them grow upon us like a cancer, and now nothing but destruction and a new beginning can save us."
>
> "Have you considered the chaos?"
>
> "Yes. It too is necessary. We will not be men without the freedom to know suffering. In it is also enlightenment. Through it we travel beyond ourselves, beyond earth and stars, space and time, to Mystery."
>
> "So you maintain that there is some undefined ultimate vagueness behind the measurable universe? . . . Please offer me a little proof."
>
> "No," I say. "Prove to me instead, beyond any doubt, that there is *not* something we cannot understand with words and equations. Prove to me likewise that I have no right to seek for it."

How strange and different to see Anderson laying the burden of disproof on the rationalist, endorsing Chaos, and pointing to the ultimate value of Mystery. Having embraced Chaos, Anderson's Harper speaks these words, poles apart from the ruminations of his engineer hero in *Three Hearts and Three Lions*:

> My enemies say I call forth ancient bestialities and lunacies; that I would bring civilization down in ruin; that it matters not a madman's giggle to me whether war, famine, and pestilence will again scour the Earth. . . . We need a gale, to strike down SUM and everything It stands for. Afterward will come the winter of barbarism. And after that the springtime of a new and (perhaps) more human civilization.

That Samson-like determination to bring down the temple of rationality and materialism, and the hope of a (perhaps) more human civilization were the best expression that early-Seventies' sf could bring itself to make. Poul Anderson's own familiar rational doubts were still sufficient to cause him to question the value of his own vision in "Goat Song" and hold the story back from publication for several years after it was written.

For the most part, those in the Seventies who remembered the energy and promise of the Sixties, and hoped for a fulfillment of the promise, were offered only the cold comfort of a story like Alexei Panshin's "How Can We Sink When We Can Fly?" (1971). Here there was a long enumeration of the horrors of the present moment and a fleeting glimpse of a future ecological utopia. And the question—how are we to get from one to the other? But no answer.

5

The question remains to be answered. How does one get from here to there?

Worldviews are the collective mental state of a society, the ground for all thought and action. They come into being, contend with their predecessors, for a time dominate and direct the affairs of a society, and then are themselves replaced, in a regular pattern of succession. There seem to be three stages in the appearance of a worldview.

The first stage is a theoretical expression. An example of this is the new biology, and the first tentative statements to be found in the sf of the Fifties. Inevitably, there is a reaction to this theoretical expression. It is threatening and contrary to the prevailing mood of the time. It seems dangerous. There is a retreat from it, as there was a retreat into the hard-nosed materialism that marked sf at the end of the Fifties.

The second stage is a romantic expression—an imaginary displacement of the emerging worldview to a distant setting—combined with social contention. If the new worldview has no present actuality, it still can be dreamed of, and battles fought in the name of the dream, and converts made. Just so, the handful of Beatniks in the Fifties became the tribe of hippies in the Sixties. Just so, the battles and protests of the Sixties. Just so, the romantic insistence on interdependence and human plasticity that marked the sf of the Sixties.

But, again, there is a period of reaction in which it seems that all the battles have been lost, that the dreams of the romantics have no place in reality, that the new worldview has been defeated by the old. We can see seeming defeat of this kind in President Nixon's decision to ignore 500,000 people marching in protest against the Vietnam War and watch football on television instead; in the disastrous crash of hippie hopes of togetherness at Altamont; and in the simultaneous invasion of Cambodia and murder of students at Jackson State and Kent State.

But this defeat is only seeming. The new best understanding of the universe is embodied in the emerging worldview—as its very foundation. And this cannot be escaped. In our time, the physics that underlies the old deterministic worldview has come to pieces. The biology that underlies the Sixties' counter-culture continues to advance.

In the absence of contention, all of the flaws in the old worldview—vainly pointed to by the protesters—are given leave to express themselves. And inevitably do. Just so, the disastrous end of U.S. intervention in Vietnam. Just so, the self-defeat of Richard Nixon.

As the institutions based on the old worldview crumble, with consequent extreme social upheaval and dislocation, the new worldview begins to replace it and become the common standard of the society—a flower emerging from ruin. The third stage. Until, of course, in its own time, the new worldview becomes static and self-satisfied, no longer an incubator of creativity but a basis for entrenched privilege, and must itself be struggled against and replaced.

We may perhaps be able to see this process—and our own moment—more clearly by looking at the rise of the last worldview, the deterministic, mechanistic state of mind now in shambles, and its reflection in the sf of its own time.

The theoretical basis of the last worldview was established at the end of the Nineteenth Century. Between 1893 and 1905, a new physics was conceived, the physics of atomic particles, quantum theory, and relativity. The universe of this new science appeared unimaginably remote from ordinary human experience, divorced from all human values, incomprehensible to all but a few superior human intellects.

The parallel in science fiction is chiefly to be seen in the early work of H.G. Wells. In a series of short stories that began in 1893, in novels like *The Time Machine* (1895), *The Island of Dr. Moreau* (1896), and *The War of the Worlds* (1898), and culminating in the theoretical expression of *A Modern Utopia* (1905), Wells presented a new and unsettling vision of the universe and man's place within it.

The universe, to Wells, is a machine, indifferent to ethical values, doomed eventually to run down. Humanity is a cosmic accident, the result of blind chance. Nothing stands between mankind and sudden extinction or supersession by another species. Survival is the only ultimate value, and mankind can hope to survive only through the exercise of reason. Through reason man can control the blind processes of the universe. Therefore, in *A Modern Utopia*, Wells advocated the collapse of the old class structure and the rise of a new elite of technicians and engineers.

Some of the flavor of the new ideas can be seen in this quote from a letter written in 1899 by Jack London, who would become a sometime sf writer:

> The different families of man must yield to law—to LAW, in-
> exorable, blind, unreasoning law, which has no knowledge of good
> or ill, right or wrong.

There was no room for God, no room for purpose, no room for sentiment, no room for the soul, in the new worldview. London, like Poul Anderson in our own time, was in some sense caught between worldviews. He appended this epigraphic verse to his auto-biographical novel, *Martin Eden* (1909):

> Let me live out my years in the heat of blood!
> Let me lie drunken with the dreamer's wine!
> Let me not see this soul-house built of mud
> Go toppling to the dust a vacant shrine!

Martin Eden, London's fictional self, commits suicide, unable to bear the emptiness and lack of value he perceives in the world. London himself committed suicide in 1916, at the age of forty.

The new ideas were desolating, but they were also liberating. They were like a fresh breeze in a stuffy Victorian drawing-room. They restored awe and wonder to an over-tidy universe. They promised to overthrow the constraints of Victorian gentility, which had been based on the sense that the human soul was the only element of spirit in an otherwise mechanical universe. They were a glittering weapon against all stuffiness and inhibition.

The first expression of the new worldview, in all its danger, was followed by a period of retreat comparable to the end of the Fifties. The first decade of the century was a time of general complacency and conformity.

In 1911 and 1912, however, there was a quickening of the arts and a new romantic sf made an appearance in the pulp magazines of the period. The chief master of the early Teens was Edgar Rice Burroughs, particularly notable for his John Carter of Mars stories. Burroughs' plots and characters were still Victorian, but his Mars was Wellsian, a dying planet on which the struggle for existence is the pre-eminent fact.

As the Teens continued, the sf of the pulp magazines grew more lushly romantic in themes and style, and the new vision came more into focus. Thus we find in A. Merritt's *The Moon Pool* (1919) this direct invocation of Wells:

> "The Englishman, Wells, wrote an imaginative and very entertaining book concerning an invasion of earth by Martians, and he made his Martians enormously specialized cuttlefish. There was nothing inherently improbable in Wells's choice. Man is the ruling animal of earth today solely by reason of a series of accidents; under another series spiders or ants, or even elephants, could have become the dominant race."

In the social sphere, this was the period in which Greenwich Village was established as a center of Bohemianism—the living antithesis of all that was Victorian. It was also the time of World War I, which in many ways was an experimental application of the new worldview —a brute struggle for survival using new and soul-less means like poison gas.

The climax of the period, comparable to 1967-68, came in 1918 to 1921. In 1918, Oswald Spengler published his *The Decline of the West*, suggesting that every civilization goes through a cycle from birth to maturity, to old age, to death, and that ours had now entered its period of decline. In 1918, the world was ravaged by a great flu epidemic which killed twenty million people and seemed a confirmation of the blind hostility of nature. In the wake of World War I in Europe, there was revolution and near-anarchy. In this country, there were unsuccessful strikes and massive political repressions. It was not for nothing that Warren G. Harding, the period's equivalent to Richard Nixon, based his successful 1920 political campaign on the promise of a return to normalcy.

The ambivalence and decadence that characterized the Twenties were if anything more marked than the ambivalence and decadence of the first half of the Seventies. The new worldview seemed more of a horrifying inevitability than a happy promise.

1919 was the high point in the pulp scientific romance story. At the end of the decade, magazines failed, receptive editors left the field, and even Edgar Rice Burroughs found the doors of his usual magazine markets closing in his face.

The sf of the early Twenties was dominated by intense ambivalence on the part of the old high literary tradition. The continued seriousness of the tradition was dependent on accepting the new worldview with its scientific underpinnings—but the very existence of the tradition depended on the elite values of the old worldview.

In the sf of the Twenties, there was a reaction to Wells in the form of utopias of disenchantment—dystopias which presented the new worldview without accepting it. These horrified visions of the future included Eugene Zamiatin's *We* (1924), E.M. Forster's "The Machine Stops" (1928), and, ultimately, Aldous Huxley's *Brave New World* (1932).

Contrasting with these were hyper-esthetic fantasies like James Branch Cabell's *Jurgen* (1919) and its successors, and E.R. Eddison's *The Worm Ouroboros* (1922). In these, there was likewise a presentation of the new worldview without acceptance. The fantasy form was in some sense an attempted evasion. But even Jurgen's romantic and erotic adventures were set in the context of a central vision of ultimate purposelessness, against which Jurgen's egotism rails in vain:

"Facts! sanity! and reason!" Jurgen raged: "why, but what non-sense you are talking! Were there a bit of truth in your silly puppetry this world of time and space and consciousness would be a bubble, a bubble which contained the sun and moon and the high stars, and still was but a bubble in fermenting swill! I must go cleanse my mind of all this foulness. You would have me believe that men, that all men who have ever lived or shall ever live here-after, that even I am of no importance! Why, there would be no justice in any such arrangement, no justice anywhere!"

Not by accident alone were both *Jurgen* and *The Worm Ouroboros* circular novels, ending just where they began.

To the extent that there was acceptance of the new worldview, as opposed to evasion, it was to be found in the continuation of the pulp tradition of sf. In *Weird Tales*, founded in 1923, and in particular in the writing of H.P. Lovecraft, there is outright horror expressed—but without evasion.

We can see, then, that as of the Twenties, science had established a new concept of nature—a nature of blind laws, mechanical and purposeless. Man was seen as being at the mercy of cosmic forces that had no special concern for him. Nineteenth Century gentility was now seen as weakness, and there was a horrified presentiment of human extinction.

The transition between worldviews called for a radical readjust-ment of thought—far more radical than any readjustment required in our own time. What was necessary was a new concept of man—a new kind of man suited to live in this bleak and hostile universe. The man intimated in *A Modern Utopia*. He must be intelligent, with a command of science and technology, so as to master the laws of nature. He must be hard-boiled, a ruthless manipulator of people and events, with the power to survive and subdue his enemies.

No one who clung to the civilized values of the past could become such a person. But in the midst of the Twenties, while civilized men like Eddison and Forster were lamenting the lost past and recoiling from the future, a new kind of sf was making its appearance. In 1926, a new magazine was founded, *Amazing Stories*, which called its offerings *scientifiction*—scientific fiction. The founder of the magazine, Hugo Gernsback, was just such a man as the time required.

Gernsback was not appalled by the vision of Wells. Far from it. Here is the blurb he wrote to *The War of the Worlds*, which he republished in *Amazing* in 1927:

> Wells has often been condemned because of his pictured ruthlessness of Martians, but, after all, why should they not be ruthless? Are we not ourselves as ruthless when we dissect insects and low animals for our scientific investigations? If there were a superior intelligence, to which, by comparison, ours was as inferior as that of a chicken compared to a man's, there would be no good reason why it should not be ruthless if it wanted to conquer the planet for its own designs. We humans ourselves would not hesitate to do the same thing if we sent an expedition, let us say, to the moon, if we found what we considered a low species there.

This amorality—this cool pragmatic appreciation of *fact*, no matter what its consequences—has continued to be characteristic of modern science fiction, as it has developed and evolved along lines that Hugo Gernsback never anticipated and eventually grew to disapprove of. Science fiction has been a strange unpopular popular literature. It has never been accepted by the heirs of the decaying old high literary tradition, who rejected it for its crudity and its low pop-cult appeals. And it has never been accepted by that large portion of the public that did adopt the new worldview as a practical actuality, but felt alienated from the lofty hyper-intellectuality of contemporary science. Science fiction has found its continuing audience chiefly among engineers and technocrats and among emotionally-repressed male adolescents. But, nonetheless, it is science fiction among all literature that has provided the truest reflection of contemporary beliefs and hopes.

The old Victorian worldview came crashing down in the Twenties, first in the scandals that marked the Harding Administration, then in the stockmarket disaster of 1929. Resisted though the new worldview was, it inevitably came.

In the crucible of the Depression, a new man was forged—intelligent, ruthless, powerful, the master of technology. The triumph of the rational, deterministic worldview came in the Forties. It may be seen in the Allied victory in World War II, in the Dresden fire-bombing and in the dropping of the Atomic Bomb on Hiroshima and Nagasaki.

6

The new worldview presented in Sixties' science fiction was a vision of a multiplex universe whose parts are nonetheless ecologically interconnected and interdependent. In this universe, reality was seen as plastic, not a single thing which endures forever, but a constantly changing flux. And man's nature was likewise seen as plastic.

This was presented at the time as Chaos. But it seems clear now that the new worldview is chaotic only when seen from the perspective of the old narrow determinism. To a hard-boiled, rationalistic manipulator of facts, flux must necessarily appear to be irrational Chaos.

Just as in the Twenties, a new worldview demands a new kind of man suited to live within it. The disasters of our own moment, like the Depression of the Thirties, are a crucible in which the new man will be forged. The new man must be empathetic, capable of understanding and accepting difference when he encounters it. He must be ruthlessly honest in his approach to himself and others. And he must exercise his power to evolve and transcend his own limits. Instead of being a manipulator, standing outside nature, he must become a functioning part of the eco-system.

In the Seventies, a certain measure of guidance in becoming this new kind of man has been transmitted to us from other cultures in the form of books by writers like Carlos Castaneda and Idries Shah. And in the science fiction of the last several years, here and there, in imperfect works, some measure of positive suggestion has begun to appear once more, harbingers of the final emergence of the new worldview.

An interesting example is the uncompleted series of books by Roger Zelazny that began with *Nine Princes in Amber* (1970). In the first book, Corwin, Zelazny's protagonist, is a near-solipsist, a ruthless manipulator of men and the universe, bent on his own narrow-

minded search for vengeance. In the second book, *The Guns of
Avalon* (1972), Corwin attains to power, but is nearly overwhelmed
with feelings of guilt and self-hatred. In the third book, *Sign of the
Unicorn* (1975), Corwin is a changed man, accepting responsibility
for his world. In the two books that yet remain to appear in the
series, we are promised an ultimate confrontation with self and
changing reality at the Courts of Chaos.

Something of the same progress is visible in a series of Zelazny
novelets. In the first, "The Eve of RUMOKO" (1969), Zelazny's
protagonist is so outraged and disgusted by all the products of
narrow-minded scientific civilization that he deliberately causes a
great catastrophe. In the most recent story, "Home Is the Hang-
man" (1975), this same protagonist and a sentient robot hold a
mental dialog on the possibilities of redemption that come through
an acceptance of guilt. The robot thinks:

> *Guilt has driven and damned the race of man since the days of
> its earliest rationality. I am convinced that it rides with all of us
> to our graves. I am a product of guilt—I see that you know that.
> Its product, its subject, once its slave . . . But I have come to terms
> with it, realizing at last that it is a necessary adjunct of my own
> measure of humanity. I see your assessment of the deaths—that
> guard's, Dave's, Leila's—and I see your conclusion on many other
> things as well: what a stupid, perverse, shortsighted, selfish race we
> are. While in many ways this is true, it is but another part of the
> thing the guilt represents. Without guilt, man would be no better
> than the other inhabitants of this planet—excepting certain ceta-
> ceans, of which you have just at this moment made me aware. Look
> to instinct for a true assessment of the ferocity of life, for a view
> of the natural world before man came upon it. For instinct in its
> purest form, seek out the insects. There, you will see a state of
> warfare which has existed for millions of years with never a truce.
> Man, despite his enormous shortcomings, is nevertheless possessed
> of a greater number of kindly impulses than all the other beings
> where instincts are the larger part of life. These impulses, I believe,
> are owed directly to this capacity for guilt. It is involved in both
> the worst and the best of man.*
>   *—And you see it as helping us to sometimes choose a nobler
> course of action?*
>   *—Yes, I do.*

Another science fiction book with relevance to the transition to the new worldview that we are presently embarked upon is Joanna Russ's *The Female Man* (1975). In this book, the old insensitive, exterior, materialistic headstate is symbolized as male and the new state of mind as female, and some description is made of an all-female utopia that originated in a catastrophe which destroyed all gross maleness. Here is the testimony of a citizen of that society:

> I was born on a farm on Whileaway. When I was five I was sent to a school on South Continent (like everybody else) and when I turned twelve I rejoined my family. My mother's name was Eva, my other mother's name Alicia; I am Janet Evason. When I was thirteen I stalked and killed a wolf, alone, on North Continent above the forty-eighth parallel, using only a rifle. I made a travois for the head and paws, then abandoned the head, and finally got home with one paw, proof enough (I thought). I've worked in the mines, on the radio network, on a milk farm, a vegetable farm, and for six weeks as a librarian after I broke my leg. At thirty I bore Yuriko Janetson.

This vision of protean becoming is emphasized by a device of the book which presents this character and others, including a submissive little woman and a ferocious man-killer, as avatars of the author. The point being made is that no one's nature is permanently fixed. Like Patty Hearst, who and what we are depends on the environment we find ourselves in.

In these mid-Seventies, the fears of the worst awfulnesses of the last worldview continuing forever are losing their grip on us. The Vietnam War has ended. The Nixon Administration has been disgraced. And those in science fiction who wrote of eternal static futures of despair, desolation, decadence and doom are changing their tune or leaving the field.

The Female Man is an example of a new note in science fiction, books that might be called "ambiguous utopias," after the subtitle of one of them. Their ambiguity is in part a result of the moment. We are still early in our transition and though our fears are passing, their grip has not yet been completely lost. The new utopias are also ambiguous because of the recognition of the new worldview that no static vision of perfection can possibly be permanent and complete. Nonetheless, the societies presented in these new books —including Samuel R. Delany's *Triton* (1976) and Ursula K. Le Guin's *The Dispossessed* (1974)—are intended to serve as laboratories for an improved humanity, non-selfish, non-manipulative and in balance with the environment. Visions of possibility that can help to promote and guide present belief and action.

In *The Dispossessed*, a winner of both the Hugo and Nebula awards, Earth has been made into a place of awfulness through that mode of behavior we are now trying to reject:

> "My world, my Earth, is a ruin. A planet spoiled by the human species. We multiplied and gobbled and fought until there was nothing left, and then we died. We controlled neither appetite nor violence; we did not adapt. We destroyed ourselves. But we destroyed the world first. There are no forests left on my Earth. The air is grey, the sky is grey, it is always hot. It is inhabitable, it is still inhabitable, but not as this world is. This is a living world, a harmony. Mine is a discord."

Two worlds figure at the heart of *The Dispossessed*. One, Urras, is a "rich, real, stable present," a comfortable and easily prosperous place much like the United States was in 1960. To the citizen of a barren Earth, it looks like Paradise, but it looks like Hell itself to a person from the second planet, Anarres. His world is an anarchist utopia—even now only a half-promise of itself—established through hard work and sacrifice on a desert planet by people who had deliberately chosen to reject the comfort of Urras.

In a crucial dialogue, the protagonist from Anarres strikes to the heart of the Earthwoman's preference of the easy actuality of Urras to the unknown potentialities that lie beyond the difficult attempt to make a garden bloom in a desert. He says:

> "You do not believe in change, in chance, in evolution. You would destroy us rather than admit our reality, rather than admit that there is hope!"

The Earthwoman is rocked:

> "I don't understand—I don't understand," she said at last. "You are like somebody from our own past, the old idealists, the visionaries of freedom; and yet I don't understand you, as if you were

trying to tell me of future things; and yet, as you say, you are here, now! . . ."

And, she comes to add:

"I thought I knew what 'realism' was."

The anarchist replies:

"How can you, if you don't know what hope is?"

7

A little more remains to be said.

The middle Sixties were a magical time, a visionary moment. The act of rejection of the old worldview was only the outer shell of that moment. The inner kernel was a sense of intensely heightened perception that was generally associeted with psychedelic drugs, but which was not dependent on them. The high glory of 1967 lay in a shared certainty, based on personal experience, that the universe is a place of magic and purpose. The promise of 1967 was that when we discovered our own true nature, we would find ourselves to be gods from whom magic and meaning flow.

As Samuel R. Delany had it in *The Einstein Intersection*, published in that year of 1967:

> Something new is happening . . . something we can't even define with mankind's leftover vocabulary. You must take its importance exactly as that: it is indefinable; you are involved in it; it is wonderful, fearful, deep, ineffable to your explanations, opaque to your efforts to see through it . . .

At the end of the Sixties, the vision became dulled. The sense of underlying purposes turned to paranoia; the magic became demonic. Psychedelics became merely one more high. And the Seventies have been a time of blight.

But the glory and promise of 1967 cannot be dismissed as the product of a moment of euphoric over-enthusiasm. Ever since *Three Hearts and Three Lions*, fantasy has insisted more and more strongly on the reality and mystery of magic—in contrast to the Forties' certainty that magic is only technology under another name. And ever since *More Than Human*, *Childhood's End* and "The God Business," one sf writer after another has made his contribution to envisioning the evolutionary leap that humanity is to make.

The succession of worldviews that occurred in this century was a unique transition. It now seems apparent that the hyper-materialistic, hyper-rational state of mind that our culture resisted so hard, and that we presently find so painful and deadly, was not an aberration, but a necessity. It was a Dark Night of the Soul, a means of passage from one broad orientation of consciousness to another.

For as long as we humans trace our history, we have been oriented to the past. The creation of humanity, the gods who created us, and the decreeing of our destiny were all sought in the past. If there was anything moral, anything of meaning, anything miraculous in the universe, its sources lay in the past as well. Dreams of past truth might serve to guide men into the future—but the impulse was always from behind.

For the past three hundred years, however, the members of Western Civilization have been leading humanity in breaking the hold of the past, in doubting all of the ancient truths that gave us our reasons to live and to act for so long. Bit by bit, as we moved from one increasingly materialistic worldview to the next, the ancient truths were discarded.

The final and most difficult step was taken with the first change of worldviews in this century. We did not want to give up our last shreds of virtue and purpose—to which the Victorians had clung so desperately—in exchange for no meaning at all, for emptiness and desolation. But we did it, even though we came to suffer for it.

And the result, achievable in no other way, has been that new sense of truth and meaningfulness that we are awakening to now. We have known since the Forties and the Existentialism of Sartre that humanity itself must create whatever meaning it is to find in the universe, that it must be the source of its own morals and its own destiny. When first stated, that seemed a slim hope.

But when we seek answers, not in our present insufficient selves, but in the future selves immanent within us, the picture changes. In the beings that we may become, and in the beings that we may encounter in the universe, lie all the mystery and truth of the old gods that we conceived in our past.

During the Dark Night that was the period of the last worldview, we left the old past-oriented fantasy behind us. In its place has arisen the literature called science fiction, oriented toward the future and toward the task of self-creation. No longer need we be shoved from behind by an understanding of truth that allows for no revision as time passes, as the fluid world changes, as our minds and nature alter.

In time, sf itself—in whatever new forms it takes—may be over-taken by the miraculous actuality of our future. In time, the succession of worldviews may be discarded as an unnecessary restriction on what we can think or do or become. Gods have no need of myths.

Until that time, we may hold in mind this question and this proposal by Jalaludin Rumi, a Sufi master who died a little more than 700 years ago:

> How long shall we, in the Earth-world, like children
> Fill our laps with dust and stone and scraps?
> Let us leave earth and fly to the heavens,
> Let us leave babyhood and go to the assembly of Man.

—March 1976

Part V: A Season of Change

19/ THE PAST AND THE FUTURE OF SF

[*Fantasy and Science Fiction*, June 1978]

A few years ago, in the course of reviewing Brian W. Aldiss's *Billion Year Spree*, his account of the history of science fiction, we ran into basic internal contradictions of outlook that we could resolve only by the suggestion that there were two Brian Aldisses. One was the young rebel who had discovered SF pulp magazines sent to England as ship ballast and sold cheap in Woolworths' (3p at the counter marked "Yank Mags"), and loved them for their breadth and vitality. The other was a mandarin, an elitist who proposed to divide science fiction into two parts, juvenile junk and high literature, and to cast his lot with the second of these, and never mind the fact that doing so might mean throwing out all the qualities of SF that first brought Aldiss to the genre so many years ago.

If contemporary psychological research is to be credited, the split between head and heart, between rationality and intuition, is not Brian Aldiss's problem alone. Mending the split—which is the result of varying specialization in the two hemispheres of the brain—is the psychic challenge of the era, made more difficult by the fact that the rationalistic processes are "louder," more verbal, easier to attend to than the holistic flashes of intuition. Writing here four years ago, we criticized *Billion Year Spree* for its fragmentary nature, its divisiveness, and its insistence on the application of standards derived from conventional mimetic literature which seemed inappropriate to the actualities of SF. But if the new psychology is correct, we cannot dwell too long and too hard on anyone's verbalisms and formal ideas, including Aldiss's, but instead should look at the whole of what they have to offer. We might notice, for instance, that while it was the rationalistic mandarin Aldiss who wrote the introduction to his compilation *Science Fiction Art*, it was the non-rational, open-hearted lover who edited what is clearly the broadest and warmest of the SF art books of the last several years.

In the new two-volume anthology, *Galactic Empires*, it is again the lover and holist Brian Aldiss who is dominant. It is this Aldiss who says: "You have to love the throw-away explanation . . . You have to love the way villains or heroes flee across the remote star galaxies in pursuit of each other. You have to love the way Elder Races, Hideous Secrets, Ancient Forces or plain sneaky old teleporters crop up at every turn. And you have to love the imperial women." And it is this Aldiss who identifies the non-rational values of these pulp space operas (which a pure rationalist could only consider worthless juvenile junk of the most patent sort): "What the authors do in the main is to tell a story adorned with alien creatures, swordplay, fascinating gadgets, and—for preference—beautiful princesses. The story itself is fairly traditional, the crux being resolved by quick wits, courage, and brute strength. If this sounds like the recipe for a fairy-tale, the point about fairy tales is that they enchant us and enlarge our perceptions . . . Science is thin stuff beside this legendary material."

True, true, all true.

There are twenty-six stories contained in the two volumes of *Galactic Empires*, detailing the rise, maturity and decay of interstellar civilization. The book is not a mere theme anthology; it is an historical record, a summing of a specific phase in an earlier period of science fiction. The bulk of the stories are from the five years 1950-54, the heyday of the galactic empire theme. There are three earlier stories, clearly precursors, and a handful of later stories, clearly vestiges.

Aldiss has done his homework, digging through the pages of *Planet Stories*, *Super Science* and *Startling*, as well as *Astounding* and *Galaxy*. Most of what he found will be unfamiliar to contemporary readers, and the book is so well-integrated that stories which might appear weak or frivolous or questionable when taken on their own assume power and even dignity within the larger context. Through philosophical introductions and quotations from Olaf Stapledon, Aldiss establishes a perspective encompassing many races, many eras, giving *Galactic Empires* a scope and weight as a whole that is simply not present in the stories taken individually.

Galactic Empires is a most readable anthology, lively, vigorous and entertaining. If it has one single obvious limitation, this defect is not in the conception or in the execution of the editing, but is inherent, the reciprocal of the great virtue of the book. That is, the material of the anthology forms a whole, indeed, can be *perceived* as forming a whole, can be arranged as a whole, only because it is stuff of the past, the mirror of yesterday's problems, and yesterday's solutions, too. The stories derive in the main from one concentrated early Fifties period because they are the direct reflection of the head state of the time.

Aldiss says: "Some commentators have claimed to find something sinister in the idea of a galactic civilization, linking it to American Imperialist designs. This seems to me absurd; the stories do not bear that sort of weight of interpretation."

We feel compelled to disagree with Aldiss here, at least in part. The stories do not seem to us sinister, and neither would we speak of "American Imperialist designs." But it seems to us undeniable that they reflect (in the main) the macho, materialistic, might-makes-right attitudes that dominated American thinking in the early Fifties. In fact, what is to be found in these stories is not so much sinister imperialist designs as the theme of the lusty space barbarian injecting vitality into a universe grown effete. How far is it to leap from Poul Anderson's "Star Plunderer" to Graham Greene's American naif in Indo-China in *The Quiet American*? And from there to the American conduct of the war in Vietnam? To an American observer in 1977, blessed with the gift of hindsight, not far at all.

The case against American thinking of twenty years ago is so potentially "provable" that we can only be grateful that some bright Italian Communist, say, did not beat Aldiss to this theme. A careful choice of stories could be damning. But Aldiss has not been doctrinaire in his selections. He has represented a wider reality than the merely materialistic, merely political. The stories that he includes by Clifford Simak, Algis Budrys and Harry Harrison question the assumptions of galactic empire and human dominance (read "American dominance"). They reflect that innocence and idealism that were also present in American thinking in the early Fifties—those qualities that have enabled us to survive the period just concluded, the period of Vietnam and Watergate. Most interestingly, all three of these stories express a longing for communion with aliens—a theme far more characteristic of present-day SF than of the science fiction of the time in which these stories first appeared.

Thank you, Brian. A model anthology.

The *Weird Heroes* series, edited by Byron Preiss, is an attempt to capture the virtues of the pulp magazines of yesteryear and present them in contemporary paperback format. Preiss writes:

> These pulp artists, heroes and authors are to a large extent the literary heritage of *Weird Heroes*. The adventure pulps provided readers with characters that were *fun* to read, whose exploits invited the purchaser to immerse him- or herself in the story on hand. The sf pulps were a visual treat, giving the readers a glimpse of worlds yet unseen, tantalizing them with panoramas of depth and movement which often excelled the stories themselves. If the pulps were to be criticized for anything, it was that in their zeal to entertain, they also lapsed into mindless use of racist, sexist and violent situations which, frankly, showed up in most media of the time. So, our purpose: to develop a *new* showcase in the seventies; to establish a place where characters reflecting current times could have their adventures; to lay the groundwork for a continuing publication which gives ample room for the presentation of new fantasy graphics.

Is it possible or even desirable to revive the pulp magazines in this new format? Can it be done, and is it worth doing?

For the graphic side of *Weird Heroes, Volume Six*, Preiss has drawn upon comic artists like Alex Nino and Ralph Reese and given them full pages in which to display their talents. In art and design, *Weird Heroes* is something new and dynamic. We are not sure that the pulp magazines at their best have been surpassed, but it does seem quite likely that Preiss has hold of a live wire here, an area for exploration and development.

The fiction printed in *Weird Heroes* is by established SF writers Ron Goulart, Ben Bova and Philip José Farmer, and recent SF writer Arthur Byron Cover. It seems much less successful than the artwork. It often lapses into mindless sexism and violence. Even more often, it is not genuinely heroic. Instead, what we are given is an emotionally affectless smerging together of worn-out popular story conventions from an earlier day, locked-room mystery dissolved into galactic SF, *Unknown*-type fantasy explained in unmagical terms, Raymond Chandler mated with Beowulf. This last is Arthur Byron Cover's "Galactic Gumshoe." About it, Cover says, "What I do like about 'Galactic Gumshoe' is the smart-ass quality of the narrative, the smooth prose (save for a few paragraphs), and the way it glorifies [*sic*] in its punk existentialism." In short, what we have here is the debased and degenerated attitudes of an earlier time presented to cynical young comic-book grads. The fictional side of *Weird Heroes* does not seem ultimately viable, but a living fossil, the last expression of those attitudes and materials that Aldiss has collected in *Galactic Empires* in fresher and more sincere form.

The fact is that the Seventies are not the Thirties. It is not possible today to write or think like Raymond Chandler, or like E. E. Smith. And travesty of the pulps is not a true route to recapturing the virtues of the pulps.

The most worthy piece in *Weird Heroes, Volume Six* is a final memoir by Edmond Hamilton, author of seminal Interstellar Patrol stories in the late Twenties, of Captain Future novels, and of Superman comic book scenarios. Hamilton died in February 1977, and is sincerely mourned by us. The era he represents is also dead. There is no going back.

The three remaining books we have for review are not recapitulations like *Galactic Empires* or degenerations like *Weird Heroes*, but honest (if not wholly successful) attempts to express the problems of the present time in SF form. These novels are truly of this present unique moment, the mental configuration that is the latter Seventies. Their authors are all writers to read and writers to watch.

Catchworld is a first novel by a young Scotsman, Chris Boyce. It was a joint winner of a Gollancz/London *Times* SF prize. In an effort to bring the book to the attention of the American SF audience, Ian Watson—perhaps the most purely brilliant of the new SF writers of the Seventies—has nominated *Catchworld* for an SFWA Nebula Award. With these recommendations behind us, it should also be said that if *Catchworld* were not a first novel by a young author published in a time of uncertainty and confusion, it would seem less endorsable and far more questionable than it does.

The initial situation of *Catchworld* is very old head in appearance: a fleet of starships newly set out from Earth on a mission of retaliation against crystalloid beings from Altair who have launched an unprovoked attack against our planet. At the outset, the story appears very technically oriented, not unlike, say, the middle sections of *2001*. As we get deeper into the book, however, the novel reveals itself as something quite different from its initial appearance. It becomes a reality trip exported to interstellar space. The real issue of the book is revealed to be the question of whose "reality" will dominate: the commander of the ship, one or another of the crew, the Machine Intelligence that operates the ship, the programmers of the mission, the aliens that are encountered, or the mysterious force known as the Crow.

The virtues of *Catchworld* are its vigor, its pace, its ceaseless inventiveness, its willingness to plunge headlong into the unknown, and its sometimes brilliant suggestions—as, for instance, the idea that communication with aliens may be achieved on emotional rather than intellectual grounds. The sheer energy generated by *Catchworld* is a rare and valuable quality in a decade when the horizons of SF have been drawn tight around unresolvable knots of defeat, madness and eco-catastrophe.

As to the limitations of *Catchworld* . . . The events of the story are often so murky as to be nearly unintelligible. Characters, events and plot lines are introduced and then never developed, never resolved, never used for anything beyond the immediate zap of a cheap thrill. Ultimately, the book comes perilously close to fitting that situation described by H. G. Wells where anything can happen and nothing is interesting.

Catchworld is a work where much is risked. It is a dance on the razor's edge. Is what is attempted successfully achieved in the end? Probably not. But we would be the last to say that the risks were not worth taking. This book's failures are worth more than many another book's easy success. Look for *Catchworld*, and look, too, for Boyce's next book. If he gets his act together, he could be SF's next resident wildman.

A Place Beyond Man by Cary Neeper is a far more straightforward and intelligible first novel. It is very much a book of this moment, imbued with an overwhelming sense of the negative consequences of those commonplace ideas and attitudes of yesterday that are expressed so offhandedly in the stories included in *Galactic Empires*. Neeper is freaked and nauseated by the ruthless, power-oriented, masculine, "rational" left-brain thinking that threatens to ruin the delicate balances of the biosphere and redound on mankind. As late as the Fifties, power could still be held to be an all-in-all. Neeper knows that power without an equivalent sense of responsibility is corrupt and perverse.

In the near-future we are shown in *A Place Beyond Man* there is "little remaining on Earth that one could call beautiful, few moments that one might call peaceful—but no one there seemed to care. Most human beings let economic pressures downgrade all other considerations to secondary importance." Great suffering and massive die-offs are in prospect. "Meanwhile, those human beings who could obtain enough food and fuel to maintain their mental acuity lived an existence in a dulled awareness, the increasingly lowered minimal standards for air and water purity slowly squeezing thin their hope that they might escape the worsening health statistics for one more year."

You get the picture. And if this were a book published five years ago, you would have the whole picture. Final scene: the last man on Earth going glug-glug-glug as he drowns in a puddle of purple glurp. But this is a later moment, and the book offers more than this.

In *A Place Beyond Man*, there is an observation base on the Moon occupied by (shrewd stroke, token of the new moment) *two* different species of good-guy humanoid aliens, the varoks and ellls, living in harmony, more-or-less, and watching us as we go glug-glug-glug. In an opening sequence that has altogether too much Gothic Romance about it, sensitive, idealistic young microbiologist Tandra Grey is approached at a party by a tall, dark elllonian stranger who gives her the option of accompanying him to the Moon—and off she goes.

Once this initial lump is swallowed—and it's a small lump—*A Place Beyond Man* has much to offer: the aliens and their base, as we get to know them in intimate detail, are fascinating. The story (unlike *Catchworld*) is centered on character interactions. The story is sincere (oh rare virtue in the cynical Seventies) and dedicated to the highest values that the author can imagine. Perhaps the best thing in the novel is Tandra's growing awareness that the froggy elllonians are not human, not to be forced into her conventional mental categories, but are truly different in ways that must be respected. A far cry from the "might makes right and human beings are the rightest of all" attitudes of Campbellian SF.

The ending of the book is a bit of a disappointment. Cary Neeper cannot solve the fundamental problems she has set for herself. Tandra Grey, after her alien education, returns to Earth, but cannot make a dent in the attitudes that are ruining the planet. This is token of our times, when sensitive human beings like Neeper can *see* the changes that must be made, but cannot yet really believe that they will be made. At the end, all Tandra can do is call on her new-found friends and go away with them to a better world elsewhere, murmuring, "So much for Earth."

Not enough. Not enough. Not for all of us readers (and Cary Neeper) who are still faced with the prospect of that purple puddle.

Not enough—but still a far better than ordinary first novel.

C. J. Cherryh, like Cary Neeper, is one of the large number of female writers who have begun to write SF in the Seventies, visible token of those changes in attitude and priority that have made star plundering and galactic barbarianhood the stuff of another now than the present one. Once upon a time, thirty years ago, there were only C. L. Moore and Leigh Brackett at work in the SF domain, disguised behind names that could be taken for male, writing stories that could be taken for the work of men. That simply isn't the case now. After the handful of women writers who became prominent in the Sixties —Kate Wilhelm, Anne McCaffrey, Joanna Russ and Ursula K. Le Guin—a deluge has ensued. It is possible to name half-a-dozen promising new male writers of the Seventies, but it is just as possible to name fifteen or twenty women. A sign of basic change, and one that should be welcomed. If we are to solve the overwhelming problems of this moment, we need the thoughts and ideas that women have held private. We need new and broader mythic expressions.

Of the three novels that are reviewed here, it is *Hunter of Worlds* that is most deeply rooted and most original. Cherryh is a woman in her thirties who has been writing novel after novel in private since she was a young teen-ager. The practice has served her well. *Hunter of Worlds* is the third novel by Cherryh to be published in the space of little more than a year. The first of these, *Gate of Ivrel*, was introduced enthusiastically by Andre Norton, who wished aloud that she could write like Cherryh, and was reviewed with equal enthusiasm in these pages by Algis Budrys, who called Cherryh "a born storyteller." A born storyteller? We can't be too sure of that, not with all those years and years of hard work behind her. That may be selling Cherryh short. But there can be no doubt that she is a pure storyteller in a sense that Boyce and Neeper are not—or are not yet. Storytelling, in this sense, encompasses not just event, as in Boyce's novel, or character, as in Neeper's, but the two woven together in dynamic interaction.

Like other young writers who came of age in the Sixties, and like so many of the new female writers in particular, Cherryh's impulse has been to combine the virtues of traditional science fiction and heroic fantasy. Her roots can be seen to lie in works like *The Lord of the Rings*, *Dune*, and the early romantic novels of Ursula Le Guin. But *Hunter of Worlds* is cast not as sword-and-sorcery or as after-the-bomb melodrama, but as a new sort of galactic adventure, clearly related to the work that Aldiss reprints in *Galactic Empires*, but just as clearly work of a new order.

What is the difference? Perhaps it lies in the fact that humanity is relatively peripheral in this novel, not the central locus of interest, not the lusty muscular rulers of the universe. There are, in fact, no less than three other races of alien beings, each with its own distinct psychology, that stand closer to the center of this story. A situation of this sort would simply not have existed in that earlier era. That it can exist now is token, perhaps, of the passing of American insularity and parochialism. It is an admission that other modes of thought than our own exist, and that some of them may be older and more central than ours. This is underscored by a device that *Hunter of Worlds* shares with Neeper's *A Place Beyond Man*—the frequent use of alien terms. Language is the wellspring of autonomous realities, as Tolkien, in effect, has taught us. But where Neeper gives us one glossary, Cherryh presents us with no less than three.

The result is *real*, but it also makes for slow, hard reading. At any moment you may be faced with a sentence like this: "He is a peculiar being, this *m'metane*, a little rash with us, and without any sense of *takkhenes* to feel his way over the most deadly ground; but his *chanokhia* appeals to me." It is another case, perhaps, of a virtue carrying with it its own defect. The alien vocabularies of *Hunter of Worlds* are both an evidence of other states of mind and an impediment to full identification, full rapport, with the ongoing story.

The other chief limitation of *Hunter of Worlds* is the smallness of the problem posed and resolved, particularly small when compared with the scope of the setting. Cherryh's characters are forced into slavery by the dominant race of the book, the Iduve, forcibly jammed into a mental menage by the Iduve, in order to attack a problem of social dominance and honor raised by an Iduvian renegade. The Iduvian problem is settled, but at the end of the story the focal characters are still slaves and the fundamental imbalance between species still remains. Again, not enough. But again, this insufficiency, this inability to resolve problems on the widest scale that is shared by all three of the novels we are reviewing may be a factor of the cloudiness and uncertainty of the decade in which they were written.

In any case, stick with Cherryh. She's really going to be good.

20/ THE END OF THE GHETTO?

[*Galileo*, October 1977]

Science fiction has entered a season of change. It is not possible yet to say with any surety what things will be like when the period of fluidity is over. Not now. Not when those most centrally and intimately involved in the processes that are changing are in no agreement among themselves about what is happening. Like a flea on an elephant, we are involved in a dynamic process so immense that our precedents, our facts, our hopes and wishes are beside the point. All that we can do is hang on for the ride and see where we are when we arrive.

Here are some of the signs of change in the science fiction universe, as best a curious flea can see them:

The movie *Star Wars* has been the cinema success of 1977. For the first time, some of the delights of (forty-year-old) science fiction have been realized on film. A vast new audience—immensely larger than the special superior few who read Jack Williamson's *The Legion of Space* and E. E. Smith's *Galactic Patrol* when they were serialized in *Astounding Stories* in those long-ago pre-Campbell days—has been thrilled out of its socks by tractor beams, rayguns and galactic rebellion, stuff that written SF long ago left behind it. Even blasé SF readers have been tickled, their sense-of-wonder revived. How neat to see it, not just to imagine it, but to see it happen! It's enough to make a person trade in his Farrah Fawcett-Majors T-shirt for a newer and more potent display. It's enough to make people who don't ordinarily see movies return to movie theaters to see *Star Wars* over and over again.

And *Star Wars*, seemingly, is only the beginning. In November, a cartoon production of *The Hobbit* is to be shown on television. And shortly thereafter, *Close Encounters of the Third Kind*, a major SF movie made by Stephen Spielberg, the young director whose last movie was *Jaws*, is scheduled for release.

Already, as a result of the success of *Star Wars*, there is talk of many new SF film productions. Most of these, no doubt, will be exploitation quickies—*The Creature from the Black Lagoon* or *The Blob* in 1978 disguise. But surely, not all will be of this nature. From our own experience, we can say that there is currently a seemingly very serious interest in making a movie of *Rite of Passage*. The technology now exists to produce SF effects on film. If the audience is ready to view genuine SF movies—and to pay for the privilege—the money to make genuine SF movies will be found. Hollywood may be stupid, but it's not dumb, not where profits are concerned.

We are left with a question which only time will resolve. Is the success of *Star Wars* an isolated phenomenon, a fluke? Or is *Star Wars* a first sign of a fundamental change? Along about 1985, will SF films be the commonplace product of Hollywood, as, say, historical costumers were the common romantic format of an earlier era? It is a sign of change in itself that the question can be seriously raised, even if it cannot yet be answered.

The magazine publications that feature SF are a second area of change within the science fiction microcosm. From 1926, when science fiction was first defined as a distinct publishing category, until the late Fifties, SF was primarily a magazine literature. At first, the science fiction magazines were fashioned in imitation of Hugo Gernsback's popular science magazines. In the Thirties, SF magazines took on the appearance of the racy pulp story magazines of the day, a publishing form that died with the advent of television and the paperback book. Since the late Fifties, magazine fiction of all kinds has become rare, the emphasis of SF publishing has clearly shifted to the paperback, and the few remaining SF magazines have been digest-sized pulps, remnants from another period, fossils confined to a tuckaway corner of the newsstand. New readers of science fiction, like students of ours at Cornell a few years ago, could feel that *Galaxy* and *Analog* and *Fantastic* and the like may safely be ignored, secure in the knowledge that anything in them worth the bother of reading would show up pretty soon as a paperback novel or in an anthology.

But there are special things possible in a magazine that are impossible in a book. A sense of continuity, of editorial direction, of community and mutual growth, of cumulation and common discovery. Books are sold to faceless consumers; magazines are continuing centers of attention for coherent audiences. Feedback is possible in magazines, and their regular publication schedules enforce on them a quality of being in the moment. This is valuable to SF, a literature that makes a conscious effort to reflect current best knowledge.

Without the magazine format of the early *Amazing*, which defined both the genre of science fiction and the community of science-fiction readers, the present SF microcosm of fans, writers, editors and artists, of fanzines, conventions, awards and amateur and professional associations would never have existed. That is an historical fact. It is also safe to say that the Golden Age of *Unknown* and *Astounding* orchestrated by John Campbell in the early Forties would not have had the cumulative impact that it did without the benefit of the special power of regularly-issued, time-reflective, specific audience-addressing magazine publishing.

The power and virtue of magazine publication of SF continues to cast a spell. In the last year, we have seen no less than four new American SF magazines—*Galileo, Cosmos, Unearth* and *Isaac Asimov's Science Fiction Magazine*. Only the last of these has been cast in the old familiar digest-sized, scaled-down pulp format we are used to. The other magazines have been experiments, attempts to present SF magazines in new and contemporary form.

The visible limitations of these new magazines, however, seem to be the result of initial undercapitalization. At best, the new magazines hope to equal the pay scale and other finances of the old lame fossil SF magazines. At worst, they can offer less than the resources of the magazines they hope to supersede.

One is led to wonder . . . If, say, a magazine were to be launched with the verve and power and contemporary feel of a *Crawdaddy*, a *High Times*, a *Heavy Metal*, with graphics as advanced as those to be found on contemporary record jackets, with money to pay two times or five times the rates of *Analog*—could a magazine like that achieve 500,000 or 1,000,000 circulation? Does the whole basic conception of what is proper or possible in SF magazine publishing stand ready to be revolutionized?

The possibility of a magazine like this, even as a talking point, a mere hypothesis, is new. When we traveled to New York recently to collect fact, opinion and rumor about science fiction, we were told that *Penthouse* was seriously considering launching a new-form, new-scale SF magazine earlier this year.* The gamble offers itself. A risk. A leap into the unknown. It seems inevitable that someone will like the odds well enough to try to discover whether a large audience for a dynamic contemporary SF magazine can be gathered.

What *would* be the effect of the focused attention of an SF magazine audience one million strong? It is almost frightening to think about—but we may yet find out.

A third area of change in science fiction is its growing social respectability. In former times, SF was clearly disreputable. It was associated with Buck Rogers and Flash Gordon, with pulp magazines and paperback books, with uncouth engineers with wild hair and muddy boots. It was not the sort of thing that normal, sane, well-adjusted, well-educated people had to be concerned with. Occasionally, a radical young intellectual, the sort of fellow who toyed with Marx, jazz and thoughts of writing the great American novel, would catch a faint glimmering of some of science fiction's potential power and issue a manifesto: "Hey, those science fiction writers are a bunch of dumb geeks who don't know the treasure they have in their hands. We geniuses should thank them very much and take science fiction away from them." (In case you are interested, we are thinking specifically of an essay by Seymour Krim that appeared in *Commonweal* in 1953.) A small, backhanded sort of recognition, that, but to be savored, especially since SF never was and never could be taken over

* This magazine did eventuate, and was called *Omni*.

from outside by usurpers. To write science fiction successfully, one cannot be an outsider, a slummer. No. To write science fiction, you have to *know* science fiction.

Science fiction could never be truly respectable until it was accepted for itself, as it is. SF cannot be cleaned up, cosmeticized, simplified, bastardized, ripped-off or naturalized and remain its true self. And twenty-five years ago, nobody gave a damn about pure-quill SF. Libraries excluded it. Many science fiction classics saw publication only in paperback or fan press editions that were deemed unworthy of admission to most libraries. Academics ignored science fiction.

Oh, but today how different things are! In these Seventies, there are at least four major series designed to resurrect long-forgotten antecedents of science fiction and to give classic science fiction paperbacks and serial novels the respectable surround of critically-introduced hardcover editions—books deliberately aimed at libraries and schools. SF is taught everywhere, in high schools and in colleges. There are academic journals devoted to science fiction, and academic studies of science fiction. Art books are published collecting old pulp SF covers and illustrations—and, as a direct result, Frank R. Paul covers for *Science Wonder Stories* are consciously imitated in art published in *Rolling Stone*. Reference works on science fiction from thoroughly respectable sources like *The New York Times* and R. R. Bowker are common. And perfectly sober publishers like John Day issue strange special books like Damon Knight's recent historical memoir devoted to the late Thirties and early Forties New York science fiction fan group, the Futurians (who, as proof that commitment to science fiction is indeed necessary to those who write and edit it, included Frederik Pohl, Donald Wollheim, Cyril Kornbluth, Isaac Asimov, Judith Merril, Robert Lowndes, Richard Wilson, James Blish and Knight himself).

Where does scholarship end and nostalgia begin? What is intriguing is that with many of these critical and historical publications it is almost impossible to draw the line. It is as though secret young readers of science fiction from twenty-five years ago had grown up into positions where they might certify and attest to the acceptability of science fiction and seek to remind others like them of what science fiction was like. Repeat that. What science fiction *was* like. For all of this work looks backward. It has about it the odor of an end-of-an-era summation, as though all of modern science fiction's past, from Gernsback in 1926 through the death of John Campbell in 1971, was a thing safely dead that might be hashed, sliced, dissected, analyzed and arranged with total impunity. No longer an unfathomable ongoingness; rather, a body of work produced in a former time that now can be seen whole. The appearance of encyclopedias of science fiction seems an irrefutable sign of this. Encyclopedias are graveyards.

Social respectability for long-disreputable science fiction at exactly the moment when the era of science fiction in the Gernsback-Campbell mode has come to an end. What does it mean? What does it portend?

Difficult to say, but here is a possibility to chew upon. Seymour Krim and Frederik Pohl were born near the beginning of the Twenties in New York. Many of their experiences and orientations were similar. But Pohl imprinted on science fiction when he was young, and grew up to agent it, and edit it, and write it. Krim only encountered science fiction much later, envied its energy, perceived its mythic significance, and at least for a moment entertained the thought of seizing it. But could not, as he was an outsider—foreign to science fiction. He simply did not know enough to write science fiction. But the effect of all this present-day publication of SF history, criticism, bibliography, art, reference, memoirs, classics and whatnot must surely be that what was once the special property of a favored few, like Pohl and the Futurians, has now emerged as public history, public culture. Anybody who wants to now can identify with the struggles of the Futurians, groove on Virgil Finlay illustrations, read Delany in the public library, and study Heinlein and Bradbury in school. In short, it seems possible that everybody ten years from now, as a matter of course, may assume that science fiction's past is not something alien, but *their* past. There may be no more Frederik Pohls and Seymour Krims, no more insiders who know and outsiders who yearn. *Everybody* may be an insider. Anybody who reads then may be reading science fiction. Anybody who writes then may be writing science fiction.

Could this happen? The publications of today are that which can make a general acceptance of this sort possible. And it is a fact-in-becoming that children whose daily bread in the Sixties was *Star Trek* must surely be the readers and writers of the new SF of the Eighties. It is they, if anyone, who are the new audience prepared to love *Star Wars*, and the new audience that may be waiting to be gathered by the so-far-unborn contemporary, high-powered, high-financed SF magazine we were suggesting above.

The ferment in SF book publishing visible in the past few years—a fourth area of current change—may be confirmation of this. Since 1972, the number of SF book titles published annually has risen steadily and dramatically, from about 350 titles in a year to nearly a thousand in 1976. *Children of Dune*, the novel version of *Star Wars* and the Tolkienesque fantasy *Sword of Shannara* have all been best-sellers. Publishers who formerly disdained science fiction are now not only issuing it, but advertising it as heavily or more heavily than their conventional product. The advance for three books by Arthur C. Clarke is reported as amounting to $500,000; for a paperback re-print of a Joe Haldeman novel, a reported $100,000; for a first novel by a young SF writer, $30,000. This is heady stuff for SF writers long used to $2000 advances. Twenty years ago, it was said that there were only a half-dozen science fiction writers able to make a full-time living from their work. Today there must be many more than that—together with a good many SF writers not yet graduated from $2000 advances but still attempting to live as full-time writers.

Strange and new. So strange, indeed, was the prospect of staid old art book publishers issuing new profusely illustrated editions of *The Hobbit* for $35 and of full-page ads for the latest Frank Herbert novel that *Galileo* phoned us to ask what was happening. We didn't know and couldn't say for certain, but as readers and writers of SF we were intrigued to find out.

In an effort to get a line on current fact and opinion, we made two recent journeys. First, we drove to East Lansing, Michigan, for a combined Milford and Clarion Writers' Conference reunion celebrating twenty years of one and ten years of the other. The East Lansing area, home of Michigan State University, which has become a permanent location for the intensive Clarion workshops for would-be SF writers, is seemingly a locus of science-fictionism. There is an active SF club at the university. The town boasts The Curious Bookshop which specializes in nostalgia items and science fiction. And no less than four SF writers (including one of us) and one science fiction illustrator (Ed Emsh) have been produced by the immediate area. Perhaps it's the water.

We circulated at the reunion, interrupting the on-going flurry of Moopsball tourneys, filling dead spots in conversation, in public and in private asking our questions: What is happening in science fiction publishing? Is it temporary or permanent? Why all the big money floating around?

Algis Budrys, writer, editor and reviewer of science fiction and recent Clarion instructor for a week, gave one strange answer. The money, he said, is around now because the great corporate giants who control publishing find a tax advantage for themselves in strategic losses of humungous amounts of money. The writer and his work are a near-irrelevance to this process. Budrys' final advice, delivered emphatically to an audience of writers and would-be writers of SF, was "Take the money and run."

Gordon Dickson, past Science Fiction Writers of America president and by reputation one of the science fiction world's shrewdest business heads, gave a very different reading of the weather. He saw a permanent change in the fortunes of SF, an emergence from the pulp ghetto. He said, "The money and advertising now being spent on SF is no more than mainstream books have had all along. Science fiction is no longer considered sub-literature. It's the end of the ghetto, and we have to grow used to that."

Cosmic accident or fundamental change? We drove back to Pennsylvania from Michigan, paused overnight, and then traveled to New York to talk to editors and agents of science fiction in an effort to resolve the matter for ourselves.

But again, we found radical disagreement. A disagreement of interpretation, that is, after one universally acknowledged point of agreement: that science fiction book publishing is in a state of boom.

Donald Wollheim, who was a Futurian, a sometime writer of science fiction, who shaped and directed the science fiction program of Ace Books for nearly twenty years, discovering the likes of Delany and Le Guin, and now publishes his own specialty line of science fiction paperbacks, DAW Books, takes a somewhat doubtful view of the situation. He has lived through many cycles of boom and bust in science fiction publishing and sees the current situation as not fundamentally different from what has come before: "Something is very strange, and the question is, is somebody wrong? The SF market is a ghastly, overinflated situation."

Wollheim perceives the present boom as due to the ignorance of raw young editors leaping into science fiction publishing with no real knowledge or experience of the true sales of science fiction books. His own experience shows that the print order of science fiction paperbacks is among the lowest of all genres, lower than that of gothics, for instance. "Wholesalers have not increased their orders. Even an advance of $25,000 would not be profitable for me. Publishers will see how narrow the margin of profit actually is, and in about two years there will be a disastrous bust."

Judy-Lynn del Rey of Ballantine/Del Rey Books agrees with Wollheim in seeing the current science fiction publishing boom as based on illusion. And, she feels, on literary pretensions that must inevitably be exposed when sales returns come in. She sees SF as properly being a form of pure entertainment, bought by a special audience of clearly limited size.

Newer and younger editors, however, perceive things somewhat differently. Many do agree that the present publishing situation in science fiction is fevered, but see this as less dangerous than do del Rey and Wollheim. They perceive a new, permanent and wider audience for SF and mean to capture it.

Nancy Neiman of Avon Books says, "SF is no longer beyond the pale. In the last three or four years, publishers have realized that there is money to be made in SF. Readers buy books in *stacks*, and more and more are reading it into their thirties and forties. The SF market continues to grow whatever the subtrends of the moment are."

Tom Dunne, editor at St. Martin's Press, an established hardcover publishing house that only recently has begun to issue SF books and had great success with novels like Haldeman's *The Forever War* and Pohl's *Gateway*, speaks in similar terms: "The advances are higher because the audience is bigger. I see SF as being where the mystery novel was during the Twenties. Closet fans are coming out. People who read SF as kids and outgrew it are now returning. It's a matter of legitimacy, status, class and age. Publishers who still stereotype SF as a literature for 12- to 15-year olds are wrong. I was in Washington recently and discovered that Asimov's *Foundation* books are the in thing to read among senatorial assistants, committee aides and people like that."

So what is to be made of all this conflicting testimony? One point that emerged clearly as we talked to editors and agents was the degree to which their expectations and commitments determined the characterization of the facts we received.

Inevitably, our own hopes, expectations and prejudices must influence what we are able to see of this ongoing present moment of change in science fiction—and influence what we might conclude about it. The lean of our own thought throughout this essay should be apparent. We believe that all the instances of change we have named are related and part of a single phenomenon. It seems to us that a process of fundamental change is in progress, sweeping all of us along with it, believers and unbelievers alike. Change everywhere in the reception of SF, one point of change reinforcing the others so that very soon it will be undeniably apparent that Gordon Dickson is right, and the ghetto days of science fiction belong to yesterday.

That's what we believe, or would like to believe. But only time will tell.

At the very least, we can all afford to attend to a point made by Tom Dunne of St. Martin's Press: "When previous science fiction booms have ended, invariably they have left an SF audience that is significantly larger than when the boom began." And Donald Wollheim, noting that the increase in SF titles has not cut into the number of copies that individual SF titles sell, agrees that Dunne may have a point.

And at the most . . . well . . . When the two of us left the offices of St. Martin's Press to catch a subway train, we seized seats and caught our breath. And then, looking around, we noticed that the middle-aged Chinese man to our right was lost in a book, moving his lips as he read—a paperback copy of Asimov's *Foundation and Empire*.

A random member of the new and larger SF audience revealing himself?

A Chinese spy doing his homework, trying to get a line on the inscrutable thought processes of the capitalist imperialist bureaucrats in Washington?

A sign of the times?

21/ DEALING WITH HIGHER REALITIES

[*Fantasy and Science Fiction*, August 1979]

Among the other functions it serves, SF is a device for wrestling with the problem that concerns us most. Not the little nagging problems, but the major problem of relating ourselves to the universe. SF allows us to phrase our puzzlements in symbol, to write them in mythic scale, and to test possible solutions.

Modern science fiction came into being during the Great Depression of the Thirties, a time when the universe seemed to be not only alien and incomprehensible, but indifferent, even hostile. As much as Roosevelt and the New Deal, SF was concerned to present an answer to how to live, act, think and survive in such a world. The answer, arrived at in art before it was applied in life, was that a universe like that could best be coped with by a hard-boiled pragmatist armed with the facts and a .45 automatic. That answer served a generation. It explains the A-bombs we dropped on Japan to end World War II; it explains John Wayne as the model hero of the age; and it goes far to account for the nature and style of Campbellian science fiction.

But the failure of technocratic thinking is painfully evident in Vietnam and Watergate. A bulldozer and a .45 automatic are no solution to the very different dislocations that haunt the Seventies. The ecological universe we now find ourselves inhabiting baffles and frustrates us, not because it is unyielding and indifferent, but because it is so flexible and responsive. The world has now grown so inter-dependent that something as minor as political turmoil in one coun-try like Iran can shake the economics of the planet. Trying to master such a world with a table of facts and a tough-minded attitude is as inappropriate as attempting to command the tide. New and more subtle approaches are required.

In a time like this, it is appropriate to look into the mythic mirror of SF for answers. But in a new time like this one, familiar tradi-tional old "modern science fiction"—worked up to frame answers to the questions of forty years ago—is an inadequate and inappro-priate form, as out of date as John Wayne. To provide an answer to the problem of the present, SF must change. Already it is possible to see that the phrasing of the problem of discovering more sensitive modes of engagement with the universe has begun to affect the form and content of SF.

John Varley's second novel, *Titan*, is a crude, vigorous attempt to deal with present problems within the framework of science fiction. Varley is an exasperating writer to review. His novel is flimsy and awkward, like a cheap made-for-tv movie, but at the same time he is gifted with freshness of vision and a sense of the necessities of the moment. This makes him worth reading for all his limitations.

In *Titan*, a team of NASA astronauts en route to Saturn early in the next century discovers an artificial world the size of a moon— a great wheel 1300 kilometers across, like a pocket-sized version of Larry Niven's *Ringworld*, As the astronauts approach, giant tentacles reach out from the rim of the wheel to crack open their spaceship —the *Ringmaster*. Four women and three men awaken separately on the surface of the world within the wheel. The rest of the novel consists of their adventures in this giant playground.

Varley's people are two-dimensional. Their motivations are arbi-trary and unconvincing. Although he introduces seven main char-acters, Varley is unable to handle more than three at a time. It is only by elimination of other characters and the sheer accumulation of detail that two of the women—the Captain, Cirocco, and her loyal sidekick, Gaby—come to take on a certain solidity.

Varley is content to build his story out of whatever old pieces come to hand. This may be something as pulp-magazinish as those giant tentacles, or as frankly derivative as all the many explicit borrowings from contemporary SF books and movies like *Ringworld* and *2001*. At times these borrowings are amusing, at other times annoying. But in one place in particular, the climax of the novel, where an evocation of *The Wizard of Oz* leaves an aftertaste of humbug in what would otherwise be a genuine confrontation with a superior being, Varley's practice seriously undercuts the effect of his work.

If Varley is attempting to find his way into the new coming world, his route is not by thinking or by imagining, but by feeling. The freshest and most compelling things in *Titan* are certain moments of essential experience: journeying wide-eyed through a permanently daylit landscape; climbing the most giant of all staircases to heaven; snuggling up in a cozy hole with your best friend while storms rage outside.

Titan is the story of a world more self-aware, more mutually supportive, more totally alive than our own. This novel indicates what sort of characters might be able to grow and thrive in such a world. *Titan* promises that the rewards of growth in a wonder world are to break out of the straitjacket of NASAness—that travesty of the science fiction dreams of our childhood—to find a new life of true adventure and purpose.

Varley's answer to the problem of the moment is to suggest that a limited lower level organism may be restructured as the result of contact with a higher being. But Varley arrives at this answer only as a special case. It is true within his pocket world, but it is not exportable back to the larger context of Earth. In order to retain their new abilities, his protagonists must defy their NASA "rescuers" and remain behind in their special world.

Poul Anderson's giant new science fiction novel, *The Avatar*, is clearly intended as a work of ambition. A raw young writer like John Varley may be careless and crude and redeem himself by being fresh. A writer like Poul Anderson, established for thirty years, runs the opposite risk of presenting us with well-polished familiarity. And for more than half the length of *The Avatar*, what we are given is Anderson-as-before, so much the same as to verge on self-parody. How well we know these story pieces: the ruggedly individualistic entrepreneur and his minstrel-mistress; the friendly alien; the repressive schemes of Earthbound bureaucrats; the battles, ah, the battles. Anderson's touch is surer now than it was twenty or twenty-five years ago . . . but, why bother? Only distant promise of better things and our love for the Anderson of old—when all this stuff was new —kept us reading.

Anderson's premise is that on the far side of Earth's orbit explorers have discovered a T machine—an alien device for instantaneous travel to other solar systems. From it issues a robotic voice, announcing that the machine is a gift from the Others, mysterious beings who love mankind but must remain unknown to them. The machine offers access to the entire galaxy. But to set out without knowing the return coordinates—and the robot provides coordinates for but one earth-like planet—is to go forth without assurances of coming back.

What we have here, eventually, is a story like Varley's and like so many SF stories of the Thirties, a story in which a number of human individuals are abruptly thrust into an absolutely alien environment. All that they meet is strange and unprecedented. Their only resources are character and experience. The point of elemental stories like these is to discover what personal qualities and values may enable a human being to survive and grow. It is only after more than two hundred pages of macho melodrama that Anderson finally sends his protagonists on a journey Into the Unknown. Then the whole tone of the story shifts and for the first time *The Avatar* becomes something more than rote. Real purpose at last becomes clear—to continue faring in space and time, led by an unquenchable yearning for the Others and the hope of returning to Earth to offer humanity the stars.

At the same time, there is a shift in character focus. Emphasis moves from the male entrepreneur to the contrasting characters of two females—the computer-linked Joelle and the minstrel Caitlín.

Joelle is arrogant, intellectually elitist, sexually arid. Caitlín is spontaneous, life-affirming, and loving. Perhaps the most moving episode in the book is an encounter with the inhabitants of a Jupiter-like planet as seen through Caitlín's eyes—a love-feast expressed in light and music.

The visioned purpose of *The Avatar*, however, remains only partly fulfilled. The Others prove able to perceive higher realities, but they themselves are not of a higher reality. Like Varley's mother alien in *Titan*, who is her world, Anderson's Others are merely god-like. They are not gods.

If *The Avatar* fails to satisfy completely, it is only in part a matter of Anderson's personal limitations. In part, it is a matter of the limitations of traditional science fiction as a form of SF. The fundamental premise of traditional science fiction is the supremacy of science; no other gods—who aren't frauds—are admitted. If there is a human hunger for true gods as basic as the hunger for food or sex—and this is what the great quest of *The Avatar* suggests—then traditional science fiction can offer us only shadows without substance. It can arouse our hunger but never satisfy it.

Sight of Proteus is a first novel by Charles Sheffield, a technically-trained writer in his thirties whose stories have recently been attracting attention in the SF magazines.* Varley's *Titan* and Anderson's *The Avatar* are brave books, traditional science fiction novels confronting new problems and in the process becoming something other than science fiction as science fiction has been, however imperfectly. Sheffield's book invokes some of the same vision, and then turns away. *Sight of Proteus* is merely science fiction. It shows the limitations of mere science fiction in this new day.

The appearance of Sheffield's novel is of this moment. Serious issues are raised, but only in the background. *Sight of Proteus* describes an overpopulated future Earth, resources strained to the limit, a world in which social engineering is no longer sufficient to maintain stability, a world in which computer-regulated biofeedback makes

---

* An error on our part: Sheffield, the British-born President of the American Astronautical Society, is in his forties, the generation of Larry Niven rather than of Michael Bishop.

it possible for anyone to alter his face and body into other form, human or non-human.

There are wild and wonderful possibilities in this premise, great occasions for drama and confrontations, but Sheffield turns his back on them. The story he tells concerns Behrooz Wolf, a member and eventually the head of the Office of Form Control, charged with repressing illegal form-changes. But Wolf himself never changes in form—not even once for kicks on a boring Sunday. He doesn't even encounter the social breakdown we are told about.

One indication of the search for more sensitive modes of engagement with the universe in the new SF is the frequent obsession with sex and the redefinition of sexual roles. Both Varley and Anderson are able to concentrate on female characters and both their novels are filled with frantic sexual couplings. *Sight of Proteus* is most clearly old-fashioned science fiction in its masculine-minded sexlessness, like an Asimov story in the Campbell *Astounding*. Behrooz Wolf is apparently asexual. In Sheffield's novel there are no major female characters. In fact, there are no real women at all—only Marilyn Monroe clones, Pleasure Dome hostesses, and form-changers who claim to have been female once upon a time but have given it up.

By the standards of traditional science fiction, as resolutely masculine and virginal as a Boy Scout camp, all the frenzied pairings and re-pairings found in the new SF must seem bewildering, inappropriate and unnecessary. The emphasis on bisexuality, or androgyny, or on intimacy with aliens must appear perverse. But in the SF stories of today, such sexual openness seems to be one of the most valuable qualities that a protagonist can carry with him when he is whisked away into the unknown. Far more valuable than a .45. And what does it mean? It may amount to an emerging faith that there is no being in the universe whom we cannot meet with trust and love.

However, instead of confrontation with change and difference, Sheffield deflects his story into triviality—intellectual problem-solving, pursuit of an enigmatic father figure, and well-rehearsed questions about scientific amorality. The final impression left by *Sight of Proteus* is not the protean possibility promised by the title and blurb, but rather physical and emotional stasis—encased in a static fictional form. Alone of the books reviewed here, *Sight of Proteus* concludes in bitterness and regret. If the imperative of the time is to face the unknown and embrace it, a story like this one that intimates the unknown and then retreats from it can only end in bitterness.

Whatever changes of sex and sex role are to be found in current SF, it seems to be a truism that male writers still tend to write stories framed as traditional science fiction, while the new female writers of the Seventies prefer to write fantasy. In a time when there is a separation between fact and belief, these writers prefer to believe, and let the facts go hang, rather than the reverse.

Diane Duane's alternate-world fantasy, *The Door Into Fire*, is an unusually self-assured first novel. Duane has all the deftness of touch, the insight into levels of motivation, and the originality of invention that John Varley's *Titan* is missing. But perhaps her greatest virtue is that she doesn't retreat from the freedom to be mythic that fantasy offers—and that traditional science fiction is shy of. In Duane's novel there is a true Goddess who created the universe and set in train an inescapable cosmic struggle of entropy and love, but who also takes on human form for the sake of human lovers. *The Door Into Fire* is pervaded by an awareness of this cosmic drama and by a sense that all the characters and events are but varying expressions of it.

In Duane's universe, there are two modes of power. One is sorcery —a cool jazzy magic, essentially static and manipulative, at its best with inert things, like our own science. Duane's description of sorcery is unique and vivid. Here, like a poetic vision of a scientist manipulating equations, spells take on form as a physical structure in the mind of a sorcerer:

> The spells had to be built, word by cautious word, each word placed delicately on edge against another, stressed and counter-stressed, pronunciations clean and careful, intentions plain . . . The balance was perilous to maintain, and once or twice he almost lost it as a word shifted under another's weight. Another one turned on

the word next to it—they were too much alike—and savaged it before Herewiss could remove the offender and put another, less violent, but also less effective, in its place. He had to make up for the loss of power elsewhere, at the top of the structure. He wasn't sure whether it would stand up to the strain or not, and the whole crystalline framework swayed uncertainly for a moment, chiming like frozen bells in the wind, like icy branches brittle and metallic—

But in addition to this sorcery, there is also Flame, the true creative ability to build and heal, possessed by only a few women and no men. Herewiss, Duane's protagonist, is the first male in many generations with the potential for Flame. *The Door Into Fire* concerns Herewiss's search for the self-knowledge necessary for him to use Flame, and the Goddess through whom and for whom his quest is achieved.

However rich it may be, *The Door Into Fire* is only a half-solution to the problem of the time, another compromise. Herewiss does engage with a higher level of being and is able to return to his world with necessary knowledge. But his world is not ours. It is another place, a place where our facts are set aside. That is the limitation of fantasy. Like Varley's pocket-sized fantastic world in *Titan*, Duane's universe is a special case. It works only so long as we and our problems are kept at a distance.

What is clear is that Duane is a writer to pay attention to. This first novel does display certain self-indulgences. Duane shows herself willing to settle for easy emotional effects. Her major characters are all young, good-looking, nobly-born and incredibly sexy. They are also self-centered and do exactly as they please without much concern for external obligations or the effects of their actions on others. When they are frustrated, they become petulant. If Duane can learn to see more deeply into her characters and be as ruthless with them and with herself in the promised sequels to *The Door Into Fire* as is appropriate, she may well become a major SF novelist. If she continues to have things the easy way, at the least she will be an entertaining melodramatist. Perhaps her next novel will tell.

Ian Watson is a young British SF writer who never makes anything easy, either for himself or for his readers. His plots are not fast-moving or melodramatic. His characters are not particularly likeable or easy to identify with. He has little patience for elaborating upon the traditional devices of SF, either science fiction or fantasy. He gives the impression of being intent upon a particular goal in a single-minded way that tolerates nothing that does not pertain to the goal. *Miracle Visitors*, Watson's fifth novel, may be his closest approach yet to his objective.

The protagonist of *Miracle Visitors* is John Deacon, a researcher into altered states of consciousness who uses his researches as a way of tiptoeing up to the bounds of the paranormal while still keeping a safe necessary distance. However, one experiment in hypnosis gets —from his point of view—out of hand, and he is plunged into the weird realm of UFOs, Men in Black, and other anomalous creatures.

Deacon's problem is to work out the nature and purpose of these creatures, which can neither be taken literally as genuine aliens nor dismissed as mere hallucinations. The answer that Watson offers is that they are expressions of the planetary consciousness of Earth. They are the means by which it communicates symbolically to the individual human consciousnesses which are among its components.

Like Duane, Watson is admitting a truly higher order, not just a similitude of the divine. But not in some fantasy universe. Here and now. Like Varley, Watson presents a consciousness that is a world —but not some pseudo-mechanical construct swimming in the range of Saturn. Mother Earth.

Watson is offering a dangerous and radical conclusion—which has its basis, as Watson knows and acknowledges, in Sufic thought. If it were taken as a premise, it would form the basis of a new SF that could incorporate both traditional science fiction and fantasy. Aliens and fairies, science and sorcery are revealed as equally real, equally partial fragments of a genuine science of consciousness. Even relating to the world with ecological propriety—the highest end that our culture in general can presently acknowledge—in Watson's order becomes merely a means to the higher goal of relating appropriately to the planetary consciousness.

In *Miracle Visitors*, John Deacon eventually does make contact with ultimate reality in the form of that Void that is pure consciousness. But even Ian Watson in this story is not permanently successful in bridging the gap that exists between higher reality and everyday life. His protagonist is no longer able to exist in our world, but can only dip an occasional toe back into it as a miracle visitor himself.

This insufficiency may mean that Watson still has a distance to travel in his unique progress. It may mean that SF is only half-able to manifest its new form as yet, like a butterfly only partly metamorphosed. But *Miracle Visitors* is the boldest attempt we know of on the part of contemporary SF to confront its own nature and purpose, and alter.

22/ THE DEATH OF SCIENCE FICTION: A DREAM

1. The Mandarin's Butterfly

In 1960—a year which memory says should have been only yesterday, but which the evidences of change assure us was a long long
time ago—a Chicago SF fan, a printer by trade named Earl Kemp,
compiled and published a significant symposium entitled *Who Killed
Science Fiction?* A strange and disturbing question, that. This publication was intended to win a Hugo Award, and it did.

In those days, Earl Kemp was frankly ambitious. He was a country
boy come to the city to make his mark. He was—he says today,
time and California having made their mark upon him—"a person
me now wouldn't approve of, except for the abundance of energy."
Science fiction fandom was Kemp's chosen field of endeavor. In the
Fifties, he was a founding partner and the initial sparkplug of Advent, pioneer publishers of SF criticism and the publishers of this
book. In 1962, Kemp would be the Chairman of a World Science
Fiction Convention. If in 1960 he aimed deliberately for a best fan
publication Hugo, it was as part of a career as a science fiction fan
—and because the Pulitzer and Nobel Prizes seemed beyond reach,
while this did not.

Because now is now and not then, the true scale of Kemp's ambition is hard to fully appreciate. Chicon III, the Worldcon in Chicago over which Kemp presided, drew 550 people from all over the

United States. So much have things changed in the years since that these days a convention held in mid-week in the second-best motel in Earl Kemp's native dale in Arkansas would likely draw that many.

Science fiction fandom today is a full order of magnitude larger than it was in 1960. In 1980, a sensibly-run regional SF convention may cut its membership off arbitrarily at 2500 attendees—if need be turning away people in order to keep the con to a tidy size. The time is at hand now when a World Science Fiction Convention will draw ten thousand people.

In 1960, Earl Kemp was out to make his stir amongst a much smaller number. In the present climate, when movie stars like Christopher Reeve may present dramatic Hugos at a World Science Fiction Convention, it takes a real leap of the imagination to see what things were formerly like and to perceive that the scale of Kemp's campaign to win his Hugo was on the order of an outside run to be elected King of High School Homecoming.

What Kemp did was to send a letter with five questions to 108 people, and to print the 71 replies he received. The questions were bad questions—sloppily formulated, presumptive of the answers that Kemp wanted to hear, repetitive and open-ended. The best of them were the first—"Do you feel that magazine science fiction is dead?" —and the fourth—"Should we look to the original paperback as a point of salvation?"

What Kemp was inquiring about was not truly "Who killed science fiction?" In fact, his questions were not really about science fiction at all, but about changes in publishing economics and practice and their effect on science fiction.

For thirty years before 1960, the chief mode of publication for science fiction was the pulp magazine. So long and intimate was the connection between the two that there were those who confused form and content—identifying science fiction with the pulps, the pulps with science fiction—and could not see how if the pulps died science fiction could continue to live. And now the pulps were dying. The magazines of science fiction that had flowered in such profusion during the Fifties were withering in bunches and who could say if any would survive?

Kemp's questions sought to know what was happening and what was going to happen and who was to *blame* for it all. From this distance, it seems that he was asking for a maximally-emotional response to a situation that his respondents were actually powerless to affect. In politics, this is called demagoguery. What it might be called in a campaign to win a Hugo Award, we know not.

In those days, science fiction fandom was a small family and science fiction professionals were fans, amongst whom they were known affectionately as "dirty pros." Kemp had a wide acquaintance and a lot of nerve. Among the people who replied to his questions were science fiction editors: John Campbell, Anthony Boucher, H. L. Gold, Robert Lowndes, Ray Palmer, Damon Knight, James Blish, Robert Mills, Donald Wollheim and Hugo Gernsback. Every one of these, of course, was a writer of SF as well as an editor. Many other writers were represented as well: Poul Anderson replied to Kemp's survey, and Marion Zimmer Bradley; Alfred Bester and Ray Bradbury; Robert Silverberg and E. E. Smith, Ph.D. Never before or since in the history of science fiction have so many people centrally involved in the production of science fiction stood and spoken to a common topic.

More or less, that is. The nature of the questions insured that the answers would shoot off in all directions.

Along with his hype title, his sensationalistic questions and his big gun contributors, it was part of Kemp's strategy to make his publication as rare as possible—an instant collector's item. He mimeographed and distributed only 125 copies of *Who Killed Science Fiction?* Seventy-one were sent to the contributors. Forty more were distributed to the membership of SAPS, the Spectator Amateur Press Society, one of a number of fan organizations for the generation and exchange of publications. Two copies went to the Library of Congress for copyright purposes. The final dozen copies were given to friends of Kemp.

So great was the prestige, the mystique of this publication—and so small and malleable was science fiction fandom then—that Kemp's strategy was completely successful. His publication did indeed win the Hugo it was aimed to garner. As Kemp says, "It was especially rewarding because it meant that the people who voted for *Who Killed Science Fiction?* were, in most instances, voting for something they had to borrow even to see, as there was no chance for them to own a copy."

And that was that. A successful coup—Kemp had his award. He went on from that to his convention chairmanship, and from there to a career in editing in California.

Years passed. Science fiction successfully completed the transition from the pulp magazine to the paperback book already in progress when Kemp set up his cry of doubt and accusation, and it even prospered. The content of science fiction and the nature of its audience changed and changed again.

And such was the lasting effect of Kemp's strategy in winning his award that for fully twenty years after 1960, no one was able to read *Who Killed Science Fiction?* It was not available unless you knew one of the contributors or a SAPS member vintage 1960. The two of us never saw a copy and never had a chance to read it in all that time.

On the other hand, such was the mystery and prestige of Kemp's award-winning symposium that the question asked by its title was given leave to take on life of its own: "Who killed science fiction?" Like the boy asking about the king's clothes, the effect of the existence of this unthinkable question was to make the unthinkable thinkable . . .

What was the degree of mortality of science fiction? Could its most fundamental materials and attitudes and assumptions become exhausted? What might follow them?

It is questions like these that underlie this book. If in these essays we have perceived SF as something like a phoenix, clearly dying in its incarnation as "modern science fiction" while simultaneously being reborn in new form—both the same SF as always and something crucially different—well, this is an image that is at least remotely owed to the existence of *Who Killed Science Fiction?*

We were reminded of this last summer when Earl Kemp's question, "who killed science fiction?", loomed up again out of nowhere at exactly that moment when we were most ready to appreciate its power and influence on our work. We were then in the earliest stages of planning this concluding essay for a new edition of *SF in Dimension*—an essay that by all rights should identify and resolve the recurring themes of this book—when a letter arrived from Earl Kemp.

Alexei had first met Earl Kemp at a World Science Fiction Convention in 1959, and after the manner of fandom had seen him half-a-dozen times over the years at science fiction gatherings. It was at one of these, and then another, in the mid-Sixties that Kemp suggested that Alexei write his critical book on the fiction of Robert Heinlein for Advent. That was in the days when Kemp still lived in Chicago and took an active role in the affairs of Advent.

Now, for old time's sake, Earl wished a favor. A new edition of *Who Killed Science Fiction?* was in progress and Earl wanted a contribution from Alexei. Four questions were enclosed.

How strange! How wonderful! There was no doubt that we would answer. The universal laws of reciprocal maintenance are inexorable, and we had no choice. But beyond that, we were as curious as anyone as to what really might be contained in the original edition of *Who Killed Science Fiction?* when Kemp's time capsule was finally opened to the light of day. We wanted to see what it had to say ourselves.

In 1960, there were none of today's dedicated collectors of interviews with science fiction writers. Interviewing science fiction writers is now a profession, even an industry, but Hugo Gernsback and E. E. Smith are long dead and there is no hauling them back for an interview with Darrell Schweitzer or Jeffrey Elliot. The opportunity offered by *Who Killed Science Fiction?* to overhear the likes of Gernsback and Smith now takes on the appearance of a special occasion—something like seeing rare silent movie footage of D. W. Griffith stalking about and flailing his arms—important for its documentary value, even though the event of record was a trivial, long-forgotten brouhaha.

If now, twenty years after, a contemporary publisher wished to reissue *Who Killed Science Fiction?* in updated and augmented form, dignifying this one-time mimeographed amateur publication with the immortality of hard covers and acid-free paper, we were more than ready to do what we could to help the project along. But it wasn't easy. Earl Kemp's questions presented difficulties.

The first one was: "Looking backward for twenty years at the fortunate turn of events that has brought us from science fiction's low reception in 1960 to today—what single event (or person) do you feel contributed most to 1980's success, particularly in academic circles and visual mediums such as television, film, etc.?"

That is a fuzzy and presumptive question. One of the things it presumes—like the original symposium questions in 1960—is that the container of science fiction is the same as the content. In 1960, there was an assumption that if science fiction publishing was undergoing transition, science fiction might be dying. In 1980, there is the assumption that the current commercial success of science fiction means that all is well with science fiction.

'Taint so.

Science fiction—modern science fiction, that flashy new form of SF that John W. Campbell mother-henned into being when he assumed the editorship of *Astounding*, the science fiction of the Golden Age, *that* science fiction—is dying.

Who killed science fiction?

Reduced to their essentials, Earl Kemp's new questions asked for comment on the current happy reception of science fiction, for looks backward twenty years, and forward, and for the choice of a favored science fiction book from the last twenty years.

The problem, the challenge, presented by the letter from Earl Kemp was to write an answer that said everything that needed to be said. In this new edition of *Who Killed Science Fiction?* it seemed only right to acknowledge just how much of a stimulation to our writing and thinking the title of this symposium had been. And since the nominal occasion for speaking at all was Earl Kemp's new questions, it seemed no less than appropriate to do our best to answer them. But, most urgent of all, it seemed proper, even necessary, to say what we really believed: that modern science fiction is an aged actor, a tired old gasper taking his last bows, with his bright young replacement already waiting in the wings preparing to take his place on stage.

How ever were we to say all of these incompatible things in almost

no space at all? But then, SF itself regularly attempts to knit together the incompatible and express the impossible. Should less be
asked of SF criticism?

Out of the materials at hand and our sense of what we had to say
came the answer. We announced that we had solved the case at last.
We knew, we said—half-serious, half-joking—who had killed science
fiction. It was Robert Heinlein in his new novel, *"The Number of
the Beast—"*.

Now it was by pure coincidence—some would say by meaningful
synchronicity—that we had just read a copy of Heinlein's immense
new fiction. As we are writing this, *"The Number of the Beast—"*
has just been published in England and will not see print in the
United States until this coming August. In the summer of 1979,
Heinlein's book was placed in auction on the literary block in New
York where it was knocked down for a reputed half-million dollars
from a paperback house whose intention it is to issue the book
in large paperback format with over fifty illustrations by Richard
Powers.

Oh my my, have things changed since 1960 when H. L. Gold, editor of *Galaxy*, could write in Kemp's symposium: "No writer should
try to make his living out of science fiction." And Alfred Bester,
who himself has prospered in the contemporary SF publishing boom,
could say: "Sensible people have always known that science fiction
is a luxury for the writer ... The man who dedicates himself exclusively to science fiction today has my sympathy, because he's fallen
on hard times, but he doesn't have my respect."

Another measure of change from former days is to be seen in
the great length of time between the sale of Heinlein's book and
its publication. These days even a hot item like *"The Number of
the Beast—"* may be in the publication pipeline for a year or year-
and-a-half. That is a far cry from the early days of modern science
fiction. Heinlein's first story, "Life-Line," saw print in the August
1939 issue of *Astounding* only four months after it was bought by
Campbell.

Because of the auction, many copies of the typist's manuscript of
"The Number of the Beast—" were in circulation in New York.

One of them drifted into our hands.

Now, this was no mere accident even if we didn't look for it to happen. We are interested in Heinlein's work. We have had more to say about his stories than anyone else. It is only natural in view of the power of an interest such as ours that the universe should arrange to grant us an early view of a new Heinlein novel.

But it never happened before.

Perhaps it is enough to say that here in our hand the Kemp questions were, and there across the room the Heinlein book was, and the two seemed to fit together. It was fate, intertwined destinies.

After all, Heinlein was the original link between Kemp and Alexei; and *Heinlein in Dimension* had been the reason that Heinlein, who abhors all discussion of his work, had ended his friendship with Kemp. So that was one reason for bringing Heinlein into our answer. Another was that if ever there was an example of the current clout of science fiction, about which Kemp was inquiring, it must surely be *"The Number of the Beast—"*, the first half-million dollar SF book. Most of all, however, if we indicted Heinlein's new book for being the culprit in the death of science fiction, it was because it was appropriate to do so. There can be no doubt at all that one of the specific intentions of *"The Number of the Beast—"* is to kill science fiction.

We wrote: "From the perspective of the year 2000, if one is concerned with the fate of science fiction, the most important book of the period 1960 to 1980 may well be Robert Heinlein's *"The Number of the Beast—"*, for Heinlein's deliberate undermining of the metaphysical centrality and veracity of the Future History series, Heinlein's fundamental contribution to modern science fiction."

If John W. Campbell, as editor of *Astounding*, was the architect of the Golden Age of science fiction, Robert Heinlein was its chief engineer. Heinlein has been the deepest as well as the most central writer of modern science fiction. That is the reason for our continuing interest in him.

Heinlein's impact upon science fiction was immediate. He sold "Life-Line" in April 1939. In the following year, he wrote no less than three short novels, four novelets and seven short stories. He was admired by Campbell and frankly hero-worshipped by Campbell's cleverest young disciple, Isaac Asimov. Asimov still remembers. In a recent anthology, *Isaac Asimov Presents the Great Science Fiction Stories: Volume 1, 1939*, Asimov, now grown gray-haired and himself become an institution, says: "No one ever dominated the science fiction field as Bob did in the first few years of his career."

No less than eight of the stories that Heinlein wrote in his first year, including "Life-Line," were part of his Future History series. The effect of these stories, set against a common structuring of time-to-come, was to take the future—in earlier SF pictured as a remote, undifferentiated and alien location—and to bring it close and make it apprehensible. In the same way, Asimov, with the inspiration of Heinlein's example and with direction from Campbell, would put spatial and political structuring around the galactic expanses in his Foundation stories.

These structurings of space and time were absolutely central to modern science fiction. Asimov had it right—they were the foundation.

The great claim of modern science fiction was to realism and to truth. Until recently, it has been hard for a child born during the era of modern science fiction to appreciate how very different was the SF that came before it. That was wild speculation, baseless fantasy. Campbell as a new editor insisted on fact and upon extrapolations from fact. All those who found this too difficult or not to their taste—as Edmond Hamilton for one did—ceased to write for *Astounding* or were swept out of the magazine.

No more fuzzy romanticism. Campbell's modern science fiction was *the way the future would be*.

This conviction of ability to weigh and measure and map and historically recount *the* future is apparent in a statement Campbell made in a 1942 issue of *Writer's Digest* describing the fiction he wished to buy for *Astounding*. Terry Carr found it in a fanzine of the period and printed it in another recent anthology, *Classic Science Fiction: The First Golden Age*. Campbell said: "We want stories of the future told for scientifically trained, technically employed adults; central theme usually problems of an ordinary technician employed in an industry of fifty to fifty thousand years hence."

This was a pose. The fiction printed in *Astounding* was not really like this. But of the fiction printed in *Astounding*, that which was most like this description—and most concerned with increments of future time, besides—was Robert Heinlein's Future History stories.

It has been more than forty years since "Life-Line" was first published and through all that time, whenever lists have been assembled of essential books of modern science fiction, Heinlein's Future History stories have invariably been at the top. As late as 1980, among the respondents to Earl Kemp's new set of questions, more than one picked Heinlein's Future History stories as their favorite book of the last twenty years.

If you speak about the Future History stories of Robert Heinlein, you are talking about the spinal cord of modern science fiction.

Heinlein's new fiction, *"The Number of the Beast—"*, is a very strange book. Like his other two novels of the last ten years, *I Will Fear No Evil* and *Time Enough for Love*, Heinlein's new book is long, windy, rambling and private—an old man's fantasy far removed from the rigor and exactitude of the modern science fiction of the Campbell *Astounding*. In fact, it would be fair to say that *"The Number of the Beast—"* is not really a novel at all. Rather, it is something more like a long dramatic meditation on the relationship between reality and the imagination, an extended headtrip.

A few years ago, we heard Heinlein give a public talk. With the masterly timing and subtle misdirection of a quick-change artist, he rapped his knuckles on the lectern, saying, "I know the difference between *this* and reality."

Heinlein has always been a tricky devil, full of disguise and deceit under his surface of simplicity and command of fact. From the very first, he has known that one of the best ways to say the incredible and get away with it is to speak with such boldness and charm that no one credits you for a moment with sincerely believing what you are saying. Heinlein is still like that, but with wrinkles.

From the first, there was more to Robert Heinlein than the Future History. During the Thirties, before he began to write, he was into weird stuff. Among the stories that burst out of him during that first year of writing were two that John Campbell immediately rejected. They didn't fit into the structure of modern science fiction that he was erecting. One of these stories was "Lost Legacy," based on the cults that cluster around Mt. Shasta and worship the knowledge of Lemuria. The other, published by Campbell only after two years and rewriting, and then under the never-again-used pseudonym Caleb Saunders, was "Elsewhen," based on the six-dimensional space/time speculations of Pyotr Ouspensky, the disciple of the pop-eyed mystical master, Gurdjieff.

When Heinlein and Campbell got their signals straight, Heinlein went on to write the strangest and most powerful stories of the Golden Age — stories in which the light of wonder and mystery shines through holes that open in apparently straight-forward reality: "They," " 'And He Built a Crooked House'," "By His Bootstraps," and "Universe."

"The Number of the Beast—" is stranger than any of these. It is the queerest thing Heinlein has ever written.

From the beginning in this book, nothing is as it seems. This is a constructional principle.

Everything is misleading here, changing its role, changing its identity, revealing itself as something other than what it has been taken for. The initial chapter begins with what proves to be a case of mistaken identity. What has the appearance at first of a story with a robust action plot of the sort Heinlein was writing thirty years ago. becomes a dimensional travelogue and four-way conversation by a gang of Robert Heinlein fans. (Yes, you may believe this: two prefer *Stranger in a Strange Land*, two the Future History series.) So tricky indeed is this book that it is at least an arguable possibility that by the end of the second of this book's forty-eight chapters, all four major characters are dead.

In this book, Ouspensky's six-dimensional space/time is brought forth again and raised to its own power and then raised again. Six to the sixth to the sixth. This is both 666, the Number of the Beast from the Book of Revelation, and ten million sextillion plus, the number of universes that are available to be explored in what at first is called, misleadingly, a time machine. This opener of dimensions, of course, the book being what it is, at first is mistaken by one of the characters for a portable sewing machine.

Heinlein's characters are goosed into flight by an encounter with what they call a "Black Hat"—an alien lobster disguised as a Forest Ranger. They identify this Black Beast with the Beast of Revelation, quoting to each other—" 'And I beheld another beast coming up out of the earth; and he had two horns like a lamb, and spake as a dragon'." Heinlein's characters chop this creature to pieces with swords, and then, in fear and trembling, off the voyagers dash into the dimensions of space, time and the imagination.

These characters are named "Carter" and "Burroughs." One is even named "Dejah Thoris." They travel first to Mars, which they jokingly call "Barsoom." And they go much further, from one story-book universe to another. They buzz Lilliput, and they travel to Oz. They even encounter E. E. Smith in the guise of a Lensman—as though after death authors were preserved as characters in their own fictions.

But here, too, there are problems of identity. "Barsoom" turns out not to be Edgar Rice Burroughs' Mars. Instead the story has British and Russian colonies locked in imperial struggle on Mars—as though this switched situation were something that Heinlein remembered from another scientific romance that he had read in boyhood. And can one completely believe and assent to an Oz where Glinda the Good speaks of *"lebensraum"*—with all the connotations of bully-boy brutality that word has had in the Twentieth Century?

But that is this book for you. At any given moment, values seem fixed and secure, but a blink of the eye, a turn of the head, and values and facts prove to have shifted.

And everywhere that Heinlein's characters travel through the ten million sextillion universes of the imagination, they encounter evidences of the mysterious Black Beast they have killed—appearing as one, appearing as many, appearing in disguise, appearing under a variety of names like "wog" and "vermin," but always hanging around.

One important clue as to what is going on in this strange book is offered in an episode where Lewis Carroll, the author of *Alice in*

Wonderland, is encountered by Dejah Thoris Burroughs Carter beside
a rabbit hole. The chosen mode of discourse between them is the
sorites. This is a logical form in which a number of apparently separate propositions are set forth—such as "When I work a Logic-
example without grumbling, you may be sure it is one I can understand" and "I can'n't understand examples that are not arranged in
regular order, like those I am used to"—and a chain of reasoning
must be followed through them to produce some proposition not
explicitly stated—such as "No kitten with green eyes will play with
a gorilla."

In the mouth of Lewis Carroll, Heinlein places a sorites borrowed
from Carroll's book *Symbolic Logic*, the implicit conclusion of which
is, "All my dreams come true." Deety replies with another sorites—
lightly adapted from another of Carroll's examples—to indicate that
the machine nearby is a time-traveling device.

It becomes apparent that *"The Number of the Beast—"* itself is
a kind of sorites. It piles one screwy statement on top of another.
The promise of this book is that if a chain of reasoning is discovered
and followed back and forth, through and around the events of the
story, unusual conclusions not explicitly stated will be forthcoming.

It has been a constructional principle of modern science fiction
for little bits of information to be scattered here and there, by the
way and between the lines. It is a requirement of the genre that out
of facts and clues and fragments of action, the reader must assemble
a picture of the on-going context and meaning of the science fiction
story. Heinlein was the originator and first master of this technique.

What is presented in *"The Number of the Beast—"* is a challenge
of integration to the reader something like this, but far more difficult
because here there are no facts that can be firmly and finally trusted.
All is tentative, all is in doubt, no matter how positively stated or
presumably true. There is no firm foundation here, unlike a traditional modern science fiction story, for a stable reality to be built
upon.

However, at least one conclusion can definitely be drawn if the
information revealed here and there in *"The Number of the Beast—"*
is carefully knitted together: The home base of the four central char-

acters of the story is not our continuum, and the Future History continuum—where they encounter and join forces with Lazarus Long—is neither their own future nor ours.

In short, *"The Number of the Beast—"* says that the Future History stories—the backbone, the life-line of modern science fiction—are not *the* future. Nor the future of any world remotely parallel to our own. According to *"The Number of the Beast—"*, the Future History is to be found at right angles to our continuum. It is as explicitly storybook a universe as Oz.

At a stroke, the pretensions of modern science fiction are ended. The chief engineer of the modern science fiction project has himself set the charge and pressed the button that must slowly, beautifully, majestically bring the modern science fiction edifice crumbling, tumbling down. Heinlein knew what he was doing and did it deliberately. It was no accident. Story and the imagination is what this book is *about*.

Who killed science fiction?

If one person is to be given credit or blame, it should be Robert Heinlein.

2. The Butterfly's Mandarin

During the summer that we read *"The Number of the Beast—"* and answered Earl Kemp's letter, on through the fall and into the winter, we considered the subject of this essay and what it should contain. The severest critic of the first edition of *SF in Dimension* wrote of it—"the book has no form or structure and is annoyingly repetitive." If we were to write a new concluding essay for our book, it should do its level best to sum all the aspects of our varying explorations of the dimensions of SF and make them one. It should show that underlying form or structure of the book that is composed partly out of repetition and partly not—like the pattern of music made out of rhythm and repetition, sounds and silence. *SF in Dimension* itself is a kind of inadvertent sorites, a sorites by accumulation. This new essay should trace the webwork of thought that weaves through these essays and binds them together.

This would mean, for instance, that Brian Aldiss, who has served as a mirror so often in these essays, should be mentioned. Since he has no further part to play in this dream, we will mention him now.

Having vowed to remedy this flaw in our book, we then came to think that this essay should do even more. It should present the philosophy of this book, and the aesthetic of this book. It should demonstrate one more time the tools and techniques we have evolved in the course of this book. It should solve puzzling questions left unanswered in earlier essays. It should be an experiment, one more exploration of SF, that multi-dimensional elephant in the dark. It should further the sorites by one more premise and conclusion.

All these "shoulds" on the shoulders of one unwritten essay.

But, at this point, we did have two necessities in hand. We had a practical aim: to satisfy—in our own terms and to the best of our ability—our sense of what might be necessary to make an indisputable whole of *SF in Dimension*. And we had an ideal goal for this essay: it should be an all-in-all, a one-hand trapeze act, a perfect dazzling expression of the nature and meaning of SF at one singular moment in time. Knowing that we were bound to fail. Knowing that All can never be told, but only indicated.

Still, that was the ideal we had in mind. You have to have an ideal in mind.

What was left for us to discover was the materials out of which our essay should be fabricated. Throughout all these essays, as far as our ideals and our speculations may have taken us, it has been our studied intent to stick to the letter of our texts, to respect the actual facts of SF. That is why we are given to quote so much.

To help us decide what we should read, and what we should write about, and how we should cast this piece, we went back to the beginning of *SF in Dimension* and read it through. Going back over things again often yields new perspectives and new conclusions. This time through we saw the essays dividing into three lines of investigation: one, probes into the nature and history of SF; two, reconsiderations of the particular strengths and characteristic limitations of Robert Heinlein as the predominant and epitomal writer of modern science fiction; three, descriptions of the current state of SF, inner and outer, in terms of books and the marketplace, as it changed through the Seventies, together with attempts to peer into the future.

Could all these different lines be braided together in a single pattern?

The materials out of which we might turn sausage into elephant were at hand. All that was required of us was to have steady nerves and to serve as transformers:

Appropriate to our first line of investigation, there was *Who Killed Science Fiction?*, which had been the long-ago, half-forgotten-'til-now stimulus for our inquiries into the nature and history of SF. Here it was again, a basis for discussion, just when we needed it. We decided to call Earl Kemp up and hustle him for a copy.

For point two, by happy synchronicity, there was *"The Number of the Beast—"*, Heinlein's first new novel since *Time Enough for Love* in 1973. This was a book immensely pertinent to the subject of modern science fiction—and we had a copy in our hands, another tool presenting itself as necessary.

For a description of the current state of SF, all we need do was look about us. In the days of the Golden Age, only a small number of novels were published in the science fiction magazines, and only the rarest SF book saw print. In our youth, science fiction books were still so rare and precious that when we saw one, we would slip it under our coat and run away chuckling. These days, SF books are published by the hundred—however slow the process for any one book—and all that is necessary is to sort amongst them to discover which of them have new things to say.

During all the years in which we wrote our regularly occasional book review essays for *F&SF*, we were always highly constrained in our choice of books. We had to find those that were not already chosen by the usual reviewer, Algis Budrys. We had to discover like books, or likenesses in books, as we could and discuss them in a very limited space. This time we had the opportunity to do something very different. We could take a broad overview of the books of the field, and not merely play with one circumscribed point of observation. Anything at all that it was appropriate to say, we could take the space to say. Any current SF book that chose to speak up and bear witness to the contemporary state of modern science fiction could be quoted, discussed or used by way of example.

We sorted through the stacks of freebie SF books from one publisher and another piled up on the library floor and chose out the most interesting. We let editors take us out to lunch and press on us their hottest new and forthcoming books. We called publishers for review copies of books that we had heard of and wanted to see. We collected hardcover books and paperbacks, galleys and manuscripts. We even bought books off the newsstand like regular civilians.

Oh, we read a mickle and a pickle of SF books. Unlike the early days of science fiction book publishing—after the Golden Age, in the years following World War II—only six of these books were short story anthologies. Three of them were the initial books in a series of retrospective best-of-the-year collections edited by Isaac Asimov and Martin H. Greenberg beginning with the first years of the Golden Age: 1939, 1940 and 1941. Another was an anthology of Golden Age stories edited by Terry Carr. There was a book of contemporary French SF stories edited by Maxim Jakubowski, and another edited by him of international SF, published for the 1979 World Science Fiction Convention in Brighton, England.

We read two slim volumes of interviews with twelve SF writers from Theodore Sturgeon to Larry Niven. *Science Fiction Voices #1* was the work of Darrell Schweitzer, while Jeffrey M. Elliot was responsible for the interviews in *Science Fiction Voices #2*. The two take very different approaches to the art of interview. Schweitzer wings his questions and sometimes revises them after the fact to bring a dim or sloppy question into line with a good answer. Elliot takes a more structured and formal approach. Both methods, surprisingly, can produce the revealing remark.

Most of all, however, we read science fiction novels in a profusion that the Golden Age never knew. There were novels by writers who, like Heinlein and Asimov, entered science fiction in 1939, at the outset of the Golden Age: novels by A. E. van Vogt, Alfred Bester and Frederik Pohl, all of them new books. We read novels by the smart-set writers of the Fifties: Robert Silverberg and Robert Sheckley. We read books by writers of our own age like John Crowley and Michael Bishop. We read books by women writers like Doris Lessing and Joan Vinge. We read books by up-and-comers like Arsen Darnay and Spider Robinson. We read British novels like Richard Cowper's *The Road to Corlay* and first novels like Rudy Rucker's *White Light*.

Here in these books and the others we gathered, and in *Who Killed Science Fiction?* and *"The Number of the Beast—"*, were the materials of this concluding essay we needed to write. Shake the beads, see the pattern.

There, from *"The Number of the Beast—"*, was to be taken a central metaphor identifiable with what we have been calling the World Beyond the Hill throughout this book: that realm of reality/imagination that contains ten million sextillion separate universes, none of which—most specifically not those of modern science fiction—are uniquely privileged. Also from Heinlein we might take warning of the Black Beast that lurks, and heed of the need to be tricky and fast on our feet.

In *Who Killed Science Fiction?*—the unknown, unread *Who Killed Science Fiction?* of our imagination, the *Who Killed Science Fiction?* to which we were chiefly replying when we wrote our answer to Earl Kemp—we might find a thesis and a title: "The Death of Science Fiction." Resolved: modern science fiction is dying, and it's not a bad thing.

And from the other thirty books, everything else. Everything else that we might need on this imaginary expedition of ours: Here in these books we could find stories from the Golden Age and memories of when modern science fiction was new, and look into them for messages. Here we could find all the evidence we might need of the limited, corrupt and decrepit state of even the best and most innovative contemporary science fiction when set beside the mathematical real/imaginary plenitudes offered by the Realm of 666. Best of all, here in these books, when things looked darkest, we could find, like germinating seeds, the symbols and materials that will provide the basis for a new and even more splendid Golden Age of SF. A happy ending!

And the form of this piece should be a story. But no, no. No merely another story—we've cast commentary in the form of a story before.

A story in the form of a dream.

A dream.

Only a dream could possibly reconcile all our disparate aims and ideals with the strange array of facts that we must set in order. Only a dream narrative could contain all the shifts and contrasts and radical alterations of value in this simple yet complex story we have to tell. And calling these memorial services for modern science fiction "a dream" just might serve to disarm and soothe those skittish readers who otherwise could find the death of science fiction too bald a thought to bear.

Of course this final exploration of ours should be a dream. And properly it should be dedicated to Lewis Carroll, too.

And so at last we were prepared to begin our conclusion. Ah, but where to begin it?

A dream and a sorites have this much in common: in either, any premise at all may be entertained and these strangenesses may occur in any order. Isn't it at least a little bit odd that the sorites, one of the classic models of formal reasoning, and the dream, the most freewheeling and least understood of ordinary human mental states, should carry us to the same place? For what else other than the land of dreams is the realm where—to quote the conclusions of a number of Carrollian logic examples—"no country infested by dragons fails to be interesting, my writing-desk is full of live scorpions, an egg of the Great Auk is not to be had for a song, no lobster expects impossibilities, I always avoid a kangaroo, and all my dreams come true."

And if it is true that a sorites is grumble-provoking to solve, not being arranged in regular order as we are used to, then what sort of laborious and torturous exercises of thought are necessary to construct one? Where ever do you begin?

Charles Fort, that great collector of anomalous data, advised (according to a contemporary T-shirt), "One measures a circle beginning anywhere."

First, however, we ought to say something about the new expanded edition of *Who Killed Science Fiction?* Earl Kemp did send us a Xerox copy of the manuscript, along with the request that we let him know what we thought of it. In the meantime, *Who Killed Science Fiction?* had run into one of those extended delays that affect contemporary publishing and been withdrawn from its new publisher by Kemp—which makes its connection with our inquiry here all the more singular and special. In the cosmic economy, has Kemp been using us, have we been using Kemp, or have we all been dancing together in some larger pattern?

Who Killed Science Fiction? is a fascinating collection of fragments, none of which, either separately or together, seem at first appearance to add up to a case for the death of science fiction. A queer book with a misleading title. Perhaps another sorites.

The new edition of *Who Killed Science Fiction?* begins with a long foreword by Earl Kemp entitled "Twenty Reconstructed/Fragmented Years"—which is as involuted and self-reflecting in its own way as Heinlein in *"The Number of the Beast—"*. In bewildered amazement at it all, Kemp tries to express how he got from the days when he was a plotter of Hugo coups to his very different present self and state of mind, age fifty.

To find a way to *say* what a long strange trip it's been (Grateful Dead), Kemp reaches to the model of Kurt Vonnegut's Billy Pilgrim, in *Slaughterhouse-Five*, who has come unglued in time and is everywhere everywhen he has ever been simultaneously in pieces, and he and we must put it all together somehow. In a collage of events and impressions, punctuated by fragments of song lyrics like "Jojo left his home in Tucson, Arizona, bought some California grass (*Let It Be*)," Kemp tells us what has made the difference: travel, sex, drugs, divorce, rock'n'roll, and conversations while in jail with a would-be Presidential assassin and a Manson Child.

Abruptly, there follows an introduction by Frank M. Robinson, "For Sale: One Cloudy Crystal Ball," detailing all of SF's apparent successes in the twenty years since the original edition of *Who Killed Science Fiction?*.

It is yet another jolt, then, to be thrown back into the murky atmosphere of 1960 and listen to those strange voices shouting answers to doubtful questions. The smell of ancient tempest in a teapot is overwhelming. But then, certain remarks still leap forth from the page:

> Science fiction is by no means dead. It is, however, being killed off by the lack of science in stories.   —*Hugo Gernsback*

> It isn't *science* fiction that's in trouble—it's *fantasy* fiction!
> —*John W. Campbell, Jr.*

> Anybody who announces that he is a science fiction writer is announcing that he is in damn bad company financially and artistically. You are trying to conduct a post-mortem without a corpse. I would love to provide you with one. I would love to see the expression *science fiction* butchered this very minute in order that stories with science in them not be identified, in the minds of intelligent readers, with pulpers, beginners and hacks.
> —*Kurt Vonnegut, Jr.*

At this distance, what it all seems to prove is that there are a lot of different points of view floating around at any given moment, and that even awkward irrelevant questions can startle forth revealing answers, as *Science Fiction Voices #1* confirms.

Three appendices follow. One, from the original symposium, is a graph showing the numbers of science fiction magazine titles and issues plunging grimly downward in 1958 and 1959. The second appendix presents a group of survivors from among the original symposium respondents, giving answers to Earl Kemp's new questions, saying, "It seems that I was right." And the third is younger persons like ourselves also giving answer to Earl Kemp's new questions and saying, "Sorry, I never saw a copy of *Who Killed Science Fiction?*." And all of these people explaining, explaining, explaining why, just as Kemp's questions asked them to do. Explaining why the implications of the graph were so *wrong*, so beside the point.

Finally, there is an afterword by Earl Kemp entitled "The Singer's Going to Sing a Song," in which, all alone with us, the original symposium, and his memories, Kemp fingers a tear and says . . . twenty years ago today . . . and . . . you're such a lovely audience . . . (*Sgt. Pepper*). He names some of the magazines that were already gone in 1960 and others that have ceased to exist since. He regrets the passing of Hugo Gernsback, John Campbell, James Blish, Anthony Boucher, Willy Ley, "Doc" Smith, and many others. He mourns a vanished world:

> Who could have foreseen, twenty years ago, that anyone would be sitting here celebrating the absence of so much that is so dear to all of us, as I am doing at the moment I write these words?

Where did it all go?

Where *did* it all go?

The 1980? edition of *Who Killed Science Fiction?* is an often fascinating and possibly useful document, but it doesn't hang together as a coherent book. It flip-flops back and forth amidst a conflict of ambivalences, doubtful answers and mixed emotions. If finally *Who Killed Science Fiction?* has anything to say to us about the state of science fiction in 1980, it must be this—this is a moment of confusion, celebration and grief.

Similarly, if *"The Number of the Beast—"* is ultimately an unsatisfying and even repellent book despite its dimensional explorations, its puzzles and games, and its assertions about the state of modern science fiction, it is partly because this headtrip of Heinlein's, too, is fragmented and inconclusive. For all the scope that is implied by a meta-universe containing ten million sextillion separate continua, the characters of *"The Number of the Beast—"* are so caught up in the toils of fear and desire, so wrapped up in themselves, that they truly go nowhere at all. Instead they bicker and banter, fuck and philosophize, swap hats and shadow-box with their own reflections.

This book is so self-involved, so ultimately self-referential, that it comes to seem a Black Hole of egotism. It is one more trick of *"The Number of the Beast—"* that what is promised is access to all possibility, but what is actually presented—the imaginary/real continuum *of the book itself*—is a featureless interior in which disembodied voices talk and talk and talk and *nothing* ever really happens.

How can anything happen? The characters in *"The Number of the Beast—"* are a fearful lot, and their first concern is self-protection.

As in *Methuselah's Children*, Heinlein's early Future History novel about Lazarus Long and the long-lived Howard Families, the pro-

tagonists of *"The Number of the Beast—"* set forth on their journey
into space and time not out of a desire to explore new possibility,
but as an attempt to escape from more trouble than they know how
to handle. In fact, the code phrase that automatically sends their
vehicle—"the Gay Deceiver"—into a safe place in another dimension is "Bug-Out."

These characters are cringing cowards. Once they are abroad in
the Realm of 666, they do their best to locate universes that are safe
and easy and cozy and warm—and that have medical facilities that
they can trust.

Above all, they do their best to avoid any universe that might contain beings superior to themselves. It is not just that they want no
part of H. P. Lovecraft's story universe, with its implacable human-
hating Great Old Ones. As Jacob Burroughs, the inventor of the
dimensional machine, puts it:

> "Supermen or angels would trouble me more than vermin. I know
> what to do with a 'Black Hat'—*kill it!* But a superman would make
> me feel so inferior that I would not want to go on living."

As Heinlein characters will, these Heinlein characters (and Robert
Heinlein fans) have the gift of mutual recognition. One glance and
they know each other to be not low unworthy vermin, not intoler-
ably superior supermen, but perfectly perfect Heinlein Individuals,
all thinking alike and talking alike, all knowing precisely the same
books and the same games.

This is an exclusive society, tightly circumscribed. Early in the
book, they pledge mutual allegiance. One character says, "All for
one, and one for all!" and another answers, "Us four, no more."

Them four, no more, hiding out in the foothills of the meta-
universe, sneaking into cardboard towns erected for their benefit,
and then high-tailing it back out of town. Always ready to bug-out.

With cabin fever such as theirs, they have nothing to do but wran-
gle with each other and wrestle for dominance. Since all these characters, regardless of nominal sex or age or role, are really the same
character—multiple persons locked inside one head, as it were, as in
Heinlein's *I Will Fear No Evil*—this is not easy for them to do.
They manage the trick by divvying up shipboard functions, and then

regularly changing the duty roster. They fight to find out which of them will make the worst Captain.

To make this question of blurred identity even more confusing, within any chapter a character is likely to be referred to only by his or her current function. Other characters may speak and not be identified. Since first-person narration is passed around among the characters, too, from chapter to chapter, it is very easy to lose track of which speaker is who.

The question arises, just how much of this confusion is a fault of the book and how much is a deliberate design? How much does Robert Heinlein know?

Since at least as early in his career as "By His Bootstraps"— another story of identity in conflict with itself—Heinlein has found it possible to present characters at the centers of his stories who are less than admirable, less than likeable, or less than sane, without directly acknowledging to the reader that these persons might be strange in his eyes. With all those many pages of nearly-interminable four-way monolog in *"The Number of the Beast—"*, there is no sign to the reader from Heinlein as to what we should think of the strange comedy game of musical chairs being played, and no direct comment at all from Heinlein on the untrustworthiness, cowardice, purpose-lessness, greed and insincerity displayed by his four cosmic stray lambs, all of whom have been given leave to sound so typically, self-confidently and dogmatically Heinleinian.

Heinlein's book has three parts and an envoy. Part One is entitled "The Mandarin's Butterfly." Part Two is entitled "The Butterfly's Mandarin." These opposed images—a reference to a traditional Chinese paradox, like the Red King's dream of Alice while Alice is dreaming of the Red King in Lewis Carroll's *Through the Looking-Glass*—ask us to say which frame of existence it is that is *really* real, whose consciousness it is that is privileged, which dreamer it is who determines the dream?

"The Number of the Beast—", then, is like Chris Boyce's novel of a couple of years ago, *Catchworld*, in asking which among a variety of contending realities will prevail in a contest of strength. But there is this difference. In *"The Number of the Beast—"* there is only one

consciousness at war with itself. The question is altered and becomes, "In a continuum that is populated solely by Heinlein Individuals, which among them is to have precedence?"

Eventually, Heinlein's party of four beats out a solution to this special problem: they call it "pantheistic multiperson solipsism." This is token of their recognition and acknowledgment that they are in a common dream. And it means that when they meet Lazarus Long, a Heinlein character who cheats for the pure pleasure of it, and Andrew Jackson "Slipstick" Libby, resurrected from the dead and altered in sex to female, Heinlein's Gang of Four is not flummoxed. They can afford to recognize these other Heinlein Individuals, wrestle with them, fuck them, and add them to the collective conscious/unconscious.

With this settled, a grand jamboree is held: "The First Centennial Convention of the InterUniversal Society for Eschatological Pantheistic Multiple-Ego Solipsism." The avowed purpose of this party is "to define the difference—if any—between 'real' and 'imaginary'."

The guests here include a wide variety of earlier Heinlein characters. Jubal Harshaw and Mordan Claude are present, Oscar Gordon, Rufo, Podkayne of Mars, Hazel Stone, even Jonathan Hoag. The official guest list includes many writers of SF, living and dead, a variety of Heinlein's favorite fictional characters, and friends of Heinlein from all over:

> "Some of the most bloodthirsty people in Known Space are attending this convention. Female authors. Critics. Harlan. Both Heinleins. I not only *insist* that you be armed but I hope you stick close to someone fast on the draw."

But even here there are special exclusions. Those critics are stuck away in a private little hell guarded by Jonathan Hoag. This special Critics Lounge is shaped like a Klein bottle, and once in, we are warned, you can be trapped there forever. Lazarus Long (why ever does *he* hate critics?) describes this special place to Jubal Harshaw:

> "I promised critics free entrance, I made no mention of exit. I promised them typewriters and tape recorders; I did *not* promise typewriter ribbons or recorder tapes. I promised them their own private bar, no charges. Wouldn't be fair to charge as the bar has no

liquor in it. There is a lavish dining room but no kitchen."

"Lafe, wouldn't it have been kinder to have liquidated them?"

"Who said I wanted to be *kind* to them? They won't starve; their commissary is by the Kilkenny Cats method. It should please them; they are used to human flesh and enjoy drinking blood—some I suspect of eating their young. But, Jubal, there is an easy way out . . . for any critic who is even half as smart as he *thinks* he is."

"Go on."

"He has to be able to *read*! He has to be able to read his own language, understand it, not distort the meaning. If he can *read*, he can walk out at once." Lazarus shrugged. "But so few critics *ever* learn to read."

And so, presumably, there we would be, we Panshins, stuck away forever in the Critics Lounge—along with Damon Knight, James Blish, Cyril Kornbluth and all the others, including Bob Heinlein, who have tried to resolve the puzzle of SF. Now left to our own devices, we'd no more hang out in a bar like this (even with this high-tone company) than we would match writing muscles in Elaine's. It's not our sort of scene. More likely, we'd be off in a convention room somewhere, Alexei toking it up with the Caterpillar and Torve the Trog, Cory sitting cross-legged and talking earnestly to the Mother Thing from *Have Space Suit—Will Travel* and the High One from "By His Bootstraps," and our eighteen-month-old son Adam grabbing tit or showing off or bouncing from lap to lap.

But this isn't our dream. We are Heinlein's critics—there is no doubt about that. If he means *anybody*, he means us. If we are going to play a role in his dream, let it be the one that he has assigned us. He wants us in that Klein-bottle-shaped Critics Lounge of his and we will please him by going. All three of us: Alexei, Cory and baby Adam.

(Don't go, we hear you say. Don't go!)

Let's say we went up there to invite Jonathan Hoag to that party in our room and we got stuck. Okay? And now we are faced with the problem that Heinlein has set for us: no way out, no typewriter ribbons, no liquor, and nothing to eat but the baby. *Just* where he wanted us.

So there we are, stuck inside of Mobile with the Memphis Blues again (*Blonde on Blonde*), with nothing to do forever but think about this piece and never be able to write it. But that's *our* problem.

Everybody else's problem is the Black Beast. Is it there, skulking around the edges of the party? Is it all the servants? Is it the "totally empty suit of armor" that takes part in the jousting tourney? Is it the original Forest Ranger, but this time presenting himself as an InterSpace Patrol Agent attempting to arrest one of the Gang of Four? It is! It is!

As soon as it is detected, the Black Beast runs away, leaving its badge, #666, behind. It runs up the Bridge of Bifrost to Valhalla (don't ask), the Bridge and Valhalla dissolve, melted into thin air, and the Black Beast tumbles and falls.

One character says: "We've seen the last of *it*."

But another answers mechanically: ". . . are you *sure*?"

And so this long convoluted constipated puzzlement comes to an end, after 686 manuscript pages. On a note of doubt.

Leaving us wondering . . .

Whatever was this fascinating, tedious and aggravating fiction *about*? As it stands, there is no obvious story, merely talk and game-playing. Is there some other meta-reality to which the movements of the characters in *"The Number of the Beast—"* can be related—like the chess moves in *Through the Looking-Glass*?

It is not the Critics Lounge, but Heinlein's book that feels like a construct from which there is no escape. (There must be some way out of here, said the Joker to the Thief—"All Along the Watchtower.")

And what is the Black Beast? That is the central puzzle of this book of puzzlements. We are obviously meant to come up with an answer.

Ah, lost in a maze, and no easy way out. Stuck in the Critics Lounge with a piece that can't be written about *"The Number of the Beast—"*, an involuted, self-involved, Satan's intestines of a book. Round and round and round.

But then, Lazarus Long *said* that there was an easy way out of the Critics Lounge if we could but *read*. What else would this place of special frustration be equipped with more appropriately than books

—Borges' infinite Library of Babel, perhaps—that cannot be written about for the lack of those typewriter ribbons? Not until, that is, the key to escape is found and we make our way outside. Or until some far-sighted critic *brings typewriter ribbons with him* into the Critics Lounge.

So let's get down to it. Let's read.

Let's read some of those new science fiction books.

3. Death and Resurrection

By now, it should be plain why we might be at least half-serious in suggesting in our contribution to the third appendix of the new edition of Earl Kemp's symposium that Robert Heinlein in *"The Number of the Beast—"* should be given credit for killing science fiction. (Bloodthirsty Bob, the fastest draw at the Universal Ego Convention.) It is certainly worth taking seriously when a writer as central to modern science fiction as Robert Heinlein turns renegade, and like some sinister Darth Vader aims a fatal blow at science fiction, the empty cloak of truth and certainty drooping limply to the floor.

But we were half-joking, as well. It isn't all Heinlein's fault.

Heinlein alone can't be blamed for the demise of science fiction any more than he can be credited as solely responsible for its birth. Heinlein didn't come to the writing of modern science fiction by himself in 1939—he came in company. And he is not departing from science fiction alone, either.

Close examination will show that over and over again through the history of modern science fiction it has been a commonplace for different writers to submit stories for publication that are highly alike at nearly the same moment. As just one example, William Tenn— among other things the author of "Me, Myself and I," a story of a character traveling in time and meeting himself that has many similarities to Heinlein's "By His Bootstraps"—has told us how haunted he felt in the early Forties by Heinlein's uncanny ability to reach John W. Campbell first, not once, but repeatedly, with stories just like those that Tenn was in the process of writing.

There are more general confluences of theme, as well. As we may remember from the beginning of this book, where we reviewed an anthology that was topheavy with them, in the year 1968 the SF magazines were full of stories about comic machines, threatening machines, and comic/threatening machines. In the same way, at the present moment, human clones are a minor or a major concern in one book after another of those we have been reading, from *"The Number of the Beast—"* to Charles L. Harness's *The Catalyst*, Joan Vinge's *The Snow Queen*, and Evelyn Lief's first novel, *The Clone Rebellion*. It is clone-time just now.

In fact, we may generalize and say that at any given moment SF is always concerned with a small number of central questions, a handful of fruitful themes and a few particularly apt metaphors. It is as though there were a common wavelength, a single source of energy and insight, from which all innovative writers of SF must draw. So that if one doesn't get the message out, another will.

In view of this, then, it should not be totally surprising if we suggest that Heinlein's new book—important as it may be for what it has to say about the Future History and modern science fiction—does not stand alone. Its most significant aspects, its metaphors and materials, its most provocative assertions, are all shared by other books, so that even if *"The Number of the Beast—"* did not exist, it would still be possible to draw the same conclusion—science fiction is dying.

Modern science fiction claimed to be the way the future would be. Heinlein's book explicitly recognizes that this is no longer so. Modern science fiction is just one among a number of possible structurings of the imagination. It is not the all-in-all that it claimed to be or tried to be.

But the title of a memoir published recently by a fellow member of Heinlein's Class of 1939, Frederik Pohl's *The Way the Future Was*, makes the same recognition. So does our own title, "Farewell to Yesterday's Tomorrow." This insight is in the air.

Nonetheless, *"The Number of the Beast—"* must serve as our major example. Heinlein has been more deeply committed to modern science fiction than any other writer and played the game out to its last implications. Let us then look one by one at a number of this book's departures from science fiction, and show them confirmed in other current novels.

How far Heinlein has come! We may recall his lecture at the University of Chicago in 1957 where Heinlein presented the orthodox position on science fiction. He even drew up parallel tables to distinguish real science fiction—realistic future fiction—from mere pseudo-scientific futuristic fantasy. Heinlein said then:

> A handy short definition of almost all science fiction might read: realistic speculation about possible future events, based solidly on adequate knowledge of the real world, past and present, and on a thorough understanding of the nature and significance of the scientific method.

But in *"The Number of the Beast—"*, Robert Heinlein has written a book where there are no solid bases at all, where no such thing as adequate knowledge can exist, and where the real world, if there is any such thing, is in doubt. *"The Number of the Beast—"* puts into question that formal distinction between science fiction and fantasy that Heinlein was trying so hard to maintain in 1957. For how can modern science fiction exist separate and distinct from fantasy when there is no longer any fundamental difference between the Future History and Oz?

This distinction was already in question even as early as 1957, or else Heinlein would not have had to print his now-abandoned rules in such large letters. One such assault was Arthur C. Clarke's well-known dictum: "Sufficiently advanced technology is indistinguishable from magic." To this dictum could be added several corollaries implicit in stories that Jack Vance was writing in the late Fifties and early Sixties, such as "The Miracle Workers" and *The Dragon Masters*: "One man's technology is another man's magic," and "Any sufficiently isolated world may have its own science—which has all the outward appearance of magic."

From this line of thought during the last twenty years has developed a whole contemporary SF school, which might be called "galactic fantasy," that does what *"The Number of the Beast—"* does, making an art out of blurring together formerly separate science fiction and fantasy symbols. In galactic fantasy, worlds populated by the spaceships of modern science fiction—often worlds formerly ruled by galactic empires—have fallen into isolation and in this state of privacy developed their own "magic."

Listen to the titles of current examples of galactic fantasy — Joan Vinge's *The Snow Queen*; Robert Silverberg's *Lord Valentine's Castle*; our own *Earth Magic*. How different they are in tone and implication from modern science fiction titles like "The Roads Must Roll," "Mechanical Mice," "Nightfall" and "Universe." What is a particularly interesting departure, moreover, is that all three of these galactic fantasy novels (once again following Jack Vance) attribute their "magical" powers not to unique technology but to special developments of consciousness.

Here these books are paralleled by *"The Number of the Beast—"* once more. Heinlein's many universes are no more in essence than differing states of consciousness. While Heinlein's story is not galactic fantasy, it can be seen as taking the propositions on which galactic fantasy is founded, treating them logically and mathematically, and exploring their permutations. Each new continuum in the Realm of 666 a different state of consciousness with its own laws and its own mode of "magic."

Just what constitutes the nature and powers of consciousness is one of the questions now under general consideration in SF. The investigation can take a variety of forms.

Robert Sheckley's recent novel, *Crompton Divided*, is about the fragmentation of consciousness. In *Crompton Divided*, a nebbish living in New Jersey determines to track down and integrate various separate and scattered pieces of his original self who are now living apparently individual lives on other planets.

Crompton Divided manages to combine within itself the multiple-persons-in-a-single-body theme of Heinlein's 1970 novel *I Will Fear No Evil* and the fragments-of-a-single-person-living-in-separate-bodies situation of *"The Number of the Beast—"*. The book is a jape. In *Crompton Divided*, reality is a constantly shifting state of disequilibrium and frustration—a series of cosmic pokes in the rib from a God who wears an electric bowtie, stammers and loves practical jokes. You'd better laugh—it hurts when you don't.

Sheckley's novel is "science fictional" in appearance, if just barely. That is, there is an absence of fantasy symbols. None of the queens, castles and magic of the galactic fantasy story. And there is no Oz here, as in *"The Number of the Beast—"*. On the other hand, in *Crompton Divided* there are science fiction-derived symbols like alien beings and travel to distant planets.

But this novel is by no means an old-fashioned modern science fiction story. *Crompton Divided* treats its science fiction devices flippantly. Sheckley's novel is completely nihilistic about the pretense to exact fact that has been so precious to modern science fiction. But then, fragmentation of consciousness and doubts about single stable realities seem to be intimately related.

Varieties of states of consciousness are another kind of exception to the claim of modern science fiction to have a lock on the one true reality. An example of one of these exceptions is dream. *"The Number of the Beast—"* is not the only current SF book in which dreams come true. In Robert Silverberg's galactic fantasy *Lord Valentine's Castle*, dream interpretation figures as a "magical" art. In this story, moreover, there are passages that seem dreamlike to the characters themselves, and there are machines through which dreams are selectively broadcast. In Frederik Pohl's near-future novel *Beyond the Blue Event Horizon*, dreams are also broadcast, but not selectively— as inchoate emotions that trouble a whole planet. In Charles L. Harness's *The Catalyst*, not only do dream events come truer than true, but computer-generated holograms take on temporary life of their own, and dead human beings continue to affect the affairs of the living.

A theory is being evolved in current SF in which units of consciousness—consciousness holons, so to speak—exist independent of bodies and matter. In Richard Cowper's *The Road to Corlay*, the consciousness of a contemporary scientist is projected forward in time through a drug, and there, almost like a parasite, inhabits the mind/body of another person. In Arsen Darnay's *The Karma Affair*, themes include survival after death, astral travel, and reincarnation.

In *Golem¹⁰⁰*, a new novel by Heinlein's contemporary, Alfred Bester, forces of consciousness that are much like demons may be aroused from another plane of being, a realm of mind called "an Infraworld," and human beings may disembody and travel as holons into this land of symbol and psyche.

To anyone who still retains a firm commitment to the hard-nosed materialism that has distinguished modern science fiction, this stuff must seem like out-and-out fantasy. Spirits and astral bodies and misty pink-and-gray dimensions were precisely the sort of occult crapola that John W. Campbell kicked out of *Astounding* after he became editor in 1937 and began the step-by-step job of altering mush-headed romantic scientifiction into realistic modern science fiction.

It was partly to define *Astounding* more sharply that John Campbell started his fantasy magazine *Unknown* in 1939. *Unknown* was to contain logical but impossible stories, while *Astounding* was to contain real possibilities. Demons and spirits and astral bodies, if treated logically and humorously enough, had their place in the fantasy magazine *Unknown*. But not in *Astounding*, the modern science fiction magazine.

However, contemporary SF novels like *Golem¹⁰⁰* and *The Karma Affair* that use these materials need not debunk them, and these books are not stigmatized and kept separate from proper science fiction. Like galactic fantasy, these fantasies of consciousness on the loose are SF without prejudice.

One such astral fantasy, which concentrates within itself a wide variety of current themes, is *White Light, or What Is Cantor's Continuum Problem?* This book, which is to see publication shortly, first in England and then in the United States, is a first novel by Rudy Rucker, said to be the great-great-great-grandson of Hegel. Rucker, a young American, wrote *White Light* while studying mathematics on a grant in Heidelberg. If Rucker's novel seems particularly fresh, it is partly because he employs neither the symbology of *Unknown* nor the symbology of *Astounding*, neither magic nor spaceships. Instead, *White Light* is a unique combination of logic and set theory, New Head culture, and fantasy of consciousness.

Rucker's narrator is a young mathematician teaching trivial courses at a backwoods education factory. His main professional concern is the problem mentioned in the book's subtitle. We are told: "On December 13, 1873, the 28-year-old Georg Cantor brought the continuum problem to light by proving that there are more points in space than there are natural numbers."

This insight places us in an infinite universe. It is another of the significant attacks that have been made by modern Western mathematics and science on the assumptions of materialism—that there is but one reality, one set of facts, and one right and proper rational state of consciousness.

But that isn't all that is leading Rucker's narrator to fall through kick-a-stone, rap-a-lectern, hard-and-fast reality. Rucker's narrator is a New Head Seventies person—not a strange anomalous amalgam of different times and places like Heinlein's characters in *"The Number of the Beast—"*, who are simultaneously represented as being of a future time and as having been hand-raised on Edgar Rice Burroughs and the Clayton *Astounding* like a person of Heinlein's and Bester's generation. It is a measure of the difference between *"The Number of the Beast—"* and *White Light* that Heinlein's fantasy takes us on a visit to Oz, while Rucker's mathematical fantasy (which also has a chapter entitled "The Number of the Beast") gives us an episode inside a flipped-out Uncle Scrooge comic book in which the narrator as Donald Duck has his heart cut out by Aztecs before Huey, Dewey and Louie can rescue him.

The Seventies were a spaced-out time. Rucker's character is the representative of a generation that isn't quite sure where truth lies, but is sure that it isn't fixed. Felix Rayman's cultural referents are all multiplex symbols of shifting realities—Neal Cassady, the Rolling Stones, acid, and Vietnam. Even without Georg Cantor, this character is already just a bit unglued.

Like Earl Kemp's foreword in *Who Killed Science Fiction?*, *White Light* is punctuated with significant quotations. The epigraph to Part III is a quote from the rock'n'roll poet-priestess Patti Smith: "Within the context of neo-rock / we must open up our eyes / and seize and rend / the veil of smoke which man calls order." It is clear that Rucker in his own way is aiming to rend the veil of smoke which man calls order, but not in the context of neo-rock. In its intent, we might call this book neo-SF.

But hold on, this isn't a complete representation of *White Light*. Along with mathematical games and hip tripping, Rucker has made his book out of materials that are not only not new, but are positively Victorian: lucid dreaming, out-of-body experiences, an encounter with the Devil and Jesus, astral travel, and a journey to "the land of dreams and departed spirits." This last we might identify with Bester's Infraworld and Heinlein's Realm of 666.

As Rucker presents it, this is entertaining stuff, so old that it is new. *White Light* is a clever and innovative book, and out of its mathematical ruminations, it comes to fascinating conclusions—that the universe may not just be infinite, but may contain level upon level of being unto Absolute Infinity. Once again, as with Heinlein, we are arrived in the place where Anything Can Happen.

Busted free of all the linearities and restrictions of modern science fiction.

It is all the sadder, then, that on its own terms as a story, *White Light* is not a success. But in this, too, it is like *"The Number of the Beast—"*. In fact, all of the contemporary SF novels we have been reading in one way or another are unsatisfactory as story.

In the case of *White Light*, early in the book the Devil and Jesus tussle for Rayman's "worthless ass"—whatever unit of body or soul that may be. Jesus instructs Rayman to travel to the dream dimension and there climb Mount On, the Absolutely Infinite mountain. And he is to take with him to the top the ghost of a young woman. Rayman is to be responsible for her. She isn't to come back to Earth.

But Rayman gets no farther than to the dream dimension and partway up the mountain. He loses track of the woman's ghost. He gets distracted into other pursuits and questions, he allows himself to be turned aside, and he never does get to the top of the mountain. Moreover, the woman's ghost comes back again to Earth, even though Jesus has said, "Be sure you don't let her come back with you. For your own good as well as hers."

So the book can't be a success. Not only is it not right to cross

Jesus and not keep solemn promises, but a story quest that is set aside and forgotten halfway through a book must mean an incomplete story.

The new SF books that we have been reading—the brightest and most innovative works we could find—are all incomplete stories. A complete story has a beginning, a middle and an end. It sets forth some problem that must be resolved. The problem *must* be resolved if the story is to be complete. The problem cannot be dodged. It cannot be set aside. It *can* be redefined—but only if the stakes of the game are raised, and the original problem is shown to be but an aspect of a problem of larger dimension. But then *that* problem must be solved.

In John Crowley's exquisitely written *Engine Summer*, a subtle horror story of a consciousness holon trapped forever short of a moment of completion and resolution, there is a significant passage comparing a bit of special local geography and the necessities of story:

> I told you about Path: Path is like a snake, it curls around the whole of Little Belaire with its head in the middle and the tip of its tail by Buckle cord's door, but only someone who knows Little Belaire can see where it runs. To someone else, it would seem to run off in all directions. So when you run along Path, and here is something that looks to be Path, but you find it is only rooms interlocking in a little maze that has no exits but back to Path—that's a snake's-hand. It runs off the snake of Path like a set of little fingers. It's also called a snake's-hand because a snake has no hands, and likewise there is only one Path. But a snake's-hand is also more: my story is a Path, too, I hope; and so it must have its snake's-hands. Sometimes the snake's-hands in a story are the best part, if the story is a long one.

But Crowley's story is not a success, either. Just like *White Light*, it loses its own Path and turns into a snake's-hand. In *Engine Summer*, a post-disaster situation that looks promising and ecological becomes altered and trivialized into a mere recording in the hands of a stagnant and fearful remnant technological society living in an orbiting satellite.

This is the sort of thing that happens again and again in these books. Some are content to be collections of fragments. Some set goals and then forget them. Some present situations of promise and then trivialize them. Some books dodge and run away. Some throw up their hands. Some even have endings where trumpet flourishes are sounded to herald what is announced as Complete Success— except that some significant awfulness, like the Black Beast, has been left out of the solution.

In fact, the most common conclusion in these novels, as it has been in so many of the novels we have reviewed in the past few years —such as Cary Neeper's *A Place Beyond Man*—is the half-solution. Viewpoint characters are permitted to find answers to their own personal problems, escaping perhaps from some imminent disaster. Invariably, however, the larger public situation, the common human condition, remains awful.

In one after another of these late science fiction books, future man is pictured as having suffered a disaster through the reckless excesses of technology, as in the Crowley. And where this has not yet happened, man is living a gray, squalid, over-populated existence, helplessly drowning in his own waste products like a self-poisoned bacterium.

The essence of this last scenario is displayed in this restaurant scene in Charles Harness's *The Catalyst*:

> Paul had already checked the list. Swiss steak—with a red asterisk. Filet of sole—likewise. Chicken creole—also. Beef pie— the same. On down the list. And the red asterisk at the bottom: The Surgeon General Has Determined That Eating This Is Dangerous To Your Health. Paul said: "The carcinogenic index seems lowest on the roast penguin. No DES, kepone, low PCB's, BHT, just a little mercury . . . ."
>
> "It's got an EPA yellow mark," said Marggold. "You are further endangering an endangered species."
>
> "Yeah, well *everything* is either poisonous, anti-ecological, or too expensive. Meanwhile, I'm hungry."

None of these books offer answers to this problem. It is merely the given condition of things. The best current SF may do, as in galactic fantasy, is to show some special isolated planet that has escaped the collapse of empire and become magical.

This was not the case in the modern science fiction of the Golden Age. In classic science fiction—in stories like Heinlein's "Coventry" and *Sixth Column* and *Beyond This Horizon*, even in Heinlein's "Solution Unsatisfactory"—personal problems are identified with public ones, and the solution to one is the solution to the other. If one fails, the other fails.

But this is no longer so. Just as in Heinlein novels since *Stranger in a Strange Land*, in contemporary science fiction novels the public situation is written off as a dead loss.

Some of these books allow no answers at all, either public or personal. In Robert Sheckley's *Crompton Divided*, for example, the fragmented Alistair Crompton eventually unites four different pieces of his psyche. He even, after a struggle with himself, hands over the captaincy of the common being to another consciousness byte nobler than himself. But the story concludes:

> The new person considered. A presentiment of disaster came over him. He was still stuck in the human situation! He said, "Hey, Alistair, fellows, are you still there? I don't think this one is going to work either."

It is not demanded and should not be demanded that every story be complete. By their very length, short stories tend to present only a portion of the complete monomyth, or a highly compressed version of it. Many admirable short stories are snake's-hands.

Neither should it be demanded that every story portray a success. It is undeniable that stories of irony, tragedy and failure should have a place. But it should be demanded of stories like these that they be honest and truthful about their nature. They should not simply cop out on a problem. They should not attempt to pass failure off as success. A story of non-success should not be a cheat.

But what is to be said of the state of a literature of the imagination that can imagine *no* complete and honest successes? That sees the human condition as a no-win situation? That foresees nothing ahead of us but trouble and disaster, which only individuals may escape or evade? What is to be said of a literature that cannot present any true Path for a reader to travel from beginning to end, but only offer snake's-hands?

That is the state of science fiction today.

At the least, it must be clear that science fiction is not the same now as it was when it was young and modern and realistic, and no problems lay beyond its practical methods and all-competent self-confidence.

The problem with mid-Twentieth Century modern science fiction is that it is the product of mid-Twentieth Century beliefs, mid-Twentieth Century attitudes, mid-Twentieth Century science, and mid-Twentieth Century world conditions. And that is all. This was an essential strength at mid-century, but now it is a fatal disease. Modern science fiction must die of it in the late Twentieth Century, with its very different beliefs and attitudes, its different standards of knowledge, and its very different problems which we see so excruciatingly presented in contemporary SF novels.

Each era produces its own form of mythic literature—its own SF —in which the dreams, the thoughts, the hopes and the fears of the culture are written in the largest possible letters so that everyone may see them. SF is sacred drama. It takes different forms in different times and places, altering as the times alter.

Modern science fiction leaped into being at the end of the Thirties —at exactly one of those moments when the times were altering and one fundamental vision of the ordering of society and the universe was giving way to another. Modern science fiction was the epitomal expression of the new mid-Twentieth Century American vision, rational and pragmatic and pluralistic, that was precipitated by the experiences of the Great Depression.

Every era has its own special vision of the laws that underlie and harmonize all the multiplicity and fragmentation that apparently surrounds us. Each such vision is a paradigm, an elaborate construction of fact and belief that makes it possible to do certain things and perceive certain things, and impossible to see and do others.

The era that was passing then was the Age of Invention, the period from the Franco-Prussian War in 1870 to the outbreak of World War II in late 1939. This was the tophat-and-tails late-Victorian and early-Twentieth Century world of Thomas Edison and H. G. Wells, the same world that is on display in *Upstairs, Downstairs*, the British series about declining aristocrats and their upwardly-mobile servants before, during and after World War I.

According to the late-Victorian vision, the order of the world was this: The laws of nature were rigid and deterministic and made no special provision for mankind. The universe was driven by inexorable historical and evolutionary forces of growth and decay. There was only one possible history, only one predetermined future, only one line of development for humans and non-humans alike. And there was an innate hierarchy of superiority based on positions in that development.

If you weren't where you belonged, you clawed and scratched to get where you did belong. And if anyone else tried to scramble up onto your rung of the ladder, you kicked him off again. Likewise, however, given the chance, someone higher up the ladder would do the same for you.

The Victorian vision can be seen in full mythic form in the classic scientific romances of H. G. Wells, written at the end of the Nineteenth Century. *The Time Machine* took leap upon leap of ever-increasing size into the future, and found there, inevitably and inexorably waiting, the prospect of human extinction and the guttering out of the sun. *The War of the Worlds* offered an intimation of how the human end might come, at the hands of superiorly-evolved creatures sweeping down on us from out of the cosmic void.

The Victorian order was very hard on people, particularly those without power. The Social Darwinism of the era expected men to struggle to show their fitness to survive. This viewpoint led to the competitive assembling of great colonial empires by the European nations, and from there, almost inevitably, to the immense historical contention of World War I. Victorian attitudes could send millions of men over the trench-tops to be indifferently gunned down or gassed. And they were the excuse for widespread indifference to massive economic suffering at the outset of the Great Depression.

In the first part of the late-Victorian era, in its period of empire-building expansiveness and relative optimism, a great deal of SF was written, particularly in England and in Europe. But after the seeming confirmation of Wells' dark prophecies in World War I, European SF writers could not bear to continue writing mythic visions. In the course of the Thirties, European SF writing and publishing became all but extinct.

SF was not much better off in Britain after World War I. At the beginning of the Thirties, what England could offer in the way of SF was Aldous Huxley's *Brave New World* and Olaf Stapledon's *Last and First Men.* Huxley foresaw an awful, automated, drug-sodden, genetically-programed, all-for-your-own-good, hierarchical hell. Stapledon, who carried the historical and evolutionary themes of the Victorian vision to their furthest extent, dreamed of man's future as no less than eighteen evolutionary metamorphoses, the last of these being winged beings living on Neptune. But there Stapledon's vision faltered. He could not imagine man making the leap to the stars, but saw him as inexorably doomed to extinction.

The one place that SF survived in the latter part of the late-Victorian era was in the American pulp scientifiction magazines. These magazines were organized around the principle of envisioning the wonders of man's future progress, specifically future technology. One of these dreams was travel to the stars in spaceships.

In 1930 or 1935, it was not yet possible to deny the Victorian vision of mankind's ultimate evolutionary decline. But it was possible to ignore it and concentrate on the nearer future—those centuries of exploration and adventure before racial senility set in.

To any properly grave and judicious Victorian eye, scientifiction —this peculiarly American form of imaginative literature—must have seemed a crude and juvenile sort of fantasy. Pure wish-fulfillment in the face of the true cold hard facts of life. However, in appropriate Victorian fashion, scientifiction was a survivor. At the very same moment that European writers were dropping SF, that Huxley was blanching at the future, and Stapledon was balking at the stars, American writers of juvenile scientifiction fantasy like E. E. Smith and Edmond Hamilton were dreaming dreams of intergalactic adventure.

It was out of this special line of imaginative literature—three frail American pulp magazines, sometimes more but usually three, irregularly published, storm-tossed by the Depression—that modern science fiction emerged at the end of the Thirties. The new vision of which modern science fiction was the mythic expression came into place in American society during the period 1937 to 1939, as a reaction to the rigidity and fatalism that had led to the disasters of World War I and the Depression.

Never again. There must be new ways and new thoughts. And so there were.

In the mid-Twentieth Century American vision, the only eternal "laws of nature" were the simple rules of physical science, like $E = mc^2$. In this new view, there were no great cosmic fiats that man was helpless to evade. Instead, natural laws were seen as the building-blocks of the universe, those rules of form and function that man could manipulate to his own advantage.

A good description of the attitude of the new mid-Twentieth Century order is given near the end of *"The Number of the Beast—"*. Jubal Harshaw is dictating a story, and says:

> "As I once heard Andrew—that's my disappearing brother—say: 'Life consists in accommodating oneself to the Universe.' Although the rest of our family has never taken that view. We believe in forcing the Universe to accommodate itself to us. It's all a question of which is to be master."

This vision is an inherently pluralistic and contentious point of view. By this ordering of value, what matters is competence, command of fact, and getting the job done. In this world, knowledge of physical law and the way things work is the ultimate source of power, and not your parents' social standing.

The metaphors for expressing this new vision in mythic terms, the bits and pieces out of which modern science fiction would be assembled, were all developed within the context of the late-Victorian scientifiction of the Thirties: multiple worlds, alien creatures to play with, and limitless scientific power.

In the great space epics written by E. E. Smith and the young John W. Campbell, Jr. at the beginning of the Thirties, men went forth in giant spaceships—inconceivably vast technological constructions—armed with blasters and ray guns, ready to zap even evolutionarily-superior aliens, if need be. And these ships discovered a plurality of worlds. In Stanley Weinbaum's stories of planetary treks written during the mid-Thirties, humans were to demonstrate that the alien inhabitants of other worlds need not be hostile and superior, but merely different. And in the stories that he published during the later Thirties under the name "Don A. Stuart," John W. Campbell deliberately set out to attack the givens of Victorian SF in a scientific manner, armed with the principles of the new probabilistic physics he had studied in college and an emerging sense of the values of the coming vision.

But we should bear in mind that these ancestral stories of modern science fiction were not altogether typical of Thirties' scientifiction. Far more common were stories of invasions of Earth by hostile aliens, stories of scientist-inventors and their beautiful daughters, and fanciful satires of the Victorian vision that criticized the Victorian world without offering an alternative. There were stories of excursions into misty dimensions of another order than our own, and stories in which the Earth proved to be the egg of some evolutionarily-advanced space-dwelling creature, and hatched. In Thirties' SF, travel to other worlds was far more commonly achieved by dimensional warp, or matter transmitter, or astral projection, than by spaceship.

At best, the new imaginary universe of interplanetary adventure posited by Smith and Campbell, Weinbaum and Williamson was some special case that might be partially exempt from the old dictatorial laws of the Victorian cosmos. But it still remained for the new principles developed in these stories to be recognized as universally applicable, the basis for a new vision capable of superseding the exhausted and discredited Victorian mythos that was no longer worthy of being believed in.

Then, as if it were fated, in September 1937, John W. Campbell, the young critic of the Victorian vision, became the editor of *Astounding Stories*, one of the three scientifiction magazines then in existence and the only monthly. Almost the first thing that Campbell did was to change the name of the magazine to *Astounding Science-Fiction*. A sign of intent. And the times were with him. In the spring of 1938, F. Orlin Tremaine, who was Campbell's predecessor as editor of *Astounding* and his overseer in his new job, left the publishing company and Campbell was given leave to do with the magazine what he wished. He was free to turn it into the first magazine of modern science fiction.

But one more piece was necessary, the key to the essential change in vision. And Campbell found it. In the August 1938 issue of *Astounding*, Campbell published the climactic story in his series of Don A. Stuart experiments—"Who Goes There?", the first story of modern science fiction.

In "Who Goes There?" a powerful, superior, shape-shifting alien monster is discovered frozen in the Antarctic ice, a horror straight out of H. G. Wells and H. P. Lovecraft that humans instinctively fear and loathe. This creature can take on the appearance of men. If it escapes, it can take over the whole world.

The problem is an essentially Victorian problem. But the answer to it is the mid-Twentieth Century solution. What defeats this horrendous being is not fortuitous accident, like the disease that suddenly overcomes the Martian invaders in *The War of the Worlds*. It is rather a calm faith in scientific law and its universal applicability: whatever higher powers this alien may possess, it is still vulnerable to detection and defeat by the simple physical facts of its own biochemistry and native environment.

Here was the insight necessary to take all the scattered new ideas and notions and inklings of the day and turn them into a new vision of order and purpose. The new prime rule was command of fact and knowledge of scientific law. Anyone armed with that rule had a grip on the real world and was competent to write real genuine science fiction as opposed to old-fashioned fantasy-tinged scientifiction.

Anyone who shared Campbell's new vision was welcome within the pages of *Astounding*, but all the writers who didn't were invited to leave. There was useful work to be done—the basic engineering job of converting the old symbols and assumptions of Victorian SF into the terms of the new vision.

In the spring of 1939, Campbell started a second magazine, *Unknown*, the magazine of rational fantasy. *Unknown* was a companion to *Astounding* and largely shared a common audience with it.

In one sense, the magazine was intended to serve as a contrast to *Astounding* — *Unknown*'s fantasy serving to set off all the more clearly the disciplined realism of the modern science fiction of *Astounding*. But, in another sense, *Unknown* was the complement and partner to *Astounding* in the good work of turning the materials of former imaginative literature into the new mid-Twentieth Century terms. The classic *Unknown* short novel was generally a story of an aw-shucks American manipulating rules of logic or laws of magic to travel into a storybook dimension and back.

In 1938 and 1939, Campbell gathered around him the new writers —mostly engineers, and newspapermen, and trade journalists, and science fiction fans—who would write for the reborn *Astounding* and *Unknown*. By the end of 1939, Campbell had published stories by Lester del Rey, L. Sprague de Camp, Clifford Simak, Henry Kuttner, C. L. Moore, A. E. van Vogt, Isaac Asimov, Robert Heinlein, Theodore Sturgeon and Fritz Leiber. As fast as modern science fiction was born, the Golden Age was on!

The good work that these new writers of the Golden Age were launched upon was the translation of Victorian SF into modern science fiction, and the presentation of a new ordering of the universe. The universe as perceived by the new practical-minded mid-Twentieth Century generation was an assemblage of disparate pieces, each with its own nature and purposes.

By this view, unlike the Victorian, objects and beings might interact with one another in complex ways—like the particles of atomic physics—but they were not caught up and bound together in a single, shared destiny. In this new view, history was not a deterministic evolutionary unfolding, but rather the record of separate, local social processes. Evolutionary fitness was no longer to be understood as all-around superiority, but rather as those particular, specialized qualities that might enable an individual creature to survive.

There was a key, however—a common denominator—to resolve all this individuality, specialization and fragmentation. It was the insight arrived at by "Don A. Stuart" in "Who Goes There?": the universal applicability of simple, rationally comprehensible physical laws. The fundamental underlying assumption of modern science fiction has been that no matter how complex and subtle the behavioral patterns of living creatures and societies may appear, it is possible to cut through all that complexity to the basic simple facts of mechanical process and bodily survival. The genuinely superior being is the man (or alien creature) who is ready to recognize the true facts and willing to apply them.

As Heinlein has it in "The Notebooks of Lazarus Long" in *Time Enough for Love*:

> What are the facts? Again and again and again—what are the *facts*? Shun wishful thinking, ignore divine revelation, forget "what the stars foretell," avoid opinion, care not what the neighbors think, never mind the unguessable "verdict of history"—what are the facts, and to how many decimal places? You pilot always into an unknown future; facts are your single clue. Get the facts!

The three writers who were most useful to John Campbell in the task of converting previous imaginative fiction into these new terms were Isaac Asimov, A. E. van Vogt, and Robert Heinlein. If these three have been the major figures of modern science fiction, it is precisely because they performed the most central work. It was they who reconceived the nature of human history, the relationship of man to technology, and the future evolution of mankind in the new mid-Twentieth Century terms.

Isaac Asimov was a precocious young Brooklyn college student and science fiction fan who wanted nothing more in all the world than the opportunity to learn from John Campbell. Campbell recognized Asimov's eagerness to learn, took him under his wing, and set him to his own purposes.

As Asimov puts it today:

> Though others still younger came his way later, I don't think that ever in his career did he have an acolyte less worldly and more naive than I was. I believe that amused him and that it pleased him to have so excellent an opportunity to do a bit of molding. At any rate, I have always thought that of all his writers I was his favorite and that he spent more time and effort on me than on anyone else. And I believe that it still shows.

What Campbell got for his investment was an able tool. Asimov has been a living demonstration of what a man given the facts can make of himself, rising from an immigrant child tending his father's candystore in Brooklyn to a Ph.D. in chemistry, and from there to his present position of universal expert in absolutely everything.

Asimov carried out two jobs in particular for Campbell. One was the rationalization of the robot, the other the Foundation series.

In Victorian SF, robots were powerful and inhuman, the embodiments of inexorable evolutionary forces. They were much given to challenging the evolutionary fitness of their makers and attempting to overtopple them. However, the "Laws of Robotics" that Campbell and Asimov worked out together provided a simple, logically-comprehensible basis for the thought-processes of robots. In story after story, Asimov showed that any robotic behavior, no matter how bizarre, hostile or irrational it might seem, could be derived from and altered by these three rules.

Having placed the most sophisticated fruits of man's technology under his control, Asimov turned to the subject of human society in its most sweeping form, the galactic empire. The idea of the galactic empire had first appeared in the SF of the Thirties, representing an attempt to squeeze the new materials of interplanetary adventure into the Victorian schema of historical progress and decay. But after the changeover to modern science fiction, the concept of galactic empires largely dropped out of SF—at least until Asimov wrote his Foundation stories. In these stories, Asimov treated human societies as he had robots, subjecting them to universal "laws"—the mathematical rules of "Psychohistory." As in the old Victorian SF, Asimov's galactic empire might be subject to fall, but under Asimov's laws, this was given as the inevitable—but purely temporary—result of normal human political balances and interactions, and not as the consequence of irreversible biological decline.

The most singular of the new writers of the Golden Age was A. E. van Vogt, older than Asimov by eight years. Van Vogt was a journeyman writer, a Canadian, who had read *Amazing Stories* as a teenager, but dropped it in 1930. He had had nothing to do with scientifiction since, until one day in 1938 when he casually picked up an issue of *Astounding* on the newsstand and began to look through it. By significant coincidence, the story he picked to read was "Who Goes

There?" Van Vogt was hooked. As soon as he had finished reading it, van Vogt wrote off to Campbell with a story idea of his own— not knowing the editor to be the author of the story that had so impressed him. Campbell wrote back to encourage van Vogt, and his career was begun.

If van Vogt was special, it was because he thought and wrote like no one else during the Golden Age. Van Vogt was a man with no sense of the specific, a man with no sensitivity to detail, a man capable of populating the far future with Studebaker cars. Fact and the extrapolation of fact, so central to most modern science fiction, meant nothing to van Vogt at all.

On the other hand, this blindness of van Vogt's was more than offset by his acute sensitivity to general cases and underlying regularities of process, those universal constants that could make the alien monster in "Who Goes There?" vulnerable to men armed with a knowledge of earthly fact. By analogy with the mathematical formulations of physics, Asimov called these regularities "laws." Van Vogt, who had his own name for everything, called them "thought systems."

The central question to which van Vogt applied his "thought systems" was the Victorian problem of evolutionary superiority. Van Vogt was fascinated by the possibility of superior beings—but was unable to accept the undifferentiated Victorian definition of superiority that said superior is *superior*, and that's that.

In his first few stories—all directly inspired by "Who Goes There?"—van Vogt presented one alien creature after another far advanced beyond man in terms of physical power, intelligence and ruthlessness, but in each case crippled and limited by an inability to see past personal appetites and a local frame of reference. In van Vogt's first published SF story, "Black Destroyer," for instance, men armed with a knowledge of Oswald Spengler's classic Victorian account of the decay of societies, *The Decline of the West*, are able to use this thought system, this broader perspective, to set a powerful but decadent Victorian-style ravening monster on his ear.

But van Vogt soon moved on from this to his true major theme —superman, man transformed, man beyond man. In one story after another, like the novels *Slan* and *The World of Null-A*, van Vogt presented men evolved past the level of current humanity—men with an increased capacity for systematic thinking, and men whom systematic thinking has altered.

If Asimov was Campbell's chief disciple, and van Vogt was unique, it was Robert Heinlein, the third major writer of modern science fiction, who was the brilliant star performer of the Golden Age. Heinlein was the one writer of modern science fiction whose version of the new understanding was comparable to John W. Campbell's in its scope and completeness.

In his fiction, Heinlein presented an ideal type for the age—the competent man. And Heinlein was the competent man embodied. He had had formal education in science, engineering and mathematics. He was a fencing champion at Annapolis. He had served as an officer in the Navy and commanded men and machines. He had had experience in business, politics and architecture. And not only did he have the encyclopedic grasp of fact of an Asimov and the awareness of system of a van Vogt, he was a practical man, a man of action and a man of the world, which they were not. Heinlein was the man who knew how things worked.

Heinlein's first story, "Life-Line," was written to earn quick money in a story contest sponsored by *Thrilling Wonder*—the retitled descendant of Hugo Gernsback's *Science Wonder Stories*. When Heinlein was finished—after only four days—he liked what he had done enough not to submit it to *Thrilling Wonder* at all. He sent it first to *Collier's*, a general magazine, and then to *Astounding*, where his talent was recognized by John W. Campbell. "Life-Line" earned $70 from *Astounding*, whereas Alfred Bester, the winner of the *Thrilling Wonder* contest, had to be coached by the editors and earned only $50 for his story. That was competence on display.

There was one other thing that gave Heinlein an advantage over his competitors. In addition to everything else he had going for him, Heinlein knew more about SF than any of the other new writers of modern science fiction. Heinlein had begun to read Victorian SF almost as soon as he could read at all, including books now long forgotten. He had read all types of SF: scientific romance, high fantasy, lost race stories, utopian stories, scientifiction, weird tales. He had read Wells, Gernsback, Burroughs, Merritt, Cabell, Huxley, Lovecraft and Smith. Other writers of the Golden Age, like Asimov, van Vogt and Bester, have testified that they only discovered SF in the later Twenties in the pages of *Amazing Stories*. None of them could begin to match Heinlein's command of the facts of SF.

More than anyone else, Heinlein was the great summator of the central themes and preoccupations of Victorian SF. Future war, time travel, utopia—one by one (and often alone), Heinlein attacked them all and rewrote them definitively in the new terms of modern science fiction.

And the heart of it all was the Future History. In these stories, with a wealth of integrated imaginative detail sufficient to make an Asimov seem tissue-paper thin and a van Vogt seem to be asleep by comparison, Heinlein took on the central preoccupation of the Victorians—the force of history—and presented it in the new mid-Twentieth Century terms of fact, exact measurement and competence to survive.

However, in the changeover from the Victorian vision to the new mid-Twentieth Century frame of reference there were losses as well as gains, as there always are in a shift of this sort. The new vision succeeded the old because the Victorian order could no longer get the job done—but compared to the grand sweep of the Victorian mythos, the mid-Twentieth Century vision was superficial and shallow.

To see that this might be so, all that is necessary is to set the Future History beside a classic late representation of the Victorian vision like Olaf Stapledon's 1937 masterwork, *Star Maker*. The Future History is more vigorous, more diverse, and more human. At the same time, the Future History is completely lacking in *Star Maker*'s great scope and majesty. The Future History is an incomplete jumble of stories—a variety of separate facts—involving a few hundreds of years, and no more. Stapledon's book is a unified work overviewing and encompassing a time scale reaching to the death of the last galaxy and beyond.

It is not by accident then that old-time scientifiction fans like Sam

Moskowitz could believe that in the transition from scientifiction to modern science fiction the sense of wonder had become mislaid. The sense of wonder—the awe-filled appreciation of the transcendent—is central to myth in every era. If Moskowitz and others were distressed, it was because they felt that without the sense of wonder there was no difference between SF and mundane mimetic fiction.

In Victorian SF, the sense of wonder was triggered by demonstrations of scale, by the presentation of new dimensions and the display of immense vistas. Where was the sense of wonder? It was to be found in the contrast between Wells' Time Traveller sitting at tea in a homey room with all his familiar friends, and the description that he gives to them of his lonely meditations on a dim beach at the end of time. Or it was to be found in E. E. Smith's perky and plucky *Skylark* voyagers as they take their ship outside our own galaxy and then look back and turn pea-green at their own audacity.

It wouldn't be fair or accurate to say that in modern science fiction the sense of wonder has been altogether missing. No, it has simply been harnessed to fact rather than to demonstrations of scale. Wonder in modern science fiction has lain in the revelation of some new fact, or, more commonly, in the realization of a hidden aspect or application of some known fact.

It is not surprising, then, that science fiction has had a tendency to fall into mundanity. Or, that next to the aching realizations and awe-inspiring spectacles of Victorian SF, the sense of wonder in modern science fiction should seem muted, rare or altogether missing.

The most purely powerful sense-of-wonder stories that modern science fiction has produced were those few grand summational stories of the Golden Age that managed to express the old-time sense of wonder and the new simultaneously. In these stories—like Heinlein's "Universe" and Asimov's "Nightfall"—a hidden fact was revealed, and the fact was a fact of relative scale. In both "Universe" and "Nightfall," for instance, the fact revealed was that a world that had imagined itself sufficient was but a pinpoint amongst the immense and myriad stars. Double zappo!—a zinger in both the new terms and the old. More purely fact-oriented later science fiction has few stories with even a fraction of the power of these two.

Again — always as it seems — there were grave potential moral flaws in the mid-Twentieth Century vision. A universe populated by creatures who consider themselves separate colliding particles with no common purpose must be inherently contentious and competitive. Immediate practical results must be the bottom line in a universe in which there are short-term local processes and conditions but no grand design. Longer-range consequences become somebody else's bookkeeping problem.

The mid-Twentieth Century order has not been marked by the incessant social class warfare and the heartless and indifferent brutality of the Victorians, but in its own way it has been just as locked into the question of dominance and subordination. The Victorians struggled to prove who was the innately superior being. Men of the mid-Twentieth Century have pushed and shoved simply to get ahead, competing to command those positions of privilege available to those most adept at marshalling and manipulating fact.

The result has been egotism, aggressiveness, factual one-upsmanship, and constant struggle for power—every man a privateer pursuing his own gain in a universe where some must win and others must lose. Both in private and public life, those in possession of power—special facts, special secrets—have felt justified in using their monopoly to gain advantage over others.

But nobody can have all the real facts all of the time. Sometimes the facts aren't known. Sometimes they are in doubt. And no one— not even a Robert Heinlein or an Isaac Asimov—knows everything.

There is a temptation, then, in the mid-Twentieth Century to clip the facts, to cut corners in the name of immediate practical results. There is a temptation to bluff and pretend to have the facts when the facts aren't really known. There is a temptation to turn lying, cheating and intimidation into a primary mode of dealing with the universe. It seems a practical way of getting along.

In view of all this insincerity, short-sightedness and concern to prevail, it may not be surprising that modern science fiction has been most uncomfortable and dishonest where the question of dominant aliens has been concerned. What does the man whose justification in life is his greater command of fact do when faced by a being with a few million years head start? What does the competent man do when faced by the truly superior being?

Jacob Burroughs, in Heinlein's *"The Number of the Beast—"*, is only expressing the common opinion of most writers of science fiction when he says:

> "Supermen or angels would trouble me more than vermin. I know what to do with a 'Black Hat'—*kill it!* But a superman would make me feel so inferior that I would not want to go on living."

So, from the very outset of modern science fiction, the question of superior aliens with a higher grasp of the facts has been avoided. So marked has this been that when L. Sprague de Camp was asked in *Science Fiction Voices #1* whether he had ever had problems with editorial restrictions, he replied:

> I have run into some curious little quirks and prejudices. John Campbell, for example, among other things, would not publish a story in which an extra-terrestrial species was portrayed as superior to human beings in a general sense. That is, morally, mentally, and physically better all around. He just didn't like that. And he was somewhat of an old-fashioned imperialist also. He thought that the United States ought to go and conquer all of Latin America. He had some rather curious ideas of that sort.

Isaac Asimov, who had a dominating Victorian father, solved this problem by working around Campbell as he was used to working around his father at home. Not wanting either to cross Campbell or to write stories in which competent human beings kick inferior alien peons around, he wrote in his Foundation stories about a universe in which there were no alien beings at all. Humanity is alone in an empty universe, free to do with it as it wills. But this was a dishonest presentation. Asimov didn't really believe at all that this was the way things would really be.

Heinlein, in his own way, did even worse with the problem. In his classic early stories, his characters—competent in all other circumstances—turn into limp lettuce before superior aliens. They run away. They go mad. They grow gray and old before their time. They turn belly up and die.

At the end of *Methuselah's Children*, the centerpiece of the Future

History, serialized in *Astounding* in 1941, the Howard families retreat to Earth after two humiliating encounters with superior aliens among the stars. In the expanded version of the story published in book form in 1958, there is a new ending in which Lazarus Long makes a vow to return to the stars and meet the highest aliens, the gods of the Jockaira, once again on more even terms.

> "Someday, about a thousand years from now, I intend to march straight into the temple of Kreel, look him in the eye, and say, 'Howdy, bub—what do *you* know that I don't know?' "

Except for the overtones of wise-ass belligerence, this could be a worthy resolve. "What do you know that I don't know?" might be a very good question to ask a superior alien, if asked in the right way.

But that's not what Heinlein represents as having happened in *Time Enough for Love*, his mammoth 1973 book about Lazarus Long, where the gods of the Jockaira are mentioned again. Lazarus is about to share an anecdote when another character interrupts him:

> "He's leading up to how he killed the gods of the Jockaira with nothing but a toy gun and moral superiority. Since that lie is already in his memoirs in four conflicting versions, why should we be burdened with a fifth?"

And Lazarus retorts:

> "It was not a toy gun; it was a Mark Nineteen Remington Blaster at full charge, a superior weapon in its day—and after I carved them up, the stench was worse than Hormone Hall the morning after payday. And my superiority is never moral; it lies always in doing it first before *he* does it to *me*."

This puff of hot air is hardly a fulfillment of the promise to look the gods of the Jockaira in the eye as an equal. Within the terms laid down in *Methuselah's Children*, it *must* be a lie. That is, higher beings who were capable in the earlier story of lifting large numbers of human beings through the air no hands, stuffing them into a spaceship, and then directing and controlling the ship to a destination thirty-two light years away, simply aren't plausibly vulnerable to toy guns like the "Mark Nineteen Remington Blaster," crackerjack weapon though it may have been in its day.

Banter, bluster, grossness and lies can't alter that. They only serve to accentuate our awareness of the underlying evasion, hostility, inferiority and fear. If Lazarus Long is not fond of critics—and he puts them down in his "Notebooks" as well as in *"The Number of the Beast—"*—it may be because he is aware that the lies he tells will not stand up to examination. In any case, he is a typical modern science fiction protagonist. All the heroes of the present period have tended to prefer having an edge to having moral superiority.

Now, in 1980, we are once again at the end of an era. The solutions, values and tools of the mid-Twentieth Century vision are no longer sufficient to deal with the urgent problems of the day. This order has had its good moments and done its good work, but its hour has passed. We are once again at one of those moments when the times alter and one vision gives way to another.

The mid-Twentieth Century order had many accomplishments to its credit. It dismantled the old Victorian colonial empires. From its tolerance of multiplicity and willingness to accept fact has arisen the present climate of concern for women's rights, minority rights, and human rights in general. Its great engineering projects have sent men to the Moon, and established the first world-wide communications network.

The time has come when a kid in Singapore may wear blue jeans and a Grateful Dead T-shirt, just the same as the kid in Topeka. The world has been united, and the mid-Twentieth Century order is responsible! Hooray! Hooray!

But, so far, what has been put into place is all exterior. It is an engineering-works-and-economics sort of unification. All money and gross fact, and little understanding. That's in keeping with the nature of the times.

Right now, however, the economic glue that holds the world together is threatening to come unstuck. Inflation, shortages of material, cartels, unemployment, weighty taxes, massive dislocations of population. And nothing seems sufficient to get things working right again. Rather than answering all questions, the facts pull in a thousand different directions.

And meantime, the sins of the mid-Twentieth Century order have mounted in number. Let us speak only of America's sins and be con-

tent to name the major fiascos of the last twenty years, one by one
—the times when American authority acted according to the values
and priorities of the mid-Twentieth Century vision and made an ass
or a villain of itself: the Bay of Pigs; the Gulf of Tonkin; the 1968
Democratic Convention in Chicago; Vietnam; Cambodia; Kent State;
Jackson State; Watergate; the Mayaguez Incident; the Great Iranian
Helicopter Raid.

Oh, and add just a few more things to make the picture more complete: the revelation of longstanding CIA and FBI misdeeds; the business and political scandals of the Seventies; the financial collapse of
giant businesses and major cities; Three Mile Island; Love Canal.

Again and again the same mistakes have been made, the characteristic mistakes of the era: The use of lies for tactical gain. The
employment of questionable methods for near-sighted ends. Willful
ignorance of the consequences of selfish courses of action. The employment of massive force to crush insignificant opposition. Most of
all, the consistent overestimation of the powers of technology.

Even more than coming out on top in the wrestle for dominance
with the Russians, the chief concern of the mid-Twentieth Century
order has been to force the universe to accommodate itself to us.
And that, finally and above all, is what hasn't worked.

Lying, cheating and intimidation are not tactics that the universe
responds to positively. Methods like these have a way of rebounding,
as we are now finding out, coming back to haunt us as chemical
dump explosions, as withered grass and malformed babies struggling
to live on old dump sites, as nuclear wastes that nobody wants to give
a home to, and as silent nuclear reactors filled with trapped radio-
active gases.

Once more a mythic vision has become exhausted and discredited.
Once more there are choruses of "never again." Once more there
is the widespread conviction that there must be new ways and new
thoughts.

The materials out of which the new vision of the late Twentieth
and early Twenty-First Centuries will be made are already on the
scene. For more than twenty-five years, the fundamental ideas and
metaphors of the next vision have been developing within the mid-

Twentieth Century order—new mathematical ideas, new scientific ideas, new social and cultural ideas. Ever-increasing numbers of people are embracing these ideas. The ideas themselves are falling together and mutually reinforcing each other.

What have been odd and contrary thoughts and practices subscribed to and fostered by individuals and minorities will soon become the basic premises of a new vision held by the majority in our society. In 1980, we stand at the very last moment of the mid-Twentieth Century era, on the verge of an almost miraculously rapid transition.

Within SF literature, we are as close to the onset of the New Head Golden Age as, say, 1937 was to 1939. In 1937, the mid-Twentieth Century era and modern science fiction were still a dream. But it was already possible in 1937 for John W. Campbell to write a series of articles for *Astounding* on the planets of the solar system that in retrospect can be seen as a primer for modern science fiction to come.

In the same way today, although the new era has not yet arrived, it is possible to identify some of its pertinent elements and key ideas. In the mid-Twentieth Century, *fact* has been the prime index. In the new organization of reality, the central concept will be *pattern*.

Pattern is the higher organization of fact into configurations that may be only partly visible and that may perform functions not predictable from a knowledge of individual bits and pieces. Once again, the elephant in the dark is a good simile. Those who touch it in various places know the facts of the matter—respectively perceiving a "fan," or a "rope," or a "pillar," or a "hose pipe"—but only one who knows the overall pattern can recognize these individual elements as being the parts of an elephant.

In a real sense, *pattern* was the central concept that the mid-Twentieth Century vision was straining after from the very beginning. The makers of modern science fiction—Campbell, Asimov, van Vogt and Heinlein, with their "laws" and "thought systems" and the like—were reaching ahead from the Forties toward this very moment. Like all good mythmakers, they were genuine seers.

What is about to change is a matter of emphasis. For the mid-Twentieth Century, fact was primary. Patterns, to the extent that they were recognized, were elaborations of fact. In the New Head vision, however, systems are going to be recognized as more fundamental than separate individual facts.

This is an insight of ecology, which perceives the ecosystem as a whole as more basic than individual creatures or species. Along with genetics and computer science, ecology is one of the model sciences of the New Head vision, a source of metaphors and analogies in the same way that astronomy and physics served as the sources of modern science fiction.

The Old Head vision claimed to be objective and realistic and to stand apart from the facts that it so blithely manipulated. But contemporary physics — the science which has been more important than any other in the making of modern science fiction—now tells us that it is not possible to stand apart and manipulate fact. There simply is no such thing as pure dispassionate objectivity. This is a participatory universe. Every action we take not only has consequences, but involves us in the outcome of the processes that we affect.

There would be no way to pretend, for instance, that this essay is objective—in spite of the care we have taken to read widely, to quote aptly and to check our facts. As readers of SF, as fans of SF, as writers of SF—we are *involved* with SF. This essay, these various pieces, and this book as a whole are not isolated and autonomous. They are factors in an ongoing process, produced by that process, and intended to affect that process. They are elements in a pattern.

If ecology, genetics and computer science are models for the New Head vision, it is because they are sciences in which pattern is central. In computering, the program is more fundamental than either the information stored and processed or the machine on which the program is run. Similarly, in genetics, the individual is perceived not as an autonomous physical construct, but as the outward expression of a pattern encoded in the genes.

What is particularly interesting is that in both computering and genetics—as in the human brain—information is stored nonlinearly. If the facts in these systems were to be taken in order of storage, they would seem to be nonsense. It is the program itself, the overall pattern, that maintains and orders the facts, and not the facts that determine the system.

There is a story to the effect that once a man was headed home from the market with a piece of liver, intending to make himself pâté, when a vulture swooped down on him and made off with the meat. The man shook his fist after the bird. "*You* may have the liver," he cried, "but *I* still have the recipe!"

There is an ever-increasing awareness of the presence of pattern, the nature of pattern, and the power of pattern in contemporary SF. We can find examples in the three galactic fantasy novels we have named—Robert Silverberg's *Lord Valentine's Castle*, Joan Vinge's *The Snow Queen*, and our own *Earth Magic*.

In *Lord Valentine's Castle*, awareness of pattern is an important detail, but not the central matter. But early in the story, Valentine takes up with a troupe of jugglers and proves to have a natural aptitude for tossing balls around. So easy does it come and so well does he do in his first attempt, that he finds himself thrown into another headspace:

> Time seemed divided into an infinity of brief strokes, and yet, paradoxically, he had no sense of sequence: the three balls seemed fixed in their places, one perpetually in mid-air, one in each of his hands, and the fact that at each moment a different ball held one of those positions was inconsequential. Each was all. Time was timeless. He did not move, he did not throw, he did not catch: he only observed the flow, and the flow was outside time and space.

In other current books, the perception of pattern is not a matter of momentary insight, or of a special state of consciousness, as here, but is the crucial fact whose revelation is the climax of the story. In *The Snow Queen*, for instance, we learn that sibyls, discounted and persecuted people who claim to have access to a source of higher knowledge, are in fact the remnants of an informational network established long ago by a now-fallen galactic empire.

That *pattern* can be treated as though it were a *fact* to be revealed as a kicker means that a book like *The Snow Queen* is still being written within the parameters of modern science fiction. The true implications of pattern taken in its own right are yet to be recognized.

And we as storytellers are as bound by this as Joan Vinge. In our *Earth Magic*, at a crucial turn the protagonist realizes that the countryside in which he was born and raised, the land he has always taken for granted as given and natural, has deliberately been altered and shaped in some former time:

> Below, the pattern of land was as deliberately made as writing on the page of a book. But the pattern was visible only to one who could sense the power that the pattern gathered. Otherwise, it was invisible, unsuspect, unimaginable. And still, the power gathered in the land, as palpable as fear and hate, as imminent as catastrophe, awaiting direction, awaiting discharge.

At this moment, in stories like *The Snow Queen* and *Earth Magic*, it is only the half-obscured outlines of ancient broken patterns that are being perceived. We are not arrived at the time when the power of these patterns is fully harnessed, directed and discharged. And as for new patterns altogether with even greater power, they yet wait to be discovered.

However, even in contemporary stories that do not concentrate explicitly on the subject of pattern as pattern, the growing awareness of pattern may still be present, manifested in the form of art. Art —unbased on fact and a requisite number of decimal points—has been an area of expression generally excluded by the fact-minded techno-heads of the mid-Twentieth Century.

It is probably no accident at all that modern science fiction has never been a well-illustrated literature—not as Victorian fiction in general and scientifiction in particular were well-illustrated. *Astounding*, the magazine of modern science fiction, was notorious for having the poorest drawings of all the pulp magazines of the Golden Age. With the exception of usually inadequate and often inaccurate cover paintings, the vast majority of SF books published during the last forty years have had no illustrations at all.

In just the past several years, however, illustrated books have appeared in increasing numbers. John Varley's *Titan*, which we reviewed last year, was illustrated by Freff. Joan Vinge's *The Snow Queen* is illustrated by J. Michael Nally. Heinlein's *"The Number of the Beast—"* has over fifty illustrations by Richard Powers, known for his SF book covers of the Fifties. That this new wave of illustration is not yet fully taken seriously by those who have commissioned it can be seen in the fact that the publishers of these three books have not thought it necessary to send copies of the illustrations to reviewers along with advance copies of the text.

There is one exception to this among the new SF books we have gathered. In Alfred Bester's *Golem^{100}*, illustration is not just a dispensable ornament to the novel, but an integral part of it. In *Golem^{100}*, trips to the psychic Infraworld are represented by clutches of Jack Gaughan drawings—perhaps the most impressive work he has ever done—as well as by dialog.

Bester says:

> I have tried to invent a brand-new style for myself. I have tried to write a story in a visual, narrative style where the visuals *lock in* with the text. The text doesn't mean anything unless you see the visuals, and they don't mean anything unless you see the text.

Perhaps even more significant than this trend toward the incorporation of illustration in SF are all the many new stories that concern themselves with music and dance. The fulfillment of an unfinished opera is a central motif in Charles Harness's *The Catalyst*. In Bester's *Golem^{100}*, it is a musical chant that summons the demonic being from the Infraworld. In Vinge's *The Snow Queen*, it is use of music that enables a character to survive a crucial ordeal. In Spider and Jeanne Robinson's *Stardance*, a collaboration between a writer and his dancer wife, there is dance in outer space and dance as a means of communication with aliens.

Music is coming to be recognized as a transcendent force. It may be taken as representative of the growing power of *pattern* in exactly the same way that the super-science wielded in the Thirties' scientifiction of E. E. Smith and the young John W. Campbell was a foretaste of the power of *fact* to come.

The purest expression of this new music of power is to be seen in the most imaginative and romantic current SF—those galactic fantasy stories and post-disaster fictions that have freed themselves from the domination of fact and technology through the suffering of catastrophe. In one after another of these stories, there is a minstrel-hero—a singer, a piper, a guitarist—whose power derives from his music.

In Richard Cowper's *The Road to Corlay*, for instance, a piper's music renders enemies senseless. In Orson Scott Card's *Songmaster*, a minstrel's song directed against a tyrant drives the man mad and causes him to rip his own guts out with his bare hands. In Arsen Darnay's *The Karma Affair*, a consciousness holon passes through a significant series of reincarnations—first it is a Nazi villain, a representative of Victorian superiority; then it is a fact-minded American engineer in the 1970's; later yet, it is a scavenger of artifacts from our crashed-out civilization; finally, this holon is reborn as a power-minstrel who can send a general and his army into flight with the magic of his finger-picking.

This multiple appearance of the same theme is a synchronicity for you! And it is a sign of change. Modern science fiction was never like this. In a modern science fiction story like Heinlein's "The Roads Must Roll," a competent man might defeat a bad guy by knowing and stating the cold inescapable fact of his deficient I.Q. score. But never ever would a Heinlein character be a minstrel who withers the unworthy with the cosmic power of song.

We should point out that for all their New Head materials, these contemporary SF stories are still being written within the parameters of the mid-Twentieth Century vision. If 1980 is the equivalent of 1937 in the last cycle, we may note that it was in 1937 that the last major works of Victorian SF were published. John W. Campbell wrote two Don A. Stuart stories, including the highly important "Forgetfulness." E. E. Smith's novel *Galactic Patrol*—the very peak and summation of Thirties' scientifiction—was serialized in *Astounding*. And Olaf Stapledon published his mythic overview of post-human and non-human development, *Star Maker*. All of these works contained materials vital to the making of modern science fiction—but these crucial stories themselves were not modern science fiction. They were written within the confines and assumptions of the Victorian vision.

In exactly the same way, the contemporary novels we have been reading while stuck away in the Critics Lounge contain metaphors and materials that will be central to the coming form of SF, but themselves are still written within the frame of modern science fiction. Many of these novels regard Old Head methods and their consequences with deep dismay, but even so the mid-Twentieth Century order of value is still honored as basic, fundamental, the way things must be. Even as they expect to be bitten by them, these stories are spellbound by the old attitudes.

It is this that accounts for all the current stories of polluted futures and technologically-induced eco-disaster. At exactly the same moment that they appear to be rejecting it, these novels are most hung up on the mid-Twentieth Century vision. It is as though until the vision changes, these writers must continue to believe that the red asterisks and roast penguin they extrapolate from the conditions of the present must inevitably be *the facts* of the future.

It is no accident at all that so many contemporary SF novels should fake successful endings, or force endings, or fall into fragments, or turn into snake's-hands. For exactly as long as the old commitments continue, they will be helpless to do otherwise.

At the same time, however, even while this is true, in contemporary SF the New Head elements become ever more visible. There is a conspicuous drift toward the new matter and attitudes. If there is a single source of energy and insight from which all innovative writers of SF must draw, producing synchronicities like all the current power-minstrels, it is New Head ideas that this source is broadcasting now.

We can see the movement toward the New Head clearly illustrated in a new novel by Michael Bishop. Bishop's first novel, *A Funeral for the Eyes of Fire*, was published in 1975. Now, five years and half-a-dozen books later, Bishop has rewritten the novel completely and issued it again under the title *Eyes of Fire*.

The differences between the two books are instructive. Even though they have nearly the same title and use the very same Szafran cover illustration, they are not at all the same book. The bones of the two stories are the same—an essentially Old Head situation of duplicity, betrayal and disaster. But the flesh is different. The pattern is the same, the facts have changed.

In *Eyes of Fire*, narrative voice is altered from first person to third. In all but a few places, the language of the book is completely new. Names of planets are different. Cultures and customs are different. Character names, ages, sexes, relationships and motivations have all been changed.

The Old Head situation that is shared by the two books is deeply important to Bishop. Even as he despises it, Bishop is committed to the deceitfulness of his characters. Even as he finds it loathesome, he is wedded to the awful inevitability of his disintegrating situation. Bishop *desires* the disaster to occur. Only if it happens can he serve us his true dish—the savory well-seasoned bitterness of innocence deliberately betrayed.

Nonetheless, essentially (anti-) Old Head as both books are, the sum of changes from *A Funeral for the Eyes of Fire* to *Eyes of Fire* is all in the direction of the New Head. We might note two changes in particular—the recognition of the female side of humanity, and the introduction of the theme of the clone.

In the Seventies, large numbers of new female writers of SF arrived on the scene. It has been these writers who have led in the writing of galactic fantasy, and in the amalgamation of formerly separate fantasy and modern science fiction symbology.

That's new. Modern science fiction, with its facts, its decimal points, its machines and its contests of dominance, has been a man's game. Women and their thoughts and values could safely be ignored as unfactual, and therefore not completely real.

Women, of course, were not all that was excluded by modern science fiction. So were non-rational states of mind, like dreams. So were non-material states of being, like astral bodies. So were art of all sorts, unorthodox sexual practices and relationships, and superior aliens.

Now, however, as *fact* gives way to *pattern*, all these formerly excluded materials are appearing in SF stories. The sign on the SF clubhouse door that for forty years has said, "Rational Heterosexual Engineers with Muddy Boots Only," is coming down. And *Eyes of Fire* is a measure of that.

A Funeral for the Eyes of Fire was published only five years ago.

It was dedicated to the author's mother. But so thoroughly a modern science fiction novel was it that there were no female characters of any kind in the story. Two different planets and characters from four separate cultures were involved in *A Funeral for the Eyes of Fire*—but women and the female side of nature went completely unrepresented.

Michael Bishop has labored to alter that in *Eyes of Fire*. Now, in the new book, the society of one planet has become female-dominated, ruled by a Liege Mistress. And the entire population of the second planet, defined as crystalline-eyed but otherwise ordinary human beings in *A Funeral for the Eyes of Fire*, has been changed in anatomy and physiology. In *Eyes of Fire*, the crystalline eyes remain, but the people have become hermaphroditic beings—not unlike the populace of the planet Winter in Ursula K. Le Guin's *The Left Hand of Darkness*.

Where once on this planet all the visible characters were male, and we were given a dominant society and a dissident community whose destruction was the central tragedy, in *Eyes of Fire*, this has been reconceived. The dominant culture is now presented as technology-minded and as hermaphro-male by choice. And the breakaway culture that is destroyed is now given as ecological in orientation and hermaphro-femme.

By these changes, Bishop not only brings female notes into his formerly all-male story, but opens the door to new, experimental sexual unorthodoxy. There is sexual unorthodoxy involved as well in the other major alteration Bishop has made in *Eyes of Fire*, the introduction of the theme of the clone.

In *A Funeral for the Eyes of Fire*, the narrator, Gunnar Balduin, is an ordinary human being who happens to have a strange, over-intense relationship with his untrustworthy and domineering older brother. In *Eyes of Fire*, the protagonist, now named Seth Latimer, and his older sib are given as "isohets," two clones of different age budded from the same isosire. Not only are Seth and his older isohet bound together by their shared gene pattern, but by a homosexual predator/prey relationship as well.

Does this constitute incest, or is it merely masturbation? This is only one question among a great number raised by the coming of clones.

Clones are to the present moment what robots were to the Age of Technology. Clones are pure *pattern* in just the same way that robots, buckets of bolts, were assemblages of *fact*. The mid-Twentieth Century had to come to terms with the robot, our mechanical image. Modern science fiction had to discover rules for the robot to follow and social roles for it to perform.

In the same way, the coming period is going to have to resolve the problems raised by the existence of clones, organic beings made in the same pattern as ourselves: our three-dimensional mirrors. How should we relate to our clones? What do an isosire and an isohet owe each other? If a man dies, which relative inherits his estate—his child or his clone? What are the rights of a clone, and what are its duties?

His newly-introduced clone theme is highly important to Michael Bishop. The title of his book, as it appears on the cover page of the manuscript, is not *Eyes of Fire*, but rather *The Isohet*. And any number of times in *Eyes of Fire*, he repeats the thought: "*We are all imperfect isohets of the same perfect progenitor.*"

Notice if you will that this perception, this appreciation of the universality of pattern, applies not merely to known clones like Seth Latimer. It is all of us who are given to be imperfect copies of the same perfect pattern.

With this in mind, it is possible to perceive *Eyes of Fire* as something more and something other than a mere redrafting of *A Funeral for the Eyes of Fire*. The two books themselves are isohets. One can wonder if someday Bishop will present the same situation yet again in a third book, resolve the problem, and complete an isotrilogy?

As things are, neither of the two existing books is satisfactorily resolved. Both are content to be indictments. *A Funeral for the Eyes of Fire* charges Old Head thinking with being guilty of violence and duplicity. The effect of the changes in *Eyes of Fire* is to make the charges more specific. Now the crimes that the Old Head is given as being guilty of are offenses against the New Head—the corruption and abuse of an innocent young clone, and the destruction of a mystical, ecological community of hermaphro-femmes.

If Bishop does write a third version of this story within the context of the next period, will the nature of the inhabitants of the second planet be altered yet again? Perhaps the one feature of *A Funeral for the Eyes of Fire* and *Eyes of Fire* that ties them most strongly to modern science fiction and the mid-Twentieth Century vision is the fact that there are no alien beings in either book. As much as Asimov's Foundation stories, Bishop's two variant novels are set in a humans-only galaxy.

Like all the other elements that have been excluded by modern science fiction, superior aliens have been knocking at the door again recently, craving admittance. Out in the darkness of the cosmos they lurk, these superior beings with unknown intentions toward us. This is the very problem that John W. Campbell banished from the pages of *Astounding* more than thirty-five years ago, presumably to keep his writers from becoming demoralized and losing their sense of possibility and optimism. What is most interesting is that the novels into which these aliens have been intruding themselves are the most technologically-minded, the most conventionally "modern science fiction" of contemporary SF stories.

It is as though now that the sense of possibility and optimism that kept them at bay has departed from modern science fiction, superior aliens have snuck back to haunt the degenerate, unhappy, techno-yucchh future. Again and again through the Seventies, in one nuts-and-bolts science fiction story after another—Clarke's *Rendezvous with Rama*, Anderson's *The Avatar*, Benford's *In the Ocean of Night*, Pohl's *Gateway*—fact-minded techno-men have discovered facts they cannot ignore. Techno-men can ignore many things, but they cannot ignore superior technology. And in all of these stories, alien artifacts have come drifting into the Solar System or turned up in parking orbit out beyond Pluto.

There is great fear and doubt. What do they want of us, these superior aliens with their cosmic greeting cards?

Now that we have ruined Earth, fouled our own nest, will superior aliens judge us for what we have done?

Or will those aliens prove to be just like us, but even more so?

Will they, too, be selfish, greedy, self-regarding manipulators of fact, but with a million years more practice at the game?

These questions are addressed directly in a new novel which popped into existence in our reality space here in the Critics Lounge only moments ago—Norman Spinrad's *Songs from the Stars*. Here is a book that is at least a half-step closer to the New Head transition than any of the other new books we've been reading. The specific advance that it offers is an understanding of higher aliens and our relationship to them that isn't bogged down in Old Headery.

It is clear from *Songs from the Stars* and other clues that the New Head will be able to cope with superior aliens without the anxiety that was displayed by a Victorian like H. G. Wells or a mid-Twentieth Century technocrat like Robert Heinlein. It's a matter of fundamental attitude. We can see the relevant attitudes on display if we state the respective answers of the Victorian patriarch, the mid-Twentieth Century engineer, and the New Head ecologist to the same question, the familiar popular problem of the chicken and the egg.

Which of the two came first?

An unorthodox Victorian—a Lewis Carroll or a Samuel Butler—out of a spirit of whimsy and perversity might answer that it was the egg. But the ordinary orthodox Victorian would give the ordinary orthodox answer—the chicken. And the ultimate reason, if pressed hard by a foolish doubter or an insubordinate offspring, would be the argument from authority: "Because I told you so."

"Because I say so" is not a fruitful method of approach to higher aliens. If they were already inclined to be hostile, as the Victorians feared, an attitude like that might make them testy. And if, on the other hand, these superior beings only wished us well, it seems more than possible that they might feel that our belligerence and dogmatism were an impossible barrier to our learning anything at all contrary to our present beliefs.

A higher alien couldn't get very far with a Victorian. He would either have to kill him or stay away from him.

The mid-Twentieth Century attitude is less purely dogmatic. Its boast is that it stands back and lets the facts prevail. Instead of saying, "Because I said so," like a Victorian, a mid-Twentieth Century person might say either, "*I* have the facts," or "Prove it!" A mid-Twentieth Century person might make a case either for the chicken or for the egg, depending on which was more convenient.

But a recent London *Sunday Times* story tells us that a man was accidentally killed in Thonburi, Thailand, in a fight with a friend over which came first, the chicken or the egg. He said it was the egg.

And so we might ask—how fruitfully might a higher alien get on with a man who is capable of fighting to the death to prove that he has the true facts? Could a superior being teach anything to a man who secretly yearns to come marching into her house, say "Howdy, bub," to her, and then chop her into tiny little bits with his Mark Nineteen Remington Blaster? That might be just a bit of a barrier to understanding. Above all, could any responsible higher alien reveal itself to the sort of man who promises to fall to pieces before any being he can't dominate, particularly one who knows more than he does?

No wonder superior aliens have stayed away from modern science fiction, or been content in recent days to send us simple technological puzzles to study. A would-be student who is *always* contending, and who wobbles between hostility and demoralization is in no state of mind to learn anything.

The New Head attitude is different from either of its immediate predecessors. It is far less concerned with matters of precedence and is much less contentious. Where the mid-Twentieth Century was constantly urging its children to compete, compete, compete, to succeed and to win, the New Head watchword—repeated again and again on *Sesame Street*—is "cooperation."

Given the question of the chicken and the egg, a New Head person would neither dictate an answer from on high like a Victorian, nor fight to the death over the issue like some mid-century type. Instead, the New Head takes its clue in this matter from the old Chinese folk song, "Inside of Every Yang There's a Little Bit of Yin."

To the New Head what is central is neither the chicken nor the egg—one of these being considered "cause" and the other "effect" —but the overall pattern of which both are necessary parts. Their relationship is perceived as one of mutual interdependence. To say that one exists is to say that the other exists—the chicken contains the egg, the egg contains the chicken.

The New Head is not an either/or way of thinking. It opts instead for both/and. It is New Head to believe in two contradictory things before breakfast.

In short, compared to its two predecessors, the New Head is more open to multiplicity and to ambiguity. It is more ready to recognize mutual interdependence. And it is willing to cooperate rather than compete. All of these qualities make the New Head person a readier subject for contact by superior aliens than either the Victorian patriarch or the mid-Twentieth Century technocrat. If a higher being did have something to tell us we didn't already know, these New Head attitudes would be the minimum necessary for a lesson to be absorbed.

Norman Spinrad is aware of this in *Songs from the Stars*, a book which more than any other epitomizes the current transition. *Songs from the Stars* is specifically about the differences between technocratic Old Head thinking and the ecologically-minded New Head.

In *Songs from the Stars*, many years after an eco-disaster there is but one viable, prospering culture in all the world—the neo-hippie, eco-society of Aquaria on the West Coast of North America. This culture divides all science into White and Black. Black Science— the mid-Twentieth Century kind of science—brought the world to ruination. Aquaria follows the "law of muscle, sun, wind and water."

Secretly, however, this sweet civilization is supported by crucial technology turned out by surviving enclaves of Black Scientists on the other side of the mountain. Two key Aquarians, the karmic judge Clear Blue Lou, perfect master of the Clear Blue Way, and Sunshine Sue, who runs the Aquarian communication network, are made aware of this dependence.

In one sense, this initial situation is artificial and unlikely. The ecological culture surviving technological catastrophe is a typical late-modern science fiction situation, an analog of the magical planet that survives the fall of galactic empire. The situation is a set-up, an exception, a special case.

But then, so were the exploratory scientifiction stories of Smith and Campbell, Weinbaum and Williamson special cases, exceptions to the dictatorial laws of the Victorian cosmos. And Spinrad's *ad hoc* situation does have a certain measure of obvious truth to it. It is only fair to recognize that any ecological society to come will build on a base established by the Black Science of the mid-Twentieth Century.

It turns out that Clear Blue Lou and Sunshine Sue are being deliberately led by the nose. They are willy-nilly acting out parts in a behavioristic scenario manipulated and directed by the chief Black Scientist, a man named Arnold Harker. Harker intends to show Clear Blue Lou and Sunshine Sue that their civilization is based on unacknowledged Black Science as one step in convincing them to join together the resources of both societies in a project to send a spaceship to a long-abandoned space station—the Big Ear.

Spinrad, author of *Bug Jack Barron* and *The Iron Dream*, has always been fascinated by Old Head power-brokers. He loves them almost as much as he hates them. He paints Arnold Harker convincingly as he pulls strings, boasts of his power, and aims for the stars. And he acknowledges the undeniable brute effectiveness of Old Head psychology and technology.

But he also sees clearly the necessity of New Head attitudes. In *Songs from the Stars*, the Old Head survives as a few thousand fanatical people living in artificial oases—not unlike the remnant technosociety living in the orbiting satellite in John Crowley's *Engine Summer*. Aquaria is following the only truly viable path in spite of its dependence on bits and pieces of Old Head science.

Harker convinces Clear Blue Lou and Sunshine Sue to join him in launching the spaceship. The prospect of re-establishing a world-wide communication system is sufficient to entice them to play Harker's game.

Clear Blue Lou and Sunshine Sue deliberately deceive their own Aquarian people in order to send the spaceship *Enterprise* to the Big Ear. They lie. They manipulate facts. They even pass Harker off as a superior alien.

It is this compromise with the worst habits of the Old Head that flaws the success that Spinrad envisions in *Songs from the Stars*.

Lying, cheating and manipulation of fact are *not* the Clear Blue Way. To pass a man like Harker off as a superior alien can only be a karmic error.

And this becomes apparent when the characters arrive at the space station. Here, in the last days before the eco-disaster, an alien information transmitter assembled itself. To use this machine is to enter the consciousness of one alien race after another, all of whom are joined together in a galactic communications network: "An interstellar brotherhood communing over thousands of years of space and time."

Harker, the technocratic man, man-the-all-conqueror, proves unable to cope with the actualities of space. He hates what he expected to love. He finds the stars overwhelming. And he looks upon this alien machine and fears it:

> "Why would beings who didn't even know we existed when they sent out their broadcasts *care* what happened to us? Why would they go to all that trouble unless . . . unless . . ."
> "Oh shit, Arnold, unless *what*?"
> "Unless they wanted to *control* us, unless they want us to follow a scenario we can't even understand, unless they want to turn us into something . . . into something that isn't *human* any more . . ."

Arnold Harker, who thinks in terms of control and forcing others to follow his scenarios, inevitably projects these Old Head attitudes onto the unknown aliens, and fears them. Clear Blue Lou and Sunshine Sue, on the other hand, are at their best in this moment. They revel in the chance to participate in alien thought processes, which Spinrad specifically calls both "dreams" and "songs."

Harker can only mutter fearfully: "As far beyond us as we are beyond crawling worms . . ." And shiver in his socks.

But Clear Blue Lou delivers the New Head answer to both the Victorians and the Twentieth Century technocrats:

> "Damn it, do you suppose that intelligent creatures could survive millions of years of their own history possessed of such enormous physical power and knowledge without being as advanced *karmically* as they are scientifically? A civilization of power-mad mindfuck artists and would-be conquerors would never last that long. Its very survival for millions of years is proof of its wisdom and goodness.

Mere superior *knowledge* wouldn't be good enough—they have to
have superior *wisdom*."

And, a moment later, Clear Blue Lou has this further thought, this
judgment of Black Scientists like Harker:

> Their arrogance had blinded them to the difference between
> knowledge and wisdom; possessing superior quantities of the former,
> they could not see their own lack of the latter. They were scientific
> geniuses, but moral morons.

Let that last sentence stand as an epitaph for the entire mid-Twentieth Century. It can serve as a last word for Arnold Harker as well.
He tests the machine just enough to assure himself that it *is* superior
aliens with a greater command of fact that he is dealing with—and
then he gives up. He commits suicide.

Perhaps the competent man is not the survivor that Robert Heinlein always said that he was. At least in *Songs from the Stars* it is the
competent man of fact, Arnold Harker, who is dead, while Clear Blue
Lou and Sunshine Sue bring their spaceship back to Aquaria. And
Aquaria lives—now connected to the stars.

In the clearest possible symbolic language, *Songs from the Stars*
tells us that the mid-Twentieth Century Age of Technocracy is passing. It treated human beings as mere facts to be manipulated. It de-
spoiled the environment without pausing to reckon costs. And its
justification was its dream of conquest of space.

But it is the very hunger, pride and greed that has driven techno-
man toward the stars that must cause him to recoil from a stellar
world populated by superior aliens, fearing their dominance and exploitation—not unlike the thirsty jackal who dodges back from the
pool of water at the sight of his own reflection. Outer space is the
mirror of inner nature, and if you press an Arnold Harker too hard
with the prospect of superior aliens—whom he must see as his own
awful reflection—he will inevitably kill himself.

The Twenty-First Century Age of Ecology is being born out of
the ruins of the Age of Black Science. And the stellar dream of the
Aquarian Age of Clear Blue Lou and Sunshine Sue is very different
than the dreams of conquest of technological man. In the mirror
of outer space, ecological man perceives not the prospect of domi-

nation and exploitation, but the promise of cosmic connection and cooperation.

The Old Head kept meeting the enemy and discovering him to be themselves. The New Head perception is "I am he as you are he as you are me and we are all together." (*Magical Mystery Tour*) This difference in perception is what causes Arnold Harker to commit suicide while Clear Blue Lou and Sunshine Sue continue on toward an unknown higher destiny.

In the land of the imagination—call it the World Beyond the Hill, the Infraworld, or the Realm of 666—what you perceive is what you get. This is our explanation for the Black Beast—Heinlein's *bête noire*—in *"The Number of the Beast—"*.

The title of Heinlein's book, as we have pointed out, is from the Book of Revelation. Through the years, and perhaps more frequently than any other science fiction writer, Robert Heinlein has used the Bible as a source for his story titles. *Stranger in a Strange Land* is one example. " 'Let There Be Light' " is another. The working title of Heinlein's first serial in *Astounding*, *"If This Goes On—"*, was *Vine and Fig Tree*—an allusion to the Book of Micah.

In *"The Number of the Beast—"*, several of the chapter titles are from the Bible—including Chapter XXXVIII, which has the title (resurrected after all these years): "—under his vine and under his fig tree; and none shall make them afraid—." But the very last chapter of the book—the single chapter contained in the envoy—has a a title that is slightly different. It is not a Biblical quotation, but a Biblical reference. Chapter XLVIII is titled "Rev. XXII: 13."

This verse reads: "I am Alpha and Omega, the beginning and end, the first and last."

The book *"The Number of the Beast—"* is an Alpha and Omega, a beginning and an end, for modern science fiction. Before there was modern science fiction, the imaginary universes visited in *"The Num- of the Beast—"* existed: Lilliput, Wonderland, Oz, Barsoom, the world of the Lensmen. The Realm of 666 described in *"The Number of the Beast—"* contains within itself not just the Future History and other Heinlein stories, but all of the imaginary continua of modern science fiction. And, by indicating the existence of iso-universes to the number of ten million sextillion plus, *"The Number of the Beast—"* suggests possibilities of the imagination far beyond the scope of modern science fiction.

Heinlein has found an organizing principle that completely surrounds and incorporates modern science fiction, and changes it from an all-in-all to an atom. The frame of reference of SF has been decisively and permanently altered by *"The Number of the Beast—"*. Modern science fiction was "realistic." It was linear. It was oriented toward space travel. Because of *"The Number of the Beast—"*, SF-to-come will be non-linear. It will be imaginary and know it. And it will discover its adventures in the meta-dimension of consciousness.

"The Number of the Beast—" opens the door to this meta-dimension—the Realm of 666—but then does not pass through it, like Moses indicating the Promised Land, but not entering into it himself. It is fear of the Black Beast who waits that keeps Heinlein from entering the full Realm of 666.

In certain significant ways, *"The Number of the Beast—"* is like Olaf Stapledon's *Star Maker*. Just as *Star Maker*, published in 1937, was a summational work of Victorian SF, so *"The Number of the Beast—"*, published in 1980, is a summation of modern science fiction.

Star Maker was also a visionary work. It delineated the universe of interstellar space that would be the ground of modern science fiction. But *Star Maker* itself was not modern science fiction. Stapledon could identify the interstellar universe to come, but Victorian convictions he could not shake prevented him from imagining human beings as active participants in interstellar affairs. Stapledon's human characters in *Star Maker* are but prophets and seers of interstellar possibility.

In the same way, *"The Number of the Beast—"* delimits the meta-universe of consciousness that will be the ground of New Head SF-to-come, without itself being a work of New Head SF. Heinlein's Gang of Four are indicators of possibility to us, but they are not full participants in that possibility. Their fear—and Heinlein's fear—of encountering superior beings prevents them.

The glory of *"The Number of the Beast—"* is that it indicates the possibility of *so much*. But the awfulness of the book is that it is so self-referential, so self-protective, so self-limited, and ultimately so self-defeated.

Heinlein rightly perceives that in a universe of consciousness, as opposed to a universe of fact, we all must be solipsists-in-collaboration. This is a conclusion that his characters come to, and they throw their grand jamboree—"The First Centennial Convention of the InterUniversal Society for Eschatological Pantheistic Multiple-Ego Solipsism" just to prove this point.

But still, Heinlein and his chief characters want to make exclusions. They want to be able to pick and choose among egos. They are capable of thinking in terms of "wog" and "vermin." They may ship a Jonathan Hoag and other persons of critical temperament off to a Klein-bottle-shaped Critics Lounge in order to be rid of them. As it always has been in Heinlein stories, okay people are okay, but not-okay people—instantly identifiable—deserve the worst fates that can be imagined for them.

That's flatly contrary to the New Head way of looking at things. To the New Head, the universe of collaborative consciousness requires the active participation of all types of human being, not just some privileged few. (We won't even go into the possibility or necessity of having non-human consciousness in the mix.) Any universe based on such a limited range of consciousness as may be found among Heinlein's Gang of Four, Lazarus Long, Jubal Harshaw and the like must be an egotistic partiality—a mental snake's-hand—and not be the true Realm of 666.

If *"The Number of the Beast—"* is a Black Hole of egotism, and if the Critics Lounge is a Klein bottle within *"The Number of the Beast—"*, we may ask—just what *is* the effect of entering a Klein bottle within a Black Hole?

There has hardly been a writer of SF from Poe, Verne and Wells to the present who has not contributed some note or essay or critical comment to the common continuing discussion of the nature and meaning of SF. And so we might inquire—just exactly who is it that still remains in attendance at the Universal Ego Convention rather than stepping aside to join the party going on in the Critics Lounge?

We Panshins first came into the Critics Lounge to find Jonathan Hoag and ask him a question. The short novel, "The Unpleasant Profession of Jonathan Hoag," published in *Unknown* in October 1942, was the last and strangest of the stories that Robert Heinlein contributed to the Golden Age before he ceased to write during World War II. In this story, Jonathan Hoag—named for a friend of H. P. Lovecraft's—is a Higher Critic from some meta-reality in which our world is the creation of a talented but immature art student. If Hoag decides that our world is lacking in artistic merit, he may cancel us out altogether.

Heinlein can't feel easy about that. Hoag is not just an ordinary superior alien of the sort that Heinlein characters have never been able to tolerate. He does not merely cast our personal purposes and competence into doubt. He is a meta-alien, a being so superior that he throws into doubt our entire universe. And yet, here he is, with dirty fingernails and a prissy expression, pretending to be ordinary, but guarding the entrance to the Critics Lounge. We must believe he is there for a purpose.

The question that we came to ask him was this: Just exactly who or what is the Black Beast that so haunts Heinlein's book?

We know very little for certain about the Black Beast. We know that it looks like a lamb and speaks like a dragon. We know that it is instantly detectable as "wrong" by Heinlein's characters. We know that if they kill it in one place, it returns in another. And we know that it has access to all the same iso-universes as Heinlein's characters. If the implication of the title *"The Number of the Beast—"* is correct, it may be the true master of the Realm of 666.

Heinlein's characters would like to trap this dragon-beast and dispose of it—possibly by dropping it down the oubliette of the Critics Lounge. But always it eludes them and defies their control. The conclusion of *"The Number of the Beast—"* is the promise that it will be back again.

Just what is this strange creature—the Black Beast?

Is it us, Heinlein's critics? We do look like lambs and speak like dragons. And there is no question that when Lazarus Long looks at us, he groks wrongness.

Can it be Jonathan Hoag, the Higher Critic from a meta-dimension?

Or is it everything Heinlein despises, everything that he fears, everything that he would exclude from the creative stewpot of his "pantheistic multiperson solipsism"?

The Black Beast must be all of these things and more. It is the essence of Outsider. It is a being of a higher order of reality, capable of manifesting itself in ten million sextillion different continua at one and the same instant. Of course it can't be killed when Heinlein's Gang of Four chop it to pieces with their swords—no more than you can be killed by skinning your knee, even though a few replaceable cells may perish.

"The Number of the Beast—" presents but a shadow of the true Realm of 666. Taken by itself, the book is all false presentation. It offers us a false Oz, a false Barsoom, and a false Realm of 666.

How can we say so? If we may recall, Lewis Carroll told us, "No country infested by dragons fails to be interesting." The true Realm of 666 is the land of the dragon. If *"The Number of the Beast—"* is often false and even more often a bore, it is because it attempts to avoid all those places where dragons might be found.

The true location of the Realm of 666, in fact, is not in *"The Number of the Beast—"*. Unlikely as it may seem, it is in the Critics Lounge, as we can demonstrate.

Lazarus Long would have us believe that the Critics Lounge is a claustrophobic and fatal place, a trap for the unwary, and a place of doom for critics who cannot read. Indeed, as Lazarus Long describes it, it sounds very much like the sort of place that we have found *"The Number of the Beast—"* to be—full of promise, but ultimately a cul-de-sac.

But the Critics Lounge cannot be like that. It is shaped like a Klein bottle, and a Klein bottle is a fourth-dimensional construct. To enter a Klein bottle is to find an automatic escape hatch from the prison of any three-dimensional continuum.

Jonathan Hoag could have told us so. So could the Black Beast. But we found the relevant information in a book lying on a coffee

table in the Critics Lounge—*The Dragon*, by Francis Huxley. On
page 28, Huxley writes:

> The dragon world seems to be formed in the manner of the Purse
> of Fortunatus—known to us as a Klein Bottle—whose singular
> property, as described by Lewis Carroll, is that "Whatever is *inside*
> the Purse is *outside* it, and whatever is *outside* it, is *inside* it."

The Critics Lounge is the dragon world. No wonder, then, that
all the time we have been inside the Critics Lounge, a woggish, ver-
minous person claiming to be "the caterer" should have been keeping the party going with constant supplies of peanut butter and jelly
sandwiches.

And so we have the answer to the question of greatest urgency
posed by *"The Number of the Beast— "*: By what route may we
depart from the Black Hole of modern science fiction and enter into
the true Realm of 666?

The route lies through the Critics Lounge. And that is the path
we have taken in this piece.

Now, waiting before us is the World Beyond the Hill, the Infraworld, the Realm of 666. We have only to enter it.

But, if we are to enter it, we cannot enter it alone. The Realm of
666 is dependent on diversity. Old Head thinking can only bar the
door to us, as it has barred the door to Heinlein. If we are to enter
this land of the imagination, we cannot go on making the same Old
Head mistakes of domination, exclusivity, hostility and rejection.

All of us need all of us. And somebody must be the first to lay
down his Mark Nineteen Remington Blaster.

Envoy

The last competent man sat alone in a room—together with his
clones and avatars. It was very crowded. The room kept shrinking
and they were starting to get on each other's nerves.

There was a knock at the door. It was the Black Beast.

"Jonathan Hoag sent us," they said. "Can you come outside and play?"

"I'll let you be in my dream if I can be in yours. I said that."
                                        —Bob Dylan

—written in the Critics Lounge with ink manufactured from peanut butter and jelly   il-May-June-J   1980

REFERENCES

Arasteh, A. Reza. *Toward Final Personality Integration: A Measure for Health, Social Change and Leadership.* Schenckman, 1975.

Bateson, Gregory. *Mind and Nature: A Necessary Unity.* Dutton, 1979.

Bennett, J. G. *Gurdjieff: Making a New World.* Harper Colophon, 1976.

Blair, Lawrence. *Rhythms of Vision: The Changing Patterns of Belief.* Schocken, 1976.

Campbell, Joseph. *The Hero with a Thousand Faces.* Pantheon, 1949.

Capra, Fritjof. *The Tao of Physics.* Shambala, 1975.

Castaneda, Carlos. *Journey to Ixtlan: The Lessons of don Juan.* Simon & Schuster, 1972.

Corbin, Henry. *Spiritual Body and Celestial Earth: From Mazdean Iran to Shi'te Iran.* Princeton, 1977.

de Chardin, Teilhard. *The Phenomenon of Man.* Harper, 1959.

de Mille, Richard. *Castaneda's Journey.* Capra, 1976.

de Santillana, Giorgio, and Hertha von Dechend. *Hamlet's Mill: An Essay on Myth and the Frame of Time.* Gambit, 1969.

Fort, Charles. *The Complete Books of Charles Fort*. Dover, 1975.

Graves, Robert. *The White Goddess: An Historical Grammar of Poetic Myth*. Noonday, 1966.

Hofstadter, Douglas R. *Godel, Escher, Bach: an Eternal Golden Braid*. Basic, 1979.

Koestler, Arthur. *The Sleepwalkers: A History of Man's Changing Vision of the Universe*. Macmillan, 1959.

Kuhn, Thomas S. *The Structure of Scientific Revolutions*. Chicago, 1970.

Ornstein, Robert E. *The Psychology of Consciousness*. Viking, 1972.

Pearce, Joseph Chilton. *The Crack in the Cosmic Egg: Challenging Constructs of Mind and Reality*. Julian, 1971.

Shah, Idries. *The Way of the Sufi*. Dutton, 1970.

Thomas, Lewis. *Lives of a Cell: Notes of a Biology Watcher*. Viking, 1974.

Watson, Lyall. *Lifetide: the Biology of the Unconscious*. Simon & Schuster, 1979.

Young, Arthur M. *The Reflexive Universe: Evolution of Consciousness*. Delacorte, 1976.

Zukav, Gary. *The Dancing Wu Li Masters: An Overview of the New Physics*. Morrow, 1979.

INDEX